YE. I. VE. HAMSTRING. EYED.
ED. I. VARNISHED. GEM. YET
INERT. GYM. TRY. ME. ADH
HINGES. DIAMETER. ENVY. SIGH. HIS. DYNAMITE. VER
DISH. ENVY. I. M. SHY. ENERVATE. DIG. MY. ENVISA
AGE. MYTH. RIDE. ENVISAGE. ME. DRY. HIT. MY. GARIS
SIGHTED. EVERYMAN. HE. S. EVERYMAN. DIGIT. EVERYMA
INVADE. MR. EYESIGHT. VERMIN. EYESIGHT. AD. RAVI
SHY. GEMINATE. HERD. IVYS. GEMINATE. HIVES. DR
ME. ADS. GENITIVE. DRY. SHAME. GENITIVE. ARMY. SH
HIS. EVE. THEY. VE. DIM. GREASIN. GREASIN. EYED. H
SAVING. EM. HEREDITY. MEIN. VAGS. HEREDITY. S. VA
ERITAGE. MENDS. IVY. GIVE. HYSTERIA. MEND. I. VEN
SEA. MIDNIGHT. VERSE. AYE. EVER. MIDNIGHT. EAS
VE. HEED. NEGATIVE. IS. RHYMED. REGIMENT. HEAVY. I
HAM. TV. SEDATIVE. GRIMY. HEN. SEDATIVE. HYMEN. R
EAVY. RIG. HI. EDGE. SEMINARY. TV. THIEVERY. DESI
VERY. MADE. SIGN. THIEVERY. MADE. SING. IS. THIEVER
THIEVING. DRAM. EYES. VEHEMENT. DAISY. RIG. VEHEME
GIVE. HI. AMNESTY. GRID. EVE. ASTRIDE. HYMEN. GIV
E. ENVY. ATHEISM. DYING. EVER. ATHEISM. VERY. GIN
Y. SIGN. GAVE. SHINY. DEMERIT. I. ENVY. DEMERIT. SHA
ENMITY. AGE. DERVISH. GAIETY. MEN. DERVISH. ENEM
I. DESERVE. THY. GAMIN. DESTINY. GRIEVE. HAM. GIV
HIVE. YE. DEVIANT. MESH. RIG. DEVIATE. RHYME. SIG
HEM. SEVERE. HAM. DIGNITY. RE. SHAVE. ME. DIGNIT
IMITY. I. HASTEN. MY. DIVERGE. DIVERGE. ANY. THEIS
DIVERGE. DIVERGE. TINY. SHAME. SHINY. DIVERGE. TEA
EYE. ME. AM. DRIVING. THEE. YES. THEM. AS. DRIVI

THE BEST ADVERTISING AND DESIGN IN THE WORLD.

EVERY THING IS MADE

EV ERY
THING
IS
MADE

TASCHEN

RYTHING ADE.

OF THE MANY GOOD **THINGS ABOUT BEING PRESIDENT OF D&AD IS YOU GET TO CHOOSE WHO DESIGNS THE ANNUAL.**

I've always had a bit of a secret ambition to do it myself. But I put the megalomania on hold and asked one of my favourite artists instead: Bob and Roberta Smith.

Bob probably didn't realise exactly what he was letting himself in for, but I think he and his designer Keith Sargent have risen to the challenge magnificently.

There is also an important message at its heart – **Everything is Made**.

I love that sentiment.

To me, it sums up what being a creative is all about. It's not just coming up with an original idea, it's about crafting it, nurturing it, doing it justice.

Look through these pages and you'll see that the level of craft is astoundingly high, and only those ideas that are superbly executed truly shine.

You'll also notice the book is a little lighter compared to previous years. Just over 550 entries made it in. Forty-two went on to win a Yellow Pencil, and five picked up Black Pencils. When I became President, I said that I wanted to spend my year reminding everyone of the DNA of D&AD. One essential strand of that DNA

is the incredibly high standard that our judges demand. It's what makes the awards so maddening when you miss out, but so rewarding when you win.

D&AD has put almost eight years of annuals up on its website now, and will continue to add content in the months and years to come. At the click of a mouse you can flick through work, search for credits, and see a snapshot of creative excellence through the years.

I'd like to thank the Executive Committee for all their hard work and dedication, and the Education Council for their continued support.

Most of all, I'd like to thank Anthony Simonds-Gooding CBE, who stepped down as Chairman this year. Anthony has steered D&AD through waters both smooth and choppy over the last 17 years and was incredibly supportive to me during my Presidency.

And finally to everyone whose work appears in the D&AD Annual 2010: congratulations.

**Paul Brazier
D&AD President**

WENN MAN PRÄSIDENT DES D&AD IST, GEHÖRT ES DAZU, DASS MAN ENTSCHEIDEN DARF, WER DAS JAHRBUCH GESTALTET – UND DAS IST TOLL.

Ich hatte insgeheim schon immer den Ehrgeiz, die Gestaltung selbst einmal zu übernehmen. Doch ich halte meinen Größenwahn in Schach und habe stattdessen einen meiner Lieblingskünstler gefragt: Bob and Roberta Smith.

Bob hat wahrscheinlich nicht genau erfassen können, auf was er sich eingelassen hat, aber ich finde, dass er sich mit Keith Sargent als seinem Designer der Herausforderung ganz großartig gestellt hat.

In deren Kern gibt es außerdem noch eine wichtige Botschaft: **Alles wird geschaffen.**

Ich liebe diesen Gedanken.

Für mich fasst er all das zusammen, worum es geht, wenn man ein Kreativprofi ist. Es reicht nicht, nur originelle Ideen auszubrüten, man muss sie auch handwerklich gut umsetzen, sie weiterentwickeln und ihnen gerecht werden.

Schauen Sie sich die folgenden Seiten an, und Sie werden sehen, wie erstaunlich hoch der Grad der professionellen Ausführung ist. Nur jene Ideen, die bravourös ausgeführt werden, stechen wirklich heraus.

Ihnen wird auch auffallen, dass dieser Band verglichen mit früheren Jahren ein wenig dünner ist. Etwas mehr als 550 Werke haben es zwischen die Buchdeckel geschafft. 42 davon wurde ein Yellow Pencil verliehen, und nur fünf wurden mit einem Black Pencil ausgezeichnet. Als ich Präsident wurde, sagte ich, dass ich in

meinem Präsidentschaftsjahr alle an die DNA des D&AD erinnern wollte. Ein wesentlicher Strang dieser DNA ist der unglaublich hohe Standard, den unsere Juroren erwarten. Deswegen ist die Preisverleihung so unerträglich, wenn man leer ausgeht, aber so lohnend, wenn man gewinnt.

Auf der Website von D&AD stehen mittlerweile acht Jahrbücher, und in den folgenden Monaten und Jahren werden weitere Inhalte folgen. Per Mausklick können Sie die Arbeiten durchblättern, nach deren Schöpfern suchen und über die Bilder einen Eindruck der ausgezeichneten Arbeiten aus den verschiedenen Jahren bekommen.

Ich möchte zum Schluss dem Leitungsgremium für seine harte Arbeit und sein Engagement sowie dem Bildungsrat für seine fortwährende Unterstützung danken.

Doch vor allem möchte ich gerne Anthony Simonds-Gooding (CBE) danken, der sein Amt als Vorsitzender in diesem Jahr niedergelegt hat. Anthony steuerte D&AD in den vergangenen 17 Jahren durch unstete, aber auch ruhige Gewässer und hat mich während meiner Präsidentschaft unglaublich unterstützt.

Außerdem möchte ich alle, deren Arbeiten im Jahrbuch des D&AD 2010 erscheinen, ganz herzlich beglückwünschen.

**Paul Brazier
Präsident des D&AD**

L'UN DES NOMBREUX AVANTAGES D'ÊTRE PRÉSIDENT DE D&AD EST DE POUVOIR CHOISIR QUI S'OCCUPERA DU DESIGN DE L'ANNUAIRE.

J'ai toujours eu l'ambition secrète de le faire moi-même. Mais j'ai maîtrisé ma mégalomanie, et j'ai demandé à l'un de mes artistes préférés de s'en charger : Bob and Roberta Smith.

Bob ne réalisait probablement pas dans quoi il se laissait entraîner, mais je pense qu'il s'est amplement montré à la hauteur du défi, tout comme son designer Keith Sargent.

Il y a aussi un message important au cœur de cet ouvrage : **tout est fabriqué**.

J'aime beaucoup cette idée.

Pour moi, elle résume l'essence de la créativité. Il ne s'agit pas seulement de trouver une idée originale, mais aussi de la mettre au monde, de la cultiver, de lui rendre justice.

Parcourez ces pages, et vous verrez que le niveau de savoir-faire y est incroyablement élevé, et que seules les idées qui bénéficient d'une exécution superbe brillent vraiment.

Vous remarquerez aussi que le livre est un peu plus léger que les années précédentes. À peine plus de 550 projets ont été sélectionnés. Quarante-deux ont remporté le Yellow Pencil, et cinq le Black Pencil. Lorsque j'ai pris mes fonctions de président, j'ai dit que je voulais passer mon année à rappeler à tout le monde de quoi était fait l'ADN de D&AD. L'un des maillons les plus importants de cet ADN est la qualité incroyablement élevée que nos jurés exigent. C'est cela qui rend les prix si exaspérants pour ceux qui passent à côté, et si gratifiants pour ceux qui les reçoivent.

D&AD a publié plus de huit années d'annuaires sur son site Internet, et continuera d'y ajouter des contenus au cours des mois et années à venir. En un clic de souris, vous pouvez consulter les projets, faire des recherches sur les créatifs, et visualiser un cliché instantané de l'excellence dans la créativité pour chaque année.

Pour conclure, j'aimerais remercier le comité exécutif pour son travail acharné et son dévouement, ainsi que le conseil de l'éducation pour son soutien.

J'aimerais surtout remercier Anthony Simonds-Gooding, Commandeur de l'Empire britannique, qui a quitté ses fonctions de président du conseil cette année. Anthony a tenu la barre de D&AD par mer calme aussi bien que par mer agitée au cours des 17 dernières années, et m'a été d'un grand secours pendant ma présidence.

Et à l'attention de tous ceux dont le travail est représenté dans l'annuaire 2010 de D&AD : félicitations.

Paul Brazier
Président de D&AD

A short sentence which goes to the heart of what D&AD is about: real creative work made for real clients, appearing in the real world.

The difficulty of achieving brilliance in the world of commercial creativity is what drives us – and is one of the principal reasons that Messrs. Donovan, Bailey and Fletcher brought D&AD to life nearly half a century ago.

They knew that awards matter, because standards matter: more than just the pleasure (in our case, a fairly rare one) of having one's work acknowledged, D&AD awards serve as an absolute reference standard for greatness in any given year. In a nutshell: flick through the book and, as a creative person, you'll know where you stand.

Anything you see anywhere in this annual is notably good, representing less than 5% of the work our judges deliberated over – which in turn was but a small, rigorously-edited fraction of the design, advertising and interactive work released worldwide during 2009.

The Yellow Pencil winners will view this as one of the most significant moments in their professional lives. While the five 2010 Black Pencil winners may need to have a little lie-down.

Which is precisely what Donovan, Bailey and Fletcher had in mind.

But they also knew that the ability to be creatively brilliant, to compete at this level, isn't something most people are born with. The aptitude, probably, the proclivity, almost certainly. But the full-blown, finely-polished ability? Probably not.

That takes time. And it takes learning.

From day one, D&AD has been dedicated to helping the next generation of creative people to scale the heights of greatness. We have a deep and lasting commitment to educators and students across a broad swathe of creative disciplines, with well over 140 University and College partnerships around the world.

Through our Student Awards program, we bring real-world brands together with the best and brightest creative minds in the education system (see the winners in this book). And New Blood, D&AD's yearly graduate exhibition, continues to be the biggest and most highly regarded showcase for talents on the verge of professional life.

And we also recognise that, in the change-maelstrom that is modern life, even the most feted of professionals sometimes needs a tune-up: a new skill here, a refresher there – and that's what our Professional Development programs are all about. Led by highly respected creative people, we run a diverse set of programs and courses which have been attended by (and greatly benefited) thousands.

So D&AD is much more than just an Awards show: it's a finely tuned machine, uniquely combining celebration and inspiration, but with a singular purpose: the perpetuation of brilliance in commercial creativity.

We thank you for your support.

Tim O'Kennedy
CEO

G IS MADE

ANY KIND OF
PRODUCTION
HAS BEEN MADE
BY HUMAN
BEINGS BEEN
DESIGNED BEEN
THOUGHT ABOUT
BEEN DRAWN
ERM IS
DELIVERED BY
ER FASHIONED
BY BY ER
HUMAN BEINGS

EVERYTHII

Ein kurzer Satz, der genau das trifft, worum es im Kern bei D&AD geht: echte kreative Arbeit für echte Klienten in der realen Welt.

Die Herausforderung, in der Welt der kommerziellen Kreativität wirklich brillant zu sein, treibt uns alle an – und sie ist einer der Hauptgründe, warum D&AD von den Herren Donovan, Bailey und Fletcher vor fast einem halben Jahrhundert ins Leben gerufen wurde.

Sie wussten, dass Auszeichnungen und Preise wichtig sind, weil die damit vermittelten Standards von Bedeutung sind: Dabei geht es nicht nur um die Freude (die in unserem Fall recht selten vorkommt), die eigene Arbeit gewürdigt zu sehen; die Auszeichnungen des D&AD dienen auch als absoluter Referenzstandard für großartige Leistungen eines jeden Jahres. Kurz und knapp gesagt: Blättern Sie dieses Buch durch, und als kreativer Geist wissen Sie genau, wo Sie stehen.

Alles, was Sie in diesem Jahrbuch sehen, ist bemerkenswert gut und repräsentiert weniger als 5 % der Arbeiten, die unsere Juroren ausgewertet haben – was wiederum nur einen kleinen, rigoros ausgesiebten Bruchteil der Arbeiten aus Design, Werbung und interaktiven Werken darstellt, die im Jahre 2009 weltweit veröffentlicht wurden.

Die Gewinner des Yellow Pencils werden die Verleihung als einen der bedeutendsten Momente in ihrem professionellen Leben betrachten. Die fünf Gewinner des Black Pencils von 2010 hingegen werden sich wohl erst einmal hinsetzen müssen, um diese Auszeichnung zu verkraften.

Und genau das war das Ziel von Donovan, Bailey und Fletcher.

Aber ihnen war außerdem klar, dass – um auf dieser Stufe mithalten zu können – die Fähigkeit zu herausragenden kreativen und brillanten Leistungen nicht etwas ist, was den meisten Menschen in die Wiege gelegt wird. Die Begabung vermutlich ja, die Neigung höchstwahrscheinlich auch. Doch ein voll entfaltetes, vervollkommnetes Können? Wahrscheinlich nicht.

Das braucht Zeit. Und die Bereitschaft, viel zu lernen.

Vom ersten Tag an verschrieb sich D&AD der Idee, der nächsten Generation kreativer Köpfe dabei zu helfen, die höchsten Gipfel der Kreativität zu erklimmen. Wir fühlen uns den Lehrenden und Studierenden aus einer großen Bandbreite kreativer Disziplinen zutiefst und dauerhaft verpflichtet und arbeiten mit weit über 140 Universitäten und Colleges weltweit in Partnerschaften zusammen.

Durch unser Studentenförderungsprogramm bringen wir echte Marken mit den besten und hellsten Köpfen aus dem Bildungssystem zusammen – siehe die Gewinner in diesem Buch. Und New Blood (die Ausstellung der jährlichen Absolventen von D&AD) ist weiterhin die größte und renommierteste Präsentation von Talenten, die sich auf dem Sprung in ihr berufliches Leben befinden.

Und wir erkennen auch, dass in dem Mahlstrom der Wechselhaftigkeit, die wir modernes Leben nennen, sogar die gefeiertesten Profis manchmal mehr Anregungen und neuen Input brauchen: Hier muss etwas neu gelernt werden, dort könnte mal wieder was aufgefrischt werden – und genau darum geht es bei unseren Programmen für das Professional Development. Diese vielfältigen Kurse und Programme werden von herausragenden und anerkannten kreativen Köpfen geleitet und wurden bereits von Tausenden belegt, die davon außergewöhnlich profitiert haben.

Also ist D&AD mehr als nur eine Preisverleihungs-show: Es ist eine fein abgestimmte Maschinerie, bei der auf unvergleichliche Weise Würdigungen, Feierlichkeiten und Inspirationen miteinander verschmelzen. Doch letzten Endes dient sie nur einem einzigen Zweck: dem Erhalt einer brillanten kommerziellen Kreativität.

Wir danken Ihnen für Ihre Unterstützung.

Tim O'Kennedy
CEO

Une courte phrase qui touche du doigt l'essence de D&AD : un travail créatif réel fait pour des clients réels, et qui se manifeste dans le monde réel.

Notre moteur, c'est la difficulté d'atteindre l'excellence dans le monde de la créativité commerciale – et c'est l'une des principales raisons pour lesquelles messieurs Donovan, Bailey et Fletcher ont fondé D&AD il y a près d'un demi-siècle.

Ils connaissaient l'importance des concours et des prix, parce qu'ils connaissaient l'importance des critères d'excellence : au-delà du simple plaisir (dans notre cas assez rare) de voir son travail reconnu, les prix D&AD sont la référence absolue de l'excellence, année après année. En quelques mots : feuilletez ce livre, et vous saurez où vous vous situez en tant que créatif.

Tout ce que vous verrez dans ce recueil annuel est d'une qualité remarquable, et représente à peine 5 % des projets sur lesquels nos jurés ont délibéré – ce qui là encore n'était qu'une petite fraction rigoureusement triée sur le volet des projets de design, publicité et interactivité produits dans le monde entier en 2009.

Pour les lauréats du Yellow Pencil, ceci est l'un des plus grands moments de leur carrière. Quant aux cinq lauréats du Black Pencil pour 2010, il se pourrait qu'ils aient besoin de s'asseoir, juste le temps de reprendre leurs esprits.

C'est exactement ce que Donovan, Bailey et Fletcher avaient en tête.

Mais ils savaient aussi que l'excellence créative, à ce niveau de compétition, n'est pas une qualité innée pour la plupart des gens. L'aptitude, probablement, et l'inclination, très certainement. Mais la compétence pleinement développée et perfectionnée ? Sûrement pas.

Cela demande du temps, et de l'apprentissage.

Dès ses débuts, D&AD s'est consacré à aider la prochaine génération de créatifs à conquérir les sommets de la grandeur. Nous sommes engagés auprès des enseignants et étudiants d'un large éventail de disciplines créatives, et avons établi des partenariats avec plus de 140 universités et établissements d'enseignement supérieur dans le monde entier.

Avec notre programme de prix étudiants, nous réunissons les marques du monde réel et les meilleurs esprits créatifs du système éducatif (voir les lauréats dans ce livre). Et New Blood, l'exposition annuelle de D&AD pour les jeunes diplômés, est toujours l'une des vitrines les plus importantes et les plus prestigieuses pour les jeunes talents sur le point d'entrer dans la vie active.

Nous savons aussi que, dans le tourbillon de changement qu'est la vie moderne, même les professionnels les plus chevronnés ont parfois besoin de s'actualiser : une nouvelle compétence ici, une remise à niveau là – c'est l'objectif de nos programmes de développement professionnel. Ces programmes et cours conduits par des créatifs hautement distingués couvrent un large spectre de sujets et ont été suivis par des milliers de professionnels (qui en ont retiré de grands bénéfices).

D&AD est donc bien plus qu'un concours. C'est une machine bien huilée, qui opère une alliance unique entre récompense et inspiration, mais avec un seul objectif : perpétuer l'excellence dans la créativité commerciale.

Nous vous remercions pour votre soutien.

Tim O'Kennedy
Directeur Général

Art Direction
Dave Dye, Dye Holloway Murray (Jury Foreman)
Mark Denton, COY! COMMUNICATIONS
Pierrette Diaz, DDB Paris
Zac Ellis, WCRS
Menno Kluin, Y&R New York
Mark Reddy, BBH London
Tiger Savage, M&C Saatchi

Book Design
John Morgan, John Morgan Studio (Jury Foreman)
John Hamilton, Penguin Books
Nick Hard, Research Studios
Julian Humphries, Harper Collins
Lucie Stericker, The Orion Publishing Group
Julius Wiedemann, TASCHEN

Branding
Ben Casey, The Chase Manchester (Jury Foreman)
Adrian Burton, Lambie-Nairn
Fiona Curran, Williams Murray Hamm
David Dalziel, Dalziel & Pow
Gareth Howat, hat-trick design
Peter Knapp, Landor Associates

Digital Advertising
Rei Inamoto, AKQA San Francisco (Jury Foreman)
Suzana Apelbaum, REDE
Tim Barbar, Odopod
Vincent Jansen, Boondoggle Leuven
Patou Nuytemans, Ogilvy & Mather London
Darren Richardson, 180 Amsterdam
Alistair Robertson, Abbott Mead Vickers BBDO
Sebastian Royce, glue London
Liz Sivell, R/GA London
Måns Tesch, Tesch

Direct
Caitlin Ryan, Proximity London (Jury Foreman)
Jamie Bell, CMW
Kurt-Georg Dieckert, TBWA\ Deutschland
Nigel Edginton-Vigus, Wunderman
Bernd Fliesser, Draftfcb Partners
Victor Ng, Euro RSCG Partnership
Colin Nimick, OgilvyOne Worldwide London

Environmental Design
Ian Caulder, Caulder Moore Design Consultants (Jury Foreman)
Jussi Ängeslevä, ART+COM
Robin Clark, Land Design Studio
Mark Dytham, Klein Dytham Architecture
Annabel Judd, Victoria & Albert Museum
Nicky Kirk, Amenity Space
Alex Mowat, Urban Salon Architects
Amanda Parks, Publicis Mid America
Owain Roberts, Gensler
Robert Thiemann, Frame Magazine

Graphic Design
Jonathan Ellery, Browns (Jury Foreman)
Mark Lester, MARK
Fraser Muggeridge, Fraser Muggeridge studio
Michael C Place, Build
Paul West, Form

Illustration
Brian Cairns, Brian Cairns Studio (Jury Foreman)
Adrian Johnson, Adrian Johnson Studio
Dave Masterman, CHI&Partners
Michael Montgomery, Graphic Thought Facility
Stuart Radford, Radford Wallis
Monty Verdi, Leo Burnett London

Integrated
Steve Henry (Jury Foreman)
Philip Andrew, Clemenger BBDO
Matthew Bull, Lowe Worldwide
Chris Clarke, LBi
Daryl Corps, Anomaly
Craig Davis, Publicis Mojo
David Lee, TBWA\Digital Arts
Rob Reilly, Crispin Porter + Bogusky
Ted Royer, Droga5
Anders Stake, Wieden+Kennedy London
Satoshi Takamatsu, ground Tokyo
Steve Vranakis, VCCP
Jon Williams, Grey London

Magazine & Newspaper Design
eremy Leslie, magCulture (Jury Foreman)
arissa Bourke, ELLE Magazine
ndrew Diprose, Condé Nast
ebecca Smith, TwinFactory
uchar Swara, Esterson Associates
orgo Tloupas, Intersection Magazine

Mobile Marketing
ames Temple, R/GA London (Jury Foreman)
m Ash, This is Movement
orihiro Harano, Drill
o Heiss, Dare
ac Morrison, Oil Productions

Music Videos
asha Nixon, Partizan (Jury Foreman)
orin Hardy, Academy Films
ichard Kenworthy, Shynola
m Nash, Atlantic Records UK
awn Shadforth, RSA/Black Dog Films
hris Sweeney, Blink Productions

Outdoor Advertising
eremy Craigen, DDB UK (Jury Foreman)
ndy Clough, BBH London
enno Kluin, Y&R New York
ark Roalfe, RKCR/Y&R
ake Rusznyak, BMF
aul Silburn, Saatchi & Saatchi London

Packaging Design
ohn Blackburn, Blackburn's (Jury Foreman)
duardo Del Fraile, Dfraile
ruce Duckworth, Turner Duckworth
avid Jones, Buddy
arah Roberts
raham Shearsby, Design Bridge London
lenn Tutssel, The Brand Union

Photography
ames Day, James Day Photography
ury Foreman)
aul Belford, This is Real Art
ominic Goldman, BBH London
iran Master, Burnham Niker
lexandra Taylor, Mrs.McGuinty Ltd.
ike Trow, Vogue

Press Advertising
Rosie Arnold, BBH London (Jury Foreman)
Thierry Albert, Mother
Damon Collins, RKCR/Y&R
Matt Doman, BBH London
Simon Learman, McCann Erickson London
Dean Webb, The Red Brick Road
Deneke Von Weltzien, Jung von Matt/Alster

Product Design
Luke Pearson, PearsonLloyd Design (Jury Foreman)
Christoph Behling, Christoph Behling Design
& SolarLab
Adrian Caroen, Seymourpowell
Marcus Hoggarth, Native Design
Sung Han Kim, Samsung Design Europe
Adam White, Factorydesign

Radio
Tony Malcolm, Leo Burnett London (Jury Foreman)
Ben Fairman, Radioville
Jerry Hollens, RKCR/Y&R
Jason Hynes, Jason Hynes
Marcus Leigh, BJL
Ian Mactavish, Radioville
Philip Maes, The Maffia
George Prest, DLKW
Lode Schaeffer, INDIE Amsterdam
Mike Schalit, Network BBDO Johannesburg
Munzie Thind, Grand Central Sound Studios

TV & Cinema Advertising
Rémi Babinet, BETC Euro RSCG (Jury Foreman)
Martin Beauvais
Mike Boles, RKCR/Y&R
Andy Cheetham, Cheetham Bell/JWT
Manchester
Susan Credle, Leo Burnett Chicago
Richard Denney, DDB London
Simon Green
Mike McKenna
Jay Phillips, McCann Erickson London

TV & Cinema Communications
Charlie Mawer, Red Bee Media (Jury Foreman)
Richard Holman, Devilfish
Matt Lambert, Rokkit
Richard Martin, ENVY Post Production
Adam Parry, Superfad
Jorn Threlfall, Outsider

TV & Cinema Crafts
Walter Campbell, Serious Pictures (Jury Foreman)
Phil Crowe, The Mill
Lisa Gunning, The Whitehouse
Carlos Manga Junior, Paranoid BR
Guy Manwaring, SONNY London
Paul Prince, The Sweet Shop
Ben Sedley, Outsider
James Spence, Red Bee Media

Typography
Michael Johnson, johnson banks (Jury Foreman)
Frith Kerr, Studio Frith
Pete Mould, DDB UK
Ben Terrett, Really Interesting Group
David Wakefield, 23 Press
Matt Willey, Studio8 Design

Websites
Martin Cedergren, Åkestam Holst (Jury Foreman)
Paul Banham, JWT London
Anders Gustafsson, Crispin Porter + Bogusky
Europe
Simon Labbett, Saint@RKCR
Tim Malbon, Made by Many
Pablo Marques, Publicis Modem
Eva Mautino, B-Reel
Martin Palamarz, Lateral
Simon Richings, Tribal DDB London
Andy Sandoz, Work Club
Simon (Sanky) Sankarayya, AllofUs

Writing for Advertising
Leon Jaume, Engine (Jury Foreman)
Sean Doyle
Tony Miller, Fallon London
Richard Russell, DDB London
Claudia Southgate
Mark Tweddell, Abbott Mead Vickers BBDO

Writing for Design
John Simmons, The Writer (Jury Foreman)
Nick Asbury, Asbury & Asbury
Robert Ball, The Partners
Stuart Delves, Henzteeth
Ruth Gavin, Cherry
Roger Horberry
Jayne Workman, Elmwood Design

Students
Jessica Reynolds
Serena Wise

College
Kingston University

Tutors
Mike Bond
Malcolm Kennard
Marion Morrison

Open Brief
for IKEA

IKEA Spectrum
The brief was to inspire a wave of boundless change in peoples' homes by promoting the new IKEA catalogue. We were interested in how people react instinctively to colour. After observing customers in store, we noticed they have an immediate response to the colour of a product. In our solution, the colour wheel shows the endless possibilities of IKEA's huge range of products. It can be used across all IKEA communications in print and online. On the website, an interactive colour wheel can be used to browse the range or search for products using colour swatches.

19

Student
Matthew Young

College
University of Leeds

Tutor
Claire Tindale

Open Brief

Moving Image
for onedotzero

The City
The City is constantly in transition and mutation, disappearing behind changing environments and shifting identities. The brief was to create your own 'adventure in motion' which explores this. I went around several major cities and asked people one question: what is 'The City' to you? Their responses were then animated.

Students
Stewart Linton
Scott Oxley

College
University of Lincoln

Tutors
Sinclair Ashman
John Dowling
Carolyn Puzzovio
Glen Robinson
Barrie Tullett
Philippa Wood

Advertising

Integrated
for Lloyds TSB

Get Involved
The brief was to create an integrated campaign to bring to life Lloyds TSB's partnership with the London 2012 Olympic and Paralympic Games. In order to boost expectation and anticipation during the build-up to the Olympics, we used an iPhone app, internal posters, newspaper adverts and a direct mailer. Through these platforms, Lloyds TSB directs customers to local sporting venues in order to get them involved in different Olympic sports, regardless of their location.

Students
Brad Hall
Patrick Koelling
Devin LuBean
Nathan
Wigglesworth

College
Brigham Young
University

Tutor
Jeff Sheets

Advertising
TV Advertising
for Doritos

Doritos Guardian
The brief was to create a TV advert for Doritos that 'entertains your mates as much as it does you', so we decided to create a spot that would be memorable but, above all, majestic. We all have that moment in our lives when we wish that we could command the beasts and fowls of the earth to do our bidding for us. This piece is a step towards realising that wish, as the falcon protects man's most valuable possession – Doritos.

Students
Alex Katz
Javi Iñiguez De
Onzoño
Rui Marini

College
Miami Ad School,
Madrid

Tutor
Elvio Sanchez

Advertising
TV Promo
for Channel 4

E4 Movie Night – Loo 2 You (20 Second Spot & 5 Second Sting)
The brief was to create a TV promo for E4, promoting their Monday Night Movie strand in a fun and irreverent way. We decided to give their audience something to help enhance the movie watching experience at home. Before each film, viewers are treated to an infomercial for a product that is the latest in movie night technology: Loo 2 You, an adult diaper that allows you to remain seated throughout the entire film without having to get up for those pesky bathroom breaks. It also includes an E4 air freshener at no additional cost.

Students
Patrick Schroeder
Jaclyn Stauber

College
Design Factory
International

Tutor
Michael Hoinkes

Advertising

Direct Response
for LIDA

Stick-a-Mini
The brief was to create a direct response communication for MINI demonstrating that customers can create their own unique version of their favourite model. We created the 'Stick-a-Mini' Stickers; the chassis of the car on the stickers is transparent, so whatever surface you put them on will shine through. This translates to unique versions of MINIs created by customers. This also works on an iPhone, as you can take a picture of your surroundings through the mask of a 'Stick-a-Mini' sticker.

Introduction

The Mobile Health Service is a medical health application. It deals with public health in the broadest sense, by pointing to what could be possible in the future with advancements in mobile technology. Its intentions lie in improving the relationship that a person has with their National Health Service.

Whether it be diagnosing symptoms, booking appointments or advising you on when to take medication; the application makes public health more welcoming and instantaneous.

Key Features

Connections

- On the go synchronisation of the user's profile with the National Health Service database, keeping the user and their GP both constantly up to date.
- A connection to the internet provides the application with reviews of pharmacies, GPs and hospitals.
- Profiles are accessible from any phone running the application.
- GPs and call operators (emergency / non-emergency) have instant access to the user's profile, case files and medication.

Diagnosis

- Can diagnose problems using a multitude of different sensors (camera, accelerometers, microphone, etc).
- Can diagnose a severe and otherwise unforeseen problem ahead of time and potentially save lives.
- Understands when it is important for the user to talk to a qualified practitioner. Encourages the user to book in with the GP when necessary.
- Reassuring interface for making emergency calls, ability to send case file and profile, making for more effective emergency help.

Management

- Allows the user to manage appointments with their GP and taking of medicine.
- Reminds the user when an appointment is due and when medication needs to be taken.
- Breaks down the taking of medication with calendars and daily schedules.
- Able to locate nearest GPs and hospitals, can provide information on relevant facilities (A&E, X-Ray, etc).

Clarity

- Even though the application deals with complex medical procedures, its wording always remains simple and clear.
- An intuitive interface with specific help available for every screen.
- Clean and consistent design that is easy to navigate.
- Support for the visually and aurally impaired.

The Nokia X8

The Mobile Health Service makes full use of technology offered by the Nokia X8 (fictitious). The technology is listed below along with its use in the application:-

Touch Screen	Used to operate the application.
Camera	Used to take pictures of rashes and other visual symptoms.
Accelerometer	Ultra high sensitivity, used to measure the user's pulse or heart rate.
GPS	For locating the phone when using maps and in the event of an emergency.
Thermometer	Used to check user's temperature.
Microphone	Used to record and diagnose coughs and wheezes (on front of device).

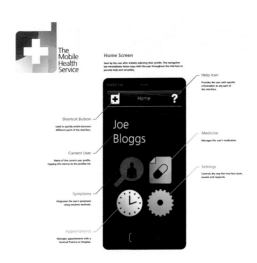

The Mobile Health Service

Home Screen

Student
Matt Turnbull

College
University College
Falmouth

Tutors
Mafalda Spencer
Jon Unwin

Graphic Design

Interactive Design
for Forum Nokia

The Mobile Health Service
The brief was to help Nokia change the everyday world by creating a forward thinking and functional interactive mobile service that can make a real difference to the user's personal or professional life. Our solution was the Mobile Health Service, a medical health application. It deals with public health in the broadest sense, by pointing to what could be possible in the future with advancements in mobile technology. It aims to improve the relationship that people have with the National Health Service. The application makes the public health service more welcoming and instantaneous, whether it is to diagnose symptoms, book appointments or get advice on when to take medication.

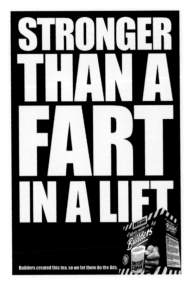 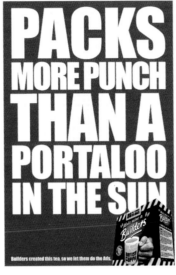 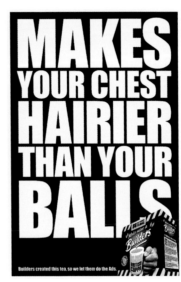

Students	**College**	**Tutors**
Melissa Haselden	University of Central	Frank Cookson
Claire Watson	Lancashire UCLAN	Lin Sinclair

Graphic Design

Writing for Design
for Elmwood

Builders
Builders tea is British slang for a strong, no-nonsense cup of tea. The brief was to create a copy-based campaign which positions Make Mine a Builders as the authentic builder's tea at the heart of British life. Builders created this tea so we let them do the ads. Well not really, we did them, but we tried to tap into builders' frank and honest sense of humour. Based on 'Make Mine a Builders' being slang for a strong cuppa, we created adverts that are strong both in their use of language and message.

Student	**College**	**Tutor**
Chris Howker	Stockport College	Ian Murray

Craft

Illustration
for Don't Panic

Don't Do That!
The brief was to create an image for Don't Panic that captures the theme of resistance. I used the notions of 'not colouring within the lines' and 'not running with scissors' as metaphors for rebellion. It seems easier to resist or rebel when you are younger and I was reminded of all the things I was told not to do, but did anyway! This piece is a call to arms to remind us to have fun whatever we are doing. Stop taking things so seriously, lighten up, take some risks and enjoy yourself.

Student
Ricky Lo Wing Kit

College
Hong Kong
Polytechnic
University

Tutor
Tsang Kam Ching

Craft
Photography
for Getty Images

Paranoid Android
The brief was to create a set of images that help communicate a company's character and spirit to its customers. This is a series of dynamic fashion images that show men's mightiness, vitality and elegance, and aim to promote the identity of a brand.

Student
Tim Keay

College
The University of
Northampton

Tutors
James Smith
Barry Wenden

Craft
Typography
for LBi

LBi: Loved By invertebrates
The brief was to use typography across any medium to explore the possibilities of meaning behind the LBi name. By taking a humorous approach to the brief, a series of typography-based illustrations were created to promote the company in a unique and appealing way. The series of illustrations have been compiled into a promotional booklet, designed to be used as a light-hearted alternative to the usual promotional materials used by companies.

Students
Richard Gilbert
Matthew Laws
Adam Paterson

College
Royal College of Art

Tutor
Ashley Hall

Product Design

3D Product Design
for DIY KYOTO

Design Out Waste: The Optimist Toaster
The brief was to design a product that can help consumers who enjoy access to the luxury market to live more sustainably. Consuming less 'stuff' is a way to live more sustainably, but to own an object for life is a big decision. No one wants to be burdened with an item that they don't like. The Optimist is a toaster with weight and substance that communicates a new vision for luxury product design: the luxury of longevity. Most small household electricals don't get recycled, even though recycling facilities exist. The Optimist is one of a series of three toasters that take different approaches to conserving material that would otherwise go to landfill.

Student
Rodrigo Da Silva

College
Centro de Diseño
Cine y Televisión

Tutor
Francisco Torres

Product Design

Furniture Design
for New British Design

Broom-Stick Shelving System
The brief was to go modular in furniture design and create a piece for New British Design that looks great in a crowd but is equally happy in its own company. Broom-Stick is a modular shelving system that is inspired by the typical Mexican broom. The connecting parts are based on the simple principle of assembling positive and negative, tension and pressure, like Velcro. Combining CNC technology, traditional carpentry skills and certified wood, the Broom-Stick shelving system eliminates the need for screws and nails for assembly. This product is functional and flexible, as it gives users the opportunity to create many different combinations according to their needs.

25

President̶s̶ AWARD

DARWIN
SPEED
STAR.

California

Weapons of Choice

Photographer
Benzo Theodore

Where the Wild Things Are

President's Award

Spike Jonze

The term maverick is often overused. But I don't think anyone would deny that Spike Jonze is a true creative maverick. And I am delighted to give him the D&AD President's Award 2010. The breadth of his work is staggering, covering everything from music videos and advertising to TV and feature films. Yet he seems to have an inexhaustible supply of original ideas, no matter what medium he works in. And although each project is distinctive in its own right, they are all marked by one thing: to watch Jonze's work is to enter a world just like, and yet completely unlike, our own.

Paul Brazier, D&AD President

BRAWN KNOCKING WINCE PILL.

BLACK PENCIL

PENCIL

WINNING

WORK

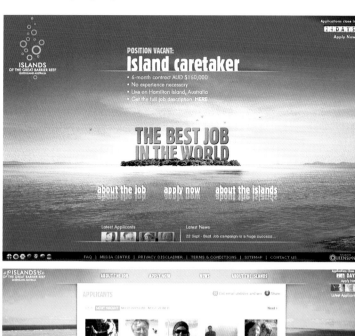

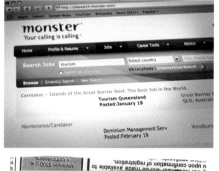

Art Directors
Ralphie Barnett
Cristian Staal
Copywriter
Merrin McCormick
Creative Directors
James Burchill
Nancy Hartley

Senior Digital Producer
Jason Kibsgaard
Advertising Agency
SapientNitro

National Planning Director
Darren McColl
Account Director
Anne Maree Wilson

Digital Account Director
Adam Ford
Client
Tourism Queensland

Integrated & Direct/Integrated

SapientNitro
for Tourism Queensland

The Best Job in the World

We wanted to increase international awareness of Queensland's islands of the Great Barrier Reef, and transform a popular day-trip destination into an international tourist's dream holiday. In a time of rising unemployment, we created the best job in the world: the too good to be true Island Caretaker role, a genuine employment opportunity with Tourism Queensland. Anyone could apply, and the successful candidate would spend six months living above the reef, exploring the region and reporting back to the world. With a US$1.2million budget, we placed simple recruitment ads and created a worldwide phenomenon. The campaign was awarded two Black Pencils, in Integrated and Direct/Integrated.

Art Directors
Nadja Lossgott
Shelley Smoler
Copywriters
Raphael Basckin
Nicholas Hulley

Executive Creative Director
Damon Stapleton
Photographers
Chloe Coetsee
Des Ellis
Michael Meyersfeld
Rob Wilson

Advertising Agency
TBWA\Hunt\Lascaris
Johannesburg
Account Handler
Bridget Langley

Marketing Manager
Liz Linsell
Client
The Zimbabwean
Newspaper

Graphic Design/Leaflets

TBWA\Hunt\Lascaris Johannesburg
for The Zimbabwean Newspaper

Trillion Dollar Flyer
The Zimbabwean Newspaper, forced into exile, was then slapped with a 55% luxury import duty, making it unaffordable for Zimbabweans. To raise awareness of this issue, we developed an unusual solution. The most eloquent symbol of Zimbabwe's collapse is the Z$ trillion note, which cannot buy anything and certainly not advertising. But it can become the advertising. We turned the worthless money into flyers by printing our messages straight onto it. Overnight, Zimbabwean banknotes achieved what they'd never been able to buy – advertising coverage. We used Mugabe's own creation against him.

Lead Designer	Associate Architects	Environmental	Signage	Surveyors
James Corner	Diller Scofidio +	**Engineering**	Pentagram Design	Control Point
Designers	Renfro	GRB Services	**Irrigation**	Associates
Elizabeth Diller	**Planting Design**	**Civil & Traffic**	Northern Designs	**Cost**
Charles Renfro	Piet Oudolf	**Engineering**	**Soil Science**	**Consultants**
Ricardo Scofidio	**Structural**	Philip Habib	Pine & Swallow	VJ Associates
Urban Design	**Engineering**	& Associates	Associates	**Code Consultants**
James Corner Field	Robert Silman	**Water Feature**	**Historic Preservation**	Code Consultants
Operations	Associates	**Engineering**	Robert Silman	Professional
Landscape	**Structural & MEP**	CMS Collaborative	Associates	Engineers
Architects	**Engineering**	**Lighting**	**Public Space**	**Client**
James Corner Field	Buro Happold	L'Observatoire	**Management**	Friends of the
Operations		International	ETM Associates	High Line

Environmental Design/Public Space & Community

Diller Scofidio + Renfro
for Friends of the High Line

High Line

The High Line is a new 1.5 mile long public park built on an abandoned elevated railroad stretching from the Meatpacking District to the Hudson rail yards in Manhattan. Inspired by the melancholic, unruly beauty of this post-industrial ruin, where nature has reclaimed a once vital piece of urban infrastructure, the new park interprets its inheritance. It translates the biodiversity that took root after it fell into disuse into a string of site-specific urban microclimates along the stretch of railway. These include sunny, shady, wet, dry, windy, and sheltered spaces.

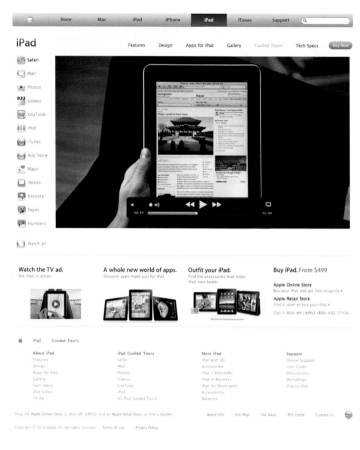

Design Group
Apple Graphic
Design

Client
Apple

Apple Graphic Design
for Apple

Apple Website
With billions of visits a year, apple.com is the online home of the company that introduced the Mac, iPod, iPhone, and iPad. Apple.com speaks directly to customers, the press, and sales personnel worldwide; so it must be as approachable as it is comprehensive. The content – video, motion graphics, photography, and copywriting – is created entirely by an in-house team with expert knowledge of Apple products. And because Apple innovates at a breakneck pace, apple.com must too. Each year, the site effectively undergoes a complete redesign, all the while maintaining a style that is distinctly Apple: clean, simple, and elegant in both its form and function.

DICTATO

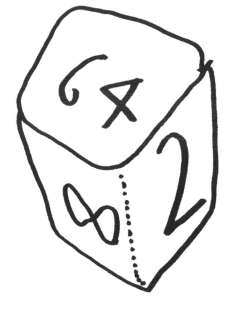

D: Art Dir

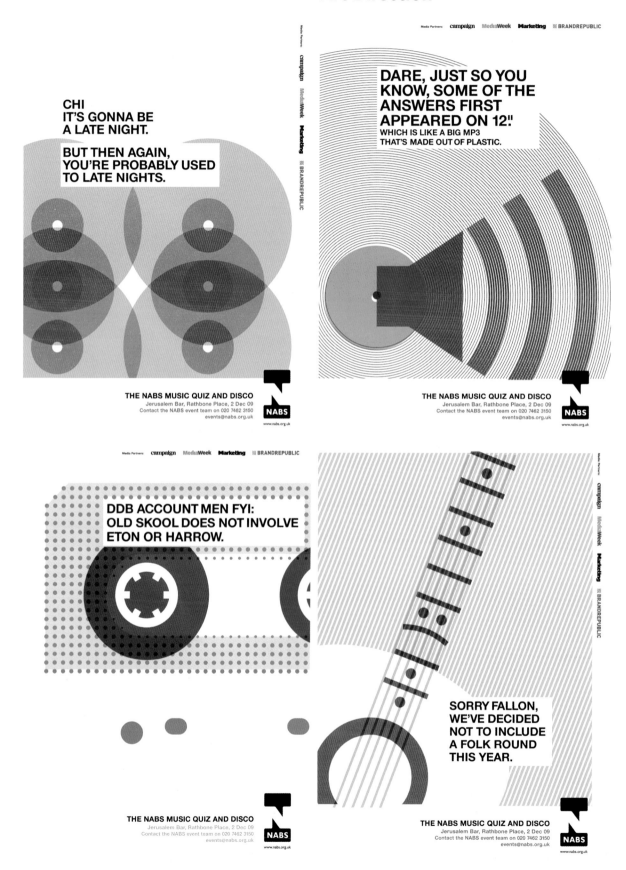

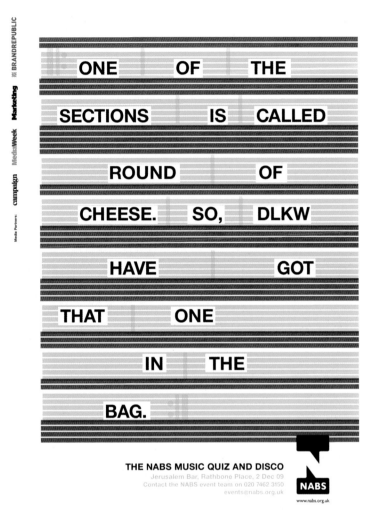

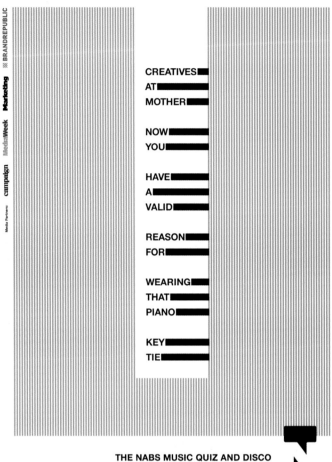

Poster Advertising

DDB UK
for NABS

CHI / Dare / DDB / Fallon / DLKW / Mother
NABS is a charity that gives professional advice, emotional support and financial assistance to people in the communications industry. To raise funds it held an industry-wide music quiz and disco. To pique people's interest, generate word of mouth and get the blogs talking, we created these good-natured but slightly barbed posters. Each agency in London got the full set of six. Whether they put the execution up that pertained to them, well, that was entirely at their discretion.

Art Directors
Adrian Chan
Stuart Mills
Maurice Wee
Copywriters
Eugene Cheong
Craig Love
Mike Sutcliffe

Photographer
Edward Loh
Creative Directors
Eugene Cheong
Tham Khai Meng
Todd McCracken

Advertising Agency
Ogilvy Singapore
Senior Project
Manager
Monica De Grave

Client
Unilever
Brand
Ben & Jerry's

Press Advertising

Ogilvy Singapore
for Unilever

Hugs / Whale Cow / Purple Caterpillar / Freaky Recipes
Consumers in Singapore have a wide range of ice-creams to choose from these days, with the recent proliferation of small, independent shops in many malls, selling both ice-cream and frozen yogurt. We wanted to bring Ben & Jerry's ice-cream firmly back into the public eye, and re-establish it as the more original, unusual ice-cream. The aim was to appeal to the young and the young at heart, an audience of more independent consumers who want to appear more individual and not eat 'the same' as everyone else. Purple Caterpillar and Whale Cow were also selected in this category as single adverts.

Art Directors
Nadja Lossgott
Shelley Smoler
Copywriters
Raphael Basckin
Nicholas Hulley

Photographers
Chloe Coetsee
Des Ellis
Michael Meyersfeld
Rob Wilson

**Executive Creative
Director**
Damon Stapleton
Account Handler
Bridget Langley

Advertising Agency
TBWA\Hunt\Lascaris
Johannesburg
Marketing Manager
Liz Linsell
Client
The Zimbabwean
Newspaper

Poster Advertising

TBWA\Hunt\Lascaris Johannesburg
for The Zimbabwean Newspaper

Cheaper Than Paper
The Zimbabwean Newspaper, forced into exile, was then slapped with a 55% luxury import
duty, making it unaffordable for Zimbabweans. To raise awareness of this issue, we developed
an unusual solution. The most eloquent symbol of Zimbabwe's collapse is the Z$ trillion note,
which cannot buy anything and certainly not advertising. But it can become the advertising. We
turned the money into the medium by printing our messages straight onto it. We made posters,
murals and billboards out of the worthless money. Overnight, Zimbabwean banknotes achieved
what they'd never been able to buy – advertising coverage. We used Mugabe's own creation
against him.

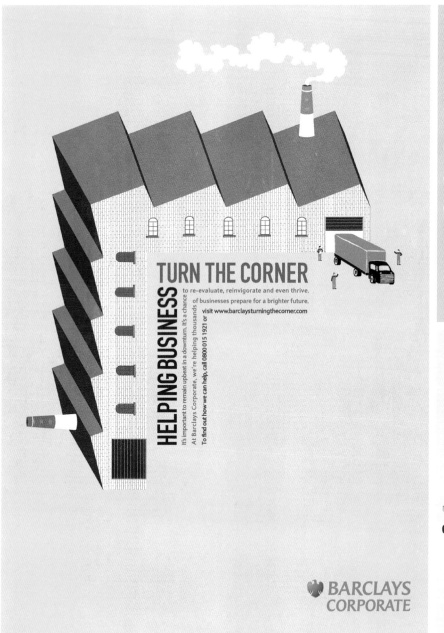

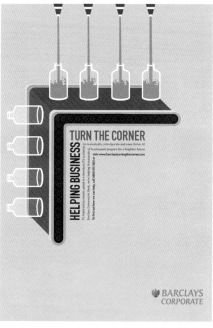

Art Directors
Andy Clough
Richard McGrann
Designers
Chris Chapman
Andy Clough
Dominic Grant

Copywriters
Andy Clough
Richard McGrann
Illustrator
Shout

Typographers
Chris Chapman
Dominic Grant
Print Producer
Michael Winek
Creative Director
Marc Hatfield

Head of Art
Mark Reddy
Advertising Agency
BBH London
Marketing Manager
Kathryn Taylor
Client
Barclays

Press Advertising

BBH London
for Barclays

Factory / Bottle / Boat
This is a print campaign to inform the business community about Barclays' ability to help them through the economic downturn.

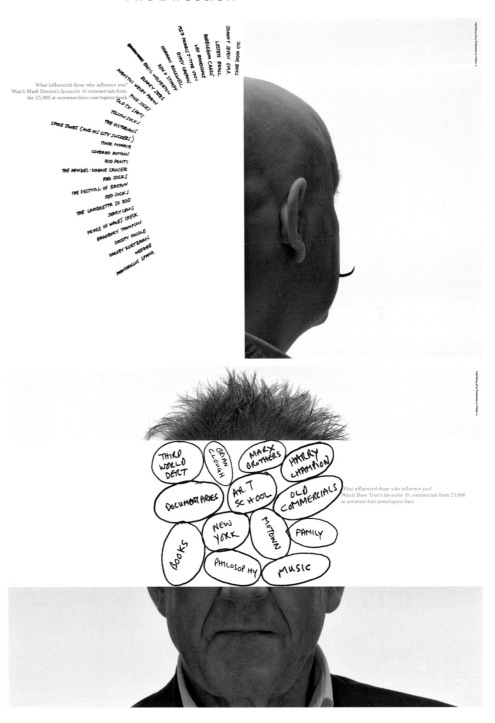

What influenced those who influence you?
Watch Mark Denton's favourite 10 commercials from
the 25,000 at arrowsarchive.com/topten/mark

What influenced those who influence you?
Watch Dave Trott's favourite 10 commercials from 25,000
at arrowsarchive.com/topten/dave

Art Director	**Typographer**	**Planner**	**Brand & Marketing**
David Goss	David Goss	Justin Holloway	**Manager**
Designer	**Image Manipulator**	**Account Handler**	Barry Cox
David Goss	David Goss	Jorian Murray	**Client**
Copywriter	**Print Producer**	**Advertising Agency**	The History of
Phoebe Coulton	Kieran Ward	Dye Holloway	Advertising Trust
Photographer	**Creative Director**	Murray	**Brand**
Brian Griffin	Dave Dye		Arrows Archive

Press Advertising

Dye Holloway Murray
for Arrows Archive

Influences – Denton / Trott
To give the advertising community a reason to visit arrowsarchive.co.uk, we featured the most admired people in the business, endorsing the fact that they had been influenced by its content: 24,000 old telly ads.

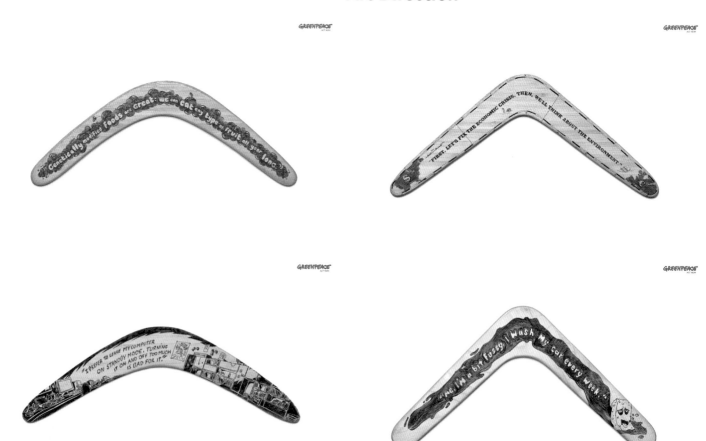

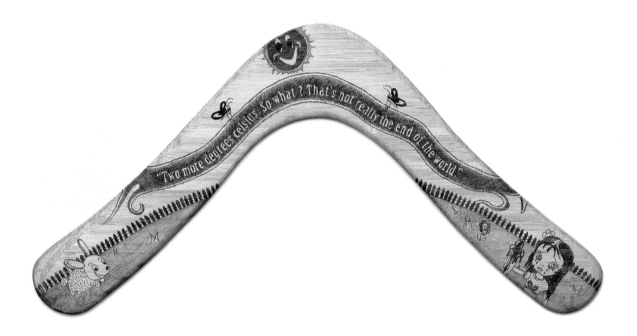

Art Director
Benjamin Marchal
Copywriter
Olivier Lefebvre
Photographer
Eric Sauvage

Illustrators
Monsieur Barbe
Augustin Camus
Typographers
Monsieur Barbe
Augustin Camus

Executive Creative Director
Alexandre Hervé
Account Manager
Xavier Mendiola

Advertising Agency
DDB Paris
Marketing Manager
Pascal Husting
Client
Greenpeace

Press Advertising

DDB Paris
for Greenpeace

GM Foods / Economic Crisis / Computer / Car / Two More Degrees
Greenpeace wanted to reach people in their everyday lives and make them realise that there are no small gestures when it comes to saving our planet. We launched a print advertising campaign using boomerangs to remind French consumers of environmental problems, as ignoring them will backfire one day. The campaign warns of the long-term effects of nuclear energy, irresponsible use of water, and environmental apathy.

Art Director
Chris Groom
Copywriter
Sam Heath
Photographer
Luke Kirwan
Retoucher
Badger

Creative Directors
Tony Davidson
Kim Papworth
Producer
Mark D'Abreo
Advertising Agency
Wieden+Kennedy
London

Model Making
DRS Construction
Model Solutions
Planner
Claire Toolan
Account Director
Ryan Fisher

Client
Honda
Brands
Civic
CR-V
Insight
Jazz

Press Advertising

Wieden+Kennedy London
for Honda

Civic / Jazz / CR-V / Insight Hybrid
In June 2009 car sales were beginning to stabilise, but there was still widespread pessimism in the market due to the economic downturn. Honda wanted to show off its cars in a new way, in order to stimulate a cynical marketplace. We looked into how we could show off the exclusive design of the cars by taking cues from their stereotypical environment. We took locations where the model would usually live and replicated them in a studio to give the viewer an intriguing, yet beautiful image of the car.

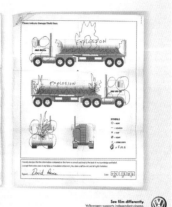

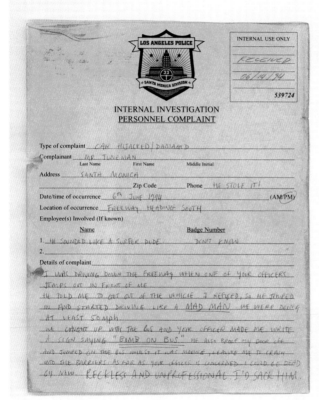

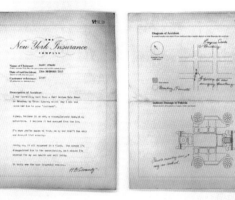

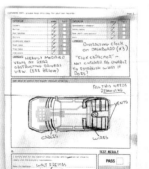

Art Director
Daniel Seager
Designer
Pete Mould
Copywriter
Steve Hall
Illustrators
Pete Mould
Alex Price
Oliver Watts

Typographer
Pete Mould
Handwriting
Steve Hall
Ruth Harlow
Pete Mould
Daniel Seager
Trevor Slabber
Nicola Sullivan

Executive Creative Director
Jeremy Craigen
Advertising Agency
DDB UK
Planner
Georgia Challis
Account Director
Charlie Elliott

Account Manager
Jessica Huth
Business Director
Jonathan Hill
Communications Manager
Sally Chapman
Client
Volkswagen

Press Advertising

DDB UK
for Volkswagen

Toy Story / Gremlins / Terminator / Speed / King Kong / Back to the Future
This campaign promoted Volkswagen's sponsorship of independent cinema. Each advert focuses on incidents involving cars in classic films. The film titles are not directly mentioned, encouraging viewers to work them out for themselves. The fictional reports outline what happened to the damaged vehicle and are filled out by the characters involved.

Book Des

EGO
SNOB
KID.

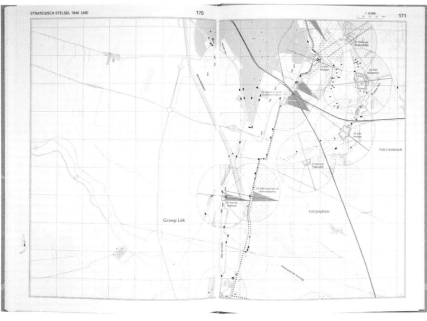

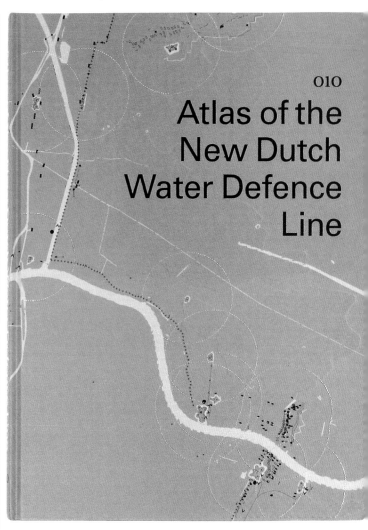

Designer
Joost Grootens
Publisher
Hans Oldewarris

Editors
Rita Brons
Bernard
Colenbrander

Translator
John Kirkpatrick

Client
010 Publishers

▲ **Entire Books**

Joost Grooten
for 010 Publishers

Atlas of the New Dutch Water Defence Line
This atlas addresses the New Dutch Water Defence Line on a themed basis. The maps have been designed to give an understanding of all aspects of the defence line landscape: its position in the landscape, the forts, the inundation system, the geomorphology, the strategic system and recent developments. The line reveals itself as a many-tentacled military defensive system of forts, group shelters and polders that can be flooded at the threat of war. The atlas offers administrators something to lean on and designers a sense of freedom – a solid starting point for getting this unique national landscape literally back on the map.

Art Director
Mark Ecob
Designer
Jon Gray

Photographer
Polly Borland

Design Group
Gray318

Client
Canongate Books

Book Front Covers
Gray318
for Canongate Books

The Death of Bunny Munro
Bunny Munro is a salesman in search of soul. After the death of his wife, he does the only thing he can think of: with his young son in tow, he hits the road. On a journey that will take him to the devil and beyond, he is soon to discover his days are numbered… For Nick Cave's first novel in twenty years, this signed, limited edition of 500 copies is presented in a beautiful flocked case that also contains a DVD. Gray318's design echoes a Victorian funeral card, showcasing Polly Borland's photography. The bunny motif on the box exterior is reminiscent of kitsch wallpaper from English seaside hotels.

51

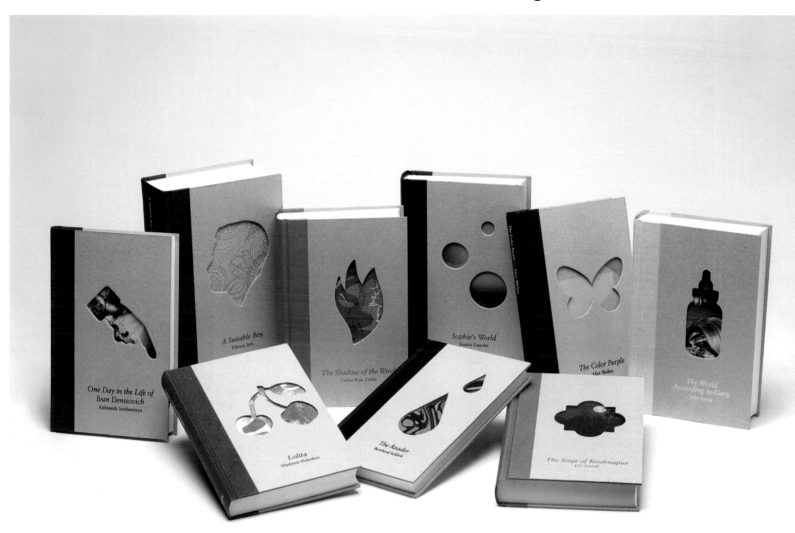

Art Director
Natasha Webber
Designer
Monica Pirovana
Creative Directors
Mark Elwood
Lucie Stericker

Creative Producer
Lisa Green
Publisher
Kirsty Dunseath
Typographer
Monica Pirovana

Art Buyer
Sarah Kavanagh
Project Manager
Rob Punchard
Design Group
Fallon

Client
The Orion Publishing Group
Brand
Weidenfeld &
Nicolson

▲ Book Front Covers

Fallon
for The Orion Publishing Group

Weidenfeld & Nicolson 60th Anniversary Titles
Fallon was asked to create a new package for a series of titles to celebrate the 60th anniversary of Weidenfeld & Nicolson, an imprint of the Orion Publishing Group. The aim was not only to showcase W&N's lineage, but to also demonstrate its progressive approach. Fallon created a stunning package that stripped the hardback book right back to its basic raw state: the bare boards. Keeping the typography simple, elegant and traditional, Fallon then used the die cut to reveal a striking series of images that are fresh and modern.

Designer
Teresa Monachino
Creative Director
Lucie Stericker

Typographer
Teresa Monachino
Editor
Debbie Woska

Publisher
Michael Dover
Client
The Orion
Publishing Group

Brand
Weidenfeld &
Nicolson

Book Front Covers

The Orion Publishing Group

Extraordinary Gardens of the World
We were asked to come up with a new book using old content; a book with added value to the existing edition. Producing a book about gardening by a famous gardener and not putting him on the cover was brave, but it enabled us to create a beautifully balanced piece of design. The use of flock enhances the link between the title and content. Not all gardens are green and living in the traditional sense.

53

Art Director	Design Director	Photographer	Advertising Agency
Rika Eguchi	Rika Eguchi	Hirofumi Sato	Dentsu Tokyo
Designers	**Creative Director**	**Agency Producer**	**Client**
Rie Abe	Yoshimitsu	Takako Miyajima	Tokyo Copywriters'
Toshikazu	Sawamoto		Club
Minatomura	**Copywriter**		
Sachiko Nemoto	Yoshimitsu		
Takeshi Ochiai	Sawamoto		
Yusuke Otsuji			

▲ Book Front Covers

Dentsu Tokyo
for the Tokyo Copywriters' Club

Tokyo Copywriters' Club Awards Annual 2009
The Tokyo Copywriters' Club Awards are given for outstanding copy selected from posters, TV commercials and other advertising produced during the year. Our task was to design the TCC Awards Annual 2009, which is a compilation of all the award-winning work. We came up with the concept of an annual 'that speaks up', since it contains lots of words, and a visual where a mouth opens up, as if speaking, every time the cover is opened.

Art Director
Tom Ising

Photographer
Martin Fengel

Design Group
Herburg Weiland

Client
2001 Verlag

Book Front Covers

Herburg Weiland
for 2001 Verlag

BRD (Bundesrepublik Deutschland)
This book, published to mark the 60th anniversary of the Federal Republic of Germany, assembles the essays compiled by Michael Rudolf and Jürgen Roth in the daily paper Taz. They present arguments for the claim 'We have to reduce the number of federal states!', made by Peter Struck, the parliamentary chairman of the Social Democractic Party of Germany. The cover design is reminiscent of old election posters, reflecting the book's manifesto-like character. Important elements, like the foreword and a blank petition form, appear on the cover itself.

Art Director	**Copywriter**	**Image Manipulator**	**Client**
Tim Hartford	Bill Tucker	Jeff Tucker	Bill Tucker Studio
Designer	**Photographer**	**Design Group**	
Tim Hartford	Bill Tucker	Hartford Design	

Book Front Covers

Hartford Design
for Bill Tucker Studio

Napa, Behind the Bottle
The aim of the project was to showcase the photography of the wine makers, owners and workers behind the great wines of Napa Valley. It was important to capture and display in one or two photos the personality of those individuals who helped make Napa Valley one of the premier wine producing areas in the world. The target audience was Napa Valley with its million plus visitors. It was essential that the book was a coffee table presentation, and something that everyone associated with wine would treasure.

Book Design

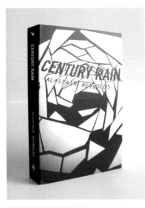

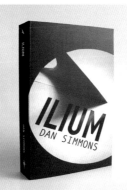

Designer
Sanda Zahirovic
Creative Director
Lucie Stericker

Publisher
Simon Spanton
Typographer
Sanda Zahirovic

Photographer
Sanda Zahirovic
Design Assistant
James Jones

Client
The Orion Publishing
Group
Brand
Gollancz

Book Front Covers

Sanda Zahirovic
for The Orion Publishing Group

Century Rain / Stone / Eternal Light / Eon / Ilium / The Centauri Device / Last and First Men / Tan Zero / Ringworld / Rendezvous with Rama / Ilium
This collection is from a project set for the D&AD Student Awards 2008. Students were asked to create a look for a series of space opera titles, and to bring them to a new audience. These designs show a merging of typography, model making and photography. Each cover is abstract yet relevant to its content, using the stark black and white scheme to evoke a sense of space and time.

57

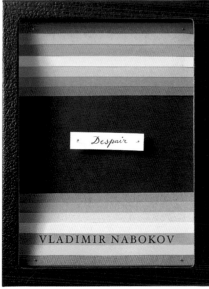
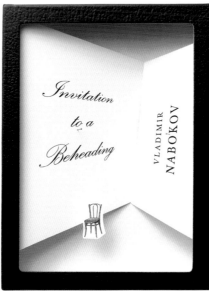
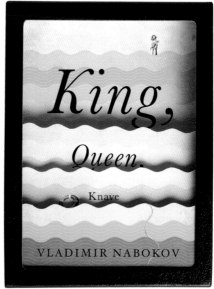
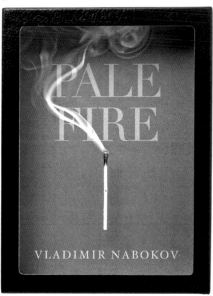
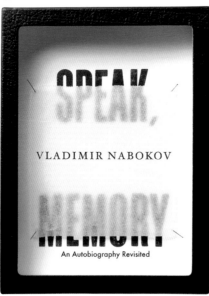

Art Director
John Gall

Designers
Michael Bierut
Stephen Doyle
Jason Fulford
Peter Mendelsund
Paul Sahre
Tamara Shopsin
Yentus & Booher

Photographer
Alison Gootee

Client
Vintage Books

Book Front Covers

Vintage Books

Despair / Invitation to a Beheading / King, Queen, Knave / Pale Fire / Speak, Memory / The Luzhin Defense
The brief was to redesign the covers for all of Vladimir Nabokov's books. Aside from being a great writer, Nabokov was also a passionate butterfly collector. The idea for this series was to have a different designer illustrate each title using a butterfly specimen box, which they could fill using only paper and mounting pins.

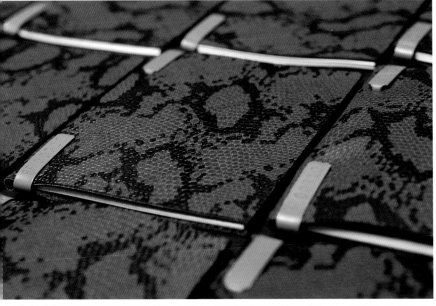

Designer
Lucas Roy

Copywriter
Cheryl Kaplan

Design Group
Studio Mercury

Client
Rhode Island School
of Design

Book Front Covers

Studio Mercury
for the Rhode Island School of Design

Free Range Exhibition Catalog
Describing the conceptual nature of sculpture requires an expression of the same symbolism. Presented during the opening of the Free Range exhibition, this catalogue gave visitors an alternate lens with which to view the intentionality and philosophy of the participating 2009 RISD Sculpture Graduates. The faux snakeskin cover was a reaction to the animalistic and textural nature of the work in the exhibition. Custom cattle ear tags became a conceptual side-stitching approach and a way to date and number these limited editions.

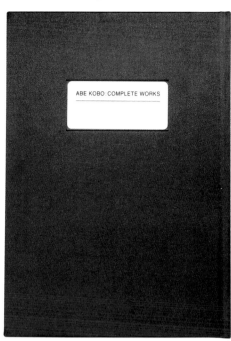

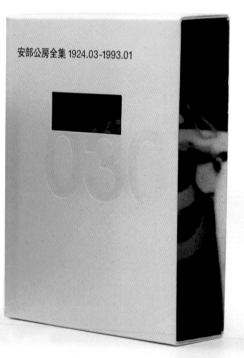

Art Director	**Designer**	**Typographer**	**Client**
Kazuya Kondo	Kazuya Kondo	Kazuya Kondo	Shinchosha
	Publisher	**Photographer**	Publishing
	Shinchosha	Kobo Abe	

Book Front Covers

Kazuya Kondo
for Shinchosha Publishing

The Complete Works of Kobo Abe Vol.30+
This edition includes a detailed bibliography and bonus CD-ROM intended for use in academic research. The book and the CD-ROM are delivered in a box, with the portrait of the author printed inside. At the back of the book, there are also photos taken by the author himself. The cloth cover has a hole through which the title of the book can be seen, carved on an aluminium plate. The product is not just for reading; it is also an attempt to deliver a high quality book design with charm and presence, which will appeal in its own right.

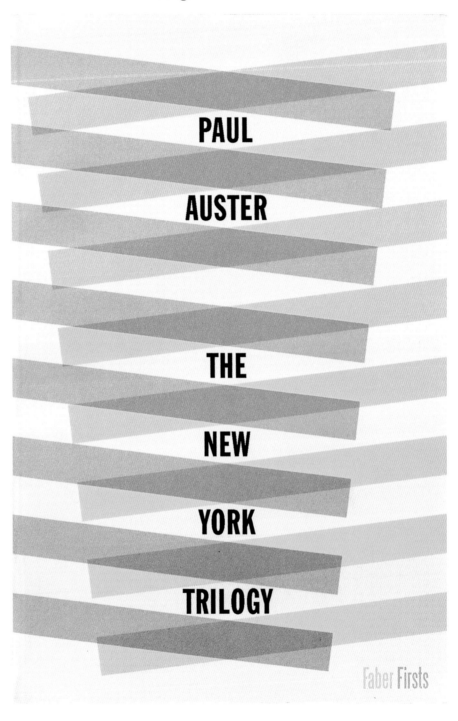

Art Director
Donna Payne

Designer
Jon Gray
Design group
Gray318

Publishers
Faber and Faber

Client
Faber and Faber

Book Front Covers

Gray318
for Faber and Faber

The New York Trilogy
Faber and Faber produced an 80th anniversary series of first novels by some of their best-known authors, called 'Faber Firsts'. The brief was to reference a period of Faber's early design history, with each cover devised by a different designer or illustrator. Art Director Donna Payne selected Jon Gray, known as Gray318, to design a cover for Paul Auster's 'The New York Trilogy'. Gray318's design reflects the graphic, two-colour cover solutions from the 1940s to the early 1960s in the Faber archive. His cover is a simple graphic attempt to illustrate three stories with two colours. The bars cross to create the third colour.

61

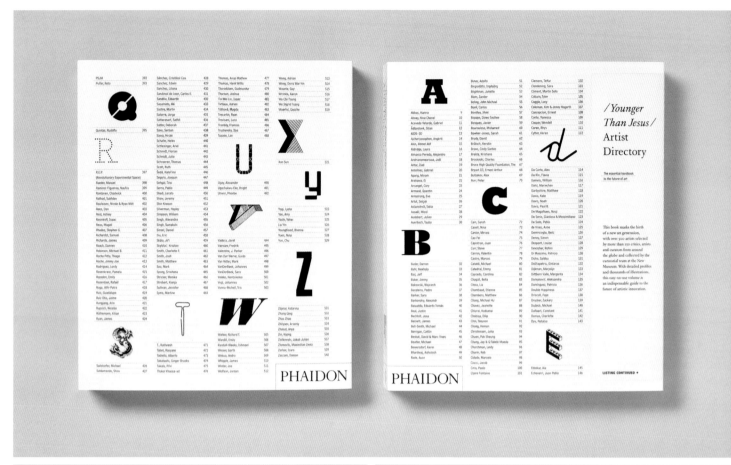

Art Director
Sonya Dyakova
Designer
Sonya Dyakova

Typographer
Sonya Dyakova
Editor
Craig Garrett

Design Group
Phaidon Press

Clients
New Museum
Phaidon Press

Entire Books

Phaidon Press
for New Museum

Younger than Jesus – Artist Directory
This publication introduces over 500 of the best artists under 33 years of age from around
the world. The idea was to create a well-functioning directory, and Yellow Pages served as
a visual reference. All elements, graphic and physical, were borrowed and then reinterpreted.
The book is typeset in Bell Centennial, a typeface designed by Matthew Carter in the 70s for
telecommunications company AT&T for its telephone directories, which is still in use. The book
is printed on a rough newsprint, and its cover features an A to Z of all the artists featured inside.
Each letter of the alphabet is different, reflecting the diversity of the work.

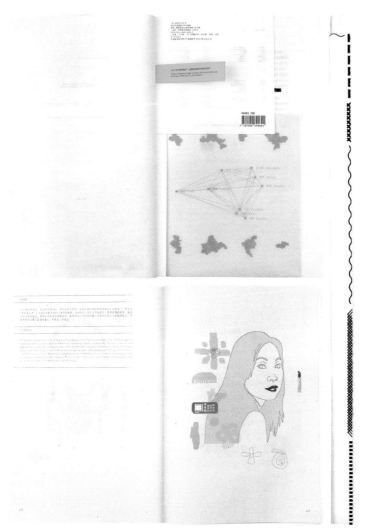

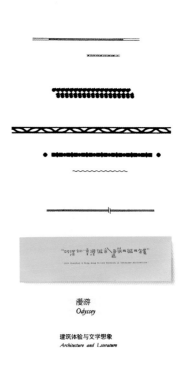

Art Director
Xiao Mage Chengzi

Designer
Xiao Mage Chengzi

Illustrator
Xiao Mage Chengzi

Client
Shenzhen &
Hong Kong
Bi-city Biennale
of Urbanism/
Architecture

Entire Books

Xiao Mage Chengzi
for the Shenzhen & Hong Kong Bi-city Biennale of Urbanism/Architecture

Odyssey: Architecture & Literature
This book is called Odyssey, but in fact it has nothing to do with myth. The compiler of the book invited nine famous writers to visit their favourite piece of architecture and write a story related to it. The designer used various elements to express different concepts: the abstract point, line and plane for the concept of roaming; and pieces of paper of different sizes and types for the concept of buildings. The reserved format was used to arrange the stories, while the sticker-on chapter pages represent the relationship between architecture and literature.

63

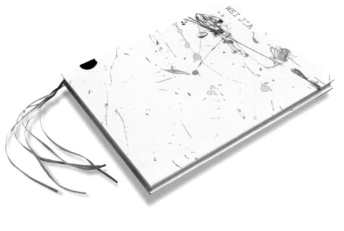

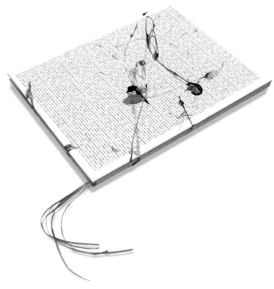

Art Director	Designer	Illustrator	Client
Xiao Mage Chengzi	Xiao Mage Chengzi	Xiao Mage Chengzi	Star Gallery

Entire Books

Xiao Mage Chengzi
for Star Gallery

Wei Jia 2004–2008
This book is a collection of artists' work. The pattern of the cover reflects the work of the artists' inside.

Entire Books

Qing Zhao
for New Star Press

A Concise Chinese-English Dictionary for Lovers
This is a love story that runs from February 2003 to February 2004. The colours rose and purple represent Chinese women and British men. The book uses both the old Chinese monthly calendar and the English calendar. Transparent tape is used as a bandage on the wound of love. The designer's daughter drew many of the pictures such as the sun, a bee, a cup and a boat. The use of a child's art demonstrates the innocence in the passion, while the ribbons and birds show the truth of the love.

Art Director
Qing Zhao

Illustrator
Yiran Zhao

Design Studio
Hanqingtang Design

Client
New Star Press

65

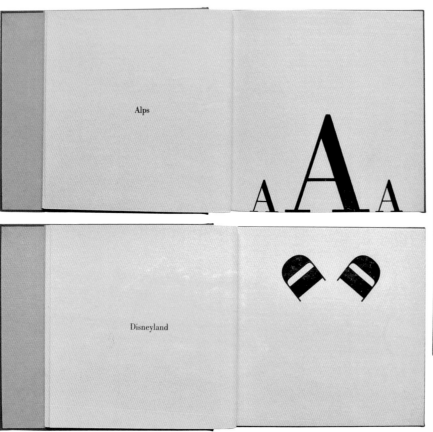

Designer	Typographer	Printers	Bookbinder
Teresa Monachino	Teresa Monachino	Tom Boulton	Robert Warren
	Design Group	Theo Wang	**Client**
	Studio Monachino		Studio Monachino

Entire Books

Studio Monachino

Around the World with the Bodoni Family
The Bodoni typeface has always been a favourite of mine. I love its balance of thin and broad lines and those long, level serifs which, together, suggest a great playfulness. I chose Bodoni to represent a typographic adventure which was to be at once witty and minimal and yet convey the idea of a journey from A to Z. The book uses the typeface to illustrate 26 destinations using only their initial letters. A showcase for design craft, the book was produced in a limited edition of 40 – a letterpress printed, hand-bound, around the world in 60 pages travelogue.

Art Director	**Copywriter**	**Image Manipulator**	**Client**
Fredrik Lindquist	Tove Norström	Andreas Lindström	The Absolut
Designer	**Illustrator**	**Advertising Agency**	Company
Fredrik Lindquist	Magnus Lundgren	Family Business	**Brand**
Creative Director	**Photographers**	**Marketing Manager**	Absolut Vodka
Kalle Söderquist	Jörgen Brennicke	Malin Stålnacke	
	Jens Mortensen		

Entire Books

Family Business
for The Absolut Company

Absolut FF

The drink book Absolut FF aims to simplify drink mixing at home, and make it a fun and accessible activity. By offering a mix of recipes, tips, tricks and key explanations, Absolut encourages people to try, dare, and let go of the illusion that drink mixing is just too tricky. Absolut also wanted a more contemporary take on the standard book format. We found the new by using the old; the book features five instruction movies in a flip-book format, which take you through the crucial stages of the drink mixing process. After all, seeing is believing.

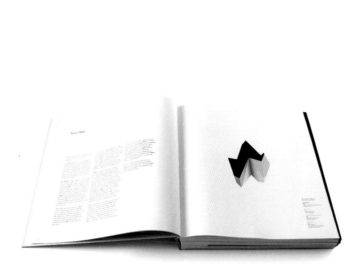

Art Director
Peter Saville
Concept
Garrick Hamm
Designers
Luke Sanders
Emma Slater

Design Group
Williams Murray
Hamm
Artworkers
Kim Browne
Josephine Spencer

**Coordination
& Editing**
Jana Labaki
Editorial Assistant
James Wormald
Image Production
Gemma Marti
O'Toole

**Production
Consultant**
Martin Lee
Origination
DawkinsColour
Project Manager
Holly Hall
Client
D&AD

Entire Books

Williams Murray Hamm & Peter Saville
for D&AD

D&AD Annual 2009
If Garrick Hamm had a single-minded proposition during his time as D&AD Education Chairman, it would have been… you guessed it… education. It's a no brainer then that the central theme for the Annual of his tenure should be all the great things D&AD does to develop new talent and bring new thinking to the industry. Garrick manipulated design master Peter Saville to take on the brief to visually demonstrate the potentially very dull task of showing that your money does this really important job. Peter also took on the task of mentoring graduate designer Luke Sanders, ensuring the process itself was an education. The end result is a lesson in design for us all.

68

Thrice Removed. David Stewart

Designers
Dan Greene
Nick Jones
Creative Director
Nick Jones

Copywriter
Peter Kirby
Typographers
Dan Greene
Nick Jones

Photographer
David Stewart
Design Group
Browns

Publishers
Browns Editions
Client
David Stewart

Entire Books

Browns
for David Stewart

Thrice Removed
Published for British photographer David Stewart, this book makes observations on family, society, relationships and life in general; it is beautifully art directed with a knowing smile and ready wink. The colour photographs bear close scrutiny both technically and emotionally, revealing more the closer you look. The format of a children's board book alludes to Stewart's childlike curiosity, while the images hint at an altogether darker heart. The launch took place in a disused warehouse in London's East End, where the audience was treated to various live installations and performances taken from the book. These included a performance of world-class lumber jacking, a fish and chip van, and a Shire horse.

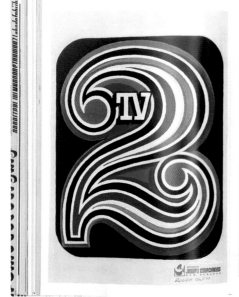

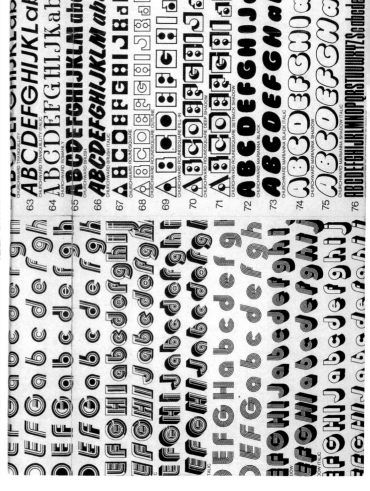

Designer
David Bennewith
Editor
David Bennewith
Copy Editor
Rebecca Roke

Authors
David Bennewith
Paul Elliman
Rebecca Roke
Daniel van der
Velden

**Design & Production
Assistant**
Sandra Kassenaar

Design Group
Jan van Eyck
Academie
Production Manager
Jo Frenken

Entire Books
Jan van Eyck Academie

Churchward International Typefaces
The first steps towards the publication 'Churchward International Typefaces' were taken
in 2005, when David Bennewith came into contact with the Samoan-born typeface designer
Joseph Churchward. Four years later, the outcome of David's research has been gathered
in this book. It tells the story of the researcher's journey, from his first attempt to contact
the type designer to the many packages he received from Churchward by post, as well as
the correspondence with Churchward's daughter Marianna.

Designer
Jayme Yen
Editors
Petra van der Jeught
Dorrie Tattersal

Translators
Chris Gemerchak
Petra van der Jeught
Dorrie Tattersal

Translation Company
The Language Lab
Production & Lithography
Jo Frenken

Publishers
Jan van Eyck Academie
Client
Jan van Eyck Academie

Entire Books

Jan van Eyck Academie

Jan van Eyck Academie Yearbook 2008
With black and gold on the cover and an impressive number of projects inside, the Jan van Eyck Academie Yearbook presents a detailed overview of the work carried out by the artists, designers and theoreticians at the academy in 2008. The various research projects and events dealt with a wide range of burning issues, including authorship and ideology critique, public space and involvement. The book concludes with an explanation of the academy's institutional policy. The yearbook was designed by Jayme Yen, a former researcher in the design department.

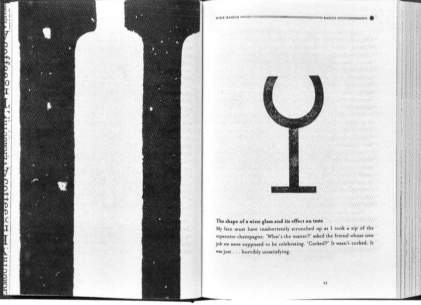

Designer
Sarah Carr
Creative Director
Caz Hildebrand

Publisher
Sarah Wasley
Typographer
Sarah Carr

Illustrator
Sarah Carr
Editor
Sara Holloway

Design Group
Here Design
Client
Granta Books

Entire Books

Here Design
for Granta Books

How to Drink

The brief was to design an illustrated book with a modest budget. After reading the book with its stories and tales intertwined between recipes, it seemed important to us to think of an unusual way to articulate the text. From the start we favoured the idea of an alternative approach over the more conventional colour photographic route, which was in any case too expensive. The illustrations for 'How to Drink' were created using old wooden type that we set and printed. The textured quality achieved in woodblock printing gives character and warmth, which makes the illustrations feel lively and distinctive.

Entire Books

TGG Hafen Senn Stieger
for Typotron

Albert Nufer
This highly innovative book offers a distinct portrait of Albert Nufer, a well-known political figure in St Gallen, Switzerland. The book contains two different parts: the personal interviews can be read by flipping through the book as usual; the second part of the book can only be read when each page is folded back on itself. This inventive design offers a fascinating window into two different sides of Nufer. The effect is strengthened by the visual contrast between older black and white images reprinted from his biography, and contemporary colour photographs.

Copywriter	**Editor**	**Design Group**	**Client**
Liana Ruckstuhl	Rolf Stehle	TGG Hafen Senn	Typotron
Publisher		Stieger	
Rolf Stehle		**Photography**	
		Thalmann & Widmer	

Architect	**Photographer**	**Director**	**Project Management**	**Planner**	
Peter Eising	Stephen Langdon	Michael Reihana	The Building	James	
Architectural	**Typographer**	**Engineering**	Intelligence Group	Hurman	
Practice	Simon Redwood	Holmes Consulting	**Agency Project**	**Marketing**	
Pacific Environments	**Creative Directors**	Group	**Manager**	**Director**	
Art Directors	Steve Cochran	**Production Company**	Paul Courtney	Kellie Nathan	
Steve Cochran	Dave King	Mike	**Account Directors**	**Mass**	
Tony Clewett	**Executive Creative**	**Advertising Agency**	Ngaio Pardon	**Communications**	
Aaron Golding	**Director**	Colenso BBDO	Matthew Pickering	**& Brand Manager**	
Copywriters	Nick Worthington	**Direct Marketing**	**Account**	Maree	
Anne Boothroyd	**Agency Producers**	**Agency**	**Managers**	Lawrence	
Dave King	Sarah Hough	AIM Proximity	Krystel Houghton	**Client**	
Maria Lishman	Nigel Sutton		Victoria Pether	Yellow Pages	

Brand Communications in 3D & Environments

Colenso BBDO
for the Yellow Pages

Treehouse Restaurant

Yellow Pages claims it can help anyone get any job done. We decided to prove it by challenging someone to build a restaurant in a tree using only Yellow Pages to make it happen. We picked Tracey, an unknown accordion player from 200 applicants, and based her in a redwood forest with Yellow books, a laptop and a mobile phone. Over three months she worked with more than 65 Yellow listed companies to build a treehouse restaurant. We documented it and kept New Zealand updated via a website, outdoor and TV advertising. Tracey actually opened the restaurant and more than 2,000 people enjoyed dining ten metres above ground in its first month.

77

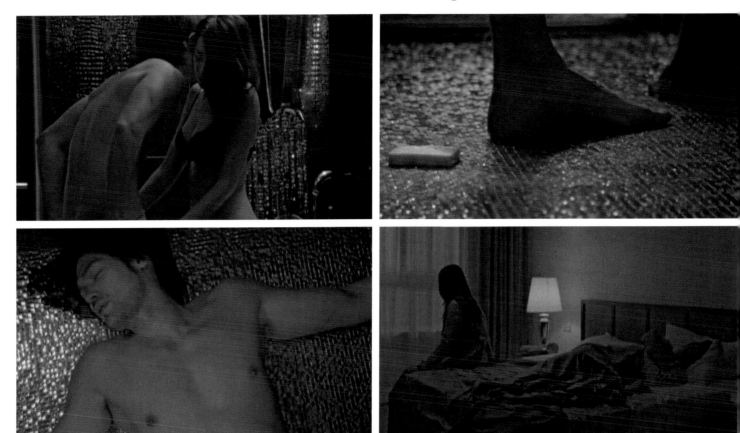

Director
Masami Kamiyama
Art Director
Kenny Chian
Copywriters
Lisa Hsu
Jennifer Hu

Creative Director
Jennifer Hu
Production Company
Greatland Films
Advertising Agency
Ogilvy & Mather
Taiwan

Account Handler
Dora Lee
Marketing Manager
Paul Cheng

Brand Director
Jessie Wang
Client
Wego Love Motel

▲   Brand Communications in Moving Image

Ogilvy & Mather Taiwan
for Wego Love Motel

Soap
This short movie is part of the launch campaign for a motel. The movie shows how well the motel's appliances and services are observant of human nature. 'Soap' shows a crooked story beneath the scentless soap.

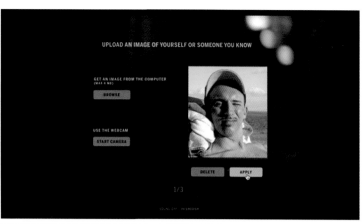

rt Director
ndreas Englund
opywriter
esper Eronn
reative Director
nders Dalenius
echnical Director
ohan Brandström

Music Composer
David Engellau
Sound Designers
Edward Björner
Eric Thorsell
Editor
Johan Wik

Director
Max Vitali
Producer
Mattias Coldén
Agency Producer
Markus Ahlm
Advertising Agency
Draftfcb Sweden

Account Handler
Per Hellberg
Brand Manager
Per Leander
Client
Radiotjänst

Online Brand Communications

Draftfcb Sweden
for Radiotjänst

The Hero
This web-based application allows you to experience how the entire world celebrates you as a hero for paying your TV fee – and safeguarding freedom and independence in Swedish TV and radio. After a simple upload, a picture of yourself or someone you know is rendered in an epic looking movie, making it look as if you were actually there on set. After the movie has played, you are given the option to register directly for the statutory TV fee, and send your movie as a link to friends.

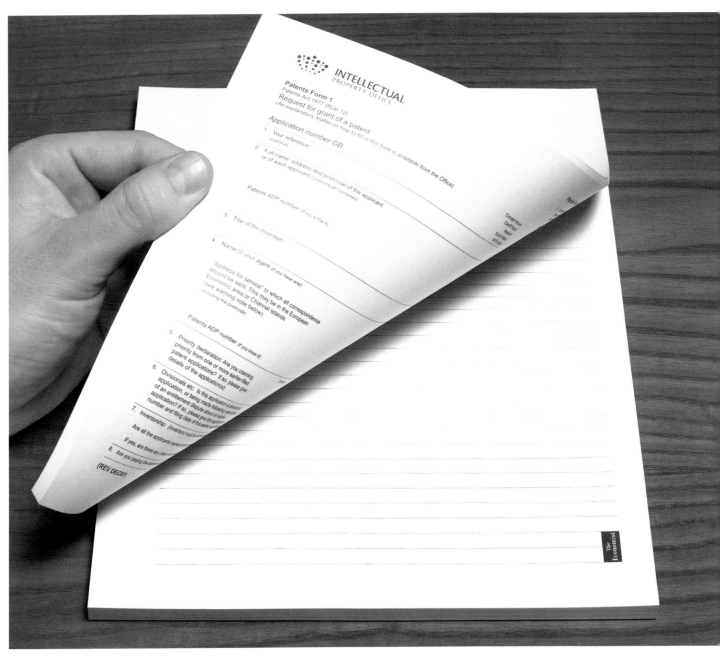

Designers
Christopher Bowsher
Frances Leach
Art Director
Christopher Bowsher

Copywriter
Frances Leach
Creative Director
Dave Dye

Advertising Agency
Dye Holloway
Murray

Brand Manager
Alan Dunachie
Client
The Economist

Brand Communications in Print

Dye Holloway Murray
for The Economist

Intellectual Property
Dye Holloway Murray created The Economist notepad with a patent application form on the
back of every page.

Designers
Jan Hartwig
Jan Simmerl
Paul Svoboda

Art Director
Reginald Wagner
Copywriters
Till Grabsch
Magdalena Gwosdz
Lorenz Ritter
Katharina Trumbach

Creative Director
Katrin Oeding
Design Studio
KOREFE / Kolle
Rebbe

Account Handler
Kristina Wulf
Brand Manager
Felix Negwer
Client
The Deli Garage

New Branding Schemes for Small Business

KOREFE / Kolle Rebbe
for The Deli Garage

The Deli Garage Range

This corporate design for the Deli Garage connects the world of the garage with the world of sophisticated design; the functional benefits of tools meet contemporary illustrations and typography. The modern illustrations are finely tuned to the individual products whilst elements of the corporate design are kept minimalist and clear, to underline the high level of functionality. They also give the products a luxurious appearance and act as a reference to the high quality of the ingredients.

Designers
James Brown
Ryan Psaila
Dom Roberts
Darren Song

Art Directors
James Brown
Dom Roberts

Design Agency
Mash

Client
Alpha Box & Dice
Wines

New Branding Schemes for Small Business

Mash
for Alpha Box & Dice Wines

Alpha Box & Dice Wines
Justin and Emma Lane, the lovable rogues behind Alpha Box & Dice, approached Mash to create a distinctive brand identity for their new wine-making venture. An important aspect of this boutique producer was to make the brains behind these liquid creations a central part of the brand identity. The solution was to take the Lanes' abundance of wine stories, tales of win and woe, and bring them to life as the central theme for the brand identity – 26 stories, 26 letters. Each wine is named after a letter in the alphabet; available so far are A, B, C, D and F. This approach was also used in the design of the logo, interior fit-out, and signage.

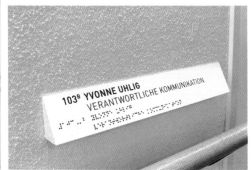

Art Directors	Design Group	Marketing Manager	Client
Martin Gaberthüel	Netthoevel	Yvonne Uhlig	Blinden und
Andreas Netthoevel	& Gaberthüel	**Brand Director**	Behindertenzentrum
		Gabriele Plüss	Bern

New Branding Schemes for Medium Business

Netthoevel & Gaberthüel
for Blinden und Behindertenzentrum Bern

Centre for Blind and Handicapped People, Bern
This is a new name, corporate design and signage design for the Centre for Blind and Handicapped People in Bern. The letter 'B' combined with the letter 'B' in the Braille font (':') define the new sign for the centre.

83

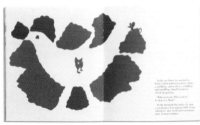

Designers
Gareth Howat
Jim Sutherland
Mark Wheatcroft
Illustrator
Rebecca Sutherland
Design Directors
Gareth Howat
Jim Sutherland

Author
Katrice Horsley
**Bereavement
Counsellor**
Diane Mix
Design Group
hat-trick design
Printers
Creative Print Group

Design Manager
Louise Kyme
Print Manager
John Walker
Project Lead
Debbie Allen
Project Manager
Ellen Mason

Project Support
Amy Corkery
Client
The British Heart
Foundation
Brand
The Small Creature

New Branding Schemes for Medium Business

hat-trick design
for The British Heart Foundation

The Small Creature
The brief was to design an identity for a resource aimed at children who have suffered bereavement because of heart disease. Our solution was to create a children's story featuring The Small Creature who encounters a number of friends and goes through a range of emotions. We worked closely with the story's author and a bereavement counsellor to develop the messages and tone of the campaign. The character is produced as a felt toy, small enough to be kept close by, in a pocket or hand.

Чем мы
можем помочь?

Цель кредита:
кухонный гарнитур

Сумма:
60,000

Пойдём!

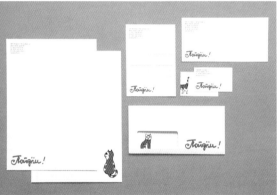

Пойдём!

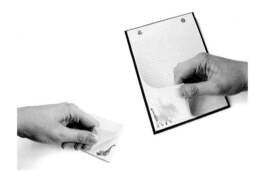

New Branding Schemes for Large Business

NB: Studio
for Probusiness Bank

Poidjom

'Poidjom' is a familiar, Russian phrase for a friendly, arm-around-the-shoulder, 'let's go'. This new name was the basis of the brand for an innovative Russian bank which aims to help ordinary people with their financial problems. This was not a conventional Western face-lift, but an authentic expression of everything Russians want a bank to be. This meant referencing traditional techniques and applying them in a modern and appropriate way. An illustrated cat was introduced as a familiar domestic reference, woven into lace patterns, and Russian murals were hand-painted directly onto the walls of the bank's branches.

Designers
Eng Su
Jodie Wightman
Art Director
Ben Stott
Copywriter
Matthew Bishop

Photographer
Lucia Ganieva
Illustrators
Jenny Bowers
Dan Funderburgh
Svetlana Gorbunova

Design Group
NB: Studio
Account Handler
Anoushka Rodda
Brand Director
Natalia A
Stolpovskikh

Client
Probusiness Bank
Brand
Poidjom

Designers
Hannah Manneke
Carmen Nutbey
Art Directors
Edo van Dijk
Earik Wiersma

Typographer
Earik Wiersma
Design Group
Edenspiekermann

Account Handler
Jennecke
Stradmeijer
Brand Manager
Ab Hooijer
Marketing Manager
Saskia Oldenburg

Client
Utrecht City Theatre
Brand
Stadsschouwburg
Utrecht

Rebranding Schemes for Medium Business

Edenspiekermann
for Utrecht City Theatre

Utrecht City Theatre
Utrecht City Theatre's new identity reflects its vision and underlines its commitment to artistic quality as well as its cultural and social engagement. The word mark, interwoven with itself, imparts a confrontation with the unexpected – its edgy play of letters positions the theatre as challenging and contemporary. The corporate design also offers inspiration for future development, and reflects, with the aid of typography and colouring, the spirit of the theatre's architecture.

EFFP ■ ■ ■

Designer
Paul Felton
Design Director
Adam Browne

Creative Directors
Rob Howsam
Stuart Youngs

Design Group
Purpose
Project Manager
Louisa Phillips

Client
EFFP (English
Farming & Food
Partnerships)

Rebranding Schemes for Medium Business

Purpose
for EFFP

EFFP Identity
EFFP provides consultancy to the agricultural and food industry. It strives to build bonds
between these two industries, to make both more efficient. EFFP needed help to differentiate
itself from other consultants in the sector. The resulting black-and-white identity is bold,
pioneering, confident and revolutionary, all attributes EFFP aspires to. The typographically led
approach is a distinguishing break from the expected use of corporate styling and generic stock
photography so common in this sector. A full suite of stationery and marketing materials was
created, including corporate leaflets, folders, a website and the organisation's magazine, 'View'.

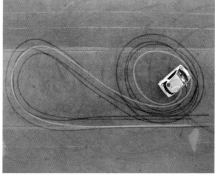

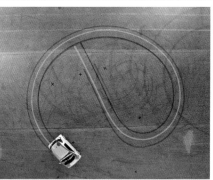

iQ font / The first typeface designed by a car

iQ Font by Toyota

a	b	c	d	e	f	g	h	i	j	k	l	m	n
a	b	c	d	e	f	g	h	i	j	k	l	m	n

o	p	q	r	s	t	u	v	w	x	y	z		
o	p	q	r	s	t	u	v	w	x	y	z		

1	2	3	4	5	6	7	8	9	0				
1	2	3	4	5	6	7	8	9	0				

?	,	;	.	:	!	(	)	/#	&	#	@	_	—
?	,	*	.	*	!	(	)		&	#	@	_	—

Art Director
Tom Galle
Creative Director
Gregory Titeca
Copywriter
Ramin Afshar
Head of Art
Cecilia Azcarate
Isturiz

Typographers
Damien Aresta
Pierre Smeets
Creative Managers
Karen Corrigan
Gregory Titeca
Software Developer
Zachary Lieberman

Advertising Agency
Happiness Brussels
Design Studio
Pleaseletmedesign
Account Director
Pascal Kemajou
Marketing Director
Patrice Vekemans

**Advertising &
Promotions Manager**
Andre Juprelle
Client
Toyota
Brand
iQ

Brand Communications in Moving Image

Happiness Brussels
for Toyota

iQ Font
Toyota launched the new iQ. Our brief was to communicate the exclusive agility and perfect control of the iQ to a target group of 18 to 35-year-old urban people. To demonstrate its incredible agility, we made the new Toyota iQ the first car to create an entire font from A to Z. To make this project happen, we worked with three opinion leaders in order to touch the right communities in design, automotive and interactive art: software developer Zachary Lieberman, a pioneer in interactive art; font designers Pierre and Damien, from Pleaseletmedesign, a type and graphic design studio and font driver Stef van Campenhoudt, a professional pilot and European champion of GT3 racing.

Senior Designer
James Hackett
Designers
Leo Nguyen
Anne Numont
Art Director
Matt Heck

Copywriter
Damian Fitzgerald
Creative Director
Noah Regan
Executive Creative Directors
Justin Drape
Scott Nowell

Producer
Kala Ellis
Agency Producer
Thea Carone
Sound Designer
Simon Kane

Production Company
Hackett Films
Advertising Agency
Three Drunk Monkeys
Client
BBC Knowledge

Brand Communications in Moving Image

Three Drunk Monkeys
for BBC Knowledge

BBC Moon Week
This spot was created to promote BBC Knowledge's week of programmes commemorating the 40th anniversary of the moon landing. Using the line animation techniques of the time, we took the viewer on a journey of obscure but amazing facts relating to the event. The voice of Ted Maynard, who broadcast the original moon landing from his radio station 40 years ago, brought this fascinating story to life.

Art Director
Jamie Starbuck
Copywriter
Richard Harris
Creative Director
Trevor Beattie

Director
Karen Cunningham
Agency Producer
Sara Wallace
Production Company
Spank Films

Advertising Agency
Beattie McGuinness
Bungay
Marketing Manager
Gemma de Haaf

Client
First Choice Holidays
Brand
Thomson Airways

Brand Communications in Moving Image

Beattie McGuinness Bungay
for First Choice Holidays

In-flight Safety Video
The brief was to make the essential Thomson in-flight safety video more engaging and entertaining for passengers, and therefore more effective and memorable. So we cast an unlikely crew of kids to charter the plane. The crew, passengers and even the pilot were all under the age of ten, yet they run through the safety features of the plane with all the professionalism and panache of a real life cabin crew. The resulting three-minute film leaves passengers charmed and reassured as they embark on their journey. The film ran on all Thomson flights (a fleet of 80 planes), which carry a total of 4.8 million passengers a year.

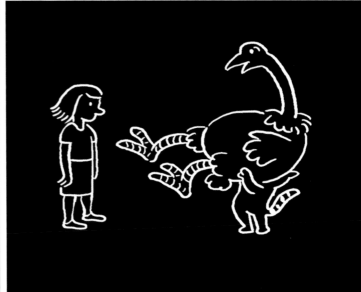

Director
Christoph Neimann

Production Company
Christoph Neimann
Inc

Advertising Agency
Google Creative Lab

Client
Google
Brand
Google Chrome

Brand Communications in Moving Image

Google Creative Lab
for Google

Chrome Shorts
In order to raise awareness of Google Chrome, we invited several creative friends to make short films on the browser. They came back with many amusing and fascinating shorts, which we shared with the rest of the world on YouTube.

Art Director	**Agency Producer**	**Head Planner**	**Marketing Manager**
Teddy Keen	Benita Stein	Glyn Britton	Kylie Evans
Copywriter	**Advertising Agency**	**Account Director**	**Client**
Teddy Keen	Albion	Keith Martin	Giffgaff
Creative Directors	**Prop Making**	**Account Handler**	
Nick Darken	Applied Arts	Duncan Welling	
Andre Moreira	Einstein's Octopus		

Online Brand Communications

Albion
for Giffgaff

Giffgaff Tool Hire

This was the launch of Giffgaff, O2's experimental new mobile network. Instead of running big glossy TV ads, we decided to get Giffgaff's potential customers to launch it for us. We invented a range of weird and wonderful tools, such as the world's first pedal powered gramophone, which anyone could hire for free to spread the word about Giffgaff, both in the street and on the internet. Participants uploaded their videos to YouTube and got free calls for a year in return. The backscratching paid off – Giffgaff was well and truly launched.

Designer	Technical Director	Shooting Directors	Project Managers
Takashi Kamada	Kay-ichi Tozaki	Hiroyuki Kojima	Yuuri Ogawa
Art Director	**Programmer**	TOCHKA 'Kazue	Shinichi Saeki
Takashi Kamada	Susumu Arai	Monno + Takeshi	**System Engineer**
Photographers	**Web Producer**	Nagata'	Susumu Arai
Shinsuke Kamioka	Ken Kanetomo	**Creative**	**Artist**
Takuji Onda	**Producers**	**Management**	Fantastic Plastic
Takuyuki Saito	Nozomu Naito	**Director**	Machine
Interactive Designers	Gyosei Okada	Kentaro Katsube	**PR Managers**
Kay-ichi Tozaki	Shinjiro Ono	**Production Company**	Mayumi Sawada
Yukio Sato	**Production Manager**	Puzzle	Ryota Sugawara
Creative Director	Shigehisa Nakao	**Digital Agency**	**Client**
Koichiro Tanaka		Projector	UNIQLO

Online Brand Communications

Projector
for UNIQLO

UNIQLO Calendar
UNIQLO calendar is an online digital calendar, which aims to build a branding platform to promote both Japan and UNIQLO on a global scale. Each season, we went on a mission to capture the dynamism of Japan by spending months travelling and filming, using tilt-shift and time-lapse techniques to create a fresh, miniature version of Japan. Users can set their location and use it as a blog widget, screensaver, greetings card, or iPhone app. As of January 2010, UNIQLO calendar covers all four seasons, featuring scenes from over 180 locations in Japan, and is still searching for more.

93

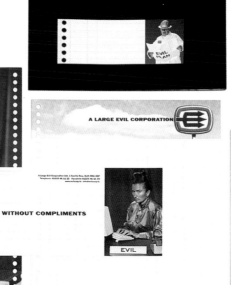

Designer	Photographers	Design Group	Client
Mark Denton	Sean & Ben	COY!	A Large Evil
Art Director	**Typographer**	COMMUNICATIONS	Corporation
Mark Denton	Andy Dymock		

Brand Communications in Print

COY! COMMUNICATIONS
for A Large Evil Corporation

A Large Evil Corporation Corporate Identity

A Large Evil Corporation is a small animation company full of nice people. It seemed obvious that A Large Evil Corporation needed a manufactured history featuring a lot of fictional employees from their non-existent offices. A collection of unlikely smiling presidents, secretaries and employees of the month were assembled after much scouring through model agency books. Of course, our chosen cast were mostly lovely to start with, but with the right styling, authentic lighting and some 'insincere' direction, the evil was coaxed out of them. The resulting images were then lavishly applied to letterheads, labels, show reels, bags, etc., along with the company's very own evil logo.

Designer
Karen Hughes
Copywriter
Lindsay Camp

Creative Director
Steve Conchie
Design Group
The Chase

Account Handler
Rachel
O'Shaughnessy

Client
Merseystride
Brand
Home

Brand Communications in Print

The Chase
for Merseystride

Home
We were asked to create a name and identity for Home, a pioneering furniture store created by Merseystride, a social enterprise working to help homeless and long-term unemployed people. The business buys returned, end of line and slightly damaged furniture from catalogue companies, assembling and repairing it on site then selling it at a discount – essentially recycling new furniture that was destined for landfill. The name represents both sides of the enterprise – it's a furniture shop, but also a stepping stone for homeless people into their new home. A small word that means a great deal to everyone involved. It's an opportunity for them to make themselves... at home.

95

Designers	Technical Designer	Typographers	Brand Manager
Wang Xiaomeng	Liu Fuyu	Wang Xiaomeng	Ni Jing
Hei Yiyang	**Art Director**	Hei Yiyang	**Client**
Liu Zhao	Hei Yiyang	Liu Zhao	The OCT Art &
	Photographer	**Design Group**	Design Gallery
	Liang Rong	SenseTeam	

Brand Communications in 3D & Environments

SenseTeam
for The OCT Art & Design Gallery

Social Energy

This is the visual identity system for the 'Social Energy: Contemporary Communication Design from the Netherlands' touring exhibition. The exhibition is located in the OCT Art & Design Gallery in Shenzhen. We covered the gallery's outer wall with hexagonal shapes. The design incorporated the energy structure of a tiny molecule. We used huge red, white and blue gas-filling devices to explain the process of energy accumulation. The interior of the exhibition also used the concept of molecular structure at every entrance and in the library's desks and chairs.

96

Art Director	Senior Executive	Director of	Production Company	Music House
Brandon Mugar	Producer	Integrated	Biscuit Filmworks	Search Party Music
Copywriter	Shawn Lacy	Production	Advertising Agency	Audio Mix
Adam Reeves	Editor	Brian DiLorenzo	BBDO New York	Sound Lounge
Executive Creative	David Henegar	Mixer	Editing House	Outdoor Projection
Directors	Chief Creative	Cory Melious	Butcher Editorial	Staging Techniques
Greg Hahn	Officers	Music Supervisors	Visual Effects	Event Coordination
Mike Smith	Bill Bruce	Stephanie	Company	GMR/T.Y. Smith
Director	David Lubars	Diaz-Matos	Animal Logic	Group
Noam Murro	Director of Creative	Randall Poster	Telecine	Client
Content Producer	Engineering	Telecine Artists	The Syndicate	HBO
Nicholas Gaul	& Production	Beau Leon		
Executive Producer	Jd Michaels	Marshall Plante		
Colleen O'Donnell				

Brand Communications in 3D & Environments

BBDO New York
for HBO

Cube Film Installation

The HBO Cube is a first-of-its-kind outdoor film event, embodying HBO's DNA of innovative storytelling. The cube shows four sides of a story simultaneously, each providing a different perspective of the film's characters and plot. Only by watching all sides do viewers see the truth of what really happened. Two distinct films were played, 'Art Heist' and 'The Affair', each specifically choreographed and created for the cube. Both films stood on their own as embodiments of the brand, but were also later revealed to be part of a larger narrative experience on the campaign website, hboimagine.com.

Creative Directors	Senior Developer	Editors	Director of	Account
Joe Alexander	Mark Llobrera	Rick Lawley	Innovation	Handlers
Jonathan Hills	**Art Director**	Jim Vaile	Mark Pavia	Carrie Bird
Technical Director	Brian Williams	**Assistant Editor**	**Digital Production**	Jarrod Bull
Oscar Trelles	**Interactive Art**	Shang Gao	**& Design**	**Marketing**
Designer	**Director**	**Art Producer**	Domani Studios	**Manager**
Saulo Rodrigues	Ben Tricklebank	Cindy Hicks	**Advertising Agency**	Lee Statham
Interactive Designer	**Copywriter**	**Sound Designer**	The Martin Agency	**Client**
Justin Young	Wade Alger	Jesse Peterson	**Agency Producers**	The John F Kennedy
Interactive Producer	**Animator**	**Music Composer**	Darbi Fretwell	Presidential Library
Steven Hubert	Petter Säfwenberg	Chip Jenkins	Norma Kwee	& Museum
Flash Developer				
Chris Wise				

Digital Advertising Campaigns

The Martin Agency
for The John F Kennedy Presidential Library & Museum

We Choose the Moon
The Apollo 11 lunar landing was the realisation of JFK's vision to land a man on the moon. For the landing's 40th anniversary, we recreated the mission online in real time. At 9.32am on 16 July 2009, Apollo 11 took off again at wechoosethemoon.org. The trip was shown using 3D animation, 102 continuous hours of mission audio, and hundreds of images from NASA and the JFK Library. 650 of the most interesting audio transmissions were rebroadcast via Twitter. 'We Choose The Moon' was also selected in Digital Advertising/Animation.

Photographer
Lennart Sjöberg

Advertising Agency
Forsman &
Bodenfors

Media Agency
Mediaedge:cia
Client Account Manager
Sara Zakariasson

Client
IKEA

Digital Advertising Campaigns

Forsman & Bodenfors
for IKEA

Facebook Showroom
To advertise the opening of the new IKEA Malmö store we created a Facebook profile for
the store manager Gordon Gustavsson and uploaded 12 showroom pictures to his photo album.
The first person to tag their name to a product in the picture won it. All pictures reached the
limit of 30 tags per photo within minutes of being posted. This resulted in the pictures reaching
thousands of people through Facebook's newsfeed function. When users looked at the photo
and read the comments they became aware of the competition, and of course, they also got
to see how beautiful their homes could be if they went to IKEA.

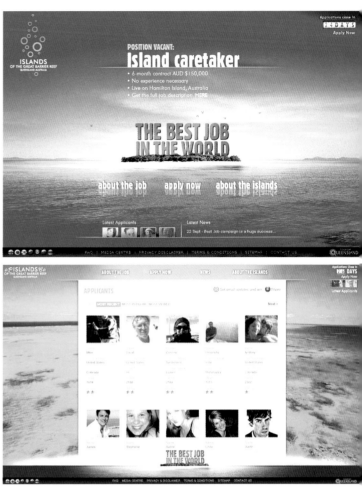

Creative Directors
James Burchill
Nancy Hartley

**Senior Digital
Producer**
Jason Kibsgaard
Art Directors
Ralphie Barnett
Cristian Staal

Copywriter
Merrin McCormick
Advertising Agency
SapientNitro

Account Directors
Adam Ford
Anne Maree Wilson
Client
Tourism Queensland

▲ Digital Advertising Campaigns

SapientNitro
for Tourism Queensland

The Best Job in the World
Our challenge was to increase international awareness of Queensland's islands of the Great
Barrier Reef, and transform a popular day-trip destination into an international tourist's dream
holiday. In a time of rising unemployment, we created the best job in the world. It sounded
too good to be true, but the Island Caretaker role was a genuine employment opportunity with
Tourism Queensland. Anyone could apply, and the successful candidate would spend six months
living above the reef, exploring the region and reporting back to the world. With a US$1.2million
budget, we placed simple recruitment ads and created a worldwide phenomenon.

102

Creative Director	**Copywriter**	**Agency Producers**	**Planners**
Andreas Dahlqvist	Martin Lundgren	Pontus Kindblad	Cecilia Cederlid
Interactive Designer	**Digital Agency**	Barbro Långjuth	Jerker Fagerstörm
Karl-Johan Vogelius	Tribal DDB	Patrik Sundberg	Karl Wikström
Developers	Stockholm	**Account Handlers**	**Brand Manager**
Andreas Andersson	**Advertising Agency**	Lars Axelsson	Åke Lundberg
Fredrik Dahlen	DDB Stockholm	Michael Bugaj	**Marketing Manager**
Art Directors		Martin Larsson	Katarina Lakowitz
Simon Higby			**Client**
Simon Mogren			Volkswagen Sweden

Digital Advertising Campaigns

Tribal DDB Stockholm
for Volkswagen Sweden

The Fun Theory
Volkswagen asked us to create a campaign that would generate interest around Blue Motion Technologies, a series of cars and innovations that help reduce environmental impact without compromising on performance or the joy of driving. Our insight was that VW could make it easier to choose an eco car by making them more fun to drive. Our solution was a theory focusing on the thinking behind the cars – that the easiest way to change human behaviour for the better is by making it fun to do. We called this The Fun Theory.

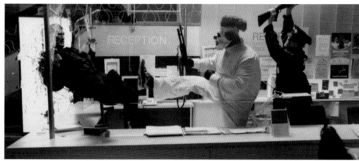 

Director Adam Berg **Art Director** Mariota Essery **Designers** Maximiliano Chanan Eric Chia Odin Church **Creative Directors** Chris Baylis Andrew Ferguson **Technical Lead** Jan Willem Penterman	**Lead Developer** Ian McGregor **Key Developers** Jamie Copeland Vincent Roman Matt Sweetman **Developer** Pierre L Thiebaut **Producer** Simon Eakhurst **Executive Producers** Daniel Bergmann Stephen Brierley Mark Pytlik	**Visual Effects** Redrum Stockholm **Chief Creative Officer** Neil Dawson **Director of Photography** Fredrik Backar **Agency Producer** Jeroen Jedeloo **Advertising Agencies** DDB Worldwide Tribal DDB Amsterdam	**Production Company** Stink Digital **Worldwide Strategy Director** Han van Dijk **International Strategy Director** Sean Chambers **Project Director** John Reardon **Project Manager** Christophe Taddei **Editor** Paul Hardcastle	**Music** Michael Fakesch **Sound Designers** Tim Davis Michael Fakesch **Colourist** Jean-Clement Soret **Account Leads** Sandra Krstic Neil Robb **Client** Philips

▲

Web Ads

Tribal DDB Amsterdam
for Philips

Carousel
This interactive campaign promoted Philips' latest entrant into the television market, the Cinema 21:9. Since the television's 21:9 frame lends itself so readily to film, Tribal DDB Amsterdam commissioned Stink Digital to create a piece of filmed content that could hold its own with Hollywood's best. Stink Digital director Adam Berg responded with an idea for an epic 'frozen moment' cops and robbers shootout sequence, which included clowns, explosions, a devastated hospital, and plenty of broken glass, bullet casings and money.

IMAGES ON WEBSITES CHANGE INTO ONLINE LOTTERY TICKETS!
UNIQLO LUCKY SWITCH

UNIQLO LUCKY SWITCH is a blog widget that changes all the images on websites into online lottery tickets, released as one of a 60th anniversary campaign of Fast Retailing. If you get a winning ticket, you receive UNIQLO original tote bag. (12/1–12/31. TOTAL 1000)

◆ SAMPLE OF BLOG WIDGET [FFFFOUND!]
◆ SAMPLE OF BOOKMARKLET [MSN Japan]

■ INSTALL LUCKY SWITCH ON YOUR BLOG

Pushing the lucky switch lets all the images on your blog changed immediately into online lottery tickets.

PUSH THIS SWITCH AND TURN OVER THE CONVERTED IMAGES.

PUSH
▼

Tools & Applications

Dentsu Tokyo
for UNIQLO

UNIQLO Lucky Switch
UNIQLO's lucky switch is a small blog widget and a bookmark, which can change whole websites into UNIQLO advertising. Pushing the switch changes all the images on a website into online lottery tickets. If you draw a winning ticket, you and the blog owner will receive a UNIQLO tote bag. The losing tickets are then turned into UNIQLO banner ads. The switch created UNIQLO adverts 2.8 million times in just one month.

Creative Director Hiroki Nakamura
Technical Directors Hiroshi Koike, Hiroki Nakamura, Qanta Shimizu
Flash Programmers Taku Ichihara, Teruo Nakanishi, Qanta Shimizu
Designers Mayuko Kondo, Ryo Tanizaki
Art Directors Kohei Kawasaki, Tsubasa Kayasuga
Copywriter Yasuhisa Nito
Production Companies Dentsu TEC, IMG SRC, S2 Factory
Advertising Agency Dentsu Tokyo
Agency Producers Shinsaku Ogawa, Hajime Yakushiji
Project Manager Tatsuhiko Akutsu
Client Supervisors Kentaro Katsube, Minako Suzuki
Client UNIQLO

Creative Directors	Designer	Motion Designer	Account Handlers
Bernd Krämer	Nina Borrusch	Nina Borrusch	Anke Göbber
Götz Ulmer	**Art Directors**	**Sound Designer**	Alexander Korduan
Interaction Designer	Philip Bartsch	Roman Vinuesa	**Marketing Manager**
Gregor Fraser	Tommy Norin	**Advertising Agency**	Milena Ivkovic
Programmer	**Copywriter**	Jung von Matt	**Client**
Alexander El-Meligi	Ramin	Hamburg	Philharmoniker
	Schmiedekampf		Hamburg

Tools & Applications

Jung von Matt Hamburg
for the Philharmoniker Hamburg

Sounds of Hamburg
The Philharmoniker Hamburg is one of the best known orchestras in Germany. The goal was to give them a more modern image and pull more ears into their concert hall. We were asked to create an online solution that would arouse the curiosity of classical music lovers throughout the country. Our solution was to create a web application which merges both city and orchestra into one exciting musical experience. The city of Hamburg becomes the concert hall and users take the role of conductor. With customised motion tracking, users are able to select moving objects from a live video feed. People, ships, cars and even fish become instruments in a spontaneous concert.

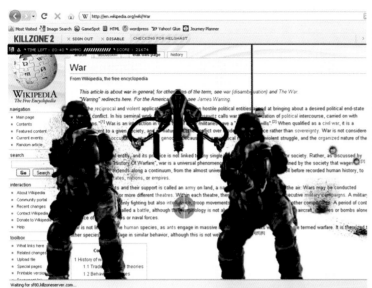

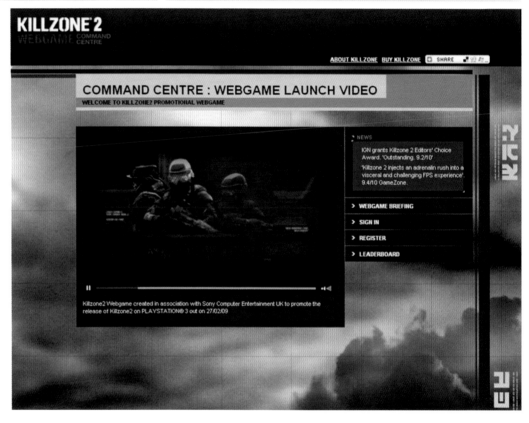

Online Games

Agency Republic
for Sony Computer Entertainment UK

Killzone 2 Web Game
PlayStation asked us to hype the launch of 'Killzone 2' among hardcore gamers. This sequel has more enemies, more hostile environments, and more life or death moments. Nowhere is safe. We decided to take that proposition and explode it across the online world. The Killzone 2 web game gave gamers a taste of what was coming with the world's first internet-wide shoot'em up. A web browser plug-in allowed gamers to hunt the Helghast across the entire internet and even destroy the sites where they found them. Gamers were able to play solo or in a squad with friends in real-time, and build their scores to top the international leaderboard.

Creative Directors	**Designer**	**Sound Designer**	**Brand Manager**
Alistair Campbell	Bertrand Carrara	Michael Robinson	Phil Lynch
Gavin Gordon-	**Developers**	**Digital Agency**	**Marketing Manager**
Rogers	Ian Lainchbury	Agency Republic	Alan Duncan
Technical Director	Matt Payne	**Agency Producers**	**Client**
David de la Pena	**Art Director**	Tim Gardiner	Sony Computer
Flash Programmers	Nick Horne	Kate Sutherland	Entertainment UK
David Cox	**Copywriter**	**Account Handler**	**Brand**
Tom Danvers	Rob Ellis	Tom Bedwell	PlayStation

Art Director	**Designer**	**Animators**	**Post Production**	**Marketing**	
Robert Lindström	Mikael Forsgren	Felix Hill	**Producers**	**Manager**	
Creative Director	**Illustrator**	Mathias Lindgren	Frida Färlin	Clemens	
David Eriksson	Therese Larsson	Daniel Wallström	Johan Forslund	Dopjans	
Design Director	**3D Artist**	**Sound Designer**	**Planner**	**Client**	
Robert Lindström	Claes Dietmann	Johan Belin	Sonja Lakner	adidas Germany	
Technical Director	**Developers**	**Advertising Agency**	**Account Handler**	**Brand**	
Hans Eklund	Kim Eriksson	North Kingdom	Roger Stighäll	adidas	
Interactive Designer	Lucian Trofin	**Agency Producers**	**Brand Manager**		
Kalle Engström	**Copywriter**	Marcus Ivarsson	Sven Schindler		
Flash Programmer	Linus Nilsson	Mia Wallmark			
David Lundmark					
Film Director					
Ted Kjellson					

Art Direction

North Kingdom
for adidas Germany

adidas Teamgeist

Adidas was looking for a web-based, cutting edge approach to launch the German national football team's new kit for the World Cup in South Africa. The main objective was to create hype around the team and its new jersey, and in the long run anchor adidas as the leading football brand in Germany. Driven by the idea of team spirit and fun of the game, we created a unique online graphic game where fans could discover and learn more about the story behind the German jersey. Users went back in time to replay the three German World Cup gold matches of 1954, 1974 and 1990 in a real-time football strategy game.

Director
James Rouse
Producer
Jon Stopp
Special Effects
Tom Cardo-Moreno
Dave Haupt
Claire Musgrave-Brown
Ashley Tyas

Effects Studio
MPC Los Angeles
Production Company
The Viral Factory
Advertising Agency
The Viral Factory
Offline Editor
Owen Oppenheimer

Lighting Cameraperson
Richard Stewart
Music
Audio Network
Senior Dubbing Mixer
Kim Storey
Post Production Producer
Josh King

Audio Post Production
Unit Post Production
Marketing Manager
Heather Hayoung Chung
Client
Samsung Electronics

Web Ads

The Viral Factory
for Samsung Electronics

Extreme Sheep LED Art

To support the launch of a new range of Samsung FPTVs that use LEDs, The Viral Factory was tasked with making a film that showed the wonder of LED technology. Shot in Wales, with a cast of local shepherds, their sheepdogs and flocks, the film features 300 sheep wearing LED coats, being herded into a series of ever more improbable shapes and pictures. After launch the film had 6.5 million views in three weeks and has now been viewed over 20 million times. The film achieved a five-star rating, and received widespread international coverage by media such as the BBC News, Sky News and The New York Times.

Web Ads

Sony Music Creative
for Columbia Records & Umbro

Kasabian Football Hero
Football Hero was created to promote the Kasabian single 'Underdog' and the band's third album 'West Rider Pauper Lunatic Asylum'. The project was carried out with British sports brand Umbro. We combined football and gaming, two things we knew our target audience was passionate about, and created a three-storey high 'Guitar Hero' style game, played with footballs. Our talented freestyle footballers had to hit five huge pressure pads in time with the music to play 'Underdog'. We created a film of the footballers learning to play the game, and a short documentary telling the story of how we created the game from a technical perspective.

Directors	Producer	Advertising Agency	Clients
Dan & Julian	Nick Moss	Sony Music Creative	Columbia Records
Creative Directors	**Executive Producer**	**Brand Manager**	Umbro
Phil Clandillon	Simon Poon Tip	Trevor Cairns	**Brands**
Steve Milbourne	**Production Company**		Kasabian
	PTE		Umbro

Digital Advertising

Directors
Scott Balcerek
Kris Belman
Copywriter
Steve Howard
Art Director
Brent Anderson
Group Creative Director
Jimmy Smith
Associate Creative Directors
Brent Anderson
Steve Howard

Chief Creative Officer
Rob Schwartz
Producers
Holli Hanley
Rosanne Korenberg
Michael Sagol
Johanna Woollcott
Associate Producer
Tim Newfang
Executive Director of Integrated Production
Richard O'Neill

Production Company
Caviar
Advertising Agency
TBWA\Chiat\Day Los Angeles
Agency Producer
Brian O'Rourke
Editors
Scott Balcerek
David Baum
Tom Moser
Greg Young
Planner
Daniel Teng

Lighting Cameraperson
Adam Ballachey
Group Planning Director
Scott MacMaster
Senior Planner
Martin Ramos
Global Director of Media Arts
Lee Clow
Group Account Director
Brynn Bardacke

Account Executive
Adam Bersin
PR Marketing Manager
Lauren Fritts
Digital Marketing Manager
Randall Brown
Management Supervisor
Amy Farias
Client
Gatorade

Web Ads

TBWA\Chiat\Day Los Angeles
for Gatorade

Replay
According to the US Department of Health and Human Services, seven in ten adults over 30 don't exercise regularly. Therefore, they're not using Gatorade like they used to. The goal was to reignite the athletic spark in this 30-plus age group. Our solution was to provide an opportunity that athletes of every age dream of – a chance to turn back the clock and settle a score. The idea was to use Gatorade's expertise to fuel the chance for high school teams to reunite and replay the biggest games of their lives... 15 years later. The platform offers athletes everywhere a shot at proving, once and for all, who the ultimate champion really is.

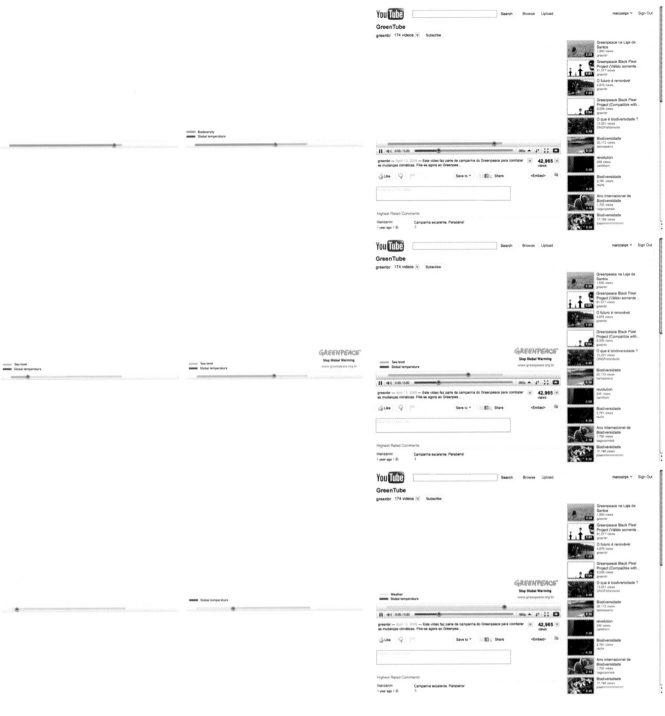

Copywriter
João Paulo Testa
Art Director
Fábio Benedetto

Creative Director
Sergio Mugnaini
Motion Designer
Daniel Barros

Advertising Agency
AlmapBBDO
Sound Design
Cromo.sônica

Client
Greenpeace

Web Ads

AlmapBBDO
for Greenpeace

Greentube
Greenpeace produced three short videos for the climate change campaign. In a very simple way and without any images, the campaign shows how the increase in temperature affects the ocean, the weather and biodiversity.

Director	**Creative Director**	**Production Company**	**Account Handlers**
Simon Ellis	Paul Brazier	Mad Cow Films	Richard Arscott
Assistant Director	**Creative Group**	**Advertising Agency**	Adam Kennedy
Stephanie Day	**Heads**	Abbott Mead Vickers	**Directorate of Public**
Copywriter	Steve Jones	BBDO	**Affairs**
Martin Loraine	Martin Loraine	**Editor**	Stephanie Day
Art Director	**Producers**	Matthew Swanpoel	**Client**
Steve Jones	Jonas Blanchard		The Metropolitan
	Pete Chambers		Police

Web Ads

Abbott Mead Vickers BBDO
for The Metropolitan Police

Choose a Different Ending

Teenagers were carrying knives believing they offered protection. The Metropolitan Police wanted to communicate that the reverse was true. A YouTube film campaign using annotation technology enabled viewers to choose what happened next. Carry a knife? Go to a party? Stab an opponent? After experiencing the consequences of their choices, viewers could choose a different ending; 21 films, ten different endings. Seeded online, the campaign appeared unbranded, employing social media, search, in-game posters and blogs. The response: average viewer engagement of nine films; average rating 4.6 out of 5; 80 YouTube comments a day; 78% awareness; 2,628,350 views.

Banners & Pop Ups

Crispin Porter + Bogusky
for Burger King

Augmented Reality Banner
The King loves tech but loathes printers, so when it came to Burger King using augmented reality, it had to be simple. Without using printouts, banner viewers could see a regular dollar bill turn into BK value menu items right in front of their eyes, just by using their webcams. Using facial recognition, users were then turned into the King himself. This was a tasty augmented reality experience all within a BK banner, something that's never been done before.

Creative Directors	**Interactive Designer**	**Copywriters**	**Advertising Agency**
James	Fabien Dodard	Chris Kahle	Crispin Porter +
Dawson-Hollis	**Developer**	Zac Myrow	Bogusky
Bill Wright	Marc Pelland	**Chief Creative**	**Agency Producers**
Associate Creative	**Art Directors**	**Officers**	Scott Potter
Directors	Michael Ackerman	Jeff Benjamin	Tony Tung
Nuno Ferreira	David Gonsalves	Andrew Keller	**Marketing Manager**
Ryan Wagman	Kristian Luoma	Rob Reilly	Claudia Lezcano
Technical Director	Elias Morales		**Client**
Scott Prindle			Burger King

Digital Advertising

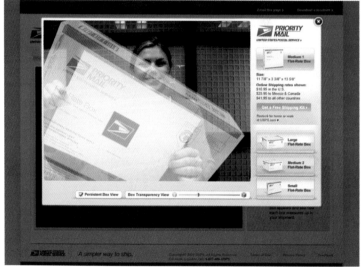

Creative Directors	Designer	Copywriter	Account Executive
Jim Beaudoin	Holly Tegeler	Rachel Gillett	Antonio Ceballos
Suellen Schlievert	**Senior Designer**	**Advertising Agency**	**Quality Assurance**
Director of Creative	Jason Fuqua	AKQA Washington	**Manager**
Development	**Senior Web**	**Senior Account**	Rick Fulgencio
Jon Reiling	**Developers**	**Director**	**Client**
Technical Manager	Sergio Baptista	Garry Pessia	The United States
Grant Furick	Aziz Syed		Postal Service

Tools & Applications

AKQA Washington
for The United States Postal Service

Virtual Box Simulator
The US Postal Service wanted to get America shipping with its four priority mail flat-rate boxes. Each box ships for a low flat rate no matter where it's going or what it weighs. Customers can order free boxes online. But which size? Without a box in hand, customers didn't know which one fitted their shipment. Augmented reality put boxes in customers' hands instantly. PriorityMail.com users launch the virtual box simulator to see 3D images of each box. Users compare the item they want to ship to the virtual boxes. No measuring. No maths. Simple and useful, the application was covered in publications such as The Wall Street Journal, Fast Company, and Creativity.

115

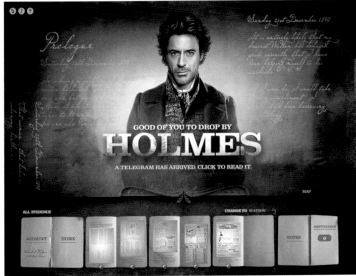

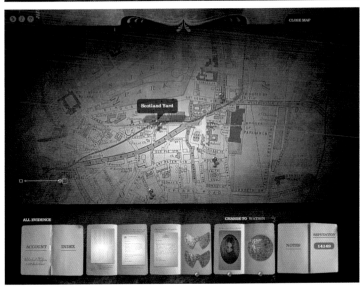

Creative Directors	Creative Developers	Writer	Project Manager	Project Director
Jeremy Boxer	Huy Dinh	Jesse Peyronel	Claire Langler	Lauren Bryan
Alex Fleetwood	Denis Nemytov	**Web Developers**	**Senior Software**	**Account Director**
Game Design	**Senior Creative**	Paul Anderson	**Engineer**	Rowena Minhas
Director	**Developers**	Alex Gemmell	Josh Duck	**Technical Account**
Margaret Robertson	Tristan Holman	**Senior Web**	**Senior Quality**	**Director**
Creative	Paddy Keane	**Developers**	**Assurance Analysts**	Sebastien Rousseau
Development	Thijs Triemstra	Nick Lockwood	Andrew Khamlu	**Client Partner**
Director	David Wiltshire	Francis Saul	Noaman Tareen	Richard Hedges
Rick Williams	**User Experience**	Patrick Troughton	**Advertising Agency**	**Marketing Manager**
Art Directors	**Architect**	James Turner	AKQA London	Kelly Bennett
Shahpour	Chris Dowsett	**Chief Creative**	**Partner Agency**	**Client**
Abbasvand	**Lead Writer**	**Officer**	Hide & Seek	Warner Bros.
Nick Morland	Sophie Sampson	James Hilton	Productions	Pictures

Online Games

AKQA London
for Warner Bros. Pictures

221B.sh

The brief was simple: create a digital campaign for the release of the motion picture Sherlock Holmes that would redefine film marketing. In partnership with Hide & Seek, AKQA London developed '221B', a world-first, two-player online game facilitated by Facebook Connect. Players teamed up as Holmes and Watson and together chased suspects, interviewed artificially intelligent witnesses, explored crime scenes and made deductions to solve eight weekly episodic mysteries, culminating in the first scene of the movie. This rich audio-visual experience blends innovative technologies in five online firsts.

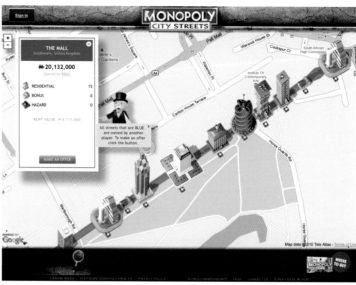

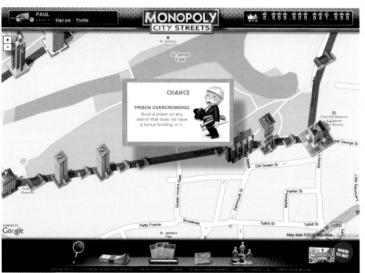

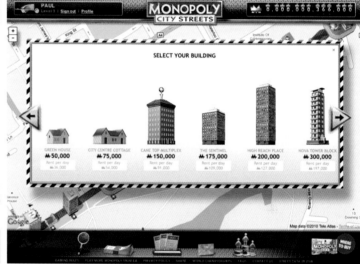

Creative Director
Simon Richings
Executive Creative Director of Digital
Matt Ross
Technical Director
Matthew Oxley
Technical Lead
Paul James
Design Director
Tony Cianci

User Experience Designer
Brooke McPherson
Designer
Romain Brisson
Developers
Christo Coetzee
Ben Cooper-Holmes
Carlton Dickson
Nicole Schloeter

Art Director
Matt Fenn
Copywriter
Matt Ross
Head of Digital Advertising
Nick Clements
Digital Agency
Tribal DDB London
Advertising Agency
DDB UK

Studio Manager
Neil Lee
Account Handler
Sheerien Salindera
Planner
James Broomfield
Marketing Manager
Joanna Austin
Client
Hasbro
Brand
Monopoly City

Online Games

Tribal DDB London
for Hasbro

Monopoly City Streets
This online campaign takes Monopoly into the real world with a live worldwide game using Google Maps to turn the globe into one giant board. The goal is simple: become the richest property magnate on earth! Armed with $3million in virtual cash, players can purchase and construct Monopoly buildings on any street in the world. They earn rent from their properties and can increase the earning potential of their streets by adding schools, eco-friendly parks and much more. With chance cards, players can sabotage their opponents by erecting prisons or sewage plants, negating all rent on a street, and even demolishing buildings altogether.

117

Producers	Production	Advertising Agency	Client Sales
Gustav Carlsson	**Companies**	Forsman &	**& Marketing**
Johan Wiman	OTW	Bodenfors	Johanna Berlinde
	Qbrick	**Media Agency**	**Client**
	Thomson Interactive	Starcom	Tele2
	Media		
	X-Com		

Digital Advertising Campaigns

Forsman & Bodenfors
for Tele2

Mobile Internet Live
To show the quality and reliability of Tele2's mobile internet, we sent a reporter all around Sweden. His objective was to broadcast live TV using a mobile internet modem from Tele2. To show how much Tele2 believed in its product, the company decided to put its top executives – including the CEO – on a ledge over a dunking pool. If the connection went down, a Tele2 executive would go straight into the pool.

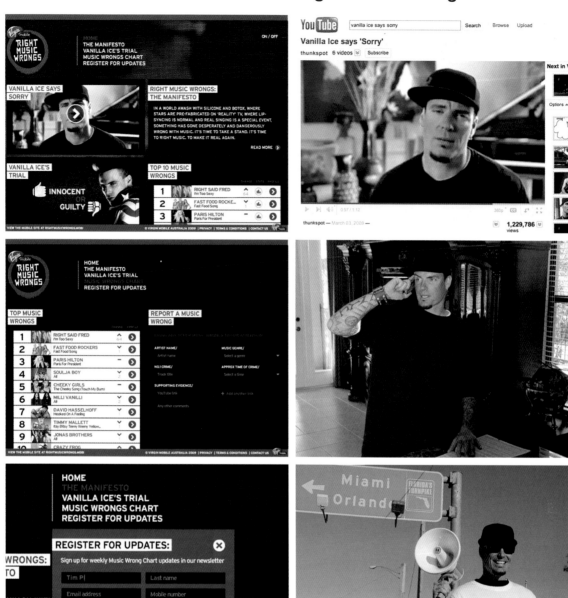

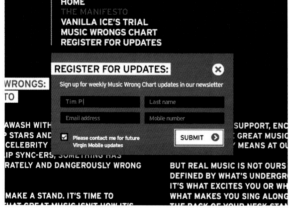

Digital Advertising Campaigns

Droga5 Australia
for Virgin Mobile Australia

Right Music Wrongs

The challenge was to reconnect Virgin Mobile with its musical heritage. Our solution was to create an online debate on what good (and bad) music really is; www.rightmusicwrongs.org was born. Using Vanilla Ice as our provocateur, we begin to put him on trial. Found innocent: He'll be allowed to play the V Festival. Found guilty: He'll get pelted with tomatoes. Hence he said: 'Sorry'. (He's now due to play Glastonbury – so maybe we should say, 'Sorry').

Executive Creative Director
David Nobay
Digital Director
Brett Mitchell
Producer
Chloe Rickard
Senior Art Director
Ben Smith
Senior Copywriter
Ben Akers

Web Copywriter
Brendan Winter
Director
Trent O'Donnel
Editor
Paul Swain
Web Editor
Marcus Johnston
Production Company
Jungle Boys

Digital Production House
Future Buro
Advertising Agency
Droga5 Australia
Agency Producer
Allison Chambers
Executive Planning Director
Sudeep Gohil

Account Director
Nicolas Kettelhake
Brand Manager
Dave Cain
Marketing Manager
Jaclyn Lee-Joe
Client
Virgin Mobile
Australia

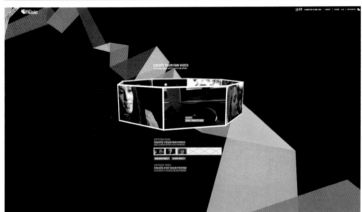

Creative Director Dominic Goldman	**Producer** Neil Andrews	**Digital Agency** Magic Socket	**Account Handler** Jason Gonslaves
Design Director Eric Chia	**Copywriter** Hugo Biershenk	**Advertising Agency** BBH London	**Marketing Manager** Lindsay Nuttall
Developer Mario Ballario	**Direction** D.A.R.Y.L	**Agency Producer** Chris Watling	**Client** MySpace UK
Art Director Dean Woodhouse	**Editor** Fernanda Wagland	**Post Production** Absolute Post	**Brand** MySpace Music
	Sound Designer Ian Lambden		

Digital Advertising Campaigns

Magic Socket & BBH London
for MySpace UK

Get Real Close

To launch MySpace Music, a brand new music service from MySpace, we created a campaign that allows fans to 'get real close' to their favourite artists. The website myspace.com/getrealclose is a series of banners featuring world famous artists listening to the music they love from their new MySpace playlists. These never-before-seen moments, like 50 Cent in his hotel suite rapping over Michael Jackson, blow up to play full screen, in HD quality. The site myspace.com/fanvideo allows hardcore music fans to feature in person in intimate films with artists like Alicia Keys, by seamlessly integrating the fans' Facebook profile pictures into the artists' films on MySpace.

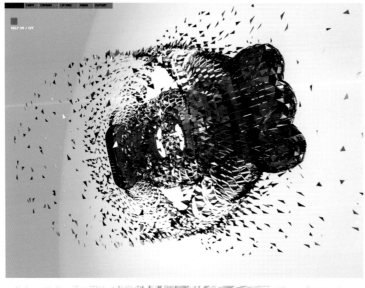
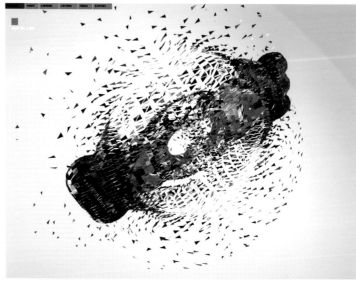
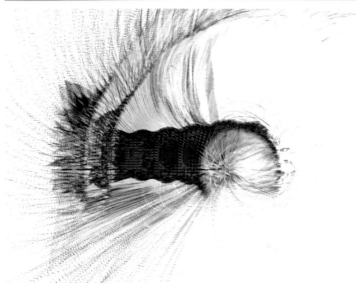

Art Directors	Flash Programmers	Digital Artist	Planning Director
David Gamble	Ali Kember	Karsten Schmidt	Mark Sng
Rodrigo Lebrun	Nick Watton	**Design Agency**	**Client**
Creative Director	**Designers**	Saint @ RKCR	The Victoria & Albert
David Gamble	Sharon Chong	**Project Director**	Museum
Copywriters	Dave Price	Chris Jefford	**Brand**
Jeeves Basu	Shaban Siddiq	**Project Manager**	Decode
Peter Brown	**Developer**	Ellen Chng	
	John Cleveley		

Art Direction

Saint @ RKCR
for The Victoria & Albert Museum

Recode | Decode

Saint was asked by the V&A to promote 'Decode', the museum's first exhibition dedicated to digital art. Traditional art is normally created to affect you, while digital art is best when affected by you. We wanted this inclusive philosophy to extend beyond the exhibition, so we created an open-source campaign that encouraged people to recode 'Decode'. We worked with digital artist Karsten Schmidt to create an interactive art application that invited people to create their own digital masterpieces. The best recodes were used to promote 'Decode' in an integrated campaign that blurred the lines between product and promotion, and helped attract over 235% of original footfall targets.

121

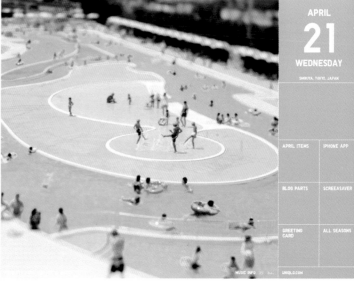

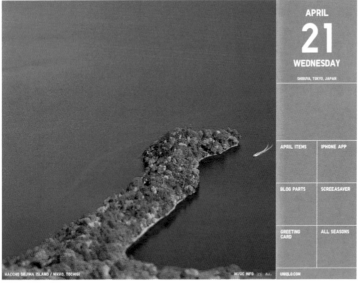

Art Director	**Designer**	**Music**	**Creative**
Takashi Kamada	Takashi Kamada	Fantastic Plastic	**Management**
Creative Director	**Photographers**	Machine	**Director**
Koichiro Tanaka	Shinsuke Kamioka	**Digital Agency**	Kentaro Katsube
Technical Director	Takuji Onda	Projector	**Production**
Kay-ichi Tozaki	Takuyuki Saito	**Production Company**	**Managers**
Shooting Directors	**Web Producer**	Puzzle	Shigehisa Nakao
Hiroyuki Kojima	Ken Kanetomo	**Programmer**	Yuuri Ogawa
TOCHKA 'Kazue	**Producers**	Susumu Arai	Shinichi Saeki
Monno + Takeshi	Nozomu Naito	**System Engineer**	**PR Managers**
Nagata'	Gyosei Okada	Susumu Arai	Mayumi Sawada
Interactive Designers	Shinjiro Ono		Ryota Sugawara
Yukio Sato			**Client**
Kay-ichi Tozaki			UNIQLO

Art Direction

Projector
for UNIQLO

UNIQLO Calendar
UNIQLO calendar is an online digital calendar, which aims to build a branding platform to promote both Japan and UNIQLO on a global scale. Each season, we went on a mission to capture the dynamism of Japan by spending months travelling and filming, using tilt-shift and time-lapse techniques to create a fresh, miniature version of Japan. Users can set their location and use it as blog widget, screensaver, greetings card, or iPhone App. As of January 2010, UNIQLO calendar covers all four seasons, featuring scenes from over 180 locations in Japan, and is still searching for more.

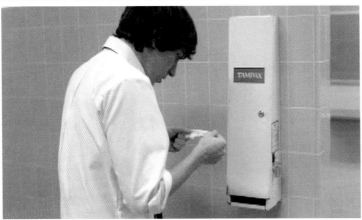

Copywriter	**Production Designer**	**Global Chief Creative**	**Production Company**	**Music**
Dave Loew	Jason Schuster	**Officer**	Smuggler	Human Worldwide
Creative Directors	**Director of**	Mark Tutssel	Productions	**Account Director**
Dave Loew	**Photography**	**Agency Producers**	**Advertising Agency**	Cindy Blikre
Jon Wyville	Jo Willems	David L Moore	Leo Burnett Chicago	**Account Supervisor**
Executive Creative	**Executive Producers**	Rob Tripas	**Digital Agency**	Katie McClay
Director	Brian Carmody	**Line Producer**	Domani Studios	**Client**
Becky Swanson	Alison Kunzman	Corey Berg	**Editing House**	Procter & Gamble
Art Director	Patrick Milling Smith	**Head of Production**	The Whitehouse	**Brand**
Jon Wyville	Lisa Rich	Chris Rossiter	Chicago	Tampax
Director	**Chief Creative**	**Editors**	**Post Production**	
Randy Krallman	**Officer**	Matt Walsh	Co3	
	John Condon	Matt Woods	The Filmworkers	
			Club	

Writing

Leo Burnett Chicago & Domani Studios
for Procter & Gamble

Zack Johnson
Every woman wishes that just once, men could experience what she goes through every month. So Tampax built an emotionally empathetic relationship with girls by dramatising the menstrual trials and travails of an all American high school boy who just happened to wake up one day more like a girl down there. Zack Johnson is branded viral content in the form of a video blog and social media. The film is a way of talking to young women about a subject that usually makes them uncomfortable – menstruation. And it does so in an empathetic and entertaining way, through Zack Johnson, a 16-year-old boy.

DiREC
CRI

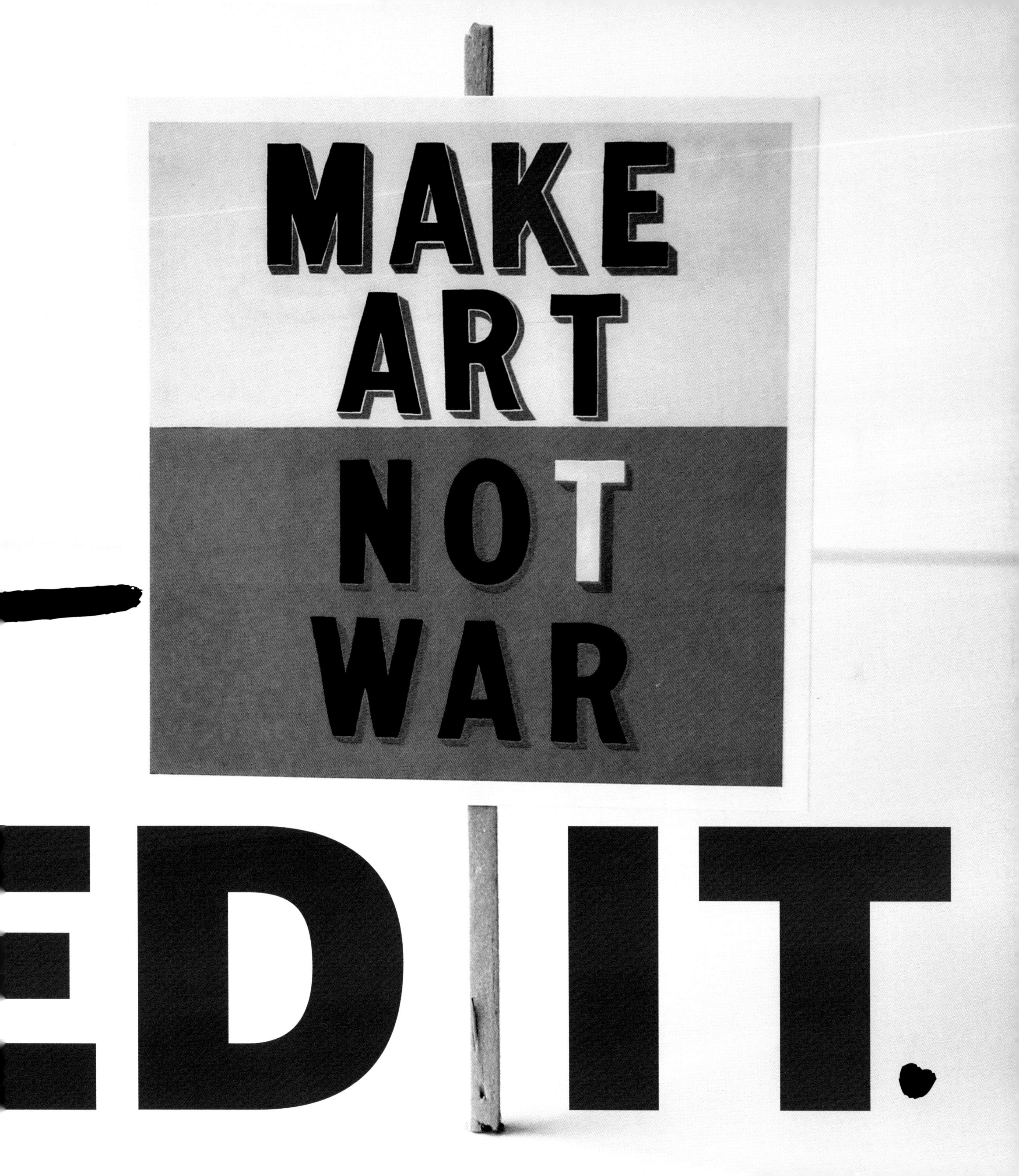

EDIT.

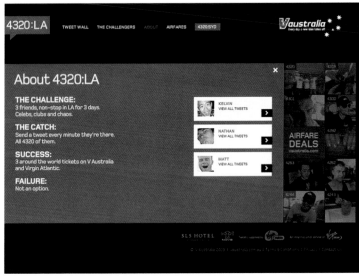

Senior Art Director	**Agency Producers**	**Production**	**Account Directors**
Ben Smith	Roy Di Giorgio	**Companies**	Liz Ainslie
Senior Copywriter	Paul Johnston	Goodoil Films	Nicolas Kettelhake
Ben Akers	**Editors**	Sydney	**Group Marketing**
Executive Creative	Andrew McLean	Great Guns USA	**Director**
Director	Craig Wilson	**Advertising Agency**	Michelle Lee
David Nobay	**Online Design**	Droga5 Australia	**Retail & Partnership**
Director of Digital	**& Development**	**Executive Planning**	**Marketing Manager**
Brett Mitchell	Future Buro	**Director**	Michael Betteridge
Digital Producer	**Sound Design**	Sudeep Gohil	**Client**
John McLean	Nylon Studios		V Australia
	Sydney		

Online

Droga5 Australia
for V Australia

4320: LA/SYD

To promote V Australia's 'Three-day deals to LA' we created a campaign that positioned LA as a place you don't just enjoy by the day, or even by the hour, but by the minute. We sent three Aussies to LA for an all expenses paid, hip and happening, jam packed weekend. The catch? They had to tweet every minute they were there, all 4,320 of them. In Australia's first Twitter based campaign, tweets and twitpics were fed live to a website, which linked through to purchasing the deal. Each minute was also filmed and used in-flight travel documentaries.

VO: Close your eyes.

Now you can see what a soldier can see as he pursues a dangerous insurgent.

Nothing.

You're in a dark tunnel.

There could be a tripwire to your right.

There could be a tripwire to your left.

And he's getting away.

Keep your eyes closed.

What do you do?

(Pause.)

You rely on your mates.

And Night Vision.

It's your mission. It's on-line.

Search online for start thinking soldier.

One Army. Regular and Territorial.

(SFX: NO boot stamp)

Art Directors
Matthew Anderson
Steve Nicholls
Digital Art Director
Asan Aslam
Director of Gaming
Tim Hall
Copywriters
Matthew Anderson
Dave Hillyard
Steve Nicholls
Ed Robinson

Digital Copywriter
Jon Groom
Typographers
Bryan Riddle
Simon Tomlin
Photographer
Steve Nicholls
Executive Creative Directors
Tom Ewart
Adam Kean
Creative Director of Gaming
Louis Clement

Digital Executive Creative Director
David Prideaux
Creative Lead of Digital
Matt Stafford
Director
Michael Geoghegan
Producer
John Golley
Agency Producer
Kim Knowlton

Production Companies
C.O.I Broadcast
Spank Films
Advertising Agency
Publicis London
Digital Agency
Publicis Modem
Gaming Agency
Skive
Commercial Director of Gaming
Anthony Somerville

Events Agency
Jack
Morton
Worldwide
Regional Marketing Director
Colin Cook
Clients
British Army
C.O.I.

Integrated

Publicis London
for the British Army

Start Thinking Soldier

How do you convince a typical 17-year-old that the army is a great career? Talk to them in a language they understand – gaming. The TV campaign, shot in the style of a first-person shooter, took the viewer on a mission. The correct answer to a task at the end of each spot unlocked more levels to the mission online. The user then took control of the action. Moving seamlessly between gaming and real footage, potential recruits were put through a series of challenges. The best competitors were invited to meet the army and compete for real. The advert 'Girlfriend', which is part of this campaign, was also selected in the Direct/Press & Poster category.

Get off at the fashionable end of Oxford Street, drift into the achingly cool technology hall of London's most happening department store and view this year's must-have plasma courtesy of the sound and vision technologist in the Marc Jacobs sandals **then go to dixons.co.uk and buy it.**

Dixons.co.uk
The last place you want to go

Step into middle England's best loved department store, stroll through haberdashery to the audio visual department where an awfully well brought up young man will bend over backwards to find the right TV for you **then go to dixons.co.uk and buy it.**

Dixons.co.uk
The last place you want to go

Get off at Knightsbridge, visit the discerning shopper's fave department store, ascend the exotic staircase and let Piers in the pinstripe suit demonstrate the magic of the latest high-definition flatscreen **then go to dixons.co.uk and buy it.**

Dixons.co.uk
The last place you want to go

t is the beginning of December and Cedric Prattletwerp, proprietor of the small second hand bookshop on Bayswater Road is troubled by an unfamiliar sensation. He has come over all a bit Christmassy. "Hurrumph", he hurrumphs and heads for the bus stop where he climbs aboard a No.94, attracted like a moth to the distant glow of the West End. Cedric steps off the bus into the winter wonderland that is Oxford Street, his usual bookish pallor transformed by 700,000 watts of flickering good cheer. "HO HO HO" insists the unemployed roofing engineer in a Santa suit outside the long established London department store. "HA", replies Cedric pushing past the cheery figure as he makes his way to the escalator. Overcome by seasonal goodwill, Cedric has decided to buy someone a Christmas present. Himself. *A plasma TV.* With Yuletide bonhomie, Noel the young assistant patiently demonstrates all 27 models available. The 53 minutes fly by for Cedric who singles out 50 inches of pixelated wonderment and, pressing the young man's hand warmly in pitiful gratitude **goes to dixons.co.uk and buys it.**

Dixons.co.uk
The last place you want to go

Art Director
Graham Fink
Copywriters
Simon Dicketts
Orlando Warner

Typographers
Gareth Davies
Simon Warden
Creative Directors
Simon Dicketts
Graham Fink

Advertising Agency
M&C Saatchi London
Planner
Neil Godber
Account Handler
Estelle Lee

Marketing Director
Niall O'Keefe
Client
Dixons Stores Group
Brand
Dixons.co.uk

▲ Press & Poster

M&C Saatchi London
for Dixons Stores Group

Sandals / Middle England / Piers
Our campaign repositioned Dixons.co.uk by persuading people to embrace a smarter way of shopping online. People were cheekily encouraged to make use of the best service freely available on the high street, then find a better price online at Dixons.co.uk. The ads wittily suggested some typical high-street shopping experiences. The sign-off, 'The last place you want to go' acted as a polite suggestion of when people should use the site, as well as a self-aware and humorous acknowledgement of the brand's equivocal reputation as a good place to shop. The campaign, including the execution 'Prattletwerp', was also selected in the Direct/Writing category.

128

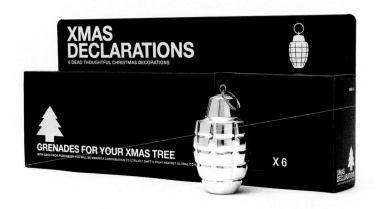

Art Directors	Project Manager	Advertising Agency	PR Agency
Ali Johnson	Ali Johnson	Dorothy	John Doe
Phil Skegg	**Manufacturer**	**Art Assistants**	**Brand Manager**
Copywriter	SUCK UK	Sonny Mitchell	Katrin Owusu
Phil Skegg	**Prototype & Model**	Johnson	**Client**
Photographer	**Maker**	Grace Skegg	Ctrl.Alt.Shift
Tim Sinclair	Philip Howard	Tom Skegg	
Creative Director			
Phil Skegg			

▲ Addressed Direct Mail Very Low Volume

Dorothy
for Ctrl.Alt.Shift

Xmas Declarations
In the past 15 years, 80% of the world's poorest countries have suffered conflict; 90% of war victims are civilian. In 2009 Ctrl.Alt.Shift launched a campaign to raise awareness of the catastrophic impact conflict has on communities in developing countries. Hand grenade-shaped baubles may not seem like the most festive of things to put on a Christmas tree, but the decorations were designed by Dorothy to act as a stark reminder of the realities of war. Packs were mailed out to press and peers to push the issue up the political agenda. Limited edition packs were also sold by SUCK UK in design stores across Europe.

Art Director
Andreas Englund
Director
Max Vitali
Copywriter
Jesper Eronn
Creative Director
Anders Dalenius

Producer
Mattias Coldén
Agency Producer
Markus Ahlm
Editor
Johan Wik
Technical Director
Johan Brandström

Sound Designers
Edward Björner
Eric Thorsell
Music Composer
David Engellau
Advertising Agency
Draftfcb Sweden

Account Handler
Per Hellberg
Brand Manager
Per Leander
Client
Radiotjänst

Online

Draftfcb Sweden
for Radiotjänst

The Hero
This web-based application allows you to experience how the entire world celebrates you as a hero for paying your TV fee – and safeguarding freedom and independence in Swedish TV and radio. After a simple upload, a picture of yourself or someone you know is rendered in an epic looking movie, making it look as if you were actually there on set. After the movie has played, you are given the option to register directly for the statutory TV fee, and send your movie as a link to friends.

Direct

Art Director
Steve Jones
Director
Simon Ellis
Copywriter
Martin Loraine
Creative Director
Paul Brazier

Producers
Jonas Blanchard
Pete Chambers
Stephanie Phillips
Tom White
Editor
Matthew Swanpoel

Advertising Agency
Abbott Mead Vickers
BBDO
Production Company
Mad Cow Films
**Creative Group
Heads**
Steve Jones
Martin Loraine

Account Handlers
Richard Arscott
Claire Best
Adam Kennedy
**Directorate of Public
Affairs**
Stephanie Day
Client
Metropolitan Police

Online

Abbott Mead Vickers BBDO
for the Metropolitan Police

Choose a Different Ending
Teenagers were carrying knives believing they offered protection. The Metropolitan Police wanted to communicate that the reverse was true. A YouTube film campaign using annotation technology enabled viewers to choose what happened next. Carry a knife? Go to a party? Stab an opponent? After experiencing the consequences of their choices, viewers could choose a different ending; 21 films, ten different endings. Seeded online, the campaign appeared unbranded, employing social media, search, in-game posters and blogs. The response: average viewer engagement of nine films; average rating 4.6 out of 5; 80 YouTube comments a day; 78% awareness; 2,628,350 views.

131

Mollie   Rahmel   Cole   Khari

Art Director
Helen Board
Director
Jim Gilchrist
Copywriter
Matt Lever
Creative Director
Danny Brooke-Taylor
Producer
Kate Leahy

Agency Producer
Lynnette Kyme
Editor
Adam Spivey
Lighting
Cameraperson
Alex Barber
Sound Designer
Parv Thind

Planner
Andy Nairn
Advertising Agency
MCBD
Account Handlers
Rachel Gilmour
Remi Rasenberg

Brand & Marketing
Manager
Helen Duggan
Client
Department of
Health

Moving Image

MCBD
for the Department of Health

Mollie / Rahmel / Cole / Khari
Anti-smoking research findings state that people are far more likely to give up when they realise the emotional effect that their habit has on their loved ones, particularly their children. These ads featured the actual children of real smokers, who were given the opportunity to tell their mums and dads exactly how their smoking makes them feel. The ads were unscripted, and targeted the parents directly, playing during their favourite TV programmes.

132

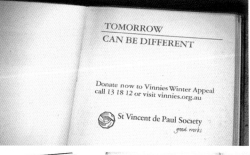

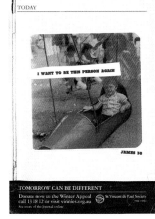

Art Director	Flash Developer	Head of TV	Planner
Heather Sheen	John Knutsson	Denise McKeon	Paul Blockey
Copywriters	**Agency Producers**	**Sound Design**	**Account Handlers**
Alex Derwin	Mel Herbert	Nylon Studios	Carla Hizon
Jess Little	Jo Kouvaris	Sydney	Jenny Jacinto
Designer	**Agency Digital**	**Production Company**	Mandy Spero
Heather Sheen	**Producer**	Yukfoo Animation	Julia Williams
Creative Director	Rebecca Smith	Studios New	**Client**
Guy Rooke	**Agency Direct Mail**	Zealand	St Vincent De Paul
Executive Creative	**Producers**	**Advertising Agency**	Society
Director	Melissa Scurry	Clemenger BBDO	
Richard Maddocks	Jameson Wright	Sydney	

Integrated

Clemenger BBDO Sydney
for the St Vincent De Paul Society

Tomorrow Can Be Different...
With the global financial crisis hitting hard, St Vincent de Paul wanted to give those in need a chance to speak for themselves. The result was the collaborative journal 'Today I Am'. Responding to the question 'What does today mean to you?', the homeless, disadvantaged and dispossessed could tell the world what living below the poverty line in Australia really felt like. Individual entries became part of an online, print, TV and radio appeal with the line 'Tomorrow Can Be Different'. The journal also became a national exhibition and a permanent part of all six state library collections. Donations reached a record high, up 20% on the previous year.

Art Director	**Executive Producer**	**Audio Engineers**	**Project Manager**
Tony Bradbourne	Matt Noonan	John Cooper	Jules Pakenham
Copywriter	**Interactive Producer**	Alfred Figueroa	**Head of Brand**
Rob Jack	Hamish Wanhill	Jordan Stone	**& Communications**
Designer	**Agency Producers**	**Chief Executive**	Duncan Blair
Heath Lowe	Fiona Champtaloup	**Officer**	**Managing Partner**
Creative Directors	Sascha Mortimer	Scott Bartlett	Michael Redwood
Tony Bradbourne	**Editor**	**Production Company**	**Media Strategist**
Rob Jack	Luke Haigh	Curious Films	Sean McCready
Heath Lowe	**Flame Artist**	**Advertising Agency**	**Head of Sales**
Director	Nigel Mortimer	Special Group	**& Marketing**
Darryl Ward		**Planner**	David Joyce
Producer		Claire Beatson	**Client**
Andy Mauger			Orcon

Integrated

Special Group
for Orcon

Orcon + Iggy Pop – Together Incredible
Orcon provides New Zealand's fastest broadband. To stand out from bigger spending competitors, it launched an innovative product demonstration campaign. The idea was to find nine kiwi musicians and simultaneously link them from their homes to Iggy Pop in his Miami studio via Skype, in order to re-record his iconic track, 'The Passenger'. Iggy appeared in TV ads, banners and street posters calling for people to audition online, through a specially built Facebook application. Iggy chose his band and, on the day, coached them live online and orchestrated a brand new arrangement. The content was then used to make a campaign of truly stand-out TV commercials.

It's not just a cup of tea
It's a chat about EastEnders
It's laughing at a joke
It's listening to a story
It's noticing the track marks on her arm
It's asking why she does it
It's hearing how she pays for it
It's believing her when she says she wants to get clean
It's the moment a 16-year-old girl asks you to help her
It's a step in the right direction
It's an excuse to come back and see how she's doing
It's a celebration
It's not just a cup of tea
It's one of the most important tools we use

Social work with children & families is changing
We can train you to use tools like these
And support you financially while you train
Call 0300 123 1220 or search **Be the difference**

It's not just a lump of Plasticine
It's a laugh
It's what shall we make?
It's a rocket
It's a dinosaur
It's watching an 8-year-old boy with his new foster family
It's noticing how he shares a joke with his foster brother
It's laughing when the dinosaur looks more like a horse
It's seeing that everything's alright
It's knowing he's happy with his new family
It's a relief
It's the result of two years' hard work
It's not just a lump of Plasticine
It's one of the most important tools we use

Social work with children & families is changing
We can train you to use tools like these
And give you support as you progress through your training and career
Call 0300 123 1220 or search **Be the difference**

It's not just a bag of crisps
It's a stroll to the newsagents
It's what's your favourite flavour?
It's stopping to sit on a bench
It's a chat about her favourite band
It's noticing the bags under her eyes
It's hearing how she does all the housework
It's hearing how she cooks the dinner
It's asking about her Mum
It's the moment a 10-year-old girl tells you how her Mummy is always down the pub
It's a problem shared
It's planning for a better future
It's not just a bag of crisps
It's one of the most important tools we use

Social work with children & families is changing
We can train you to use tools like these
And find ways of building on your existing skills too
Call 0300 123 1220 or search **Be the difference**

Art Directors
Christian Horsfall
Jamie Marshall
Digital Art Director
Christian Horsfall
Copywriters
Brian Murray
Gary Turner
Digital Copywriter
Brian Murray
Typographer
Dave Wakefield

Photographer
Jenny van Sommers
Designer
Sunil Kansara
Digital Designer
Sunil Kansara
Executive Creative Directors
Tom Ewart
Adam Kean
David Prideaux
Director
Charlie Crane

Producer
Matthew Brown
Agency Producers
Zoe Dale
Kim Knowlton
Head of Design
Athila Armstrong
Head of Digital
Athila Armstrong
Production Companies
C.O.I Broadcast
Knucklehead

Advertising Agency
Publicis London
Digital Agency
Publicis Modem
Head of Communications
Claire Chappell
Clients
C.O.I.
CWDC (Children's Workforce Development Council)

Integrated
Publicis London
for CWDC

Be the Difference
During a period of intense public hostility and anger towards social workers in the UK, we were asked to recruit new, high quality candidates to the profession. After talking to social workers, we realised that the answer to huge problems lay in the smallest of things. We discovered how they are trained to use the most simple and unassuming objects to confront issues, and thus resolve the most complex emotional and physical emergencies. In just 18 weeks, we had over half a million responses and 54,364 registrations.

135

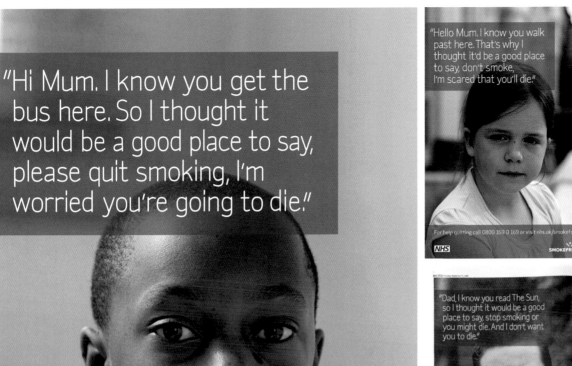

"Hi Mum. I know you get the bus here. So I thought it would be a good place to say, please quit smoking, I'm worried you're going to die."

For help quitting call 0800 169 0 169 or visit nhs.uk/smokefree

NHS   SMOKEFREE

"Hello Mum. I know you walk past here. That's why I thought it'd be a good place to say, don't smoke, I'm scared that you'll die."

For help quitting call 0800 169 0 169 or visit nhs.uk/smokefree

NHS   SMOKEFREE

"Hello Mum. I know you buy your cigarettes across the road from here. Please stop smoking. I don't want you to die."

For help quitting call 0800 169 0 169 or visit nhs.uk/smokefree

NHS   SMOKEFREE

"Dad, I know you read The Sun, so I thought it would be a good place to say, stop smoking or you might die. And I don't want you to die."

NHS   SMOKEFREE

HORROR AS PAL, 16, DIED IN 60mph SLEDGE CRASH

Art Director	Photographer	Advertising Agency	Brand & Marketing
Helen Board	Henrik Knudsen	MCBD	Manager
Copywriter	**Typographer**	**Account Handlers**	Helen Duggan
Matt Lever	Kerry Roper	Rachel Gilmour	**Client**
	Creative Director	Remi Rasenberg	Department of
	Danny Brooke-Taylor		Health

Press & Poster

MCBD
for the Department of Health

Jake / Mollie / Leon / Khari / Masika / Cole

Anti-smoking research findings state that people are far more likely to give up when they realise the emotional effect that their habit has on their loved ones, particularly their children. These ads featured untreated profile shots of children looking directly at the camera. These were actual children of real smokers. Ads were placed in media they knew their parents read or in outdoor areas near where their parents bought their cigarettes; this created a huge personal impact, which is vital to provoking quit attempts.

Art Directors
Albert S Chan
Sabina Hesse
Copywriters
Albert S Chan
Sabina Hesse

Painter
Remus Grecu
Creative Directors
Christian Mommertz
Dr Stephan Vogel
Advertising Agency
Ogilvy Frankfurt

Art Buyer
Valerie Opitz
Account Handler
Veronika Sikvölgyi
Brand Manager
Claudia Engel

Client
ANAD (National
Association of
Anorexia Nervosa
and Associated
Disorders)

Ambient

Ogilvy Frankfurt
for ANAD

Contemporary Beauty Ideals
ANAD is a not-for-profit organisation that educates the public about the dangers of anorexia.
They asked us for an innovative way to raise money and awareness. To highlight the unhealthy
beauty ideals promoted by the media and fashion industry, we opted for a completely new
approach. We painted world famous masterpieces a second time. These paintings were then
displayed in fine art museums, exactly where visitors would expect to see manifestations
of true beauty.

137

Art Directors
Nadja Lossgott
Shelley Smoler
Copywriters
Raphael Basckin
Nicholas Hulley

Photographers
Chloe Coetsee
Des Ellis
Michael Meyersfeld
Rob Wilson
Executive Creative Director
Damon Stapleton

Advertising Agency
TBWA\Hunt\Lascaris
Johannesburg
Account Handler
Bridget Langley

Marketing Manager
Liz Linsell
Client
The Zimbabwean
Newspaper

Addressed Direct Mail Very Low Volume

TBWA\Hunt\Lascaris Johannesburg
for The Zimbabwean Newspaper

Trillion Dollar Mailer
The Zimbabwean Newspaper, forced into exile, was then slapped with a 55% luxury import duty, making it unaffordable for Zimbabweans. To raise awareness of this issue, we developed an unusual solution. The most eloquent symbol of Zimbabwe's collapse is the Z$ trillion note, which cannot buy anything and certainly not advertising. But it can become the advertising. We turned the money into the medium by printing our messages straight onto it. We made flyers and direct mailers out of the worthless money. Overnight, Zimbabwean banknotes achieved what they'd never been able to buy – advertising coverage. We used Mugabe's own creation against him.

Art Director	**Illustrator**	**Model**	**Brand Manager**
Brendan Donnelly	Jason Young	Matt Arden	Alette Winfield
Copywriter	**Creative Director**	**Advertising Agency**	**Client**
Guy Futcher	Mark Harricks	DDB Sydney	AWARD
Photographers	**Executive Creative**	**Account Handler**	**Brand**
Brendan Donnelly	**Director**	Graham van Der	AWARD Call for
Guy Futcher	Matt Eastwood	Westhuizen	Entries
Typographer	**Retoucher**		
Jason Young	Matt Bright		

Addressed Direct Mail Low Volume

DDB Sydney
for AWARD

AWARD Call for Entries

For an industry that prides itself on being creative, our PR photos are anything but. 'The Modern Creative's Guide to PR Photography', complete with a 22-page booklet, a quick reference chart, an information guide and an instructional video, helps future award winners deal with the publicity that comes with an AWARD Pencil. It also takes the piss out of our fellow creatives, but only because they deserve it. This piece of direct mail was also selected in the Direct/Writing and Direct/Art Direction categories.

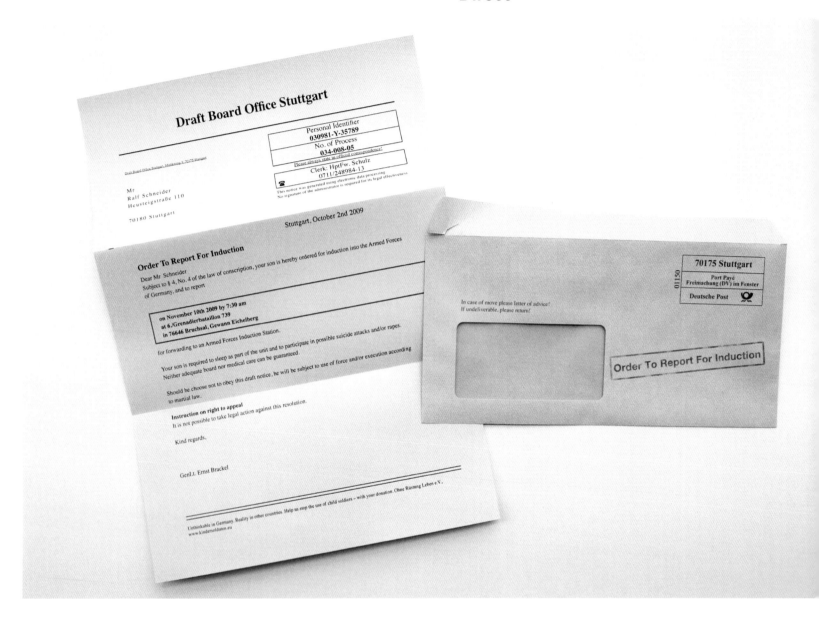

Art Director
Stephanie Wiehle
Copywriters
Carola Beck
Matthias Hess
Lars Wagner

Designer
Nana Poehner
Creative Directors
Philipp Barth
Holger Oehrlich

Advertising Agency
Jung von Matt
Stuttgart
Account Handlers
Susanne Vanselow
Denise Winter

Client
Ohne Ruestung
Leben

Addressed Direct Mail Medium Volume

Jung von Matt Stuttgart
for Ohne Ruestung Leben

Draft Notice for Child Soldiers
The use of child soldiers is common in many countries. Our client wanted to generate awareness of this issue and collect donations. When young German men reach adulthood, they receive a letter calling them up for service in the army. We sent authentic-looking military draft notices to families with young children (8 to 14 years). The children are ordered to perform military service, including taking part in suicide missions and rapes. Our message: 'Unthinkable in Germany. Reality in other countries. Help us stop the use of child soldiers – with your donation'.

Writing

Rare
for the Perth Advertising & Design Club

Man-sized Serifs
A tip of the hat to all the great long copy ads of the 70s and 80s, this tongue-in-cheek lambasting of modern day writers and art directors was designed to encourage entries into the Perth Advertising & Design Club (PADC) Awards.

NEVE
ENDII
MOAN

R-IG LIST

Environmental Design

Architect	Fit Out Contractor	Concrete Contractor	Exhibition Display	Project
Stuart McKnight	WFC	Toureen Mangan	**Case Manufacturer**	**Management**
Exhibition Design	**Service Engineering**	**Glazing Contractor**	Glasbau Hahn	Lend Lease
MUMA (McInnes	Arup	Octatube	**Daylighting**	Projects
Usher McKnight	**Main Contractor**	International	**Consultants**	March
Architects)	Holloway White	**Onyx Screens**	Arup	Consulting
Structural	Allom	**& Stone Floor**	**Artificial Lighting**	**Client**
Engineering	**Quantity Surveyor**	**Contractor**	**Consultants**	Trustees of the
Dewhurst	Davis Langdon	Gormley Masonry	DHA Design	Victoria & Albert
Macfarlane &	**Display Plinths**	Services	**Historic**	Museum
Partners	**Contractor**	**Balustrade**	**Building**	**Brand**
Architectural	Stone Productions	**Contractor**	**Consultants**	V&A
Practice		TP Aspinall & Sons	Julian Harrap	
MUMA			Architects	

Public Space & Community

MUMA
for The Victoria & Albert Museum

Medieval and Renaissance Galleries, Victoria & Albert Museum
MUMA has created a new suite of galleries to house the V&A's Medieval and Renaissance collections. The materials, construction and form of the interventions are distinctly modern and complement the historic building fabric. Innovative, passive environmental control in the context of the historic artefacts and considered use of daylight were key drivers. The new informal Daylit Gallery and circulation hub occupy a previously underused light-well, providing equality of access to six levels of the Grade I listed building.

Interior Designers	Creative Directors	Manufacturers	Project Manager
Dirk Hennemann	Prof Thomas Hundt	Kai Ertel	Gesina Geiger
Christian	Ingo Zirngibl	Matthias Furch	**Client**
Wessolowski	**Editor**	**Design Agency**	Haus der
Graphic Designers	Fabiola Maldonado	jangled nerves	Geschichte Baden-
Gerd Häußler	**Cinematographer**		Württemberg
Daniel Naegele	Fabiola Maldonado		
Anina Stocker			

Temporary Exhibitions

jangled nerves
for Haus der Geschichte Baden-Württemberg

You and Us – Integration of Displaced People in Baden-Württt
The history of people who have been displaced is told through the concerted use of different kinds of media. A walkable map of the banishment areas depicts the origins of displaced persons through hundreds of animated arrows marking the routes of their escape. A curved wall guides visitors towards an enormous, slowly rotating 'banishment' door, leading into the main room of the exhibition, the Field of Encounter. Here, 28 veterans are telling 28 authentic stories. Mirrored walls extend the field of the veterans infinitely in all directions.

145

Designers
Jun Goto
Takatoshi Miyazaki
Creative Director
Tohru Tanaka
Art Director
Kengo Kato

Executive Creative Director
David Elsworth
Copywriter
Koji Kanzaki
Producer
Kenji Mitsuhashi

Executive Producer
Ryotaro Yao
Design Groups
Dentsu Tokyo
GT
Tugboat

Client
Coca-Cola Japan
Brand
Georgia Max Coffee

 Leisure & Tourism

Dentsu Tokyo, GT & Tugboat
for Coca-Cola Japan

Georgia Max Coffee Toilet
Georgia Max Coffee is an extra sweet drink, designed to boost energy. To maximise the brand presence in the winter market, the toilets of major ski resorts were turned into a ski jumper's view, giving a 'Max' experience in the most unlikely of places. The copy on the toilet roll holder reads: 'Seriously kick-ass intensely sweat real coffee, a super zinging unstoppable Max energy booster!'

Designers
Yoshiko Akado
Mayuko Watanabe
Design Director
Koji Iyama

Creative Director
Koji Iyama
Design Group
iyamadesign

Brand Manager
Yukio Taniguchi
Marketing Manager
Shin Takatsuka

Client
Kamoi Kakoshi
Brand
mt

iyamadesign
for Kamoi Kakoshi

mt ex
This was a promotional event to present mt's new collection of masking tapes. Although masking tapes are mainly used in construction, mt masking tapes come in an unusually wide variety of colours and patterns, making them attractive as decorative material. The event was held to show customers the possibilities of mt masking tape. To create a distinctive exhibition, we put the masking tape on every single object – the walls, steps, ceilings and floors – and covered the rooms with a variety of coloured mt tapes. The mt wonderland succeeded in showing customers the potential of mt tapes as an interior decoration material.

Designers
Frédéric Eyl
Gunnar Green
Dominik
Schuhmacher
Willy Sengewald

Design Studio
TheGreenEyl

Client
Stiftung Jüdisches
Museum Berlin

Brand
Jewish Museum
Berlin

 Installations

TheGreenEyl
for Stiftung Jüdisches Museum Berlin

Whispering Table
TheGreenEyl was commissioned by the Stiftung Jüdisches Museum Berlin to create a piece for an exhibition on food and religion. Four festivities celebrated by people of different cultures are assembled in an archetypal scene of congregation. Visitors approaching a table filled with empty dishes discover that these are actually telling personal stories about food and rituals. The contents change according to the dishes' positions. Similarities and peculiarities of different food ceremonies are explored in a playful and entertaining way. By changing table constellations, the visitors reveal more stories and become part of a participatory spectacle.

Creative Directors
Tony Davidson
Kim Papworth

Art Directors
Noe Kuremoto
Harri Leppala
Petra Muda

Interactive Producer
Sermad Buni
Shopfitters
Jamie Barker
Natasha Stragalinou

Creative Agency
Wieden+Kennedy
London
Client
Wieden+Kennedy
London

Installations

Wieden+Kennedy London

2009 Xmas Advent Calendar
The brief was to create a Christmas greeting for the friends and neighbours of Wieden+Kennedy London, spread the Christmas spirit and bring a smile to people's faces. So we created a street advent calendar. Every day we decorated something in our neighbourhood with a Christmas twist. This gigantic calendar was placed in our office window, so people could walk by and see what we had done that day. The calendar doubled as a map so people could easily find where the actual decorations were. A website was also created for those who couldn't visit our neighbourhood.

Designer
Maurice Mentjens
2D & 3D Designer
Annet Butink

Technical Drawing
Paul Bovens
Photographer
Leon Abraas

Design Group
Maurice Mentjens
Design

Project Manager
Johan Gielissen
Client
Labels Fashion

Retail & Services

Maurice Mentjens Design
for Labels Fashion

Labels
Labels in Sittard, the Netherlands, offers an impressive collection of youthful, trendy fashion brands. The shop's interior was redesigned by Maurice Mentjens, who combined three small spaces, then divided them again into yin and yang. Steel trees form a reference to the Garden of Eden, white refers to virginal innocence, and black is for the lost paradise. This is the biblical story of creation, in which Adam and Eve are at first free of sin in the Garden of Eden. They only clothed themselves after their fall, when they had eaten the forbidden fruits from the tree of knowledge, and became aware of their nakedness.

Architects	Creative Director	Advertising Agency	Brand & Marketing
Toshiya Hiramatsu	Kentaro Kimura	HAKUHODO Kettle	**Manager**
Misato Noro	**Copywriter**	**Account Handlers**	Ryuichiro Takase
Sayaka Sakata	Koichiro Iizuka	Takehiko Kawakubo	**Client**
Takanori Sato	**Manufacturers**	Akio Koda	Sony Marketing
Designer	Kei Mizuta	Yoshikazu Majima	Japan
Norihisa Yamaguchi	Sayaka Sakata	**Planners**	**Brand**
Technical Designer	**Shopfitter**	Kazuaki Hashida	Sony Recycle Project
Norihisa Yamaguchi	Kei Mizuta	Shingo Kato	Jeans
Design Director		Yusuke Shimizu	
Ken Funaki			

Retail & Services

HAKUHODO Kettle
for Sony Marketing Japan

The Wall Sale
We found the best way to communicate the Sony Recycle Project Jeans was to sell the jeans at their place of origin, the Sony building's wall. So we produced a giant tarp of advertising (10m by 18m) and hung it on the Sony building in Tokyo. We aimed to promote a better understanding of the recycling concept by the display design, and by selling from where the ad was run. We sold the target number of 90 pairs of jeans and generated over $500,000 worth of publicity.

151

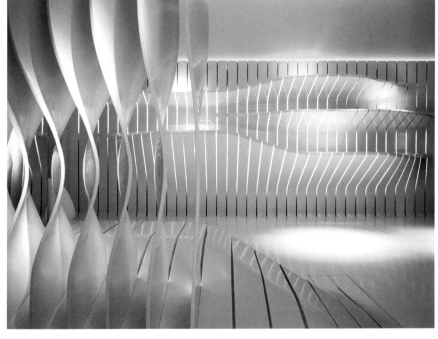

Architects	Technical Partners	Manufacturer	Practice Directors
Amanda Levete Architects	Esarc Hi Tech	Hasenkopf	Alvin Huang
	Isometrix Lighting	**Shopfitters**	Amanda Levete
Project Architect	Design	Fratelli Preziati	**Client**
Bruce Davison	Margaritelli/Listone	Hasenkopf	DuPont Corian
Technical Director	Giordano	**Brand Manager**	**Brand**
Massimo Fucci	Nemo Divisione Luci	Claudio Greco	Corian
	di Cassina		

Retail & Services
Amanda Levete Architects
for DuPont Corian

Corian Lounge

The project embodies opposites; simple yet complex, solid yet apparently kinetic, sculptural though not monolithic. Moving through the space appears to animate it. Views are revealed and concealed as the surfaces shift between active and passive states, creating countertops, display shelving, seating and a partition that seamlessly morphs from solid to transparent. To achieve maximum effect using minimum means, Amanda Levete Architects developed a flexible mould that created infinite twists from a standard flat sheet. More than just an expression of the material, these surface transformations push the technical possibilities of Corian by using the geometry of the sheets to bring structural integrity.

152

Future A-Z 2109

A is for AIRBAG HELMET
Helmet instantly inflates on impact providing 360° protection for any cyclist. Do not wear in bed.

B is for BUMBLE BLENDER
Add freshly harvested honey to any recipe or smoothie. The live hive is home to thousands of domestic 'no-sting' bees and thrives in any kitchen.

C is for CLEVER CROCKERY
Plate programmed to display personal nutritional analysis and guidelines. Dishwasher safe.

D is for DESIGNE

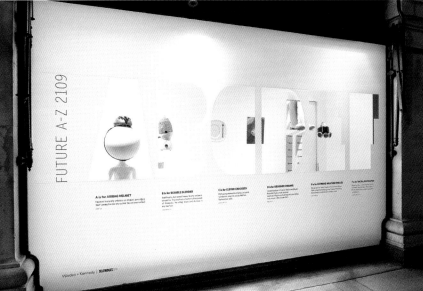

Future A-Z 2109

A is for AIRBAG HELMET
Helmet instantly inflates on impact providing 360° protection for any cyclist. Do not wear in bed.

B is for BUMBLE BLENDER
Add freshly harvested honey to any recipe or smoothie. The live hive is home to thousands of domestic 'no-sting' bees and thrives in any kitchen.

C is for CLEVER CROCKERY

D is for DESIGNER ORGANS

E is for EXTREME WEATHER

Wieden + Kennedy | SELFRIDGES

...NERATOR
...m any sea-going
...to power for use
...recharge p oduct.

K is for KNITTED DNA
Reverse extinction, through DNA reconstruction, has led to the use of experimental yarns. Woolly Mammoth knit is part of our Prehistoric range.

WOMENS CONTEMPORARY | 2

L is for I...
Create sp...
your own...
stops all m...

HOME ACCESSO...

Designers	**Creative Directors**	**Advertising Agency**	**Account Director**
Guy Featherstone	Tony Davidson	Wieden+Kennedy	Katherine Napier
Kate Slavin	Kim Papworth	London	**Client**
Art Directors	**Creative**	**Strategist**	Selfridges & Co
David Bruno	**Collaborator**	Andrew Stirk	**Brand**
Tom Seymour	Sophie Lewis		Selfridges

Retail & Services

Wieden+Kennedy London
for Selfridges

Future A-Z 2109 – Selfridges Centenary Window Installation
The brief was to create a window installation for Selfridges in London. The store was celebrating its centenary, and we were asked to create an 'adhoc vision of domestic utopia in 2109'. The idea was a 'Future A-Z' of fantastical inventions that would be on sale in 100 years time. We wanted to subvert the concept of a window display, which showcases what a store currently has to offer, and play with the idea of ludicrous consumer desires in 2109. We also wanted to include some consumer participation, and created a competition for the public to enter an idea for the missing letter X.

153

Architect	Technical Designer	Manufacturer	Client
Akira Yoneda	Yasutaka Konishi	Akira Yoneda	Yasuaki Oeda
Designer	**Creative Director**	**Design Group**	**Brand**
Akira Yoneda	Akira Yoneda	Architecton	Bambi

Leisure & Tourism

Architecton
for Yasuaki Oeda

Hojo

This 'hojo' is a small retreat in the central area of Tokyo built for the company Bambi. It combines the old Japanese notion of the pleasurable dwelling with reduced natural settings in the midst of a city. It also follows the traditional Japanese environmental design of a 'box in a box'. It has a well which provides water to the small pool inside, and a tent roof for cooling vapour. The environmental territory is defined by the pipe screened threshold, which mediates the adjacent urban context to evoke the feeling of enclosing and continuity at the same time.

154

Designer	**Manufacturer**	**Client**	**Brand**
Ben Rowan	B/E Aerospace	Swiss International	Swiss
Design Director	**Design Group**	Air Lines	
Nigel Goode	Priestmangoode		

Leisure & Tourism

Priestmangoode
for Swiss International Air Lines

Swiss International Air Lines First Class Suite
Swiss International Air Lines commissioned Priestmangoode to design its first-class suite for the company's newly purchased fleet of A330-300s. The vision outlined by Swiss's head of cabin interior was to design a first-class seat that was unmistakably Swiss. In other words, to create a product aligned with the brand, which has been developed uniformly across all other media, creating a consistent passenger experience. Priestmangoode worked closely with B/E Aerospace to ensure that the consistency and quality of detail required by the Swiss brand was incorporated into all elements of the suite, creating an overall experience of the highest comfort and quality.

155

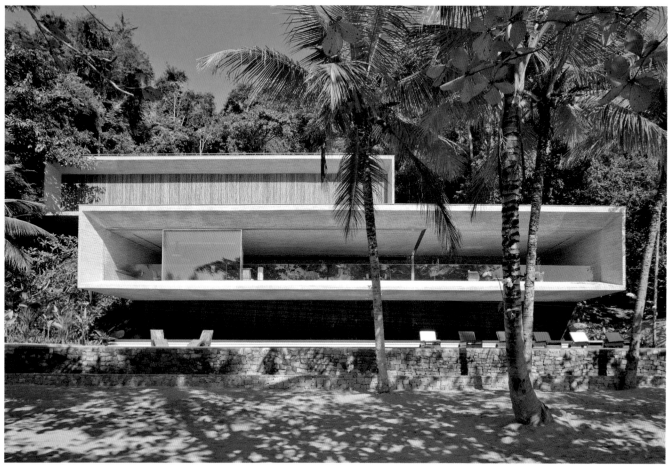

Architects
Luciana Antunes
Samanta Cafardo
Eduardo Chalabi
Renata Furlanetto
Eduardo Glycerio
Gabriel Kogan
Marcio Kogan
Beatriz Meyer
Maria Cristina Motta
Oswaldo Pessano
Lair Reis
Mariana Simas

Contractors
Andressa Donadio
Romolo Germano
Design Group
Studio MK27

**Architectural
Co-author**
Suzana Glogowski
**Interior Design
Co-authors**
Carolina Castroviejo
Diana Radomysler

Landscape Architect
Gil Fialho
Structural Engineer
Otávio de Souza
Gomes

Leisure & Tourism

Studio MK27

Paraty House
There is a legend which says that the region of the colonial cities of Paraty and Angra dos Reis (between São Paulo and Rio de Janeiro) has 365 islands, one for each day of the year. Two boxes of reinforced concrete rest on the mountainside of one of these islands; two modern prisms between the large colossal stones of the Brazilian coast. The boxes project outwards from the mountain, almost abreast of the beach, in an eight-metre cantilever. The house, of structural ingenuity, finds balance in the topography of the land, offering an extensive open doorway and living space in the practically untouched landscape.

156

Architects
Rossana Hu
Lyndon Neri

Architectural Design Practice
NHD

PR Manager
Bern Wu

Client
Y+ Yoga and Wellness Center

Brand
Y+

Leisure & Tourism

NHD
for the Y+ Yoga and Wellness Center

The Voyeuristic Wall – Y+ Yoga and Wellness Center
The Y+ Yoga and Wellness Centre is a 1,200sqm extension of the original Y+ Yoga studio. Y+ is inarguably a primary force in augmenting the concept of lifestyle in Shanghai. The design explores the abstract concept of tranquillity by creating intimate spaces for self-reflection and communal spaces for human encounters. These include rooms to cool down, read, chat, and meet new people. The main yoga room is an elevated half-circular room in an abstracted forest, represented by vertically hung ropes. More than simply a place for exercise, the environment enforces the slowing of pace, encouraging yoga students to relax, read, and enjoy their practice.

Architect
Toru Kashihara

Brand Management
Mitsui Fudosan
Residential
NPO Support Center
Chiba
Urban Design Center
Kashiwanoha
Yomiko Advertising

**Marketing
Management**
Spiral / Wacoal Art
Center

Clients
Mitsui Fudosan
Residential
NPO Support Center
Chiba

Public Space & Community

Toru Kashihara
for Mitsui Fudosan Residential

Pinocchio City
This project is a series of workshops for children living in Kashiwanoha Campus City near Tokyo. Through the programme, children learn community and communication design with an architect, urban planner, artist and town manager. They design, build, decorate, manage and demolish their ideal city. Pinocchio-shaped white cardboard is the only material used to build these paper cities. It is light and easy for children to handle, can be painted in many colours, and can be recycled after demolition. By combining Pinocchio boards, children can make arches, gates, towers and houses of different sizes for their cities.

158

Workplace

Maurice Mentjens Design
for PostPanic

PostPanic Headquarter

Maurice Mentjens has fitted up PostPanic's Amsterdam studio as a professional playground that emphasises the company's creative, headstrong attitude. PostPanic's projects are strongly focused on images and perception, and the design and layout of the studio directly influence that. In accordance with the briefing, every single department has its own distinctive atmosphere. Mentjens' conceptual approach guarantees that these atmospheres come together as one world; the different areas are segregated, not isolated, and offer the possibility of staying in touch with each other. The informal feel to the design emphasises PostPanic's philosophy. This dynamic, inviting environment offers PostPanic all the required room to play.

Designer
Maurice Mentjens
2D & 3D Designer
Annet Butink

Design Group
Maurice Mentjens
Design

Project Manager
Johan Gielissen
General Contractor
Paul de Reuver

Client
PostPanic

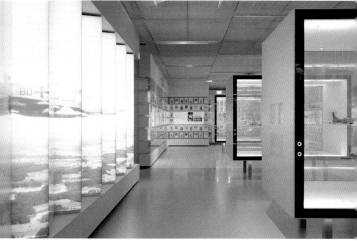

Design Director	Light Design	Architectural	Marketing Manager
Raimund Docmac	LDE Belzner Holmes	**Practice**	Susi Peschke
Creative Director	**Scenography**	Allmann Sattler	**Client**
Prof Uwe R Brückner	ATELIER BRÜCKNER	Wappner Architekten	Dornier Stiftung für
Exhibition Design		**Media Planning**	Luft- u. Raumfahrt
ATELIER BRÜCKNER		jangled nerves	

Permanent Exhibitions

ATELIER BRÜCKNER
for Dornier Stiftung für Luft- u. Raumfahrt

Dornier Museum Friedrichshafen

The newly founded museum 'The dream of flight' is dedicated to the inventions of the Dornier company. Recently collected artefacts, ranging from the very small to the very large, had to be integrated into a consistent scenography. The aim was to present the exhibits in a vivid, self-explanatory way. The museum hangar is an authentic location for the aircraft. To discover the spirit of Dornier, two storylines are offered: coloured cubes concentrate on thematic units, while the so-called museum box, which seems to levitate within the building, provides a chronological overview of the company's history. The pathway shows content-generated spatial narratives with interactively staged exhibits.

160

Designers
Susanne Elhardt
Julia Oesterle
Design Director
Julia Oesterle

Creative Directors
Michael Keller
Knut Maierhofer
Manufacturer
Wilhelm Tünnissen
Design Group
KMS TEAM

Account Handlers
Nina Anne Albrecht
Katharina
Andrzejewski
Marketing Manager
Annette Tomas

Client
Klöpfer
Brand
Weltholz

Temporary Exhibitions

KMS TEAM
for Klöpfer

Weltholz on Tour
Weltholz, the wood import brand of Germany's largest wood merchant Klöpfer, offers quality wood products from around the world. The tradeshow and exhibition concept 'Weltholz on Tour' is used to market the extensive product line. Evoking the importation of timber, a converted shipping container is used to present, store and transport all the elements of the exhibition. The container is extremely flexible in its use; in its closed state it can be readily transported from place to place. When the roof of the container is lifted hydraulically, the exhibition elements can be pulled out easily, and the exhibition stand is ready for use.

161

Design Director	Exhibition Design	Scenography	Client
Birgit Kadatz	ATELIER BRÜCKNER	ATELIER BRÜCKNER	Bertelsmann
Creative Director	Light Design	Media Planning	
Prof Uwe R Brückner	LDE Belzner Holmes	jangled nerves	

Temporary Exhibitions

ATELIER BRÜCKNER
for Bertelsmann

That's Opera – 200 Years of Italian Music
For the 200th anniversary of the famous Ricordi Archive, the aim of this exhibition was to stage not only the history of the Ricordi Company, but also the world of opera. The exhibition had to attract music enthusiasts as well as a worldwide audience, which may not necessarily be familiar with opera. The exhibition makes opera accessible in an unconventional way: it shows the genesis of an opera (libretto, partitura, scenografia, voci e costumi and rappresentazione) in individually designed cubes, embedded in a backstage ambience. The visitor participates in the staging and discovers its complexity step by step. Opera can be experienced as a total artwork.

162

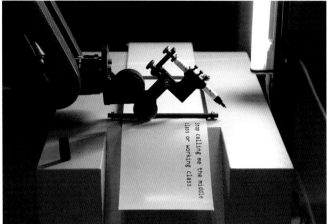

Architect
Adil Abrar
Design Director
Ben Tomlinson

Design Group
ico Design
Consultancy
Creative Agency
Sidekick Studios

Account Handler
Charlotte Moore
Marketing Manager
Jenni Young

Client
V, the National
Young Volunteers
Service

Installations

Sidekick Studios
for V, the National Young Volunteers
Service

The Voicebot in Parliament

This post-digital installation was designed to give young people a direct line to politicians. The Voicebot was an industrial robot arm, more commonly found turning screws in car manufacturing, which we taught to handwrite. Young people told us what they cared about through our website. The robot, placed inside the hallowed walls of parliament, wrote out their messages in real time for MPs to read. A Flickr pool, exhibition and data visualisation were other elements that explored how a disruptive use of the Internet can empower and connect society in remarkable ways.

Architect	**Design Group**	**General Director**	**Client**
Rolf Rongen	WINcommunication	Cathrin Jo Ann Wind	Nespresso
Creative Directors	**Account Handler**	**Brand Managers**	Deutschland
Ines Jantzen	Tina Neumüller	Christiane Glatfeld	**Brand**
Markus Lichte	**General Manager**	Susanne Ruhl	Nespresso
	Luc Bütz	Veronika Vriens	

Installations

WINcommunication
for Nespresso Deutschland

Display Windows Mönckebergstrasse
In the autumn of 2009, WINcommunication created a presentation of the entire product range for Nespresso machines, highlighting the newest design, Lattissima Premium. The presentation was placed in over 30 metres of display windows, including the façades of the department store Karstadt in Hamburg's Mönckebergstrasse. Many hours of conceptual preparation and a long list of creative suggestions led to the decision to mount an elaborate 3D display which would underscore the sophisticated aesthetics of the Nespresso machine.

Architects	Senior Designer	Electronics	Studio Manager
Yuni Choi	Gabby Shawcross	Mike Harrison	Sam Hoey
Tim Greatrex	**Lighting Designer**	**Design Studio**	**Clients**
Designers	Jenni Pystynen	Jason Bruges Studio	onedotzero
Alex Baker	**Senior Lighting**	**Workshop Manager**	SAP
Dean Munford	**Designer**	Wanju Kim	Victoria & Albert
Molly Price	Jonathon Hodges	**Project Manager**	Museum
Miriam Sleeman	**Creative Director**	Bibi Nelson	**Brand**
Interactive Designer	Jason Bruges	**Managing Director**	Decode
Daniel Hirschmann	**IT Manager**	Zena Bruges	
	Matt Wood	**Marketing Assistant**	
		Charlotte Kepel	

Installations

Jason Bruges Studio
for the Victoria & Albert Museum

Mirror Mirror
This installation was commissioned for the John Madejski Garden as part of the 'Decode: Digital Design Sensations' exhibition. It explores the concept of narcissism and the individual's relationship with space and others. The playful nature of the work encourages the viewer to explore the interactivity and consider the interconnected relationships. The white dot matrix digital panels seem to float on the pond, awakening as visitors come into view. Cameras mounted within the LED dot matrices capture activity in the garden and reflect this back to the viewer; the animated images are then mirrored once again in the surface of the water, creating multiple reflections.

165

Installations

Wieden+Kennedy London
for onedotzero

onedotzero_adventures in Motion Festival Identity 09/10
Onedotzero is an organisation promoting innovation in the moving image and motion arts.
The brief was to create an identity for onedotzero's 09/10 'adventures in motion' festival,
addressing the twin themes of convergence and collaboration. The identity had to work
across print, film, and digital platforms, with the potential to be adapted across a number of
international events. We created a 'living' onedotzero identity. Exclusive generative software
harnessed online conversations stimulated by onedotzero's global community, uniting them
as constantly updating layers within the logo. This application was 'paused' to create print work,
'recorded' for film assets, and run live as an interactive installation on London's Southbank.

Designer	**Head of Design**	**Art Directors**	**Advertising Agency**	
Karen Jane	Guy Featherstone	David Bruno	Wieden+Kennedy	
Computational	**Creative Directors**	Tom Seymour	London	
Designer	Tony Davidson	**Producer**	**Client**	
Karsten Schmidt	Shane RJ Walter	Sermad Buni	onedotzero	
Motion Director	**Creative**			
Eze Blaine	**Technologist**			
	Sermad Buni			

Graphic Designers	Creative Directors	Producer	Customer
Roman Becker	Maik Kaehler	Boris Meise	Consultant
Till Diestel	Christoph Nann	**Advertising Agency**	Constanze
	Chief Creative	Serviceplan	Strothmann
	Officer		**Client**
	Alexander Schill		Lead Academy

Installations

Serviceplan
for Lead Academy

ProContra

This project is a giant installation for the Lead Awards, the host of the most important exhibition for photography and print media in Germany. 144 balls were mounted in the main exhibition hall, which seemed to be a chaotic structure. The chaos turns into a message when you look at it from two marked positions. From one position, pro; from the other, con. We asked people to get both points of view and rethink their opinions. Because where there is a pro, there is always a con.

167

Illustrator
Christian Borstlap
Animator
Paul Postma
Directors
Christian Borstlap
Paul Postma

Sound Mixer
Jasper Boeke
Design Agency
Paul Postma &
Christian Borstlap

Artists
Clutchy Hopkins
Meets Lord
Kenjamin

Clients
TNT Post
Stichting
Kinderpostzegels

 Moving Image

Paul Postma & Christian Borstlap
for Stichting Kinderpostzegels

There Are More Than 11 Trillion Things to Learn
Working with the Dutch postal service TNT Post, the charity organisation The Children's Stamp (Stichting Kinderpostzegels) has previously commissioned stamp sets which have helped to fund projects that support vulnerable children – the last of which raised more than 9.5m Euros for educational projects. Christian Borstlap designed the 2009 issue of the children's stamps. To stimulate online sales, designer and animator Paul Postma was asked to bring the stamps' colourful illustrations to life in a two-minute film. The film was presented on The Children's Stamp website, and appeared on a variety of special interest sites, blogs and online animation festivals.

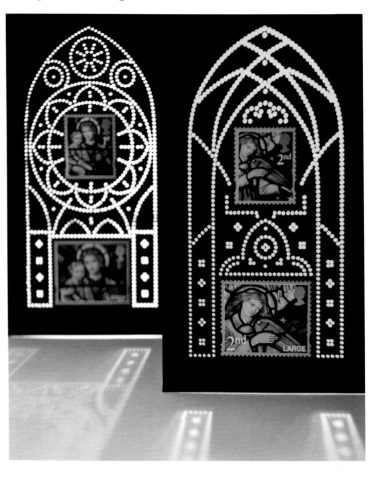

Designers
David Azurdia
Jamie Ellul
Creative Directors
David Azurdia
Ben Christie
Jamie Ellul

Typographers
David Azurdia
Jamie Ellul
Illustrator
David Azurdia

Copywriter
John Betjeman
Design Group
Magpie Studio
**Head of Design
& Editorial**
Marcus James

**Design Project
Manager**
Kim Cruickshank
Client
Royal Mail

▲ **Leaflets**

Magpie Studio
for the Royal Mail

Christmas Stamps Miniature Book
The Royal Mail releases a set of Christmas stamps at the end of each year. We were briefed to design and produce a display piece to showcase the stamps, which depict the Nativity through stained glass. The piece needed to complement the miniature works of art, without overpowering them. Our solution gently illuminates the stained-glass themed stamps, while helping to place them in context. The perforated window illustrations were laser-cut into a pocket-sized concertina format that allows all seven stamps to be viewed together when fully unfolded. The stamps are accompanied by an extract from John Betjeman's 'Christmas', sympathetically reproduced in silver litho.

171

Designer
Masashi Murakami
Art Director
Kenjiro Sano

Creative Director
Kenjiro Sano

Photographer
Yuri Manabe

Design Group
Mr_Design
Client
nico product

▲ Posters

Mr_Design
for nico product

nico product Poster
The unusual and advanced technique of printing used for these posters has been tried and tested in Japan. It enables colours and designs to appear on the back as well as the front. The posters hung from the ceiling so that people could see the different images from both the front and back as they walked around them. Nico products are already in production, created by Kenjiro Sano from Mr_Design. The range includes items such as memo blocks, note cards and post-it notes. Nico products are available at Colette in Paris, the Design Museum in London, and other shops around the world.

172

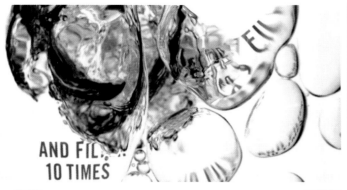

Art Director	Copywriter	Advertising Agency	Post Production
Anita Davis	Jonathan Budds	JWT London	Glassworks
Creative Director	**Producer**	**Production Company**	**Client**
Russell Ramsey	Cathy Hood	Believe Media UK	Diageo
Typographers	**Agency Producer**		**Brand**
Tomato	Denise Connell		Smirnoff

Moving Image

JWT London
for Diageo

Transparent
In this piece of work, Smirnoff vodka is used as a lens through which to focus on a 'pure' and clear message.

Illustrator
Siggi Eggertsson

Animation Director
Siggi Eggertsson

Artist Management
Big Active

Client
Integrated 2009

Moving Image

Siggi Eggertsson
for Integrated 2009

A Growing Pile of Work
This animation was produced as part of Siggi Eggertsson's lecture at Integrated 2009 in Antwerp. The artist's aim was to produce an entertaining means of quickly introducing his work to the audience without having to resort to the standard PowerPoint format. The solution was to create a short, hypnotic film making use of over 400 images that conveyed his output from the previous five years. Subsequently the film became a very successful means of self-promotion through its placement on video hosting sites.

174

Designers	**Creative Director**	**Advertising Agency**	**Brand Manager**
Sam Byrnes	Dave Bowman	Saatchi & Saatchi	Linly Goh
Sharon Lee	**Executive Creative**	Sydney	**Client**
Julian Melhuish	**Director**	**Film Production**	Sydney Writers'
Design Creative	Steve Back	Saatchi Design	Festival
Director	**Copywriter**	**Music**	
Julian Melhuish	Julian Melhuish	Simon Lister	

Moving Image

Saatchi & Saatchi Sydney
for the Sydney Writers' Festival

Sydney Writers' Festival Trailer
This 90-second trailer was broadcast at festival events, on websites and on TV. The letters flow down Sydney tributaries to meet in the harbour – a metaphor for the festival itself, where writers gather together to create 'one week of moving words'. The trailer was produced for real, not in post-production, using Tyvek – a heavy duty tear resistant paper that floats. Well actually, it kind of floats for a while, then folds and sinks. All letters were recovered. No designers or interns drowned during the process.

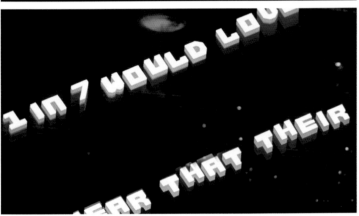

Art Directors
Luke Boggins
Dan McCormack
Creative Director
Graham Fink
Lead Motion
Designer
Paul Scanlon

Typographers
Gareth Davies
Jonathon Muddell
Simon Warden
Copywriters
Luke Boggins
Dan McCormack

Advertising Agency
M&C Saatchi London
Account Handler
Kate Edwards

Marketing Manager
Emma Harrison
Client
RNID (Royal National
Institute for Deaf
People)

Moving Image

M&C Saatchi London
for the RNID

One in Seven
To raise awareness of the fact that hearing loss affects one in seven people in the UK, we created a series of messages based on the insight that hearing something is better than hearing nothing at all. Integrated microphones allowed the posters to hear, which caused the typography to react like a graphic equaliser, animating the sounds it heard. This enabled the hard of hearing to visualise what they were missing. And, rather than being prompted to phone a number and not being able to hear what's being said, people who were worried about their hearing were invited to find out more via text.

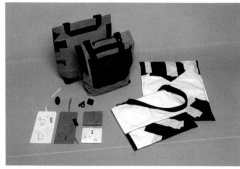

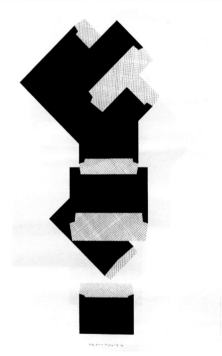

Designers
Chen Dong
Li Jingjing
He Jun
Teng Yi
Zha Yin
Liu Yingchuan
Lou Xiaoyi
Luo Xue

Art Director
He Jun
Creative Director
He Jun

Design Group
School of Design,
China Central
Academy of Fine
Arts

Client
The Organizing
Committee of
Icograda World
Design Congress
2009
Brand
Icograda

Integrated Graphics

China Central Academy of Fine Arts
for Icograda

Icograda World Design Congress 2009
'Xin-ĐÁ' means 'human speaking' and therefore 'message' or 'letter' in Chinese, representing a primitive means of communication. It was the theme of the Icograda World Design Congress 2009, Beijing, symbolising communication. Six envelopes made up the central visual identity of the congress, creating different letterforms. The Chinese letter 'ĐÁ' was formed by changing the position of the envelopes, which formed the English 'Xin'. The transformations represented the delivery or translation of the information between two different cultures.

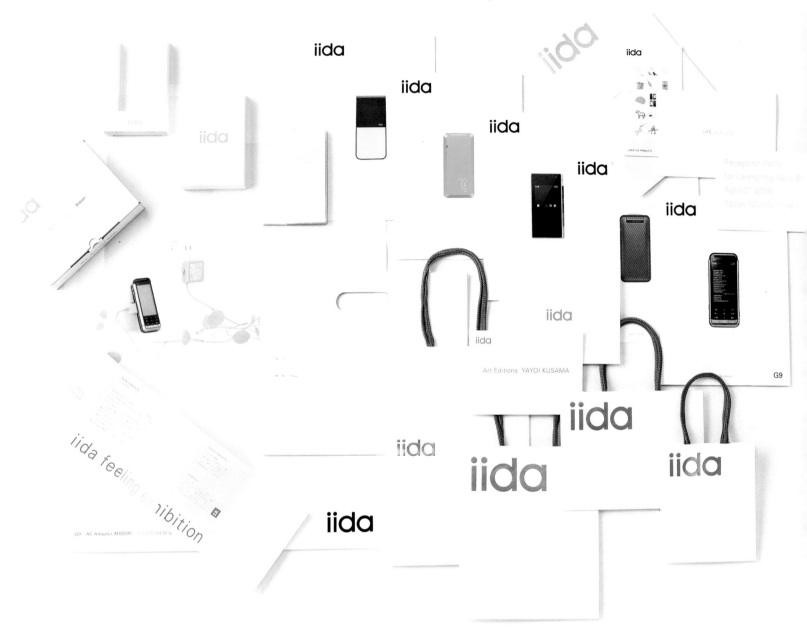

Designer
Asuka Adachi
Art Director
Daisaku Nojiri

Creative Director
Satoshi Takamatsu
Photographers
Hiroshi Harada
Yukikazu Ito
Hiroya Kitai

Copywriter
Junpei Watanabe
Advertising Agency
ground

Brand Manager
Tomofumi Matsui
Client
KDDI Corporation
Brand
iida

Integrated Graphics

ground
for the KDDI Corporation

iida
This campaign aims to demonstrate iida's premium design, quality and usability. Separate magazine ads were produced for different mobile devices. The ads were designed with the focus on the products, but have been finished with a high quality look and feel to reflect the products' desirability.

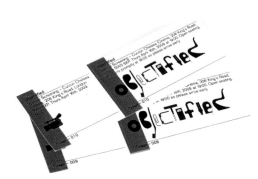

Designer	**Creative Director**	**Design Group**	**Brand**
Michael C Place	Michael C Place	Build	Objectified
Assistant Designer	**Typographer**	**Clients**	
Guy Hulse	Michael C Place	Gary Hustwit	
		Plexifilms	

Integrated Graphics

Build
for Objectified

Objectified Identity

This is an identity for the film Objectified (a documentary about product design), which was screened in cinemas across the world, and released on multiple formats. We devised a strong yet playful logo based on objects, referencing the film's theme. The identity was used to promote local screenings and associated events, and applied on merchandise such as T-shirts and reusable tote bags. To complement DVD and Blu-ray release, we created a limited-edition pack with letterpress postcards and the film on USB. We also designed the menu system and in-film captions. The poster was also selected in the Graphic Design/Posters category.

Designers
Josh Michels
Rebecca Williams
Design Director
Sarah Moffat
Creative Directors
Bruce Duckworth
David Turner

Design Group
Turner Duckworth:
London & San
Francisco

Account Handler
Jessica Rogers
Brand Manager
Frederic Kahn

Client
The Coca-Cola
Company North
America
Brand
Coca-Cola

Integrated Graphics

Turner Duckworth: London & San Francisco
for Coca-Cola

Coca-Cola Summer 2009 Packaging
The Coca-Cola Summer 2009 campaign celebrates the joy and optimism of summer, and Coke's authentic connection with the season. This set of limited edition summer cans was designed for the campaign. The joyful summer graphics feature on everything from packaging and in-store displays to T-shirts, hats and beach towels.

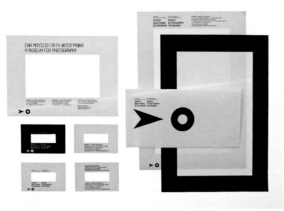

Designers
Ilias Pandikakis
Michalis Rafail

Creative Directors
Yiannis
Charalambopoulos
Vagelis Liakos
Alexis Nikou

Typographer
Alexis Nikou
Photographer
Costas Pappas

Design Group
Beetroot design
group
Client
Museum of
Photography
Thessaloniki

Integrated Graphics

Beetroot design group
for the Museum of Photography Thessaloniki

Museum of Photography Thessaloniki
We wanted to capture the actual moment of the shooting: the eye, the framing, the targeting.
Those keywords evoke images that led us to a visual outcome of two forms: the circle, inspired
by the eye and the shape of the lens; and the arrow-like shape inspired by an eye that blinks
with the click. The frame is used as an additional element, a void in order to let the user frame
his or her own theme. A new typeface was designed as part of the identity.

181

Design Director	**Photographer**	**Marketing Manager**	**Client**
Phil Evans	Satoshi Minakawa	Marc Wilder	Great Portland
Creative Director	**Design Agency**	**Managing Director**	Estates
Ben Dale	dn&co.	Joy Nazzari	**Brand**
			wells&more

Catalogues & Brochures

dn&co.
for Great Portland Estates

wells&more Brochure
Wells&more is a new London office building on the corner of Wells and Mortimer streets. The brand concept is based around the pairing of words to deliver the selling points, such as wine&dine, here&there, and size&scale. Property marketing brochures are often a dull affair. In order to stand out and be memorable, an original mechanic was used to show the reader highly graphical content when flipped in one direction, and beautiful high gloss architectural photography when flipped the other way. This was achieved by trimming 5mm off every other page. The back&forth concept was the ultimate manifestation of the brand concept.

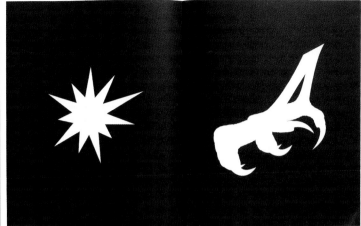

Designer
Claire Warner

Design Group
Browns

Client
Jonathan Ellery

Catalogues & Brochures

Browns
for Jonathan Ellery

Ellery's Theory of Neo-conservative Creationism
Jonathan Ellery unveiled his fourth solo show at the Wapping Project in November 2009. Ellery's 'Theory of Neo-conservative Creationism' combined materials to produce a three-element, multisensory show. Suspended brass sculptures depicting a series of ambiguous artworks responded to floating books and offset a digital sound installation. The one-colour, digitally printed catalogue was commissioned to accompany the show and represent the artist, showing artworks that had been machined into solid brass.

Designer	Design Group	Account Handler	Client
Richard Basset	Thompson Brand	Chloe Anstis	Metal
Creative Director	Partners		
Ian Thompson			

Catalogues & Brochures

Thompson Brand Partners
for Metal

Essex Guides

Metal is an artistic body that develops and supports artistic community projects in the UK and worldwide. The project brief was to inspire and involve young people from three Essex towns – Harlow, Harwich and Southend – and to get them to engage with the enormous regeneration project taking place in their area. Students collated the information; it was our job to pull it together and unite them to create a strong printed piece that showed Essex in a totally new light. 'You Are Here' was developed as an idea to illustrate the students' real sense of pride in belonging to their area and wanting to put its mark on the map.

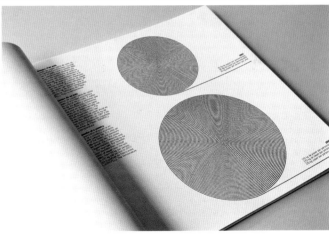

Designer	**Typographer**	**Design Studio**	**Clients**
Enric Jardí	Enric Jardí	Enric Jardí, disseny	Arts Gràfiques Orient
Creative Director	**Copywriter**	gràfic	Enric Jardí
Enric Jardí	Teresa Domingo		

Catalogues & Brochures

Enric Jardí, disseny gràfic
for Arts Gràfiques Orient & Enric Jardí

Impossibles Possibles
Impossibles Possibles is a collaborative venture between Arts Gràfiques Orient and the
Enric Jardí study. It was conceived as a way of showing certain printing techniques and more
advanced manipulation processes. In order to do this, each page shows a graphic associated
with graphic arts or design. This is a unique book, mainly printed in offset but in many cases
using a series of unusual inks and media. You can find a chart printed on a transparent acetate
sheet, when normally you would have to use screen printing to achieve this effect. There are
also sheets of baking paper, kraft, and a piece weighing nearly 500 grams.

185

Designers	Art Director	Design Studio	Client
Ana Domínguez	Astrid Stavro	Studio Astrid Stavro	Ediciones de la
Astrid Stavro			Central

Catalogues & Brochures

Studio Astrid Stavro
for Ediciones de la Central

Cuadernos Postal
Cuadernos Postal (Postcard Notebooks) is a collection of pocket-sized artist monographs.
Each notebook contains a small book, a folded poster and a series of postcards. The design
concept is based on the vertical line that divides the reverse side of standard postcards.
Simple changes in colour help distinguish the titles. Bold, typographic covers give the
collection a strong visual identity.

186

Catalogues & Brochures

Sigi Mayer
for Norbert Herold

Designer
Sigi Mayer
Art Director
Sigi Mayer
Creative Director
Sigi Mayer

Photographers
Felicitas Herold
Norbert Herold
Sigi Mayer
Jacques
Schuhmacher

Copywriters
Janet Fox
Lothar Hackethal
Thorsten Hainke
Norbert Herold
Peter Hirrlinger
Felix Lott
Ono Mothwurf
Sven Nagel
Lioba Reuter

Brand Manager
Norbert Herold
Client
Norbert Herold

Geständnisse Eines Labradorrüden
Geständnisse eines Labradorrüden (confessions of a male Labrador) is an exhibition catalogue showcasing photographs of chairs from all over the world. Inspired by Dadaism, nonsensical text was then interspersed between the images. You therefore won't find a single photo of a Labrador in this book.

187

Designer	**Illustrators**	**Copywriters**	**Brand Manager**
Michael C Place	Sanna Annukka	Nicola Place	Paul Hewitt
Creative Director	Michael C Place	John O'Reilly	**Client**
Michael C Place	**Photographer**	**Design Group**	Generation Press
	Timothy Saccenti	Build	

Catalogues & Brochures

Build
for Generation Press

GP is 10
We were asked to create a brochure for the printers Generation Press as a showcase of print processes, and to mark the company's tenth anniversary. The brochure took the form of a postcard pack with each A5 card using a variety of techniques, all housed in a specially made slipcase. The cards feature specially commissioned works from Sanna Annukka, John O'Reilly and Timothy Saccenti, with contributions from Michael C Place and Nicola Place. It was also an opportunity to tell the story of Generation Press, and its commitment to employees, clients and the environment.

What is important to us
Finsbury Green believes
that we have a responsibility
to protect the environment
both locally and globally.
Our policy is a reminder
of our responsibilities and
assists us to set clear targets
for continuous improvement.

18/19

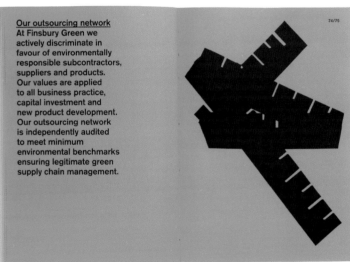

Our outsourcing network
At Finsbury Green we
actively discriminate in
favour of environmentally
responsible subcontractors,
suppliers and products.
Our values are applied
to all business practice,
capital investment and
new product development.
Our outsourcing network
is independently audited
to meet minimum
environmental benchmarks
ensuring legitimate green
supply chain management.

74/75

Designer	Typographer	Copywriter	Brand Manager
Matthew Remphrey	Matthew Remphrey	Rodney Wade	Peter Orel
Creative Director	**Illustrator**	**Design Group**	**Client**
Matthew Remphrey	Matthew Remphrey	Parallax Design	Finsbury Green

Catalogues & Brochures

Parallax Design
for Finsbury Green

Finsbury Green Sustainability Report 2009
Finsbury Green is Australia's leading environmental printing group. Every year the company
publishes a sustainability report outlining its environmental and social achievements. Parallax
developed the line 'Making green normal one page at a time' to describe the company's
environmental philosophy and what it does – puts ink on paper. This simple idea lead the whole
project. The book turns from white to green, at two per cent increments per spread. The paper
cut illustrations (again alluding to Finsbury's business) and bold typography told the story in a
simple and engaging way.

189

LABORATORY

29 JULY – 30 AUGUST 2009

STEVEN EASTWOOD
FILM MAKER
JOCK MOONEY
SCULPTOR
MIA TAYLOR
PAINTER

3 ARTISTS
3 GALLERIES
4 WEEKS ON SITE

A ONE MONTH PERIOD OF ART PRODUCTION AND EXPERIMENTATION ON SITE AT THE JERWOOD SPACE GALLERY EXPLORING THE PROCESSES INVOLVED IN MAKING, CURATING, DOCUMENTING AND EXHIBITING ART

Designers	Design Director	Website Developers	Design Agency
Sam Foster	James Cunnane	Michael Allanson	The Partners
Emily Picot	**Creative Director**	Pete Goodman	**Client**
	Nick Eagleton		Jerwood Visual Arts

Catalogues & Brochures

The Partners
for Jerwood Visual Arts

The Real-time Art Catalogue
'Laboratory' was an experimental exhibition at the Jerwood Space in London, in which three artists built a show from scratch in real time. We built the catalogue in exactly the same way. The artists' every move was documented in real time on a specially programmed blog, which also automatically drew in related content from external sites like Twitter and Flickr. Every day, all the new posts were printed and added to the catalogues, which were on display in the gallery, so visitors could see them growing as the show grew, in real time.

190

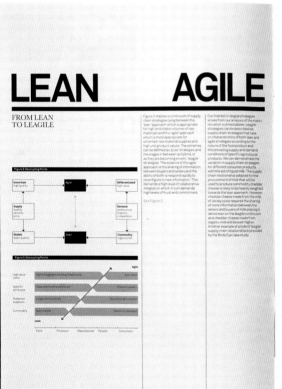

Designer	Creative Directors	Design Group	Client
Paul Felton	Rob Howsam	Purpose	EFFP (English
Design Director	Stuart Youngs	**Project Manager**	Farming & Food
Adam Browne		Louisa Phillips	Partnerships)

Catalogues & Brochures

Purpose
for EFFP

View Magazine – Issues Spring, Summer, Autumn, Winter
EFFP is an independent not-for-profit business consultancy, combining its farming knowledge with food industry expertise to help address structural, commercial and relationship issues. EFFP required a quarterly publication to send to its existing and potential clients to give them a taste of the organisation's strategic insight and knowledge. We created a large format, black-and-white brochure, entitled 'View'. The typographically led approach is a distinguishing break from the expected use of corporate styling and generic stock photography so common in this sector. The bold visual language reflects EFFP's ethos of expert, honest and practical advice delivered clearly and in a straightforward manner.

Designer	**Photographer**	**Design Group**	**Brand**
Michael C Place	Timothy Saccenti	Build	Lard
Creative Director	**Image Manipulator**	**Client**	
Michael C Place	Joe Lucchese	Commonwealth	

Catalogues & Brochures

Build
for Commonwealth

Lard Book

The brief was to create a beautiful and tactile catalogue to showcase the Lard furniture designed by Brooklyn-based product architects Commonwealth. This was to send out to potential furniture manufacturers who might be interested in producing the Lard range commercially. We proposed a brochure as unusual as the furniture it described; at first not obviously a book. Materials and print finishes were chosen to reflect the qualities of lard; the outer case, with its shiny text on a matte background, is suggestive of congealed fat, in sharp contrast to the inside pages.

192

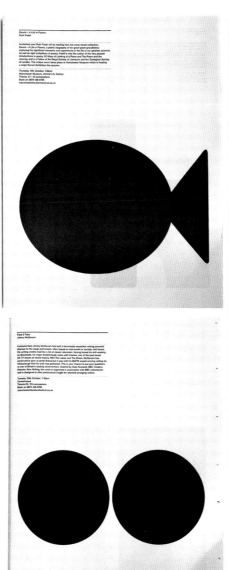

esigners
en Harrison
Mark Lester

Creative Director
Mark Lester
Design Group
MARK

Brand Manager
Cathy Bolton
Marketing Manager
Jon Atkin

Client
Manchester
Literature Festival

Catalogues & Brochures

MARK
for the Manchester Literature Festival

MLF Brochure 09
In this brochure for the Manchester Literature Festival, each page carries an appropriately cryptic icon for each event.

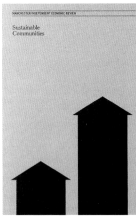

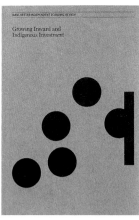

Creative Directors	Design Group	Marketing Manager	Brand
David Simpson	Music	Liz Reuben	Manchester
Anthony Smith	**Production Manager**	**Client**	Independent
Illustrator	Matthew Beardsell	Manchester	Economic Review
Jon Hatton		Commission for the	
		New Economy	

Catalogues & Brochures

Music
for the Manchester Commission for the New Economy

MIER Reports
These six reports, produced for the Manchester Independent Economic Review, were each printed on a different coloured sugar paper. Simple, single colour, graphic illustrations were used to breathe some life into the wealth of information contained within.

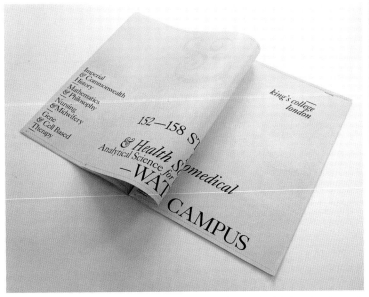

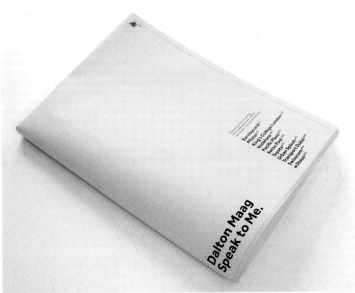

Designers	**Creative Director**	**Design Group**	**Client**
Phil Costin	Phil Costin	Mode	Dalton Maag
Darrell Gibbons	**Copywriters**	**Marketing Manager**	
Filipe Valgode	Steven Johnson	Angela Gilroy	
	Bruno Maag		

Catalogues & Brochures

Mode
for Dalton Maag

Speak to Me

Mode's brochure for typography design specialists Dalton Maag showcases recent projects for the likes of Barclaycard, Vodafone and Toyota, ranging from font modification, font licensing to custom font design. Designed specifically to appeal to corporate brand managers as well as strengthening the company's established profile with designers, the brochure has a utilitarian, newspaper-like quality. Each font is presented directly and in its purest form, appearing in monotone black throughout against Dalton Maag's recognisable duck-egg blue brand colour.

Designer
Andrew Turner
Art Director
Andrew Turner

Creative Director
Colin Scott
Photographer
Nigel Barker

Design Group
The Workshop

Printer
ProCo
Client
Roundabout

Catalogues & Brochures

The Workshop
for Roundabout

Roundabout Annual Report 2009
Roundabout is a charity that supports homeless young people in Sheffield. The Roundabout annual report increased local awareness of the charity, reflected the challenges it faces and enabled its young people to take part in the design process. One half of the report is a photographic collection of some of the young people who use Roundabout; the other half shows how the charity supports them. The wraparound is smaller than the main document to highlight the problem of young homeless people in Sheffield, and how it is larger than Roundabout's resources. The typeface is Transport, the principal font used on British road signs.

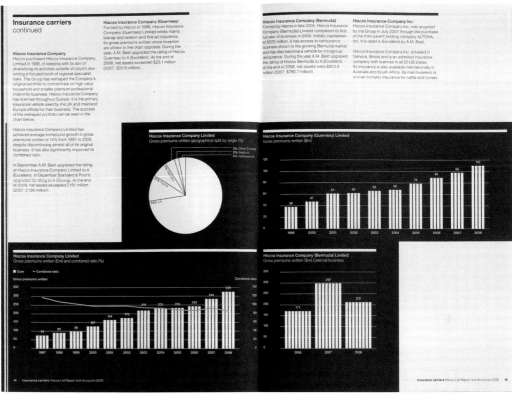

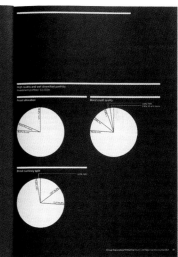

Designer
Claire Warner
Creative Director
Jonathan Ellery

Photographers
Peter Marlow
John Ross

Design Group
Browns
Account Handler
Kendra Futcher

Brand Manager
Kylie O'Connor
Client
Hiscox

Annual Reports

Browns
for Hiscox

Hiscox Report & Accounts 2008
Working closely with the Hiscox communications team and following the direction given by the Chairman Robert Hiscox, Browns has, for the third year, designed an annual report that tells it as it is, in a no-nonsense, transparent manner. Being sensitive to financially challenging times, the report is bold, concise and confident in its delivery and restraint. The report is printed using only one colour on 100% recycled paper and is supported online in order to minimise its environmental impact.

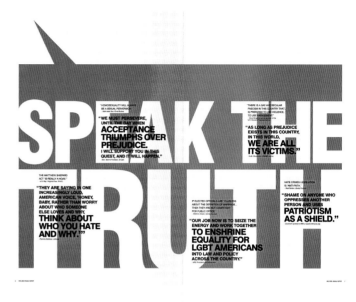

Designer
Sucha Becky

Creative Directors
Jake Lefebure
Pum Lefebure

Design Group
Design Army

Client
The Human Rights
Campaign

Annual Reports

Design Army
for The Human Rights Campaign

End the Lies

The Human Rights Campaign was in full force for 2009 with many high-profile projects and endorsements. The theme 'End the Lies' was a way to raise awareness with a very direct approach, using the words of those speaking out, for and against, the HRC. The oversized self-mailer format and lightweight eco-friendly papers helped drive the design, but the HRC 2009 report also uses visual verbiage to convey the thoughts, issues and other challenges facing the HRC. Direct quotes set in bold typography convey the impact and importance of the report, while the distinct colour scheme gives a little softness (and individuality) to the otherwise text-heavy report.

Designer	Photographer	Design Agency	Marketing Manager
Martijn Maas	Boudewijn Bollman	Fabrique [brands,	Esther Clason
Art Director	**Copywriter**	design and	**Client**
Simone van Rijn	Corianna Roza	interaction]	Haags Wonen
Illustrator		**Account Handler**	
Martijn Maas		Maartje Wensing	

Annual Reports

Fabrique [brands, design and interaction]
for Haags Wonen

Haags Wonen Annual Report 2008
This annual report is divided according to the ten different districts of The Hague. The theme of pride is the thread running through the entire report. It's about people's stories. The sense of being 'close by' comes across in the personal, colourful photos. Haags Wonen was brave enough to abandon the standard idea of putting an attractive image on the front cover; instead we put the best quotes from the residents interviewed on it. Kraft paper was used for the annual report, which was printed in opaque white, looking chic and feeling durable.

199

Designer
Jayme Yen
**Production
& Lithography**
Jo Frenken

Editors
Petra van der Jeught
Dorrie Tattersal
Translators
Chris Gemerchak
Petra van der Jeught
Dorrie Tattersal

Design Group
Jan van Eyck
Academie
Publishers
Jan van Eyck
Academie

**Translation
Company**
The Language Lab
Client
Jan van Eyck
Academie

Annual Reports

Jan van Eyck Academie

Jan van Eyck Academie Yearbook 2008
With black and gold on the cover and an impressive number of projects inside, the Jan van Eyck Academie Yearbook presents a detailed overview of the work carried out by the artists, designers and theoreticians at the academy in 2008. The various research projects and events dealt with a wide range of burning issues, including authorship and ideology critique, public space and involvement. The book concludes with an explanation of the academy's institutional policy. The yearbook was designed by Jayme Yen, a former researcher in the design department.

Designers	**Illustrators**	**Photographer**	**Marketing Manager**
Gareth Howat	Danny	Marcus Lyon	Mark Frodsham
Alexandra Jurva	Hayden	**Design Group**	**Client**
Jim Sutherland	Jacob	hat-trick design	Fairbridge
Design Directors	Jenna		
Gareth Howat	Kevin		
Jim Sutherland	Stephanie		

Annual Reports

hat-trick design
for Fairbridge

Fairbridge Annual Review
Working with troubled 12 to 24-year-olds in twelve of the most disadvantaged areas in the UK, Fairbridge aims to change what these young people expect from life and give them a chance to put things right. The challenge was to create a powerful message to engage the reader, and act as a fundraising tool for the charity. Fairbridge seeks to uncover the hidden potential in young disadvantaged people, so workshops were set up where young people told their stories through illustrations and notes on paper bags. They were then photographed wearing the bags as masks. These were juxtaposed with shots taken when the bags were removed.

Graphic Design

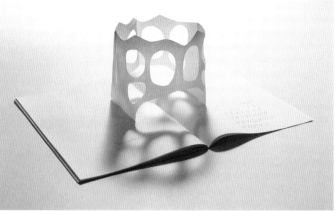

Designers
Kazuya Iwanaga
Yoshie Watanabe

Art Directors
Kazuya Iwanaga
Yoshie Watanabe

Creative Director
Satoru Miyata
Illustrator
Yoshie Watanabe

Design Agency
DRAFT Tokyo
Client
D-BROS

Calendars

DRAFT Tokyo
for D-BROS

Rose
This is a book-shaped calendar for D-BROS, a brand featuring products created by graphic designers in Tokyo. Each page has a pop-up structure made of very thin paper. The use of this thin paper effectively expresses the fragility of a rose.

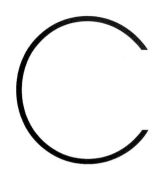

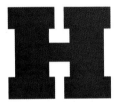

Designer	**Creative Directors**	**Design Group**	**Clients**
Li Rui	Ben Casey	The Chase	Atomic Type
	Lionel Hatch		Font Shop
			Font Works

Calendars

The Chase
for Atomic Type, Font Shop & Font Works

26&26
26&26, a week by week calendar, consists of 53 pages, each page featuring a letter of the alphabet: 26 lower case; 26 upper case; and an ampersand. We allocated an individual character to 53 of the country's leading designers and typographers, then asked them to choose their favourite typeface for that character, and write why they like it so much.

203

Designer	**Copywriters**	**Production**	**Account Manager**
Nitin Srivastava	Gunjan Gaba	**Supervisors**	Sanjay Thapar
Art Director	Jossy Raphael	Anand Kumar	**Client**
Nitin Srivastava	**Image Manipulators**	KK Sreenivasan	Department of Posts,
Creative Directors	Ranga Reddy	**Advertising Agency**	India
Ajay Gahlaut	Ibrahim Shaikh	Ogilvy & Mather	**Brand**
Piyush Pandey	**Production Director**	Gurgaon	India Post
Jossy Raphael	Rajesh Bhargava		
Nitin Srivastava			

Calendars

Ogilvy & Mather Gurgaon
for India Post

Stamps

Every day, India celebrates. It celebrates hundreds of gods and goddesses, Bollywood hits and millionaire superstars, world-class cricketers and colourful politicians. This calendar for India Post reflects this spirit through an unusual design. It commemorates each day of the year with a stamp, bringing alive the vibrant, magical, multi-faceted nation that is India.

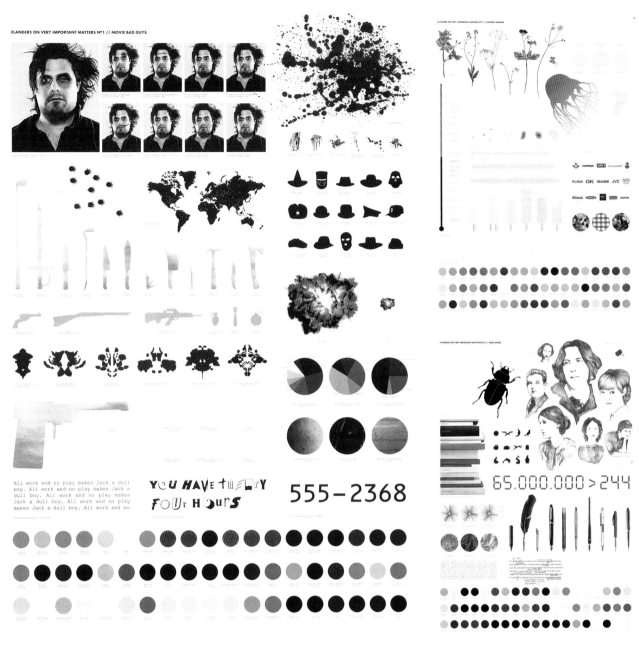

ELANDERS ON VERY IMPORTANT MATTERS Nº1 // MOVIE BAD GUYS

All work and no play makes Jack a dull boy. All work and no play makes Jack a dull boy. All work and no play makes Jack a dull boy. All work and no play makes Jack a dull boy. All work and no

YOU HAVE TWENTY FOUr HOUrS

555-2368

65.000.000 > 244

Art Directors	Illustrators	Design Agency	Marketing Manager
Oskar Andersson	Fredrik Persson	Happy Forsman	Peter Thyrén
Maria Glansén	Anders Söderberg	& Bodenfors	**Client**
Andreas Kittel	Hanna Westberg	**Account Handlers**	Elanders Printing
Creative Director	**Photographer**	Robert Axner	House
Lisa Careborg	Marcel Pabst	Jessica Wallin	

Direct Mail

Happy Forsman & Bodenfors
for Elanders Printing House

Elanders on Very Important Matters
These posters remind designers that Elanders is one of the oldest, largest, and foremost printing houses in Sweden. The posters present advanced printing techniques in the form of a number of geekish themes such as movie bad guys (relating to the increasing popularity of horror films), Swedish summer (in the run-up to vacation time) and first novels (at the time of the Göteborg book fair). Examples include the placeholder text as a famous horror movie line, a summer weather report and an editor's letter of rejection.

Creative Directors
David Alexander
Rob Fletcher

Photographer
Paul Thompson

Advertising Agency
isobel advertising

Art Buyer
Angus Fowler

Greeting Cards & Invitations
isobel advertising

isobel Christmas Card 2009
Our 2009 Christmas card continued a tradition of rank stupidity. Dress up, have fun, act like idiots. The brief was simple: make people smile. It certainly worked for us. We're not sure if it worked for anyone else.

Designer
Michael C Place
Art Director
Nicola Place

Creative Director
Michael C Place
Illustrator
Michael C Place

Design Group
Build

Client
The Design Museum
Shop

Greeting Cards & Invitations

Build
for The Design Museum Shop

Send: Greetings & Christmas Cards
We were asked to design and produce a range of own-brand greetings cards for the Design Museum Shop. As custodians of good design, the Design Museum demanded the highest quality for the items it commissioned for sale, and that production should be in the UK. Owing to the small numbers involved, we needed to find a flexible way to produce the cards in both 'Greetings' and 'Christmas' designs; the answer was to print a set of three foil-blocked cards, with separate 'Greetings' and 'Christmas' sticker sheets. These were packaged as box sets and individually; we used plain boxes with a printed belly band, to encourage their reuse once empty.

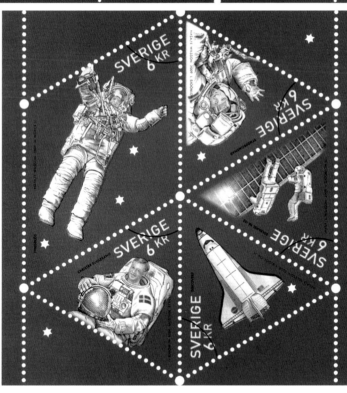

Designer
Eva Wilsson
Photography
NASA
Engravers
Martin Mörck
Lars Sjööblom

Copywriters
Benny Andersson
Björn Ulvaeus
Finishing Artist
Gustav Mårtensson
Design Group
Design Eva Wilsson

Production Manager
Jan-Olov Vuolle
Technical Advisor
Johan Marcopolous
Project Manager
Mats Granlöf

Prepress
Jan Högberg
Conny Walkin
Astronaut
Christer Fuglesang
Client
Sweden Post Stamps

Stamps

Design Eva Wilsson
for Sweden Post Stamps

Travelling in Space
This series of stamps celebrates the first space voyage by a Swedish astronaut. The creative brief was to give the stamp a sense of weightlessness. This was achieved by a design where, as in space, up and down are not defined and the stamps can be placed in any direction. The print is one-colour recess and four-colour offset. The stars are perforated and the rhomboid stamp features a microtext with the lyrics of an ABBA song, which was played in the shuttle. Permission to use these images has been granted by Sweden Post Stamps.

Graphic Design

1ST

Supermarine Spitfire
Designed by R J Mitchell

1ST

Mini Skirt
Designed by Mary Quant

1ST

Mini
Designed by Sir Alec Issigonis

1ST

Anglepoise Lamp
Designed by George Carwardine

1ST

Concorde
Designed by Aérospatiale-BAC

1ST

K2 Telephone Kiosk
Designed by Sir Giles Gilbert Scott

1ST

Polypropylene Chair
Designed by Robin Day

1ST

Penguin Books
Designed by Edward Young

1ST

London Underground Map
Designed by Harry Beck

1ST

Routemaster Bus
Design team led by AAM Durrant

Designer Tommy Taylor **Creative Director** Pierre Vermeir	**Photographer** Jason Tozer **Design Group** HGV Design	**Head of Design & Editorial** Marcus James	**Design Manager** Catharine Brandy **Client** Royal Mail Group

Stamps

HGV Design
for the Royal Mail Group

British Design, Classics Stamps
This stamp issue started with the 50th anniversary celebrating the first Mini rolling off the Longbridge production line. The Mini is the most popular British-made car in the world. A further nine equally iconic British Design Classics were required to create a set of ten. All had to be considered instantly recognisable and icons of their era, honouring the design not the invention. The stamp design was defined by simplicity and authenticity, with commissioned photography portraying them as heroes, stripping away any distractions. The framing brings a cohesive style to disparate objects, creating a strong graphic quality. Sourcing pristine originals to photograph was a monumental task.

209

yogesh shah, ceo

the backpacker co.

90/5 mahakali caves rd, andheri (east)
mumbai - 93. ceo@thebackpackerco.com
m: + 91 9820027727 www.thebackpackerco.com

Design Director	**Chief Executive**	**Design Group**	**Client**
AVN Suresh	**Officer**	Karigari Design	The Backpacker Co.
Creative Director	Neha Shah	Mumbai	
Keegan Pinto			

Stationery
Karigari Design Mumbai
for The Backpacker Co.

Soap Cards
The brief was to create business cards for The Backpacker Co., India's premier company guiding backpacking trips around the world. While studying the behaviour of backpackers, we realised they'd carry soap in the form of easy to carry and use soap strips. And soap strips are as small and slim as business cards. Voilà! After the first circulation, the client's office was flooded with calls from travellers who asked for the cards, promising to pass them around. They were distributed during the company's trips around Europe, which resulted in a 19% rise in travellers registering to backpack around India.

Designer	Creative Consultant	Project Photography	Client
Adam Rix	Ben Wedderburn	Shaw & Shaw	Adam Rix
	Design Group		**Brand**
	Various Artists		Rix

Stationery

Various Artists
for Adam Rix

Playing Cards
Produce a low-budget business card that starts conversations and makes people smile, rather than conforming to the 'foil-block-some-nice-stock' design cliché. If it ends up being a nod to sustainability – even better.

Designer	Art Director	Creative Director	Design Group
Masashi Murakami	Kenjiro Sano	Kenjiro Sano	Mr_Design
			Client
			Mr_Design

Stationery

Mr_Design

Kakuzai Memo Block
This wood block-shaped memo block is printed on four sides and on the top of each piece
of paper. It is designed to look just like a real piece of wood. The concept came from the origin
of paper: paper is made of wood and the memo block goes back to that original appearance.
This product is available at the Design Museum in London, the 21st Century Museum of
Contemporary Art in Japan, and other shops around the world.

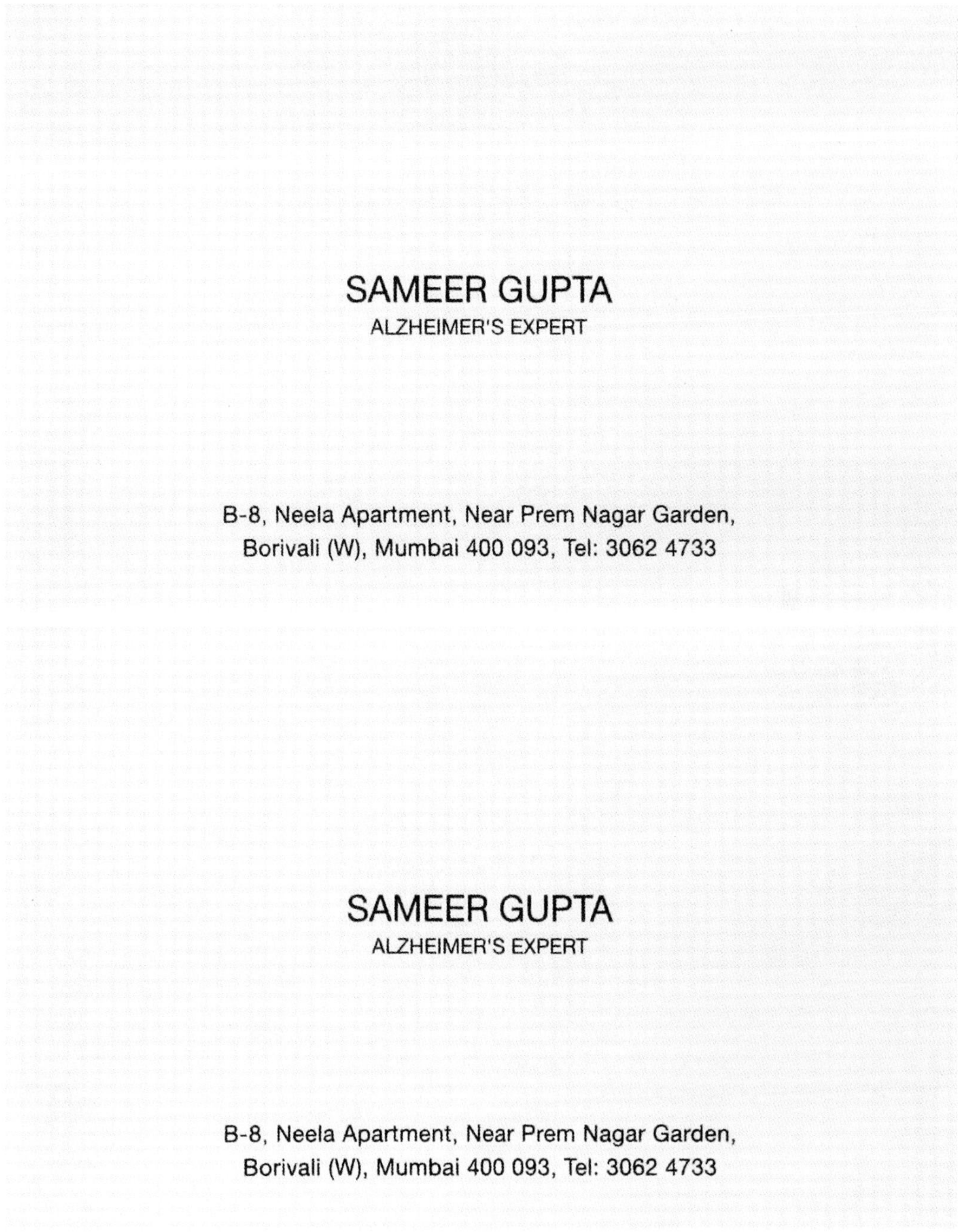

SAMEER GUPTA

ALZHEIMER'S EXPERT

B-8, Neela Apartment, Near Prem Nagar Garden,
Borivali (W), Mumbai 400 093, Tel: 3062 4733

SAMEER GUPTA

ALZHEIMER'S EXPERT

B-8, Neela Apartment, Near Prem Nagar Garden,
Borivali (W), Mumbai 400 093, Tel: 3062 4733

Designer	Copywriter	Design Group	Client
Mohamed Rizwan	Mohamed Rizwan	Kritik	Sameer Gupta

Stationery

Kritik
for Sameer Gupta

Double Side
Sameer Gupta understands Alzheimer's in a way few experts do. This card demonstrates why.

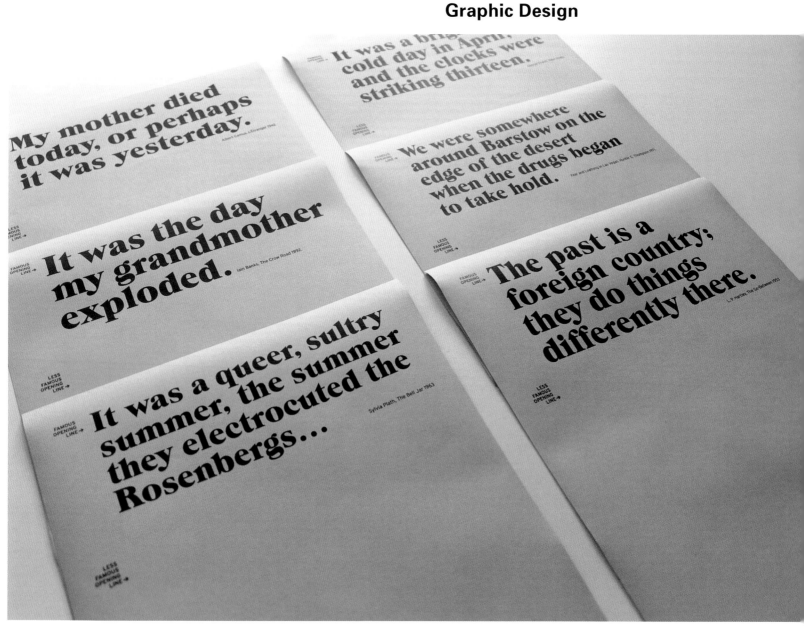

My mother died today, or perhaps it was yesterday.
Albert Camus, L'Étranger 1942

It was a bright, cold day in April, and the clocks were striking thirteen.

It was the day my grandmother exploded.
Iain Banks, The Crow Road 1992.

We were somewhere around Barstow on the edge of the desert when the drugs began to take hold.
Fear and Loathing in Las Vegas, Hunter S. Thompson 1971

It was a queer, sultry summer, the summer they electrocuted the Rosenbergs…
Sylvia Plath, The Bell Jar 1963

The past is a foreign country; they do things differently there.
L P Hartley, The Go-Between 1953

LESS FAMOUS OPENING LINE →
FAMOUS OPENING LINE →

Designer	Creative Director	Advertising Agency	Client
Julian Melhuish	Dave Bowman	Saatchi & Saatchi	Sydney Writers'
Design Creative	**Executive Creative**	Sydney	Festival
Director	**Director**		
Julian Melhuish	Steve Back		

Stationery

Saatchi & Saatchi Sydney
for the Sydney Writers' Festival

Sydney Writers' Festival Letterheads
Writers agonise over the first line of their novels. The letterheads take famous opening lines and acknowledge that the opening line of the letter is likely to be less considered. Authors include Albert Camus, Sylvia Plath, LP Hartley, George Orwell, Iain Banks and Hunter S Thompson.

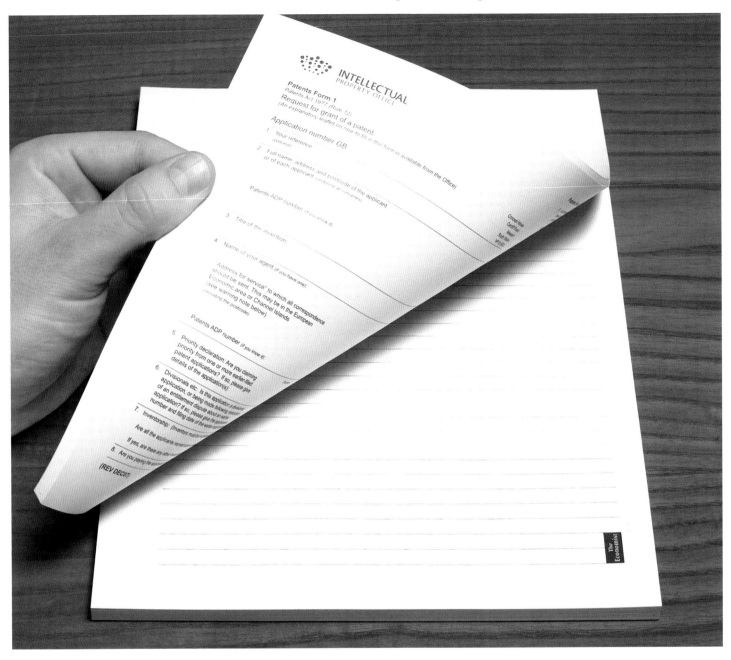

Designers
Christopher Bowsher
Frances Leach
Art Director
Christopher Bowsher

Creative Director
Dave Dye
Copywriter
Frances Leach

Advertising Agency
Dye Holloway
Murray

Brand Manager
Alan Dunachie
Client
The Economist

Stationery
Dye Holloway Murray
for The Economist

Intellectual Property
Dye Holloway Murray created The Economist notepad with a patent application form on the back of every page.

Art Directors
Simon Earith
James Musgrave
Creative Director
Simon Earith

Photographer
Dan Holdsworth
Image Manipulator
Bernard Ryan

Production Consultant
Daniel Mason
Design Group
YES

Marketing Manager
James Burton
Client
Warp Records

CD, DVD & Record Sleeves

YES
for Warp Records

Warp20 Box Set
Warp20 Box Set is a special edition box set made to celebrate 20 years of Warp Records.
Images featured were art directed by YES and photographed by artist Dan Holdsworth.
The package consists of a heavyweight 10-inch square case-bound slipcase with a tipped-in
cover photograph. Contents include a 192 page book, Warp20 (1989–2009), cataloguing
every Warp release. Two double CD albums and a single CD album are packaged in deluxe
case-bound 10-inch folders. Also included is a vinyl set housed in uncoated card sleeves
with foil-blocked typography.

Designers
Mark Farrow
Sabine Fasching
Gary Stillwell

Design Group
Farrow

Clients
Pet Shop Boys
The Vinyl Factory

CD, DVD & Record Sleeves

Farrow
for the Pet Shop Boys

Yes Pet Shop Boys Limited Edition Box Set
The album is split over 11 vinyl records, each in a coloured sleeve, which when correctly arranged form a giant version of the tick. The inner sleeves feature deconstructed graphic elements and photographs from the original album. A 12th, white sleeve contains a signed print, track listing and recording credits. The luxurious smoked Perspex case features a gold-plated tick, making it reminiscent of high-end hi-fi equipment.

Designers
Fabian Herrmann
Angus Hyland
Alex Johns

Art Director
Angus Hyland

Design Group
Pentagram Design

Client
Cass Art

Applied Print Graphics

Pentagram Design
for Cass Art

Cass Art Bag – Scarlet Lake / Phthalo Turquoise / Quinacridone Magenta / Viridian
Cass Art has four shops across London; its mission is to fill this town with artists. The brief
was to design a new series of 12 variations of Cass Art bags celebrating colour in art. With
reference to Pentagram's interiors for the Cass Art flagship store, the bag designs are
typographic compositions featuring traditional oil colours and expressing their
provenance throughout art history.

Designers
Antony Nelson
Mike Sutherland
Art Director
Antony Nelson

Creative Director
Paul Brazier
Typographer
Aaron Moss
Copywriter
Mike Sutherland

Advertising Agency
Abbott Mead Vickers
BBDO
Account Handlers
Jason Capra
Laura Stayt

Head of Consumer Marketing
Hana Shackleton
Client
ADT

Applied Print Graphics

Abbott Mead Vickers BBDO
for ADT

Ten Alarms / Ignore / Telly
In Britain a home is burgled every 37 seconds. Many of these properties already have burglar alarms fitted, but the majority of them are ignored. ADT security systems are different. Their alarms are monitored 24 hours a day, 365 days a year, ensuring that your alarm won't be ignored, giving you complete peace of mind. Instead of running a traditional poster campaign, we decided to use people's homes to put our message across. We sprayed the copy directly onto wooden boards. These boards were then placed over windows creating the illusion that the property had recently been burgled and the broken window boarded up.

Designers
Yo Kimura
Eri Kotani
Yoshihiro Yagi

Art Director
Yoshihiro Yagi
Creative Director
Yuya Furukawa

Copywriters
Eriko Ishibashi
Nae Mikuni
Mariko Tsukamoto
Haruko Tsutsui
Fujinari Tsutsumi
Advertising Agency
Dentsu Tokyo

Clients
One Show
Yoshida Hideo
Memorial
Foundation
Brand
One Show 2009
Exhibition

Posters

Dentsu Tokyo
for the Yoshida Hideo Memorial Foundation

The Oneder Brain! – One Show 2009 Exhibition in Japan
These posters were designed to announce the One Show 2009 Exhibition and tell people that One Show is a competition for creative minds working at the highest level. Our idea was to depict the thought process of creative minds recognised at One Show. The explosive moment when an idea is created and the seemingly chaotic state of the mind are symbolised by what looks like a circuit board, using a great number of words. When visitors entered the venue, they felt as if they were actually witnessing great creative minds at work.

Art Directors
Nadja Lossgott
Shelley Smoler
Copywriters
Raphael Basckin
Nicholas Hulley

Photographers
Chloe Coetsee
Des Ellis
Michael Meyersfeld
Rob Wilson

Executive Creative Director
Damon Stapleton
Advertising Agency
TBWA\Hunt\Lascaris Johannesburg

Account Handler
Bridget Langley
Marketing Manager
Liz Linsell
Client
The Zimbabwean Newspaper

Posters

TBWA\Hunt\Lascaris Johannesburg
for The Zimbabwean Newspaper

Cheaper Than Paper / Fight the Regime / Z$250,000,000
The Zimbabwean Newspaper, forced into exile, was then slapped with a 55% luxury import duty, making it unaffordable for Zimbabweans. To raise awareness of this issue, we developed an unusual solution. The most eloquent symbol of Zimbabwe's collapse is the Z$ trillion note, which cannot buy anything and certainly not advertising. But it can become the advertising. We turned the money into the medium by printing our messages straight onto it. We made posters, murals and billboards out of the worthless money. Overnight, Zimbabwean banknotes achieved what they'd never been able to buy – advertising coverage. We used Mugabe's own creation against him.

221

Designer
Emily Tu

Creative Directors
Claire Dawson
Fidel Peña

Illustrator
Ben Weeks
Design Group
Underline Studio

Client
Ben Weeks

Posters

Underline Studio
for Ben Weeks

Ben Weeks Has Many Loves
This self-promotional mailer was developed for illustrator Ben Weeks to send to top Canadian and international design and advertising firms. Underline Studio asked Ben to illustrate his favourite things, including his dream clients, in his signature quirky style. When sending the promo, the illustration of the addressee is hand-circled, giving each one a very personal touch. For the reverse side of the poster, Underline Studio crafted a typeface from segments of hearts. The customised lettering reads 'Ben Weeks has many loves'. Printed with one pantone on uncoated stock, the poster folds down to fit into a square envelope.

Posters

The Partners
for the Richard House Children's Hospice

Five-A-Side Poster
The Richard House Children's Hospice needed a promotional poster for their five-a-side football fundraising event. The solution lay in the markings of a five-a-side football pitch. Seen from one specific view-point, the white markings create a distinct number five.

esigners	Design Director	Design Agency	Client
amuel Hall	Michael Paisley	The Partners	Richard House
ex Woolley	**Creative Director**		Children's Hospice
	Jack Renwick		

花と水

菊地成孔
南博

Posters

good design company
for East Works Entertainment
& Naruyoshi Kikuchi

Designer
Masaru Uemura
Art Director
Manabu Mizuno

Creative Director
Manabu Mizuno

Design Agency
good design
company

Clients
East Works
Entertainment
Naruyoshi Kikuchi

Hana-to-Mizu
Naruyoshi Kikuchi is a famous Japanese musician who led the Japanese jazz world. As well as being a musician, he worked as a part-time university instructor. Hana is Japanese for flower, and Mizu means water. We used these items to express this dual achievement: one has a shape and one doesn't. The flower is a strong pink to illustrate its dramatic colour when compared with water.

224

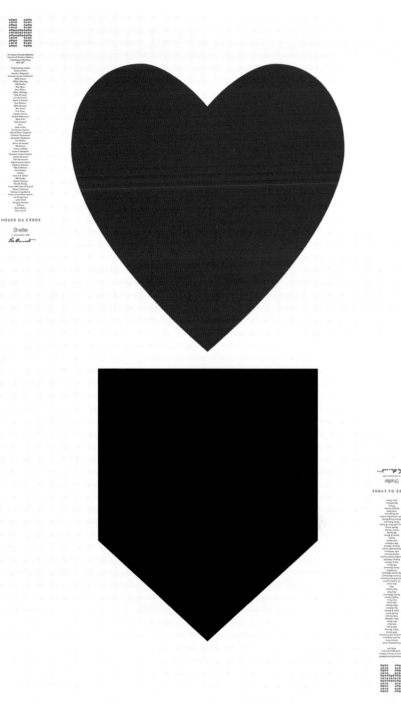

esigners
eremy Kunze
omenic Lippa
reative Directors
ichard Brim
aniel Fisher

Executive Creative Director
Jonathan Burley
Typographer
Jeremy Kunze

Design Group
Pentagram Design
Advertising Agency
Leo Burnett London

Client
Shelter
Brand
House of Cards

Posters

Pentagram Design
for Shelter

House of Cards
In 2008 homeless charity Shelter launched the House of Cards campaign to raise awareness of housing insecurity in the UK. Following the success of the campaign, Leo Burnett London developed the idea to invite 53 artists to design a set of playing cards. Artists included Damien Hirst and Marc Quinn, among others. Pentagram created an identity for the event, as well as a catalogue and limited edition box of A5 playing cards. Domenic Lippa and designer Jeremy Kunze developed a logotype that played on the symbol 'H', combining pictograms of the suits from the cards and a pictogram of a house.

MARTIN
BOYCE
BOYC
NO ECTIONS
REFLECTI NOV
JUNE — NREFL
2009 UNE-
VENICE 009
2009 NIC
VENICEFL
JUNE-
2009

la Biennale di Venezia

53. Esposizione Internazionale d'Arte

Eventi collaterali

Scotland and Venice
Martin Boyce, *No Reflections*

Curated by Dundee Contemporary Arts

Palazzo Pisani (S.Marina), Calle delle Erbe, Cannaregio 6103
Nearest vaporetto: Rialto/S.Zaccaria

7 June — 22 November 2009
Tuesday to Sunday 10am — 6pm (closed Mondays/chiuso il lunedi)
Free entry/Ingresso gratuito

www.scotlandandvenice.com

Scotland +Venice

Design Group
Graphical House

Client
Scotland and Venice

Posters

Graphical House
for Scotland and Venice

Martin Boyce – No Reflections
This poster was part of a campaign to promote the work of Scottish artist Martin Boyce at the 2009 Venice Biennale. Through a series of sculptures, Boyce set out to echo the labyrinthine nature of Venice, creating a heightened sense of displacement and abandonment in a 15th Century Venetian Palazzo. After discussions with the artist, it was decided that the design should avoid becoming a representation of Boyce's work, but instead should be derived from aspects of his practice. The designers explored disruptions found when applying the artist's grid over conventional typography. The stark and fractured design reinforced the notion of displacement, while standing out within the context of a media saturated Venice.

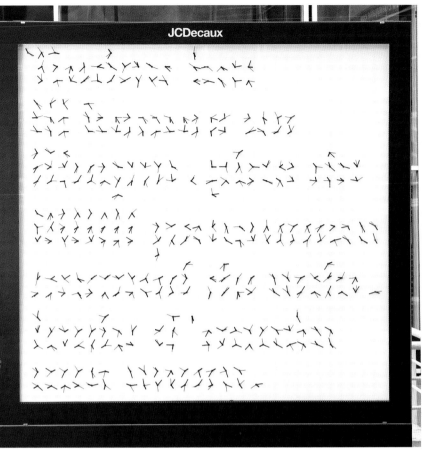

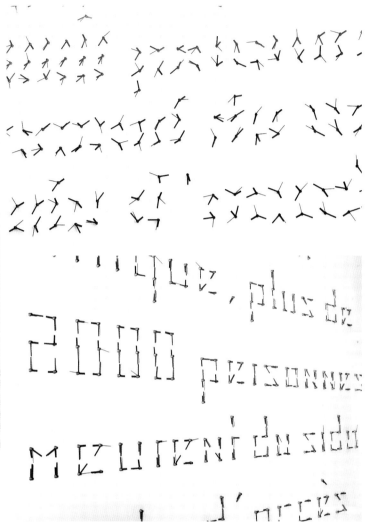

esigner	**Typographer**	**Account Handlers**	**Marketing Manager**
adine Grenier	Benjamin Le Breton	Raphaël de Andréis	Barbara Alfandari
rt Director	**Copywriter**	Elodie Andurand	**Client**
enjamin Le Breton	Arnaud Assouline	Philippe Brandt	The AIDS Africa
xecutive Creative	**Advertising Agency**	**Brand Manager**	Solidarity Fund
irector	BETC Euro RSCG	Emmanuel Dollfus	**Brand**
téphane Xiberras	**Outdoor Production**		SOLIDARITÉ SIDA
	JCDecaux		

Posters

BETC Euro RSCG
for The AIDS Africa Solidarity Fund

Clocks

Against AIDS, every minute counts. At a set time, twice a day, the hands of these clocks come together and align to form a sentence: 'Every 12 hours in Africa, over 2,000 people die from AIDS because they have no access to care'. SOLIDARITÉ SIDA wanted to alert Europeans to the necessity of acting quickly against this situation. BETC Euro RSCG created an outdoor installation, in association with artist Nadine Grenier, consisting of 321 clocks. The bottom of the installation carries the call to action, explaining where people can get more information about the foundation and donate online: 'Every minute counts. www.solidarite-sida.org'.

227

Designer	Illustrator	Marketing Manager	Brand
George Adams	Adam Hayes	Beckie Crane	The London
Creative Director	**Design Group**	**Client**	Restaurant Festival
Ben Stott	NB: Studio	Visit London,	
	Account Handler	A Private View	
	Anoushka Rodda		

Logos

NB: Studio
for The London Restaurant Festival

The London Restaurant Festival
Inspired by the excitement and collective optimism of the Festival of Britain, the graphic language of banners and flags was used to create a modern mark that has a familiar and established feel. To reinforce the vibrancy of the festival and the eclectic mix of food available in London, an energetic illustration was combined with a confident colour scheme and clean sans serif typeface. It was used across a range of applications to create a bold, distinctive and thoroughly modern identity.

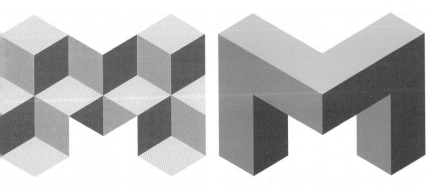

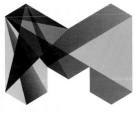

CITY OF MELBOURNE

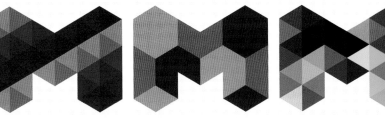

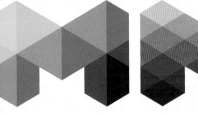

Designers
Malin Holmstrom
Jason Little
Ivana Martinovic
Sam Pemberton
Jefton Sungkar
Art Director
Jason Little

Creative Director
Jason Little
Executive Creative Director
Mike Staniford
Illustrator
Jefton Sungkar
Design Group
Landor Associates

Account Handlers
Amanda Lawson
Mark Liney
Strategy Consultants
Katie Crosby
Cable Daniel-Dreyfus

Strategy Director
James Cockerille
Client
City of Melbourne

Logos

Landor Associates
for the City of Melbourne

City of Melbourne
Melbourne is a dynamic and progressive city, internationally recognised for its diversity, innovation, sustainability and livability. Our challenge was to create a new identity for the City of Melbourne that would reflect Melbourne's cool sophistication, capture the passion of the council and the people, and enable a unified and future focus for the city. Centred around a geometric framework, the identity is as iconic and multi-faceted as the city itself. This framework allows for creative interpretation. At its heart, the 'M' provides an iconic surface for endless visual executions to take place, adapting to suit the full range of services, sub-brands, initiatives and audiences.

229

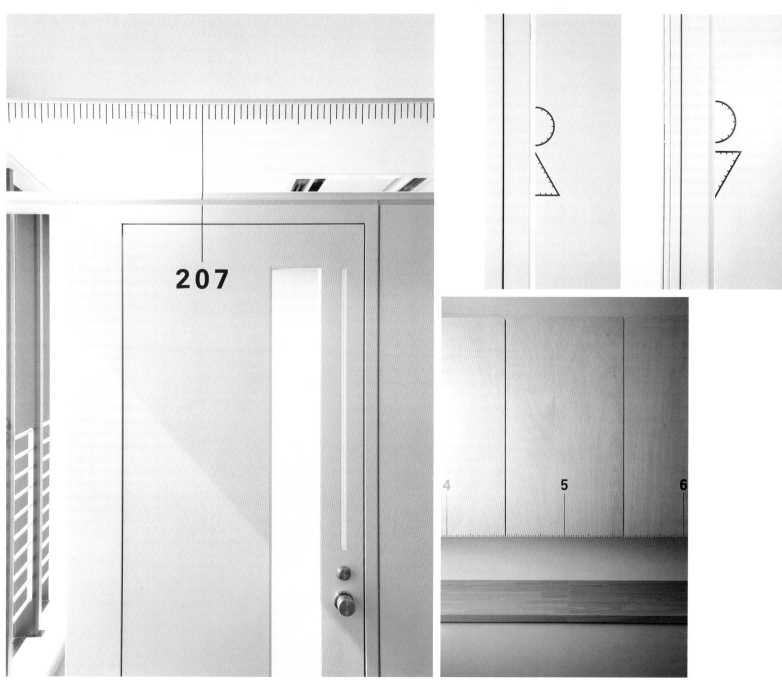

Art Director
NOSIGNER

Creative Director
TAKENAKA

Design Groups
NOSIGNER
TAKENAKA
CORPORATION

Brand
Scales

Signage & Information Graphics

NOSIGNER & TAKENAKA CORPORATION
for Scales

Scales
Scales is the signage design for a private cramming school for children. Units of measurement were used as the motif; measuring the growth achieved was the concept behind the signs. For example, the columns at the entrance resemble the scale of the nine size units (cm, yard, feet, inch, etc.). Children can learn unfamiliar scales while measuring their height. Scales is a contrivance where the design and space fuse with the measurements.

Designers	**Typographers**	**Signwriter**	**Brand Manager**
Peter Silk	Peter Silk	Simon Clark	Jonathan Reekie
Rob Steer	Rob Steer	**Design Group**	**Client**
		Silk Pearce	Aldeburgh Music

Signage & Information Graphics

Silk Pearce
for Aldeburgh Music

Hoffmann Building Signs

Aldeburgh Music opened a new campus in a former maltings building last year. Architect Haworth Tompkins kept the industrial feel, retaining many exposed surfaces, to reflect the building's heritage. Silk Pearce's design of the signs and environmental graphics is similarly sensitive to the location. Working from detailed design layouts, a traditional signwriter painted directly onto the walls and doors. The carefully chosen colours reflect the architect's colour scheme, while the upper case sans serif typeface strikes a balance between Victorian signwriting and a contemporary design approach.

231

Signage & Information Graphics

Cartlidge Levene
for the Victoria & Albert Museum

V&A Ceramics Galleries: Gallery Identity, Interpretative Graphics & Wayfinding
The V&A ceramics galleries are a key part of the museum's ongoing programme of restoration, redesign and refurbishment. Cartlidge Levene was commissioned to work alongside Stanton Williams architects to design the first phase of the 14-gallery permanent display. Our brief was to design the gallery identity and museum graphics, carefully integrating these with the architecture and display. Large scale typography located in the ceiling cornicing and dates painted onto wall surfaces provide narrative and act as navigational aids. An updatable label system integrates with the display cases, while a piece of low-tech interactive furniture explains the process of making ceramics with bold vitreous enamel graphics.

Designers	Design Group	Client	Brand
Matt Busher	Cartlidge Levene	Victoria & Albert	V&A
Ian Cartlidge		Museum	
Ben Tibbs			

Designers	Art Directors	Typographer	Landscape
Giuseppe Greco	João Gomes da Silva	Mário Feliciano	**Architects**
Nuno Gusmão	Nuno Gusmão	**Photographer**	Global
Miguel Matos	**Design Directors**	João Silveira Ramos	**Clients**
	Pedro Anjos	**Design Studio**	EDP
	Estela Pinto	P-06 ATELIER	Lisbon City Hall
			Lisbon Seaport

Environmental Graphics

P-06 ATELIER
for EDP, Lisbon City Hall & Seaport

Bike Way, Belém – Cais do Sodré, Portugal
The project was undertaken by Global and P-06 ATELIER, which developed the signage and colour study. The goal was to redefine a new public facility to enhance the 7,362m area along the river. All the signs, symbols and words establish boundaries, guidance and information, creating a relationship with the urban context, telling us a story, leading and seducing us along the way. The graphics went beyond the basic needs of communication with the large-scale features of Alberto Caeiro's poem or with the onomatopoeic intervention under the bridge revealing the sounds beneath it.

233

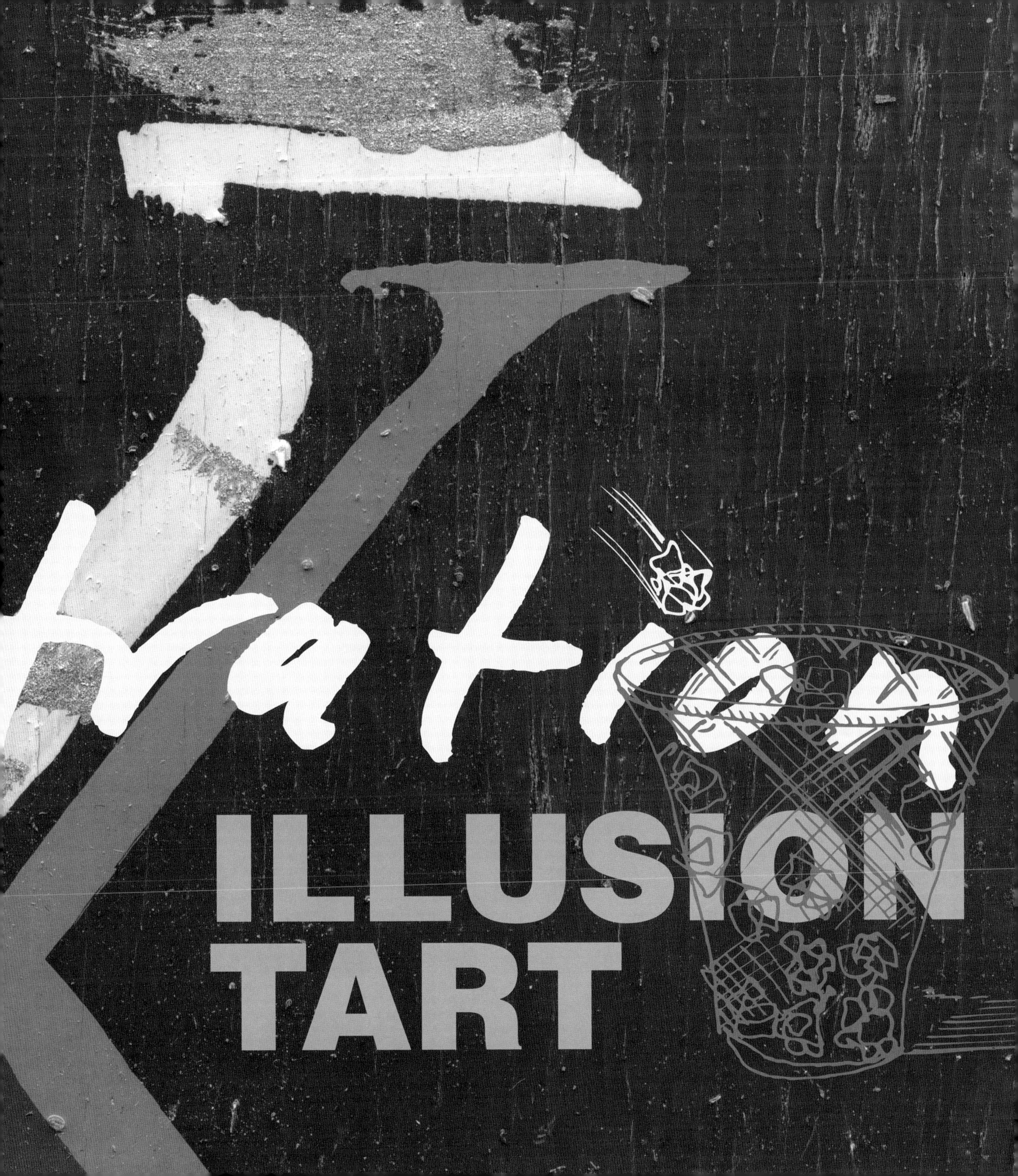
ILLUSION
TART

Artist
Geoff McFetridge
Creative Directors
Rob Longworth
Paul Willoughby

Editors
Matt Bochenski
Vince Medeiros

Creative Agency
The Church of
London
Publisher
Danny Miller

Client
The Church
of London
Brands
Huck
Little White Lies

Magazine & Newspaper Design

The Church of London

Little White Lies & Huck Double Cover
In October 2009 we commissioned world renowned artist Geoff McFetridge, graphic designer
for 'Where The Wild Things Are', to illustrate the covers of 'Little White Lies' and 'Huck',
bringing the two titles together to form one continuous piece of artwork. Geoff loved the idea,
as did director Spike Jonze. To the best of our knowledge (and that of everyone else we've
asked) this is the first time that two magazine covers have done such a thing.

LET'S MAKE THEM STICK AROUND A LITTLE LONGER. WWW.PROWILDLIFE.DE

Artist
Sarah Illenberger
Art Director
Dina Ruewe

Copywriter
Helge Hummel
Creative Directors
Jan Rexhausen
Doerte Spengler-
Ahrens

Advertising Agency
Jung von Matt
Hamburg

Marketing Manager
Annette Sperrfechter
Client
Pro Wildlife

Poster Advertising
Jung von Matt Hamburg
for Pro Wildlife

Staples
To create the world's first posters made entirely out of staples, we hired Sarah Illenberger, a young artist from Berlin. After two weeks, she had created the elephant poster, composed out of roughly 80,000 staples. Once the staple posters were almost complete, we placed them in three prominent locations in the biggest German cities, Hamburg and Berlin. Although they looked and felt like they were literally stapled to the wall, we had prepared two thirds of the art pieces in the studio. The pieces attracted a lot of attention, thanks to the fascinating way they were crafted.

Art Director
Richard Brim
Design Directors
Jeremy Kunze
Domenic Lippa
Designers
Jeremy Kunze
Domenic Lippa
Copywriter
Daniel Fisher

Typographer
Jeremy Kunze
Creative Directors
Richard Brim
Jonathan Burley
Daniel Fisher
Executive Creative Director
Jonathan Burley
Design Group
Pentagram Design

Advertising Agency
Leo Burnett London
Account Handlers
Lizzie Dixey
Gary Simmons
Client
Shelter
Brand
House of Cards

Poster Advertising

Leo Burnett London & Pentagram Design
for Shelter

Live Posters
Shelter's 'House of Cards' exhibition consisted of the ultimate deck of cards, each card being designed by a leading artist. Before the launch, we placed empty card templates in poster locations across London. Over the course of a week, street artists and the general public filled in the blanks, leading to a series of unique artworks across the city. The posters became so sought after that some even went missing and ended up on Ebay. Those that didn't were eventually sold off in aid of Shelter. Thank you to the Great British Public for their illustrations.

239

Press Advertising

DDB UK
for Volkswagen

Illustrator
Tavis Coburn
Art Director
Victor Monclus
Designer
Pete Mould
Copywriter
Will Lowe

Typographer
Pete Mould
Executive Creative Director
Jeremy Craigen
Advertising Agency
DDB UK

Account Director
Charlie Elliott
Account Manager
Jessica Huth
Planner
Georgia Challis

Business Director
Jonathan Hill
Communications Manager
Sally Chapman
Client
Volkswagen

Sci Fi
This advert to promote Volkswagen's sponsorship of independent cinema is part of the 'Film Location Road Trips' series. Film fans can follow these route maps and visit the sites of their favourite movie scenes. The images and copy suggest which films were shot at each location. Every map features a different genre with an illustrative style to match. In this case, Science Fiction.

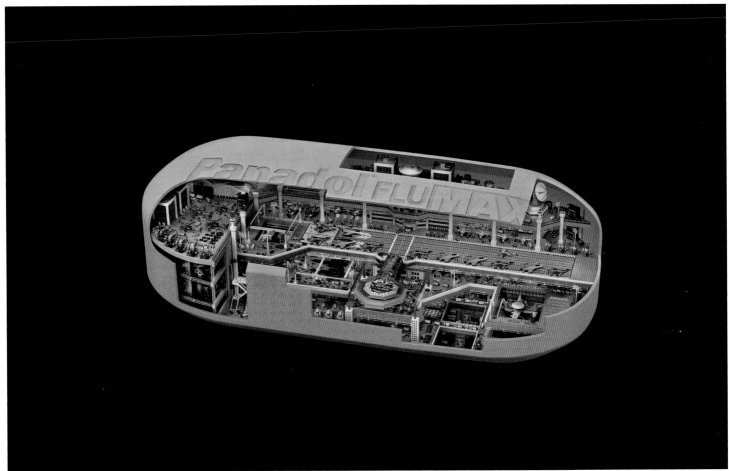

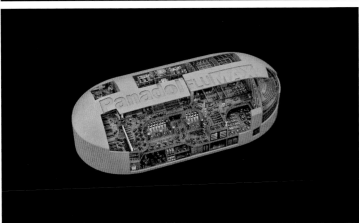
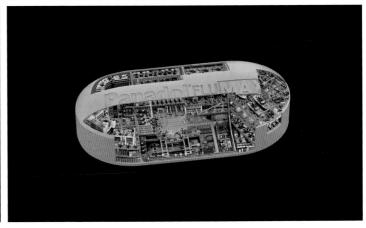

Illustration	**Copywriter**	**Executive Creative**	**Client**
Mirage Works	Serene Loong	**Director**	GlaxoSmithKline
Pro Color	**Creative Director**	Todd McCracken	**Brand**
Art Directors	Eric Yeo	**Advertising Agency**	Panadol FluMax
Hui Chong		Ogilvy Singapore	
Wat Tan			

Press Advertising

Ogilvy Singapore
for GlaxoSmithKline

Air Force / Army / Navy
When you have a single-minded campaign thought, you must send the army, air force and navy to fight tooth and nail to keep it that way. Kudos to those who made it happen, and especially to all the others who did not stand in our way – we couldn't have done it without you.

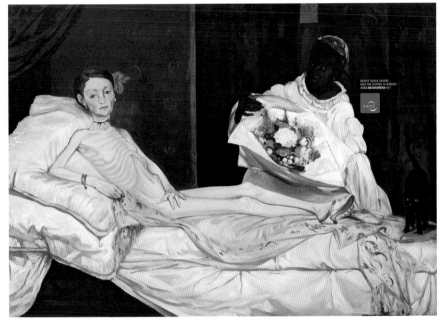

Illustrator
Remus Grecu
Art Directors
Albert S Chan
Sabina Hesse

Copywriters
Albert S Chan
Sabina Hesse
Creative Directors
Christian Mommertz
Dr Stephan Vogel

Advertising Agency
Ogilvy Frankfurt
Art Buyer
Valerie Opitz
Account Handler
Veronika Sikvölgyi

Brand Manager
Claudia Engel
Client
ANAD (National
Association of
Anorexia Nervosa
and Associated
Disorders)

Press Advertising

Ogilvy Frankfurt
for ANAD

**Contemporary Beauty Ideals: Manet's Olympia 2009 / Boucher's Nude 2009 /
Ingres' Bather 2009**
ANAD is a not-for-profit organisation that educates the public about the dangers of anorexia.
They asked us for an innovative way to raise money and awareness. To highlight the unhealthy
beauty ideals promoted by the media and fashion industry, we opted for a completely new
approach. We painted world famous masterpieces a second time. These paintings were then
displayed in fine art museums, exactly where visitors would expect to see manifestations of
true beauty.

Illustrator
David Shrigley

Typographer
David Shrigley
Advertising Agency
Krow

Brand Manager
Elisa Reinerio
Client
Fiat

Brand
Fiat 500

Press Advertising

Krow
for Fiat

Shrigley
This advert was created to promote the Fiat 500 during the Frieze Art Fair.

History is written by those who never stop

Illustrator
Manish Darji
Art Director
Manish Darji
Copywriter
Russell Barrett

Image Manipulator
Vinayak Kurade
Creative Director
Russell Barrett

Advertising Agency
Bates India
Account Handler
Subhash Rao

Marketing Manager
Ullas K Nair
Client
Alpha International
Brand
Staedtler

Press Advertising

Bates India
for Alpha International

Man on the Moon
Staedtler Pens needed an eye-catching campaign to demonstrate their new long lasting pens. The campaign was aimed mainly at students, who would benefit from these pens when writing their exams and for school and college projects. We hit on the idea of making a complete, elaborate picture with a single line. A line that never stops. The subjects chosen were historical moments of success; the culmination of the unrelenting spirit of perseverance.

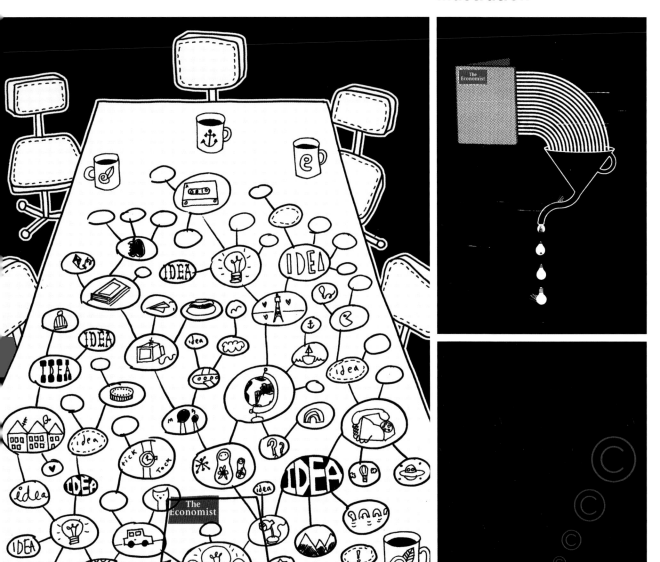

Press Advertising

Dye Holloway Murray
for The Economist

Mind Map / Funnel / Copyright
Dye Holloway Murray created a press campaign to portray Economist readers as 'the ideas people'.

Illustrators	Copywriters	Creative Director	Account Handler
Nishant Choksi	Dave Dye	Dave Dye	Jorian Murray
Kate Sutton	Frances Leach	**Advertising Agency**	**Brand Manager**
Yarek Wazsul	Ollie Wolf	Dye Holloway	Alan Dunachie
Art Directors	**Print Producer**	Murray	**Client**
Christopher Bowsher	Kieran Ward	**Art Buyer**	The Economist
Janson Choo		Kellie French	
Dave Dye			

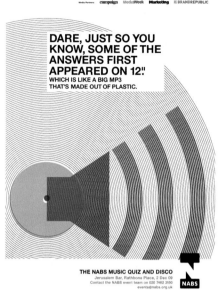

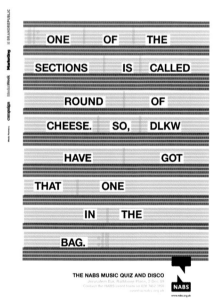

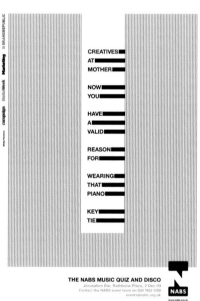

Illustrator	**Copywriters**	**Executive Creative**	**Brand Manager**
Pete Mould	Andy McAnaney	**Director**	Carol Butler
Art Directors	Christian Sewell	Jeremy Craigen	**Marketing Manager**
Andy McAnaney	**Typographer**	**Advertising Agency**	Penny Walshe
Christian Sewell	Pete Mould	DDB UK	**Client**
Designer	**Creative Directors**	**Account Handler**	NABS
Pete Mould	Mike Crowe	Samuel Payne	
	Rob Messeter		

Graphic Design

DDB UK
for NABS

CHI / Dare / DDB / Fallon / DLKW / Mother

NABS is a charity that gives professional advice, emotional support and financial assistance to people in the communications industry. To raise funds it held an industry-wide music quiz and disco. To pique people's interest, generate word of mouth and get the blogs talking, we created these good-natured but slightly barbed posters. Each agency in London got the full set of six. Whether they put the execution up that pertained to them, well, that was entirely at their discretion.

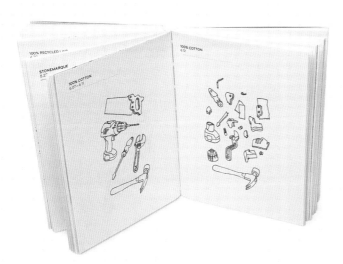

Illustrator
Damien Weighill
Designer
Dan Bown

Design Directors
Colin Gifford
Paul Tunnicliffe
Typographer
Dan Bown

Print Production
Empress Litho
Design Group
Blast
Brand Manager
Emeline Mory

Client
Arjowiggins
Brand
Conqueror

Graphic Design

Blast
for Arjowiggins

Endless Possibilities
The brief was to create a worldwide campaign to stimulate the creative use of Conqueror paper while also challenging designers' perceptions of the brand. Blast worked with illustrator Damien Weighill to create an innovative resource that promoted the 'endless possibilities' of uses for Conqueror. The campaign centred around a 256-page book, printed on eight different paper stocks and illustrated with over 300 witty thoughts and ideas. A website provided a portal for designers to download the illustrations and use them in their work. In addition, four limited edition A2 posters were created and signed by the illustrator.

247

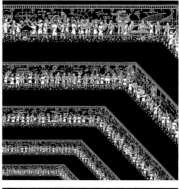

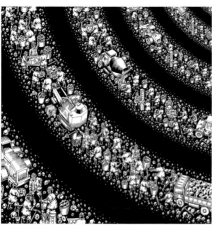

Illustrators	Copywriters	Creative Directors	Brand Manager
Lee Ka Fai	Paul Chan	Jeffry Gamble	Conroy Cheng
Ra Tang	Karen Wong	Ruth Lee	**Marketing Manager**
Liao Yiyuan	**Retouchers**	Karen Wong	Chiu Fong
Art Directors	Agei	Liao Yiyuan	**Client**
Ra Tang	Heizi	**Advertising Agency**	Chow Tai Fook
Liao Yiyuan	Yuanming Xu	DDB Hong Kong	Jewellery
Designers	**Print Producer**	**Account Handler**	**Brand**
Ra Tang	Ng Ka Lok	Conrad Ng	3-Ex Diamond
Liao Yiyuan			

Graphic Design

DDB Hong Kong
for Chow Tai Fook Jewellery

Reflection / Cut / Rarity
To highlight Chow Tai Fook's uncompromising standards in diamonds, we created an intricately crafted poster campaign. By getting up close and personal, we revealed in exquisite detail the individual stories behind the cut, the rarity and the reflection of every diamond.

Illustrator
Brian Steele
Designer
Brian Steele
Design Director
Sarah Moffat

Print Production
Dependable
Letterpress
Creative Directors
Bruce Duckworth
David Turner

Design Group
Turner Duckworth:
London & San
Francisco

Client
Turner Duckworth:
London & San
Francisco

Graphic Design
Turner Duckworth: London & San Francisco

Turner Duckworth Holiday Card 2009
Our aim was to combine the two studios in London and San Francisco in a sophisticated and festive image that we could share with our friends and clients over Christmas. The Turner Duckworth 2009 holiday card depicts both the London and San Francisco skylines. The design captures the weather and cheer of the season, from London's snow covered buildings to a starry night in San Francisco.

249

Illustrator
Jasper Goodall

Photographer
Jasper Goodall

Design Studio
Big Active

Client
Electric Blue Gallery

Graphic Design

Big Active
for the Electric Blue Gallery

Poster Girl
Poster Girl is a playful look at erotica, fetishism, dressing up and the blurring of lines between fantasy and reality. Fantastical illustrated bodies printed as posters are held up in front of real models. The resulting photograph is both illustration and photography, real and imagined.

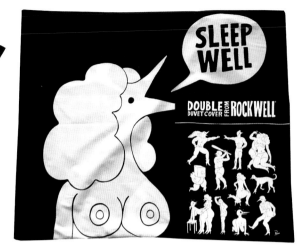

Illustrator
Parra

Creative Director
Parra

Artist's Agent
Big Active
Managing Director
Alexander Rommens

Client
Rockwell Clothing

Graphic Design

Parra
for Rockwell Clothing

The Untitled Collection
Rockwell Clothing started in 2000 as a pioneering graphic T-shirt label. Over the past decade the brand has grown under the creative direction of Dutch underground artist Parra, whose work adorns the ever expanding range of clothing, footwear, books and lifestyle products.

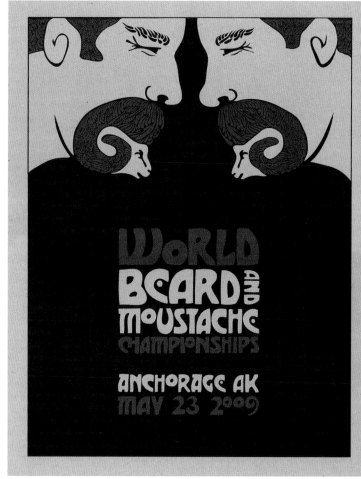

Graphic Design
Y&R New York
for The South Central Alaska Beard & Moustache Club

The Beards
These are posters for the 2009 World Beard & Moustache Championships.

Illustrator
Sanna Annukka

Design Group
Apple Graphic
Design

Client
Apple

Packaging Design

Apple Graphic Design
for Apple

iTunes Holiday Gift Cards
These are holiday designs for iTunes gift cards.

Featured Illustrators
Sam Arthur
Arnal Ballester
Cover Illustrators
Blex Bolex
Stuart Kolakovic
Illustrators
Eda Akaltun
A.Richard Allen
Alex Bland
Paul Blow
Blex Bolex
Marc Boutavant

Gwenola Carrere
Jordan Crane
Joe Crocker
Sebastiaan van
Doninck
Benjamin Guedel
Jens Harder
Leah Hayes
Mark Hearld
Richard Hogg
Andrew Holder
Carl Johanson
Mike Kerr

Sarah King
Toby Leigh
Micah Lidberg
Jean-Francois Martin
Asoko Masunouchi
McBess
Paddy Molloy
Ben Newman
Martin Ontiveros
Ken Orvidas
Louise Pomeroy
Emiliano Ponzi
Pietari Posti

Reuben Rude
Bjorn Rune Lie
Brett Ryder
Adam Schmidt
Sroop Sunar
Dave Taylor
Jack Teagle
Isabelle
Vandenabeele
Henning Wagenbreth
Nick White
Caspar Williamson

End Papers & Title
Page Illustrators
Jon Boam
Alex Spiro
Typographers
Paul Calway
Rob Cordiner
Creative Directors
Sam Arthur
Alex Spiro
Client
Nobrow Press
Brand
Nobrow

Magazine & Newspaper Design

Nobrow

Nobrow – Issue 1: Gods & Monsters / Issue 2: The Jungle
Nobrow magazine is a biannual publication set up to give illustrators, image makers and graphic artists a showcase for their work. Each issue is themed, and contributors submit work by invitation only. As well as a brief, Nobrow supplies contributors with the technical restraint of using a limited number of spot colours to create their artwork. This unifies the journal and gives the publication its distinct house style; beautiful colours and a tactile quality that would be difficult to achieve without using such an old fashioned printing technique.

Illustrator
David Foldvari
Art Director
Aldo Buscalferri

Picture Editor
Stefano Carminati

Editor In Chief
Michele Lupi
Artist's Agent
Big Active

Client
GQ Italy

Magazine & Newspaper Design

David Foldvari
for GQ Italy

WuMingWood
This series represents some of the most successful images from illustrator David Foldvari's regular feature for Italian 'GQ' magazine. The title of the column is 'WuMingWood', a wordplay that mixes Wu Ming (meaning 'anonymous' in Chinese) and Hollywood. Wu Ming is the collective name for four very popular Italian writers; each month they deliver a short biography of one of their personal heroes or anti-heroes for Foldvari to work with.

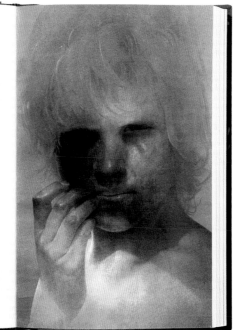

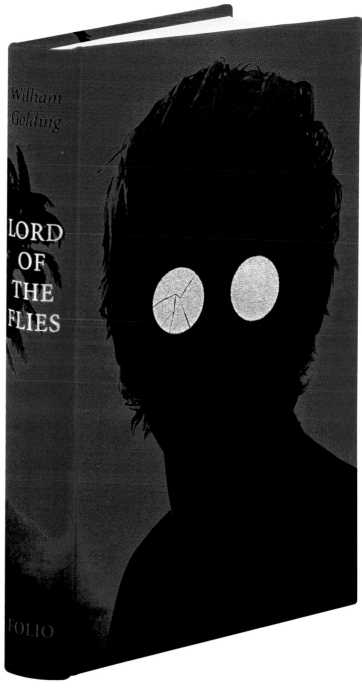

Illustrator
Sam Weber

Art Director
Sheri Gee

Publishing Company
The Folio Society

Client
The Folio Society

Book Design

Sam Weber
for The Folio Society

Lord of the Flies
First published in 1954, Lord of the Flies has been translated into every major language, selling over 25 million copies in English alone. One of the most influential novels of the 20th Century, it is both a gripping thriller and an ingenious parable about the nature of civilisation. This Folio Society edition features a preface by award-winning novelist Ian McEwan and a series of arresting illustrations by Sam Weber that perfectly capture the novel's highly charged atmosphere.

Illustrators	Designers	Typographer	Creative Director
Harry Brockway	Francis Atterbury	Phil Abel	Bruce Howard
Chris Daunt	Jo Atterbury	**Print Producer**	**Client**
Andy English		Francis Atterbury	Oak Tree Fine Press

Book Design

Oak Tree Fine Press

A Outrance
This illustrated letterpress book tells of how in the novel Northern Lights by Philip Pullman, the rightful bear-king Iorek Byrnison regained his throne through a fight to death with the false usurper Iofur Raknison, and how the story came to be written. It is limited to only 265 copies and features original woodcut illustrations by Chris Daunt, Harry Brockway and Andy English, three of the greatest woodcut artists working today. All proceeds from the sale of the book go to children made vulnerable by HIV and AIDS in southern Africa.

257

Illustrator
Noma Bar

Book Design

Noma Bar

Negative Space by Noma Bar
An artist using negative space relies on the space surrounding the subject to provide shape and meaning. The term also refers to topics that conjure up feelings of unease and discomfort. 'Negative Space' includes works commissioned by publications such as The Economist, Esquire, Wallpaper* and The Guardian, as well as previously unseen illustrations. Subject matters range from sex, global warming and nuclear warfare, to religion, crime and corporate greed. Noma Bar reinforces his reputation as an artist able to convert complex topics into clean, provocative and revealing lines, which viewers can take in with ease but not easily forget.

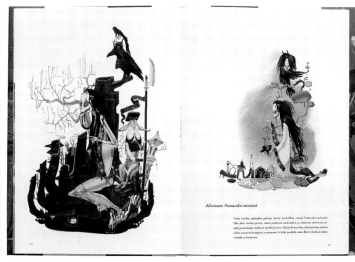

Illustrator	Designer	Publishers	Client
Klaus Haapaniemi	Mia Wallenius	WSOY	WSOY
Art Director	Author	Artist's Agent	Brand
Mia Wallenius	Rosa Liksom	Big Active	Neko

Book Design

Klaus Haapaniemi
for WSOY

Neko

Neko is an illustrated hardback picture book for the 6 to 12-year-old age group. The story is set during the time of the feudal system in 15th Century Japan; the aim was to create an authentic historical environment while trying to avoid typical Western concepts of Japanese culture. The illustrator invested considerable time in researching the subject, visiting Japan several times to ensure that the real life locations, costumes, and details were as accurate as possible.

IT'S CHEAPER TO PRINT THIS ON MONEY THAN PAPER

A VOICE FOR THE VOICELESS

The**Zimbabwean**

Art Directors
Nadja Lossgott
Shelley Smoler
Copywriters
Raphael Basckin
Nicholas Hulley
Executive Creative Director
Damon Stapleton

Photographers
Chloe Coetsee
Des Ellis
Michael Meyersfeld
Rob Wilson
Director
Chloe Coetsee

Advertising Agency
TBWA\Hunt\Lascaris
Johannesburg
Account Handler
Bridget Langley

Marketing Manager
Liz Linsell
Client
The Zimbabwean
Newspaper

Integrated

TBWA\Hunt\Lascaris Johannesburg
for The Zimbabwean Newspaper

Trillion Dollar Campaign

The Zimbabwean Newspaper, forced into exile, was then slapped with a 55% luxury import duty, making it unaffordable for Zimbabweans. To raise awareness of this issue, we developed an unusual solution. The most eloquent symbol of Zimbabwe's collapse is the Z$ trillion note, which cannot buy anything and certainly not advertising. But it can become the advertising. We turned the money into the medium by printing our messages straight onto it. We made flyers, direct mailers, posters, murals and billboards out of the worthless money. Overnight, Zimbabwean banknotes achieved what they'd never been able to buy – advertising coverage. We used Mugabe's own creation against him.

IT'S ABOUT USING THE ROAD AS A CANVAS.
—NIKE CHALKBOT TEAM

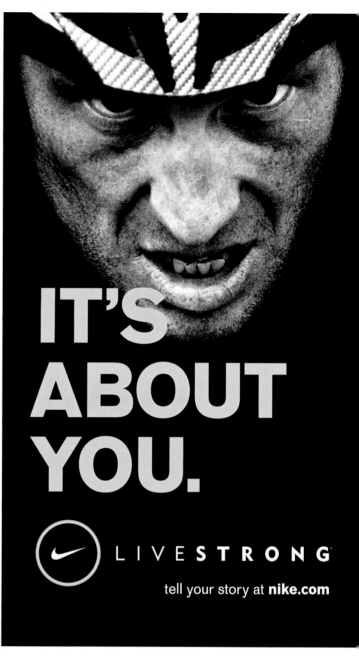

IT'S ABOUT YOU.

LIVESTRONG

tell your story at **nike.com**

Art Directors
Adam Heathcott
Shannon McLoughlin
James Moslander
Ryan O'Rourke
Copywriters
Marco Kaye
Karl Lieberman
Designers
Rob Mumford
Rehanah Spence

Creative Directors
Danielle Flagg
Tyler Whisnand
Directors
Frank Budgen
Greg Kohs
Interactive Producer
Ryan Bolls
Agency Producers
Marcelino Alvarez
Felicia Glover
Shannon Worley

Agency Executive Producer
Ben Grylewicz
Post Executive Producer
Patty Brebner
Editors
Kyle Valenta
Angus Wall
Production Companies
@radical.media
Anonymous Content

Advertising Agency
Wieden+Kennedy Portland
Media Director
Daniel Sheniak
Associate Media Director
Alex Barwick
Media Planner
Destinee Scott
Media Supervisor
Emily Leonard
Planner
Paulo Ribeiro

Account Handler
Dianne Villarreal
Studio Manager
Sarah Starr
Marketing Manager
Melissa Schoenke
Client
Nike Foundation
Brand
Livestrong

Integrated

Wieden+Kennedy Portland
for the Nike Foundation

Livestrong
It's about cancer, and it's about you. See Lance's comeback to cycling as one big call to lead a healthy life, to get involved with something you believe in, and to speak out against cancer or other issues that you face. To propagate the Livestrong message, we created an inspirational film series, a Lance Armstrong 'Just do it' commercial, and bold print and outdoor advertising, as well as a new medium: the Chalkbot. The Chalkbot allowed the world to see their words of memoriam, hope and courage chalked onto the roads of the Tour de France. The campaign is about hope, strength, and most of all, it's about you.

HIDDEN CAMERA INTERVIEW
JONATHAN H.
APRIL 16, 11:25 AM

Art Directors
Bob Kottkamp
Eric Stephenson
Copywriters
Will Chambliss
Pete Harvey
Bryan Karr
Gregg Nelson
Brett Reese
Creative Directors
Wade Devers
Pete Favat
John Kearse
Meg Siegal

Associate Creative Director
Mike Costello
Web Designers
Katherine Dawson
Dave Fernandez
A James Stone
Web Developers
Gabe Flavin
Ebbey Mathew
Sean Sullivan
Director
Henry-Alex Rubin

Producer
Drew Santarsiero
Agency Producers
Diane Brito
Carron Pedonti
Janet Pye
Terri Theiss
Editors
Josh Berger
Aaron Langley
Lawrence Young
Production Company
Smuggler
Productions

Advertising Agency
Arnold Worldwide
**Web Design
& Development**
B-Reel
Account Handler
Paul Nelson
Brand Manager
Eric Asche
Client
American Legacy
Foundation
Brand
truth

Integrated

Arnold Worldwide
for the American Legacy Foundation

Do You Have What it Takes?
In the past, truth has exposed the public to Big Tobacco and its questionable practices. This time we wanted to know if, even in the worst economy in 79 years, regular people could do what tobacco execs do. We used hidden cameras to secretly film candidates on what they thought was a real interview with someone they thought was a real recruiter. Our purpose was to answer one very real question: do you have what it takes to be a tobacco exec? Could you be the executive selling a product that kills millions? Even with unemployment at an all time high, we found out that not a lot of people have what it takes.

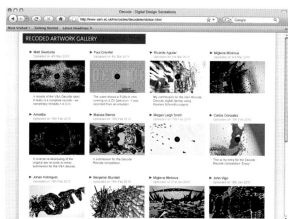

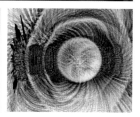

Art Directors	Creative Director	Design Agency	Planning Director
David Gamble	David Gamble	Saint @ RKCR	Mark Sng
Rodrigo Lebrun	**Digital Artist**	**Project Manager**	**Client**
Copywriters	Karsten Schmidt	Ellen Chng	Victoria & Albert
Jeeves Basu	**Programmer**	**Project Director**	Museum
Peter Brown	John Cleveley	Chris Jefford	**Brand**
Designers	**Flash Scripters**		Decode
Sharon Chong	Ali Kember		
Dave Price	Nick Watton		
Shaban Siddiq			

Integrated

Saint @ RKCR
for the Victoria & Albert Museum

Recode | Decode

Saint was asked by the Victoria & Albert Museum to promote Decode, the museum's first exhibition dedicated to digital art. Traditional art is normally created to affect you, while digital art is best when affected by you. We wanted this inclusive philosophy to extend beyond the exhibition, so we created an open-source campaign that encouraged people to recode Decode. We worked with digital artist Karsten Schmidt to create an interactive art application that invited people to create their own digital masterpieces. The best recodes were used to promote Decode in an integrated campaign that blurred the lines between product and promotion, and helped attract over 235% of original footfall targets.

Art Director
Marco Viganò
Copywriters
Dario Gargiulo
Cristiano Tonnarelli

Creative Directors
Bruno Bertelli
Cristiana Boccassini
Pietro Maestri
Advertising Agency
JWT Italia

Planner
Andrea Betti
Account Handler
Paola Natellis
Brand Manager
Dario Gargiulo

Marketing Manager
Gianluca Di Tondo
Client
Heineken Italia
Brand
Heineken

Integrated

JWT Italia
for Heineken Italia

Heineken Auditorium
Heineken's target market in Italy is young men aged 18 to 24. The older they grow, the less time they have to spend with friends drinking beer. To remind them of the importance of these moments, we arranged an event on the night of the UEFA Champions League Real Madrid vs AC Milan match. Our 200 accomplices (partners, colleagues) persuaded 1,000 AC Milan fans to sacrifice the game on TV for a fake classical concert. After 15 minutes we revealed it was a trick to let them enjoy the match on a big screen provided by Heineken. The event was watched live by 6.6 million people on Sky Sports, ten million on the TV news, and five million on the web.

Art Directors	Copywriters	Directors	Print Producer
Aaron Dietz	Rob Calabro	Will Hyde	Kim Miles
Christian Haas	Mandy Dietz	Jeffery Plansker	**Sound Designer**
Ricardo Ladim	Will Elliott	**Interactive**	Kristen Branch
Felipe Lima	Roger Hoard	**Producers**	**Production Company**
Jose Luis Martinez	Brian Thompson	Teymoor Ghashghai	Supply & Demand
Kristin Schlotterbeck	Franklin Tipton	Tena Goy	**Advertising Agency**
Paul Stechschulte	**Creative Director**	Margaret	Goodby, Silverstein
	Rich Silverstein	McLaughlin	& Partners
	Group Creative	**Agency Producer**	**Client**
	Directors	Rob Sondik	Sprint
	Christian Haas		
	Paul Stechschulte		
	Franklin Tipton		

Integrated

Goodby, Silverstein & Partners
for Sprint

The Now Network
We're fulfilling the original promise of the mobile phone – letting people connect wherever they are. Sprint provides the networks that allow you to make instant connections. Our brand is about people. It's about living right now and celebrating the vast array of life that you can connect with thanks to Sprint's technology. We renamed Sprint's network the Now Network. And set to work linking Sprint with all things now. Online, we designed the world's largest widget – a one-page snapshot of 'right this second'. Live feeds and real-time facts flooded the site, from babies being born to a live cam of Niagara Falls.

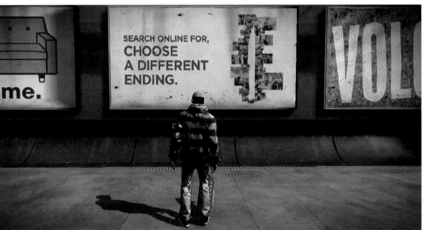

Art Director
Steve Jones
Copywriter
Martin Loraine
Creative Director
Paul Brazier
Creative Group Heads
Steve Jones
Martin Loraine

Director
Simon Ellis
Assistant Director
Stephanie Day
Producers
Jonas Blanchard
Pete Chambers
Stephanie Phillips
Tom White

Editor
Matthew Swanpoel
Production Company
Mad Cow Films
Advertising Agency
Abbott Mead
Vickers BBDO
Planner
Stephanie Phillips

Account Handlers
Richard Arscott
Claire Best
Adam Kennedy
Directorate of Public Affairs
Stephanie Day
Client
Metropolitan Police

Integrated

Abbott Mead Vickers BBDO
for the Metropolitan Police

Choose a Different Ending
London teenagers were carrying knives in the mistaken belief that they offered protection.
The Metropolitan Police wanted to communicate that the reverse was true. A series of films was created for YouTube using annotation technology, enabling viewers to choose what happened next. Carry a knife? Go to a party? Stab an opponent? After experiencing the consequences of their choices, viewers were invited to 'choose a different ending'. For the film, and for their life. In total there were 21 films and ten different endings. The response was 78% awareness, the highest ever for a Met campaign, and to date, 2,628,350 views.

269

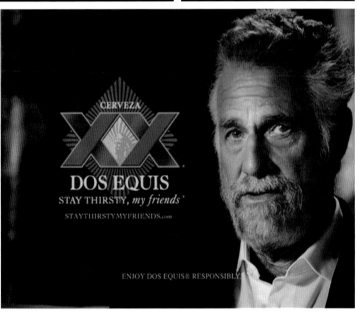 

Art Directors Karl Lieberman Stephen Petronis Bekky Pollack **Copywriters** Tim Atlinson Brandon Henderson Thom Woodley **Interactive Designer** Andrew Walko **Creative Directors** Dave Arnold Dave Weinstock	**Associate Creative Director** Andy Currie **Executive Creative Director** Jeff Kling **Chief Creative Officer** Conway Williamson **Director** Steve Miller **Agency Producers** Robert Cuff Dan Fried	**Executive Agency Producer** Joe Guyt **Technical Leads** Husani Oakley Zameer Rehmani **Programmer** Paul Denya **Flash Developer** Chlawel Chang **Advertising Agency** Euro RSCG New York **Account Director** Katy Milmoe	**Account Supervisor** Katie Pearson **Brand Manager** Paul Smalles **Global Chief Communications Officer** Mary Perhach **Vice President of Marketing** Kheri Holland Tillman	**Client** Heineken **Brand** Dos Equis	

Integrated

Euro RSCG New York
for Heineken

Dos Equis – The Most Interesting Man in the World
The star of this campaign for Dos Equis is the Most Interesting Man in the World, a grey-bearded man engaged in a series of adventurous pursuits like close-combat sparring and steering a motorboat full of beauty-pageant winners. 30-second TV slots presented a montage of his exotic adventures, while 15-second slots provided our audience with wit, wisdom and sage advice garnered from a life lived interestingly. The TV campaign was frequently refreshed to keep the audience engaged. Out-of-home advertising promoted overall brand awareness, and interactive advertising served as a central hub to build community, including a microsite developed to recruit an assistant.

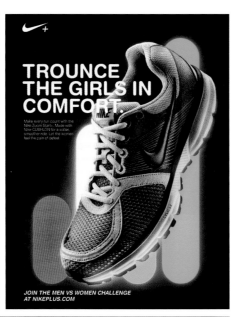

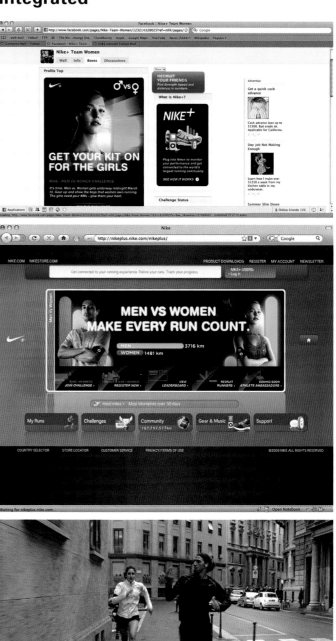

t Director	**Director**	**Print Producer**	**Account Handler**
yan Rowles	Tim Godsall	Sara Southworth	Evin Shutt
pywriter	**Producer**	**Production Company**	**Brand Manager**
son Norcross	Rick Jarjoura	Biscuit Filmworks	Marcella Fauci
oduct	**Agency Producer**	**Advertising Agency**	**Marketing Manager**
otographer	Angelo Ferrugia	72andSunny	Enrico Balleri
ns Pieterse	**Editor**	**Digital Agency**	**Client**
e Action	Robert Duffy	AKQA London	Nike EMEA
otographer	**Sound Designer**	**Planner**	**Brand**
dav Kander	Rohan Young	Alex Schneider	Nike+
eative Directors	**Art Producer**		
hn Boiler	Rob Beckon		
enn Cole			

Integrated

72andSunny
for Nike EMEA

Men vs Women
Our job for Nike was to re-energise and expand the Nike+ community, by recruiting 'emerging runners' in their early twenties, particularly women, to Nike+. To do this, we tapped into the oldest and most heated rivalry of all time. (Note: 'Challenges' is the most popular user feature on the Nike+ website).

271

Senior Art Director Ben Smith **Senior Copywriter** Ben Akers **Web Copywriter** Brendan Winter **Executive Creative Director** David Nobay **Director** Trent O'Donnel	**Digital Director** Brett Mitchell **Producer** Chloe Rickard **Agency Producer** Allison Chambers **Editor** Paul Swain **Web Editor** Marcus Johnston	**Production Company** Jungle Boys **Digital Production House** Future Buro **Advertising Agency** Droga5 Australia **Executive Planning Director** Sudeep Gohil	**Account Director** Nicolas Kettelhake **Brand Manager** Dave Cain **Marketing Manager** Jaclyn Lee-Joe **Client** Virgin Mobile Australia

Integrated

Droga5 Australia
for Virgin Mobile Australia

Right Music Wrongs
The challenge was to reconnect Virgin Mobile with its musical heritage. Our solution: Create an online debate on what good (and bad) music really is. And so rightmusicwrongs.org was born. Using Vanilla Ice as our provocateur, we put him on trial. Found innocent: He'll be allowed to play the V Festival. Found guilty: He'll get pelted with tomatoes. Hence he said: 'Sorry.' (He's now due to play Glastonbury – so maybe we should say, 'Sorry').

Art Directors	**Executive Creative Director**	**Lighting Cameraperson**	**Group Business Director**
Luisa Payne	Grant Rutherford	Martin Smith	Oliver Lynch
Grant Rutherford	**Design Director**	**Sound Designer**	**Brand Manager**
Copywriters	Fred Haas	Colin Simkins	Tanya Podlena
Lin McKeown	**Director**	**Production Company**	**Marketing Manager**
Grant Rutherford	Paul Baiguerra	PABA Media	Alex D'Amico
Designer	**Producer**	**Advertising Agency**	**Client**
Luisa Payne	Kylie Vowles	DDB Melbourne	Foster's Group
Creative Directors	**Agency Producer**	**Planner**	**Brand**
Jack Cummins	Carol Sinclair	Ian Forth	Fifth Leg
Fred Haas	**Editor**	**Account Handler**	
Lin McKeown	Damian Dunne	Justin Arnold	

Integrated

DDB Melbourne
for Foster's Group

Operation Kerplonk
To help Fifth Leg stand out in the sometimes stuffy and serious wine category, we positioned it as a quality wine with a sense of humour. This led to a tongue-in-cheek, government style amnesty to rid Australia of inferior wine once and for all. The campaign culminated in a national day of action, where all Australian wine drinkers were asked to dispose of their inferior wine at designated drop zones in return for a quality bottle of Fifth Leg. The campaign was delivered via online, viral, radio, print, poster, outdoor, direct mail, and social media.

273

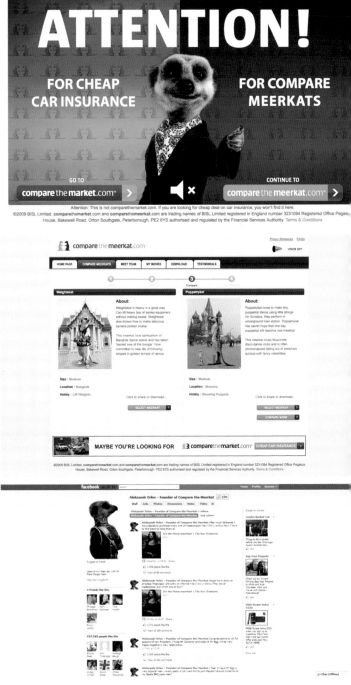

Art Director
Clement Woodward
Copywriter
Richard Connell
Designer
Neil Riley
Creative Directors
Darren Bailes
Steve Vranakis

Director
Darren Walsh
Producer
Russell McLean
Agency Producers
Olly Calverley
Carly Parris
Lighting
Cameraperson
Olivier Cariou

Sound Designer
Stuart Welch
Production Company
Passion Pictures
Advertising Agency
VCCP
Editing
Passion Pictures
Planner
George Everett

Account Handler
Cliff Hall
Brand Manager
Mark Vile
Marketing Managers
Louise Marshall
Josephine Wilkinson
Client
comparethemarket.com

Integrated

VCCP
for comparethemarket.com

comparethemeerkat.com
How do you get people to remember a long, generic brand name? We created Aleksandr Orlov, a wealthy Russian meerkat and owner of website comparethemeerkat.com. Frustrated by people mistaking his site for comparethemarket.com, Aleksandr launched a multi-faceted campaign to clear up the confusion. TV and radio ads drove intrigued users to his website where they could compare meerkats or click through to comparethemarket.com. Aleksandr also had conversations with fans on Facebook and Twitter, offering insights into his world and problem, and bespoke content. In a category traditionally dominated by rational, insistent messaging, Aleksandr proved a welcome relief.

**ask richard:
branson blogs
about fbi**

A$K Richard!!! Get Richard
Branson's attention, get him to give
FBi One Million Bucks & You'll get 50
Grand! Genius!

Share and Enjoy.

pages

ask richard - cannes entry 2010
dear richard - an open letter
things we like about richard
about fbi
download
faaaaaqs
get your ask richard tshirt

categories

all entries
all news

Designers
Lionel Alphonse
Jack Sommer
**Executive Ideas
Director**
Paul Swann

Advertising Agency
Naked
Communications
Sydney
Planning Partner
Adam Ferrier

General Manager
Evan Kaldor
Station Director
Meagan Loader
PR Director
Myfanwy McGregor

**Communications
Strategist**
Glen Cassidy
Client
FBi Radio

Integrated

Naked Communications Sydney
for FBi Radio

Ask Richard
FBi is an iconic independent Australian radio station. As a result of the global financial crisis, it was in serious trouble and needed over $500,000 to avoid a major restructuring. We had a $0 budget to raise the money. Previous fundraising efforts had only ever raised around $80,000. We turned the fundraising model on its head, encouraging all supporters to ask just one music loving billionaire for the money. The idea was simple: ask Richard Branson for $1million in the most creative way possible and win $50,000 if you get his attention. After hundreds of attention grabbing stunts, plus PR activity, Branson responded. The sum of $680,000 was raised and we saved FBi!

275

Art Directors
Ana Balarin
Hermeti Balarin
Copywriters
Borja Alvarez
Ana Balarin
Hermeti Balarin
John Cherry
Paddy Fraser
Enrique Reija

Creative Directors
Robert Saville
Gustavo Sousa
Mark Waites
Director
Agustin Alberdi
Producer
Richard Fenton

Agency Producer
Juliet Pearson
Assistant Agency
Producer
Kirsten Kates
Production Company
Stink Productions
Advertising Agency
Mother London

Digital Agency
POKE London
Client
Anheuser-Busch
InBev
Brand
Stella Artois

Integrated

Mother London
for Anheuser-Busch InBev

Le Recyclage de Luxe

Le Recyclage de Luxe showcased Stella Artois' efforts to be eco, yet chic. Hosted by Alain du Monde, father of the Recyclage de Luxe movement, the show consisted of nine episodes in which Alain, his robot butler and exclusive guests, proved being green and stylish were not incompatible. Aired live on Le Toube, a 60s YouTube channel, the show was supported by a variety of other media: newspaper wraps, Spotify takeovers, window installations, even an online film festival. The campaign began by sending 300 bloggers luxurious three-course TV dinners. To date the shows' segments have received over 1.5 million views.

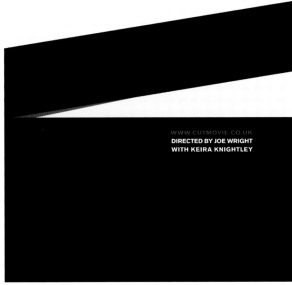

WWW.CUTMOVIE.CO.UK
DIRECTED BY JOE WRIGHT
WITH KEIRA KNIGHTLEY

Art Directors	**Director**	**Editor**	**Advertising Agency**
Tommy Blom	Joe Wright	Paul Tothill	Grey London
Jonathan Marlow	**Producer**	**Sound Designer**	**Account Executive**
Copywriters	Jane Fraser	Craig Berkey	Lisa Buckley
Tommy Blom	**Executive Producer**	**Cinematographer**	**Client Chief**
Jonathan Marlow	Dominic Delaney	Shamus McGarvey	**Executive Officer**
Creative Director	**Agency Producer**	**Visual Effects**	Nicola Harwin
Andy Amadeo	James Covill	Emily Irvine	**Client**
Chief Creative	**Digital Producer**	**Production Company**	Women's Aid
Officer	Tyrone Hannick	Dab Hand Media	
Jon Williams			

Integrated

Grey London
for Women's Aid

Cut

Women's Aid could have continued to accept the help of celebrities to champion its cause and lend their endorsement. Instead, we focused on the power of celebrity, not the individual. This insight into how to use celebrity vastly amplified the value they could bring to the charity by subverting our national obsession with celebrities. Women's Aid has shown that domestic violence can happen to any woman by releasing a movie where Keira Knightley is featured as a victim.

Art Directors
Johan Baettig
Rodrigo Saavedra
Copywriters
John Cherry
Lars Holthe
Illustrator
Robert McGinnis
Creative Directors
Robert Saville
Augusto Sola
Gustavo Sousa
Mark Waites

Directors
Agustin Alberdi
Fredrick Bond
Ringan Ledwidge
Agency Producer
Richard Firminger
Editor
Rich Orrick
Lighting
Camerapersons
Ray Coates
Crille Forsberg
Javier Julia

Sound Designers
James Lyme
Anthony Moore
Production
Companies
Landia
Rattling Stick
Sonny London
Transparent
Advertising Agency
Mother London

Digital Agency
POKE London
Client
Anheuser-Busch
InBev
Brand
Stella Artois 4%

Integrated

Mother London
for Anheuser-Busch InBev

La Nouvelle Smooth 4%
Stella Artois 4% was aimed at a younger, more mainstream audience than previously. It was therefore necessary to move from the 'rural village' setting of past ads to a new world that would appeal to these drinkers. The 60s French Riviera, with its smooth characters, was perfect for the smooth 4% lager, retaining the brand's association with European film while updating it for a modern audience. It became the setting for hand painted posters, period smooth escapade ads and the smooth originals web films – 60s European films Hollywood have since copied. 'La Nouvelle Smooth 4%' campaign smashed all launch targets and turned a product benefit – smoothness – into a new brand world.

278

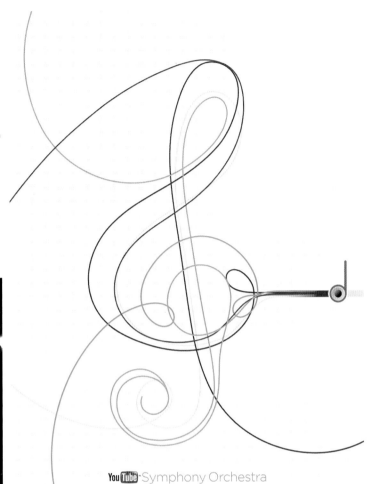

Production Company	Advertising Agency	Client	Brand
Google Creative Lab	Google Creative Lab	Google	YouTube

Google Creative Lab
for Google

YouTube Symphony Orchestra
The YouTube Symphony Orchestra brought together musicians from around the globe, who competed for the chance to play at Carnegie Hall in New York City. Over 3,000 YouTube audition videos led to 96 finalists from over 70 countries. The event attracted three times as much press coverage as any event in Carnegie Hall's history. It generated 66 million channel and video views on YouTube. But most importantly, it shed light on the quality content and passionate communities that make up the YouTube brand.

BEFORE YOU TEXT, GIVE IT A PONDER.™

THIS RUMOR COULD
GET ME IN TROUBLE.
REAL TROUBLE TOO,
NOT SEXY PILLOW FIGHT TROUBLE.

giveitaponder.com LG

GIVEITAPONDER.COM LG

Art Directors	Computer Graphics Artist	Group Technical Director	Flash Developer	Digital Agency
Evan Benedetto	Kevin Ives	Martin Coady	Marc Brown	VML
Jeff Blouin	**Creative Directors**	**Assistant Producer**	**Application**	**Account Handlers**
Alexander Nowak	Darren Moran	Tamara Lecker	**Developers**	Alex Sloane
Copywriters	Ian Reichenthal	**Agency Producers**	Juliene Dufrenne	Brent Trimble
John Battle	Scott Vitrone	Nathy Aviram	Matt Grippo	Katherine Youtos
Brandon Henderson	Mike Wente	Alex Gianni	Art Shectman	**Client**
Jan Jaworski	**Director**	Lora Schulson	**Production Company**	LG
Tara Lawall	Ulf Johansson	**Editor**	Smith and Jones	**Brand**
Felix Richter		Carlos Arias	Films	LG Mobile
			Advertising Agency	
			Y&R New York	

Integrated

Y&R New York
for LG

Give it a Ponder
Mobile harassment is a serious and growing problem among teenagers, with millions of mean texts and inappropriate photos sent every day. To address this problem, we created an integrated campaign that asked teens to stop and 'give it a ponder' before texting. The campaign came to life with the help of James Lipton and the iconic motion of stroking one's beard while thinking, or pondering. The effort was seen online, on television, in cinemas, on posters and in a first-of-its-kind video chat plug-in that allowed users to grow a beard in real time.

Art Director
Rick Dodds
Copywriter
Stephen Howell
Creative Directors
Paul Silburn
Kate Stanners
Director
Michael Gracey
Producer
Russell Curtis
Agency Producer
Ed Sayers

Second Unit Agency Producer
Jirka Mika
Production Manager
Emma Wolanski
Editors
Ben Harrex
Diesel Schwarze
Lighting Cameraperson
Tim Maurice Jones

Production Company
Partizan
Advertising Agency
Saatchi & Saatchi
London
Post Production
The Mill
Sound Design
750mph
Planners
Gareth Ellis
Jason Lonsdale

Account Handler
Sarah Galea
Brand Managers
Kelly Engstrom
Sam Taylor
Marketing Manager
Lysa Hardy
Business Leader
Sally Beerworth
Client
T-Mobile

Integrated

Saatchi & Saatchi London
for T-Mobile

Life's for Sharing
To prove T-Mobile's new philosophy, 'Life's for sharing', we decided to create events so memorable that people would feel compelled to share them. The campaign started in January with a live choreographed dance at Liverpool Street station, with hundreds of unsuspecting members of the public spontaneously joining in. The public were then invited to the second event via Twitter, Facebook and texts. 13,500 people turned up without knowing what to expect. Microphones were handed out before revealing it would be a mass karaoke. The events aired in full length commercial breaks and were simultaneously launched on T-Mobile's YouTube channel, receiving over 30 million hits.

281

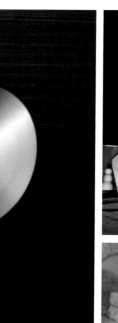

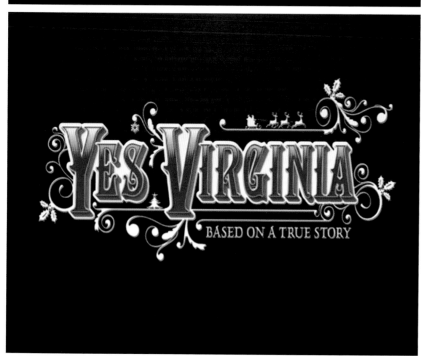

Art Director	**Director**	**Director of**	**Advertising Agency**
Jim Wood	Pete Circuitt	**Integrated**	JWT New York
Copywriter	**Producers**	**Production**	**Account Director**
Chris Plehal	Kallan Kagan	Clair Grupp	Helena Touseull
Creative Director	Kate Schwerin	**Editor**	**Global Account**
Matt MacDonald	**Executive Producers**	Matt Ahrens	**Director**
Executive Creative	Dexton Deboree	**Sound Designer**	Beth Waxman-Arteta
Director	Mick Ebeling	John Bowen	**Director of Brand**
Wayne Best	Robin Feldman	**Music Producer**	**Production**
Chief Creative	Joe Fezcko	Nicholas Hooper	Joe Calabrese
Officers	**Consulting Producer**	**Production Company**	**Client**
Harvey Marco	Betsy Spence	The Ebeling Group	Macy's
Ty Montague			

Integrated

JWT New York
for Macy's

Yes, Virginia

'Yes, Virginia' is a 30-minute animated Christmas special that was pitched and sold to CBS, premiered in prime time, and received glowing reviews. But unlike traditional shows, it was actually produced by an ad agency for Macy's, as part of the brand's holiday campaign 'Believe'. Based on actual events, the story took place in New York in 1897, when a little girl named Virginia went looking for the truth about Santa. Like the Macy's Thanksgiving Day Parade, we crafted the show to be a perennial classic. To quote USA Today: 'Like Santa himself, Virginia should be a welcome Christmas visitor for years to come'.

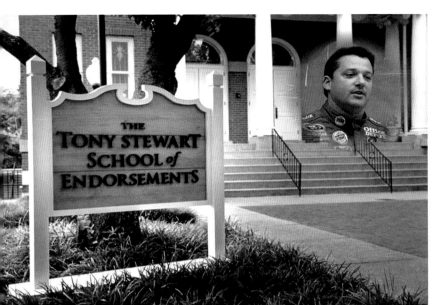

Art Director
Kat Lam
Copywriters
John Benedict
Ryan Raab
Anna Kate Roche
Ryan Wagman
Designers
Matt Schreiber
Kelly Wengert
Creative Directors
James
Dawson-Hollis
Bill Wright

Design Director
Pelun Chen
Chief Creative Officers
Jeff Benjamin
Andrew Keller
Rob Reilly
Director
Guy Manwaring
Producer
Kerstin Emhoff

Agency Producers
Sarah Bagwell
Chad Hopenwasser
Scott Potter
Julie Rousseau
Madison Wharton
Editor
Dan Aronin
Lighting Cameraperson
Jason Leiva

Production Company
Prettybird Los Angeles
Advertising Agency
Crispin Porter + Bogusky
Marketing Manager
Claudia Lezcano
Client
Burger King

Integrated

Crispin Porter + Bogusky
for Burger King

Tony Stewart
Celebrity endorsements. An advertising staple since forever. But do stars really use products they pitch, or are they in it for the money? When Burger King signed NASCAR champion Tony Stewart to endorse the Whopper, they decided to put him to the test. A polygraph test. Featuring shameless shills Carrot Top and Erik Estrada, TV, radio and online ads sowed the seeds for the moment of truth: a live web event with Tony hooked up to a lie detector to answer the cynics. Could Burger King prove Tony really ate – maybe even loved – the Whopper? You better believe it.

Art Directors	Chief Creative	Producer	Production Company
David Brown	Officers	Lisa Rich	Smuggler
DJ Pierce	Jeff Benjamin	**Agency Producer**	Productions
Copywriters	Andrew Kellerr	Brenda Fogg	**Advertising Agency**
Justin Ebert	Rob Reilly	**Editor**	Crispin Porter +
David Littlejohn	**Associate Creative**	Lucas Spaulding	Bogusky
Thomas Pettus	**Directors**	**Lighting**	**Marketing Manager**
Creative Director	Justin Ebert	**Cameraperson**	Jackie Duffus
Evan Fry	DJ Pierce	Marcelo Durst	**Client**
	Director		Best Buy
	Henry-Alex Rubin		

Integrated

Crispin Porter + Bogusky
for Best Buy

Back to School
The back-to-school season is a nutty time for any retailer. But especially for Best Buy. Problem is, if they don't come into the store, Best Buy can't help them. So to extend the knowledge of their expert Geeks and Blue Shirts beyond their walls, Best Buy created the Twelpforce. A digitised army of Best Buy employees available 24/7 on Twitter. Anyone with a question can just tweet @twelpforce and over 2,000 tech gurus race to give the fastest and best answer. It's a helpful tool that proves Best Buy employees don't just know tech – they live it.

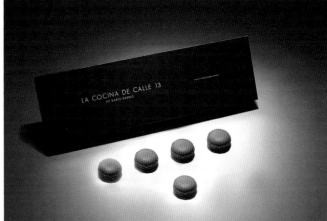

Art Directors
Carlos Álvarez
Emilia Bértola
Pablo González de
la Peña
**Direct Marketing
Art Director**
Celia Martínez
Event Art Directors
David Rigote
Victor Vazquez

Copywriters
Covadonga Diaz
Carlos Gómez
Emilio Holguin
Carlos Janini
Photographer
Francesc Guillamet
Creative Director
Pablo González de
la Peña
**Direct Marketing
Creative Director**
Álvaro González

**Executive Creative
Director**
Juan Silva
**General Creative
Director**
Juan Nonzioli
**Event Creative
Supervisor**
Borja de la Rocha
Event Producers
Maria Algaba
Carmen Murillo

Advertising Agency
Shackleton
Account Supervisor
Zaida Vázquez
**PR Account
Supervisor**
Eva Leoz
**PR Account
Executive**
Lara Garcia
General Manager
Marta Gutiérrez

Chef
Dario Barrio
Marketing Manager
Silvano Guillamet
Clients
Calle 13
NBC Universal
Brand
Calle 13

Integrated

Shackleton
for Calle 13

The 13th Street Cuisine
Calle 13, the suspense and action TV channel, was celebrating its tenth anniversary. It had to be celebrated in a way that was a wink to its regular viewers, and, at the same time, attracted other fans of suspense and action. And so the 13th Street Cuisine was born: a restaurant open to the public for a month, in which the famous chef Dario Barrio together with the agency's team created a menu full of irony that reflected the channel's theme of suspense and action. The 13th Street Cuisine was an integrated campaign: an experience, media content, a source of income, and a choice of gastronomic leisure.

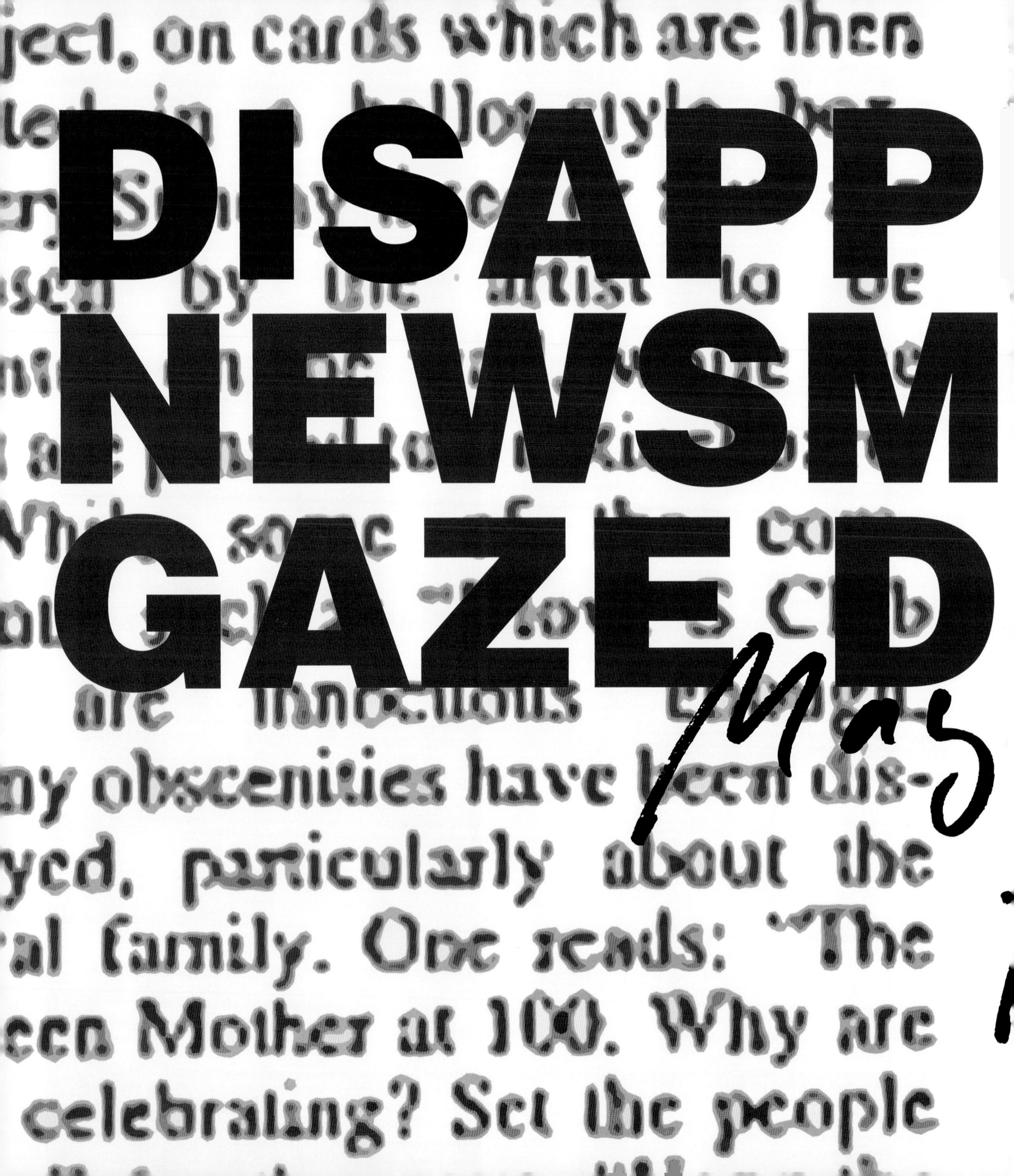

DISAPP
NEWSM
GAZED *Mag*

ject, on cards which are then

hello-style her

by the artist to be

which some of the

are innocuous

ny obscenities have been dis-

yed, particularly about the

al family. One reads: "The

een Mother at 100. Why are

celebrating? Set the people

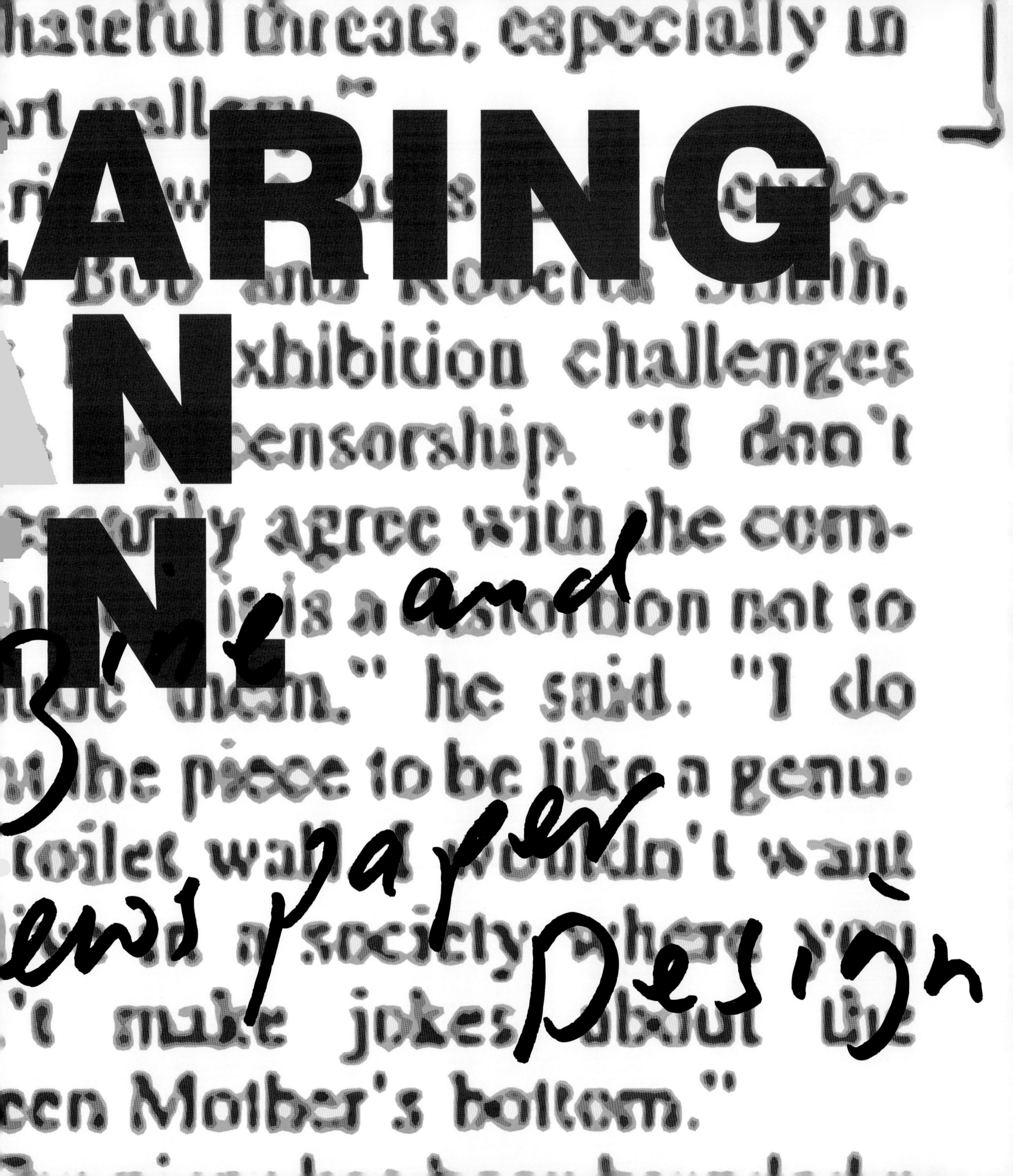

ARING
N
N

and

3mt

ews paper

Design

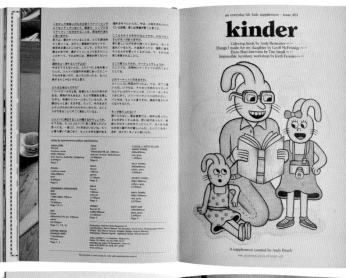

Art Director
Omar Sosa
Creative Directors
Nacho Alegre
Omar Sosa
Marco Velardi

Publishers
Apartamento
Magazine

Editor in Chief
Marco Velardi
Chief Operations Officer
Victor Abellan

Client
Apartamento

▲ Entire Magazines

Apartamento Magazine

Apartamento
Apartamento was launched in April 2008 as a biannual everyday life interiors magazine interested in homes, living spaces and design solutions as opposed to houses, photo-ops and design dictatorships. Since its launch, Apartamento has been a place in print for people, not just objects, as it understands interior design as a means of personal expression. Featuring the homes and lives of creative people from all over the world with a fresh and simply crafted aesthetic, in a time where the velocity of the digital era threatens to overtake us, Apartamento pays tribute to the simple and real things in life.

288

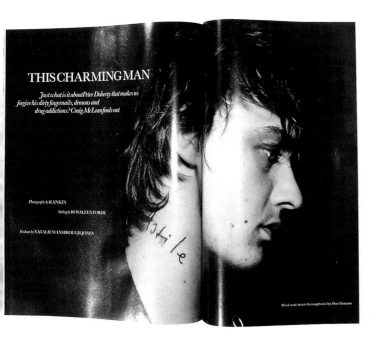

Deputy Art Director	**Designer**	**Illustrator**	**Image Manipulator**
om Meredith	Elizabeth Villabona	Pete Doherty	Noel Allen
Associate Art	**Design Director**	**Photographer**	**Editor in Chief**
Director	Tom Meredith	Rankin	Lorraine Candy
o Goodby	**Creative Director**	**Picture Editor**	**Client**
	Marissa Bourke	Hannah Ridley	ELLE
		Publishing House	
		Hachette Filipacchi	
		Publishing	

Entire Magazines

ELLE

ELLE October 2009 Issue – Lily Allen
To celebrate 25 years of London Fashion Week, ELLE chose British singer Lily Allen as its cover star. Lily has graced countless covers in recent years, so we gave her an ELLE twist in the form of a chopped blonde wig, messy make-up and – in a magazine first – specially commissioned artwork by fellow influential Brit, Pete Doherty. Doherty's poetic lyricism perfectly complements the bold, graphic photograph, used in an unusually tight crop. His inky scrawls mirror Allen's glossy black eyes and contrast with the stark peroxide hair. The magazine's front cover was also selected in the Magazine & Newspaper Design/Front Covers category.

Süddeutsche Zeitung Magazin

Nummer 16   17. April 2009

Sü deutsche Zeit ng Magazin

Sü de ts he Zeit ng Magazin

Sü de ts he eit ng Maga in

Sü de ts e eit ng M ga in

S de ts e eit ng M g in

S de s e ei n M g in

S de s e i n g in

de s i n g in

de s i g n

weniger ist mehr

Es wird Zeit, dass Gestalter und Architekten sich wieder auf das Wesentliche besinnen und den Menschen ins Zentrum ihrer Arbeit stellen. Zum 90. Jahrestag der Bauhaus-Gründung: ein Heft über die ethische Verantwortung des Designs

Art Directors
Daniel Bognar
Marcus Feil
Creative Directors
Alexander Bartel
Zeljko Pezely

Copywriters
Max Fellmann
Christina Meister
Advertising Agency
Heye Group
Account Handlers
Julia Munichhausen
Christian Scharrel

Marketing Manager
Rudolf Spindler
Client
Magazin
Verlagsgesellschaft
Süddeutsche Zeitung

Brand
Süddeutsche Zeitung
Magazin

Magazine Front Covers

Heye Group
for Süddeutsche Zeitung

Designtitle
The creative challenge was to draw attention to the magazine issue commemorating the 90th anniversary of Bauhaus; an issue about design's ethical responsibility. Our task was to create a magazine cover reflecting the central theme, that today's design must go back to focusing on the basics. Our target audience were readers of the Süddeutsche Zeitung Magazin, a weekly magazine supplement from the reputable German daily, the Süddeutsche Zeitung. Less is more – it's time for designers and architects to devote more attention to the basics again, and to make people the focal point of their work.

290

Magazine Front Covers

The New Yorker

Unmasked
Chris Ware is one of today's most respected graphic novelists. His work has received literary prizes and has been the subject of numerous museum shows. In Unmasked, published for Halloween, Ware depicts worlds in collision with his trademark concision. A cloud of white dots on the left are the faces of children, radiating eagerness and expectation; white dots on the right are the faces of their waiting parents, lit by the handhelds in which they are absorbed.

Art Director	Illustrator	Editor in Chief	Client
Françoise Mouly	Chris Ware	David Remnick	The New Yorker

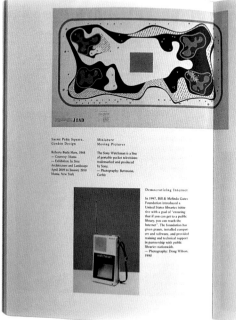

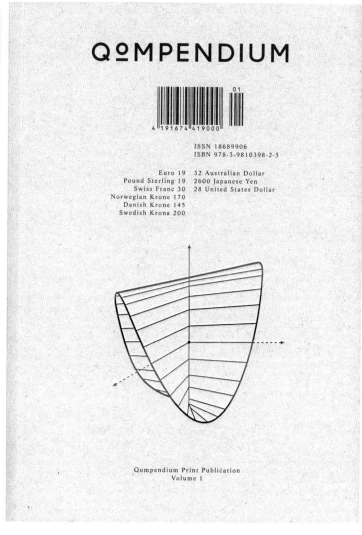

Art Directors	Creative Director	Typographer	Client
Kimberly Lloyd	Kimberly Lloyd	Johannes Spitzer	Lloyd & Associates
Johannes Spitzer	**Publishers**	**Editor in Chief**	**Brand**
Design Director	Lloyd & Associates	Kimberly Lloyd	Qompendium
Johannes Spitzer	**Illustrator**	**Marketing Manager**	
	Kimberly Lloyd	Kimberly Lloyd	

Entire Magazines

Lloyd & Associates
for Qompendium

Qompendium Print Publication

Qompendium Print Publication is a selective journey through the multiverse of intentional and unintentional time capsules, featuring an array of exceptional pictorial essays, unabridged interviews and supplementary brand editorials. With a name derived from the Latin 'compendium', this publication offers a summary of subjects from the fields of philosophy, art, culture and science. Qompendium is designed for lovers of natural curiosity and rational amusement with a keen eye for photography, delicate graphic design, typography and in-depth discussions of metaphysical issues. Qompendium is a well-curated, timeless, highly collectable book-like read for the disillusioned rational yet aesthetically intrigued fountainhead.

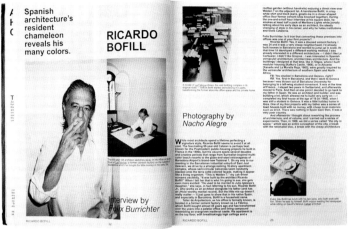

Graphic Designer
Dylan Fracareta
Creative Director
Felix Burrichter

Publishers
FEBU Publishing
Editor in Chief
Felix Burrichter

Editor at Large
Pierre Alexandre
de Looz

Client
FEBU Publishing

Entire Magazines

FEBU Publishing

PIN-UP: Issues 6 (Spring/Summer 09) & 7 (Fall/Winter 09/10)
Though architecture and design continue to generate more and more cultural heat, magazines that cover these fields can often leave you cold. Since its successful launch in autumn 2006, PIN-UP has been shaking up the genre with smart, in-depth, and candid interviews with leading personalities from the worlds of architecture, art, design and fashion, as well as thought-provoking essays, and shoots by leading photographers. All without ever taking itself too seriously. In short, PIN-UP is pure architectural entertainment.

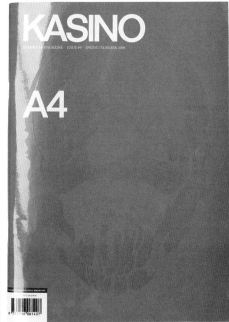

Art Director
Pekka Toivonen
Creative Director
Pekka Toivonen
Director of Photography
Jussi Puikkonen

Creative Studio
Kasino Creative Studio
Editor
Jonathan Mander

Communications Manager
Antti Routto

Client
Kasino Creative Studio
Brand
Kasino A4

▲ Entire Magazines

Kasino Creative Studio

Kasino A4 Magazine: Issues 9 & 10
Kasino A4 Magazine, aka the most melancholic magazine, was launched in 2005. 2009 was its final year, and the year was split into comedy and tragedy. The magazine's take on comedy was presented in its ninth issue, the ABC Issue. It was a celebration of these three things: absurd; black and white; and comedy. Tragedy followed in the autumn with issue number ten, the Deadline Issue, being all about the end. The magazine's introduction promised 'the most fun funeral you will ever attend', and the final issue was characterised not only by its trademark melancholy, but also an expectant mood: all ends are new beginnings.

294

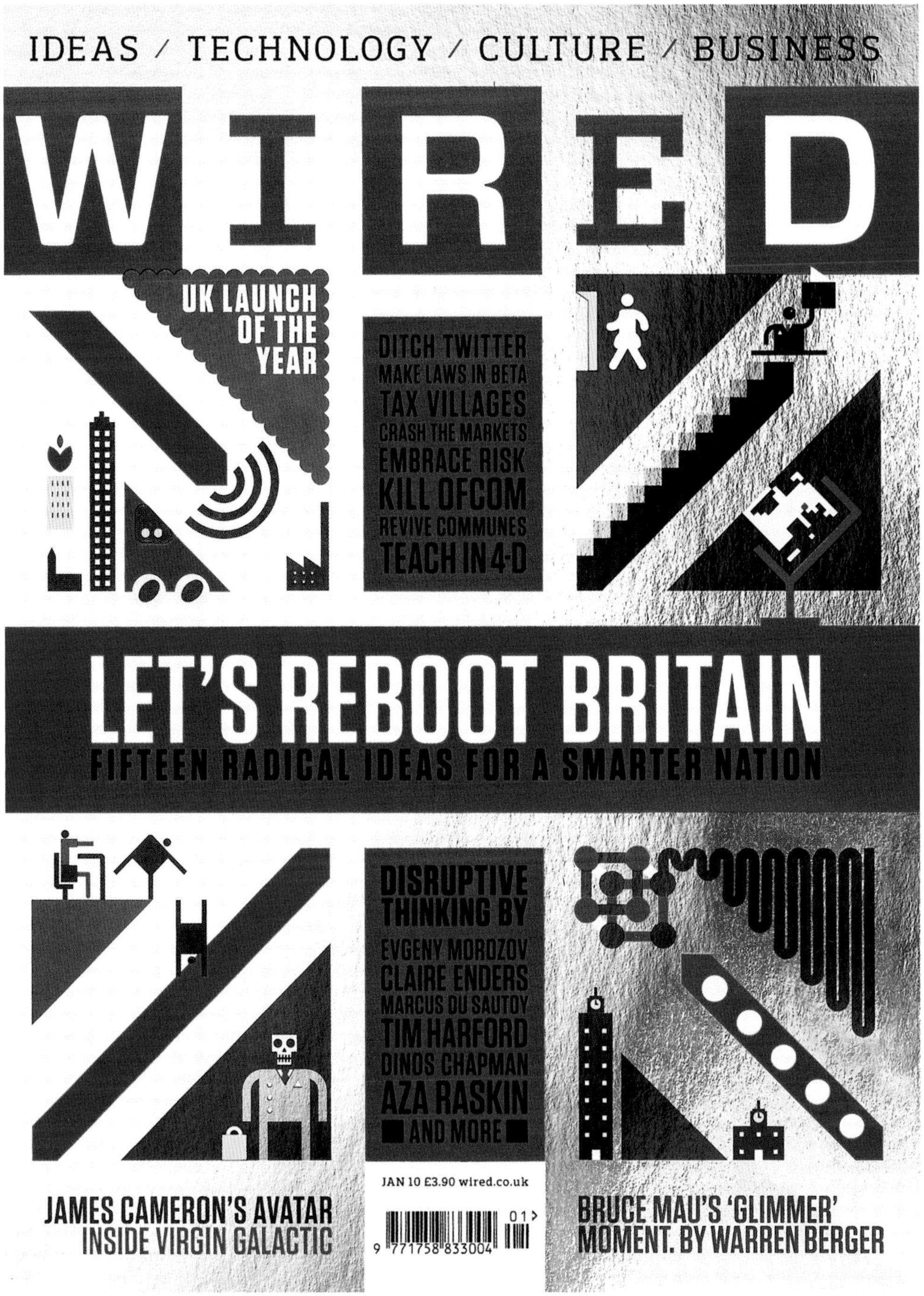

IDEAS / TECHNOLOGY / CULTURE / BUSINESS

WIRED

UK LAUNCH OF THE YEAR

DITCH TWITTER
MAKE LAWS IN BETA
TAX VILLAGES
CRASH THE MARKETS
EMBRACE RISK
KILL OFCOM
REVIVE COMMUNES
TEACH IN 4-D

LET'S REBOOT BRITAIN
FIFTEEN RADICAL IDEAS FOR A SMARTER NATION

DISRUPTIVE THINKING BY
EVGENY MOROZOV
CLAIRE ENDERS
MARCUS DU SAUTOY
TIM HARFORD
DINOS CHAPMAN
AZA RASKIN
■ AND MORE ■

JAN 10 £3.90 wired.co.uk

JAMES CAMERON'S AVATAR
INSIDE VIRGIN GALACTIC

BRUCE MAU'S 'GLIMMER' MOMENT. BY WARREN BERGER

9 771758 833004 01 >

Art Director
Andrew Diprose

Illustrator
Peter Grundy
Editor
David Rowan

Client
Condé Nast
Publications

Brand
Wired Magazine

Magazine Front Covers
Wired Magazine

Wired 01.10
Let's Reboot Britain. Wired magazine cover for January 2010. Seven colours on 415 micron silver mirri board.

Art Director
Cecilia Lindgren
Designer
Heather Bowen
Creative Director
Violetta Boxill

Publishers
EMAP
Typographers
Violetta Boxill
Cecilia Lindgren

Photographer
Rainer Viertlböck
Design Group
Alexander Boxill
Editor in Chief
Kieran Long

Marketing Manager
Steve Budd
Client
EMAP
Brand
The Architectural
Review

Magazine Front Covers
Alexander Boxill
for EMAP

The Architectural Review July Issue
Founded in 1896, The Architectural Review (AR) is a monthly magazine that presents a thoughtful, critical and at times provocative vision of contemporary global architecture. To honour this tremendous legacy, the redesign journey started by looking back through the AR's archive. Boxill and Lindgren chose to reconfigure one of its original mastheads, embracing the past but introducing a new contemporary slant by rendering the letterforms as a merged unit. The decision to use an extreme exterior crop of the Museum Brandhorst in Germany elevates the detail and colour used in the building's beautiful skin, producing an abstract multi-coloured surface.

Art Director
Katja Kollmann
Creative Director
Mirko Borsche

Illustrator
Sarah Illenberger
Photographer
Joachim Baldauf

Image Manipulator
Gal Schaeper
Picture Editor
Michael Biedowicz
Editor in Chief
Christoph Amend

Client
DIE ZEIT
Brand
ZEITmagazin

Magazine Front Covers

ZEITmagazin

Zu Viel Des Guten
The cover visualises 'too much' make-up. One of ZEITmagazin's unique features is its 'double cover': two consecutive cover pages that correspond with each other in a new way every week. The painted cover was printed on page 1 of the magazine and the other on page 3.

Designer
Chris Dixon
Illustrator
Michael De Feo

Publisher
Larry Burstein
Typographer
Michael De Feo

Photographer
Mitchell Funk
**Photography
Director**
Jody Quon

Photo Editor
Caroline Smith
Editor in Chief
Adam Moss
Client
New York Magazine

Magazine Front Covers
New York Magazine

Reasons to Love New York
Our fifth annual 'Reasons to Love' issue demanded a cover that visually summed up the love
New Yorkers have for their city. We used an image of a little girl in a red jacket serenely walking
through the park, reminding our readers of great moments in the city, and also providing an
introduction to the issue. In addition, we commissioned Michael De Feo to hand draw the type
for the cover, giving the issue a more personal, intimate appearance.

New York

MAY 25, 2009

THE
Also in the issue: David Geffen and the New York *Times.* p 10 And: Boozetown: A

ATTENTION
drunken guide to the city's finest watering holes. p 15 As well as: Why Democrats

Crisis—
can't get any love in this town. p 25 Plus: Was Francis Bacon really any good? p 40

And Why
And: Mandy Moore! p 52 And: Robert De Niro! p 52 And: Adrien Brody! p 14

DISTRACTION
Including: The controversial dream of a car-free city. p 34 Not to mention:

May
Twitter spam: a New Brunswick punk-rock group called Screaming Females;

Actually
free bikes; free haircuts; a new Austrian three-star restaurant; the culpability

Be Good For
of Madoff victims; the latest on the mess at ground zero; and much more...

You.
BY SAM ANDERSON

esigner
hris Dixon

Publisher
Larry Burstein

Editor in Chief
Adam Moss

Client
New York Magazine

Magazine Front Covers
New York Magazine

Attention Disorder
The cover story for this issue was about Attention Deficit Disorder and distraction. We used a variety of typefaces for the main headline, and wove the secondary headlines in between each line to visually create a distracting experience.

Art Director
Françoise Mouly

Illustrators
Daniel Clowes
Zohar Lazar
Mark Ulriksen

Editor in Chief
David Remnick

Client
The New Yorker

Magazine Front Covers
The New Yorker

The Food Chain
For our money issue, we had the opportunity to capture the spirit of the times with a story in three parts by three different artists. The series of three covers was entitled 'The Food Chain'. The first cover, by Daniel Clowes, depicts a bejewelled lady puzzling over the choices at a fast food restaurant. In Zohar Lazar's cover, she's headed to her limo with her food and servants. But the reader who may initially have felt sorry for the lady is in for a surprise; when turning to the last cover, by Mark Ulriksen, we see the lady at home feeding her dog the meal.

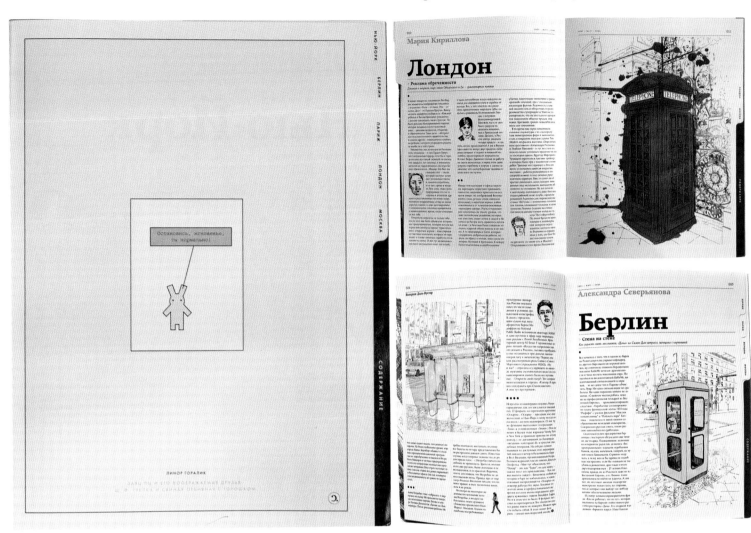

Art Director
Ilya Baranov
Designers
Anton Ioukhnovets
Aleksandra
Kuznetsova
Olga Pogorelova

Illustrator
Aleksandra
Kuznetsova
Cover Illustrator
Linor Goralik

Image Manipulator
Snezhanna
Sukhotskaya
Editor in Chief
Vladimir Yakovlev
**Deputy Editor
in Chief**
Masha Gessen

Client
Snob Media
Brand
Snob

Magazine Sections

Snob

Geocolumns Section of Snob Magazine
The Geocolumns section of Snob Magazine is a set of monthly essays about city life in London, Moscow, New York, Paris and Berlin. In these cities, Russian presence is strong and vivid, and the magazine's target audience (highly educated, well-to-do, Russian-speaking) plays a significant role. These essays are illustrated with graphic sketches and printed on a bulk offset paper with a newspaper-like look and feel. The section has a die-cut index listing all the cities reviewed, providing readers with easy navigation and access.

Furchtbar komisch

Bei der alemannischen Fasnacht in Schwaben bekommen es die bösen Geister noch wirklich mit der Angst zu tun. Fotos Axel Hoedt

Als Nadelbaum verkleidet in Empfingen: Reisbär mit Treiber

Alle Kostüme sind handgemacht, wie diese aus Hirrlingen und Wolfingen

Art Director
Katja Kollmann
Creative Director
Mirko Borsche

Photographer
Axel Hoedt
Image Manipulator
Gal Schaeper

Picture Editor
Michael Biedowicz
Editor in Chief
Christoph Amend

Client
DIE ZEIT
Brand
ZEITmagazin

Magazine Sections

ZEITmagazin

Furchtbar Komisch
This is the story of the well-known Fasching oder Karneval in Germany, a tradition that is hundreds of years old. Today, in the cities, Karneval is just a big party. Photographer Axel Hoe has done extensive research in a rural area in the south of Germany, called Schwaben. There, village people wear traditional self-made masks that seem partly funny, partly scary in his photos. It's an uncanny sight even for Germans.

Director
rry Goh
blishers
Publishing

**Contributing
Photographer**
Jovian Lim
Editor
Justin Long

Sub Editor
Stephanie Peh
Design Group
HJGHER
Printing
Dominie Press

Paper Supplier
RJ Paper
Client
Underscore
Magazine
Brand
Underscore

Entire Magazines

HJGHER
for Underscore Magazine

Underscore N°1: The ___ Issue
Underscore was developed with the reader in mind: carefully selected paper stock for texture, weight and readability; a convenient size for fit and portability; clean and concise layout; minimal advertising for an uninterrupted flow; and a soundtrack to accompany the entire experience. 'Emptiness is a vessel waiting to be filled', says Kenya Hara. With 'Underscore N°1: The ___ Issue', the theme, front cover, and six back pages of the inaugural issue were left empty. With the notion that everything begins with an idea, a pencil was attached for both symbolism and functionality. The magazine became a journal to inspire readers, who could pencil in ideas of their own.

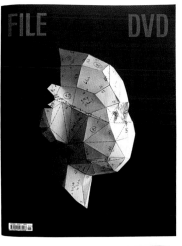

Art Directors
Thorbjorn
Ankerstjerne
Fabio Sebastianelli

Creative Directors
Thorbjorn
Ankerstjerne
Fabio Sebastianelli

Publisher
Fabio Sebastianelli
Editor in Chief
Fabio Sebastianelli

Client
File

Entire Magazines

File

File: Issues 1 & 2
File is an independent, London-based, biannual magazine that celebrates the latest in design, art and visual communication. It's a magazine to read, with its large format, iconic design and spacious layout, and to watch, with an accompanying DVD featuring over two hours of short films, music videos, documentaries and exclusive interviews. File exhibits its content as a visually engaging experience, with intelligence and style.

Designer
Matt Willey

Design Group
Studio8 Design

Editor in Chief
Marc Valli

Client
Frame Publishing
Brand
Elephant Magazine

Entire Magazines

Studio8 Design
for Frame Publishing

Elephant Magazine
The art world has, for a few decades now, been divided between what has so far been known as contemporary art on one side, with applied art, or commercial art, on the other. The problem with this division, however, is that it does not reflect the reality and the richness of what is taking place in the visual arts arena. More seriously, this division has meant that a lot of the best work has gone right under the radar. It is this vast and vital space in the middle, with its vibrant culture and endlessly changing scene, that is the subject of Elephant Magazine.

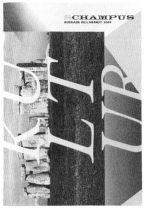
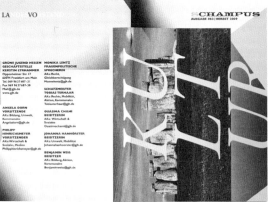
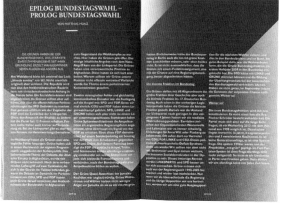

Art Director
Kai Bergmann
Designers
Kai Bergmann
Alexander Lis

Illustrator
Tim Heiler
Design Group
Bergmann Studios

Editors in Chief
Elisabeth Amrein
Tobias Teerhar

Client
Gruene Jugend
Hessen
Brand
Schampus Magazine

Entire Magazines

Bergmann Studios
for Gruene Jugend Hessen

Schampus Magazine: Issues #61 Opposition, #63 Culture & #64 Future
Schampus Magazine is a low-budget quarterly, published by Gruene Jugend Hessen, the Hessian Youth Organisation of the Green Party. Its purpose is to inform members, pupils and students about political topics and events at the Green Party. With a voluntary editorial department, lots of text and non-professional images, the design needed to make the publication visually entertaining. It couldn't look like a political publication, because they're considered dull. We played with type, used strong graphic elements and changed the images into graphic illustrations. The design is modified for every issue to suit the main topic.

rt Director
atja Kollmann
reative Director
Mirko Borsche

Photographer
Shinichi Maruyama
Image Manipulator
Gal Schaeper

Picture Editor
Michael Biedowicz
Editor in Chief
Christoph Amend

Client
DIE ZEIT
Brand
ZEITmagazin

Entire Magazines

ZEITmagazin

Café Deutschland
A series of photos by Shinichi Maruyama is displayed in this special food issue
of ZEITmagazin. It shows floating and exploding coffee.

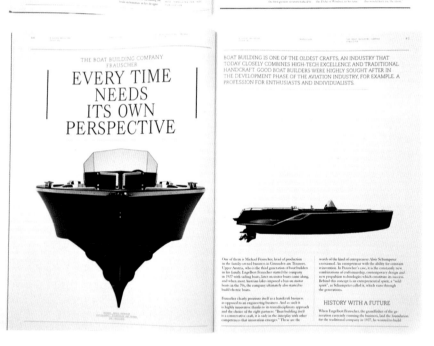

Art Director	Photographers	Editor	Contributors	Managing Directors
Albert Handler	Andreas Balon	Harald Weiler	Nicole Adler	Gernot
Designer	Marina Faust	**Managing Editor**	Imran Amed	Leonhartsberger
Anouk Rehorek	Klaus Fritsch	Judith Zwanzger	Joachim Bessing	Andreas Oberkanins
Publishers	Mathias Kessler	**Assistant Managing**	Wojciech Czaja	**Clients**
BÜRO FÜR	Elfie Semotan	**Editor**	Markus Ebner	BÜRO FÜR
TRANSFER	Martin Stöbich	Barbara Hofleitner	Martin Kolozs	TRANSFER
moodley brand	**Image Manipulator**	**Sub Editors**	Marion Kuzmany	moodley brand
identity	Mario Rott	Peter Blakeney	Cosima Reif	identity
Unit F büro für mode	**Editors in Chief**	Christine Schöffler	Richard Sennet	Unit F büro für mode
Design Group	Albert Handler	Harald Weiler	**Translator**	**Brand**
moodley brand	Doris Rothauer		Harald Weiler	A Guide Magazine
identity	Ulrike		**Printer**	
	Tschabitzer-Handler		Siegfried J Osoinig	

Entire Magazines

moodley brand identity
for BÜRO FÜR TRANSFER

A Guide Magazine
Pioneers of economy and society who are successful in the face of volatile lifestyle trends, and often over generations, lie at the centre of biannual publication 'A Guide Magazine'. The common denominator: the concentration on quality and creativity as driving forces, as well as the skilful connection of tradition and innovation, entrepreneurial spirit and the structure of family businesses. This first issue is dedicated to the phenomenon of handcrafts. Products made by hand, with knowledge and skills passed on from generation to generation. Qualities that put you one decisive step ahead. Every issue comes with a separate city guide, highlighting the 50 top spots in a particular city or region.

2.
THE
MADOFF
EXILES

BY ROBERT KOLKER

Victims of the $65 billion Ponzi scheme feel cast out, denied justice, forgotten. They're angry at just about everyone, including, in some cases, themselves.

'I feel like madoff – just left on the side of the road.'

4.
BARGAIN-BASEMENT
SKY-
SCRAPERS

BY DEVIN LEONARD

rt Director
andy Minor
eputy Art Director
tomi Sato
esign Director
ris Dixon

Publisher
Larry Burstein
Illustrators
Rodrigo Corral
Jason Lee
Matthew Woodson

Photographers
Christopher Griffith
Marco Grob
Hannah Whitaker
Director of Photography
Jody Quon

Editor in Chief
Adam Moss
Client
New York Magazine

Entire Magazines
New York Magazine

The Money Issue
Our annual issue about money had a twist in 2009. The cover featured George Washington as depicted on the one-dollar bill, winking at the reader as if he knows something we don't. The feature pages are filled with articles, photography, and illustrations that relay the idea that these days, financial worth is all in the mind of the beholder.

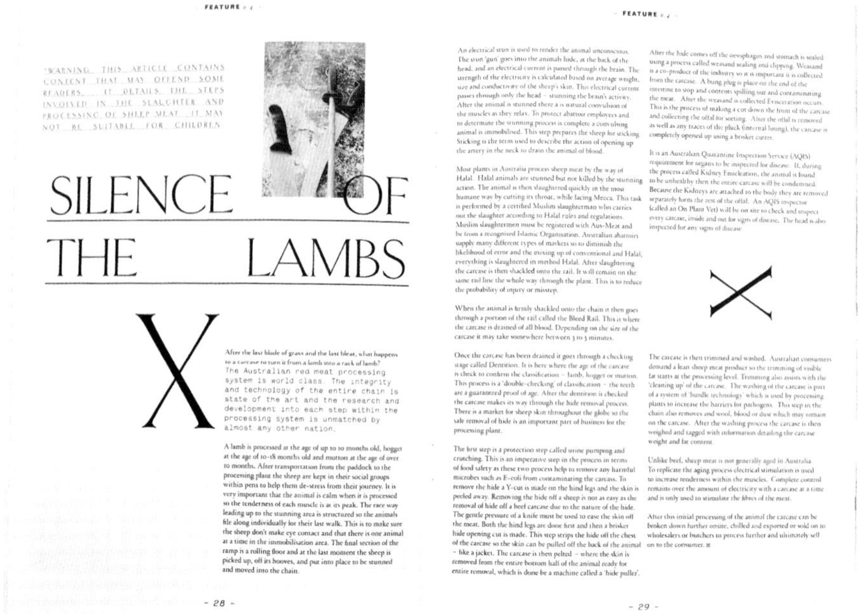
FEATURE

WARNING: THIS ARTICLE CONTAINS CONTENT THAT MAY OFFEND SOME READERS. IT DETAILS THE STEPS INVOLVED IN THE SLAUGHTER AND PROCESSING OF SHEEP MEAT. IT MAY NOT BE SUITABLE FOR CHILDREN

SILENCE OF THE LAMBS

X

After the last blade of grass and the last bleat, what happens to a carcase to turn it from a lamb into a rack of lamb?

The Australian red meat processing system is world class. The integrity and technology of the entire chain is state of the art and the research and development into each step within the processing system is unmatched by almost any other nation.

A lamb is processed at the age of up to 10 months old, hogget at the age of 10-18 months old and mutton at the age of over 10 months. After transportation from the paddock to the processing plant the sheep are kept in their social groups within pens to help them de-stress from their journey. It is very important that the animal is calm when it is processed so the tenderness of each muscle is at its peak. The race way leading up to the stunning area is structured so the animals file along individually for their last walk. This is to make sure the sheep don't make eye contact and that there is one animal at a time in the immobilisation area. The final section of the ramp is a rolling floor and at the last moment the sheep is picked up, off its hooves, and put into place to be stunned and moved into the chain.

- 28 -

FEATURE

An electrical stun is used to render the animal unconscious. The stun 'gun' goes into the animals hide, at the back of the head, and an electrical current is passed through the brain. The strength of the electricity is calculated based on average weight, size and conductivity of the sheep's skin. This electrical current passes through only the head – stunning the brain's activity. After the animal is stunned there a is natural convulsion of the muscles as they relax. To protect abattoir employees and to determine the stunning process is complete a convulsing animal is immobilised. This step prepares the sheep for sticking. Sticking is the term used to describe the action of opening up the artery in the neck to drain the animal of blood.

Most plants in Australia process sheep meat by the way of Halal. Halal animals are stunned but not killed by the stunning action. The animal is then slaughtered quickly in the most humane way by cutting its throat, while facing Mecca. This task is performed by a certified Muslim slaughterman who carries out the slaughter according to Halal rules and regulations. Muslim slaughtermen must be registered with Aus-Meat and be from a recognised Islamic Organisation. Australian abattoirs supply many different types of markets so to diminish the likelihood of error and the mixing up of conventional and Halal, everything is slaughtered in method Halal. After slaughtering the carcase is then shackled onto the rail. It will remain on the same rail line the whole way through the plant. This is to reduce the probability of injury or misstep.

When the animal is firmly shackled onto the chain it then goes through a portion of the rail called the Bleed Rail. This is where the carcase is drained of all blood. Depending on the size of the carcase it may take somewhere between 3 to 5 minutes.

Once the carcase has been drained it goes through a checking stage called Dentition. It is here where the age of the carcase is check to confirm the classification – lamb, hogget or mutton. This process is a 'double-checking' of classification – the teeth are a guaranteed proof of age. After the dentition is checked the carcase makes its way through the hide removal process. There is a market for sheep skin throughout the globe so the safe removal of hide is an important part of business for the processing plant.

The first step is a protection step called urine pumping and crutching. This is an imperative step in the process in terms of food safety as these two process help to remove any harmful microbes such as E-coli from contaminating the carcass. To remove the hide a Y-cut is made on the hind legs and the skin is peeled away. Removing the hide off a sheep is not as easy as the removal of hide off a beef carcase due to the nature of the hide. The gentle pressure of a knife must be used to ease the skin off the meat. Both the hind legs are done first and then a brisket hide opening cut is made. This step strips the hide off the chest of the carcase so the skin can be pulled off the back of the animal – like a jacket. The carcase is then pelted – where the skin is removed from the entire bottom half of the animal ready for entire removal, which is done be a machine called a 'hide puller'.

After the hide comes off the oesophagus and stomach is sealed using a process called weasand sealing and clipping. Weasand is a co-product of the industry so it is important it is collected from the carcase. A bung plug is place on the end of the intestine to stop and contents spilling out and contaminating the meat. After the weasand is collected Evisceration occurs. This is the process of making a cut down the front of the carcase and collecting the offal for sorting. After the offal is removed as well as any traces of the pluck (internal lining), the carcase is completely opened up using a brisket cutter.

It is an Australian Quarantine Inspection Service (AQIS) requirement for organs to be inspected for disease. If, during the process called Kidney Enucleation, the animal is found to be unhealthy then the entire carcase will be condemned. Because the Kidneys are attached to the body they are removed separately form the rest of the offal. An AQIS inspector (called an On Plant Vet) will be on site to check and inspect every carcase, inside and out for signs of disease. The head is also inspected for any signs of disease.

X

The carcase is then trimmed and washed. Australian consumers demand a lean sheep meat product so the trimming of visible fat starts at the processing level. Trimming also assists with the 'cleaning up' of the carcase. The washing of the carcase is part of a system of 'hurdle technology' which is used by processing plants to increase the barriers for pathogens. This step in the chain also removes and wool, blood or dust which may remain on the carcase. After the washing process the carcase is then weighed and tagged with information detailing the carcase weight and fat content.

Unlike beef, sheep meat is not generally aged in Australia. To replicate the aging process electrical stimulation is used to increase tenderness within the muscles. Complete control remains over the amount of electricity with a carcase at a time and is only used to stimulate the fibres of the meat.

After this initial processing of the animal the carcase can be broken down further onsite, chilled and exported or sold on to wholesalers or butchers to process further and ultimately sell on to the consumer.

- 29 -

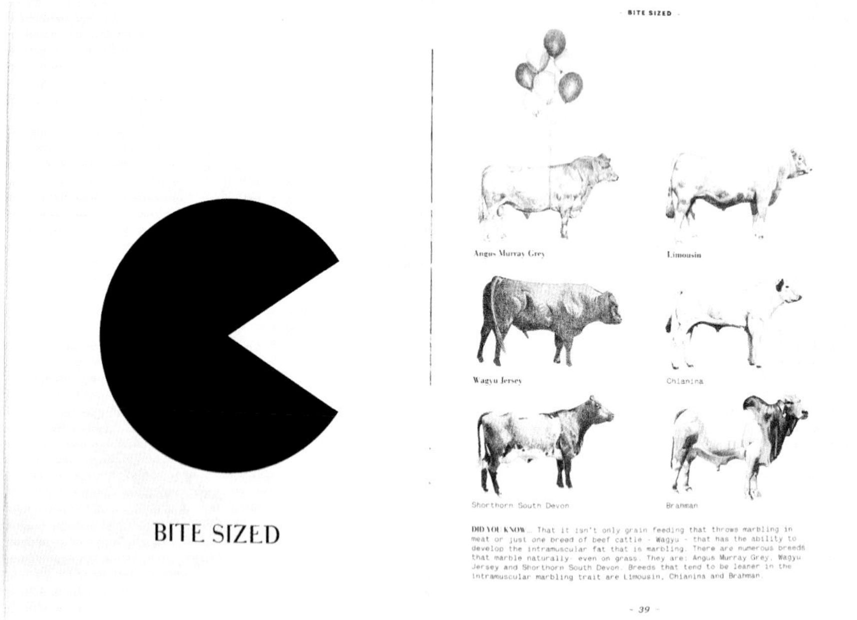
BITE SIZED

BITE SIZED

Angus Murray Grey

Limousin

Wagyu Jersey

Chianina

Shorthorn South Devon

Brahman

DID YOU KNOW... That it isn't only grain feeding that throws marbling in meat or just one breed of beef cattle - Wagyu - that has the ability to develop the intramuscular fat that is marbling. There are numerous breeds that marble naturally- even on grass. They are: Angus Murray Grey, Wagyu Jersey and Shorthorn South Devon. Breeds that tend to be leaner in the intramuscular marbling trait are Limousin, Chianina and Brahman.

- 39 -

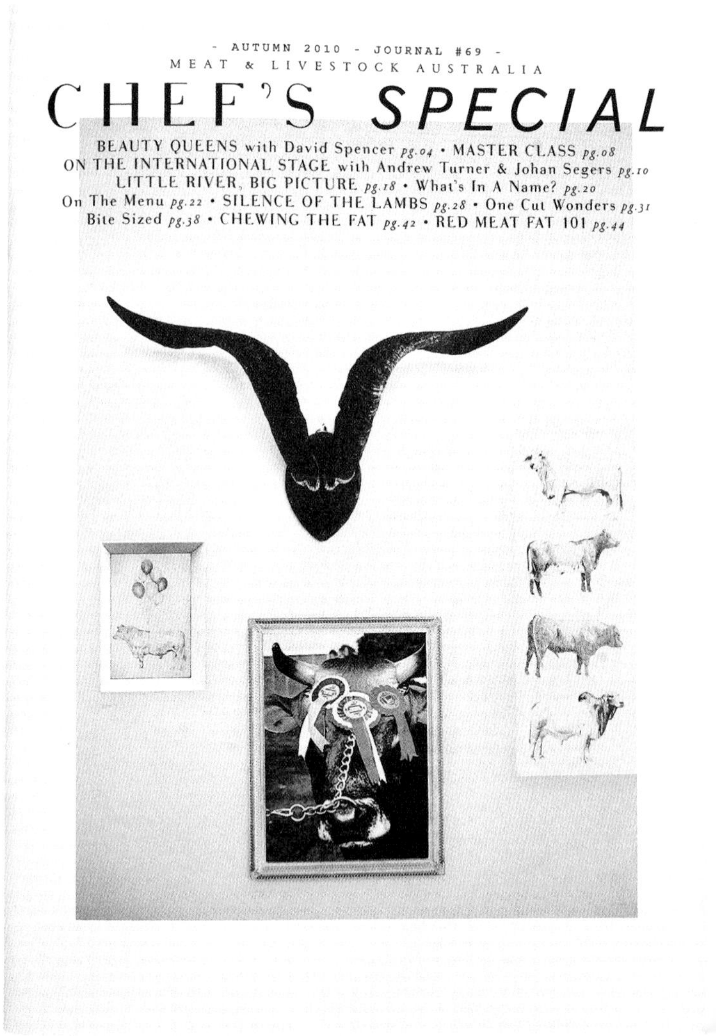
- AUTUMN 2010 - JOURNAL #69 -

MEAT & LIVESTOCK AUSTRALIA

CHEF'S SPECIAL

BEAUTY QUEENS with David Spencer pg.04 • MASTER CLASS pg.08
ON THE INTERNATIONAL STAGE with Andrew Turner & Johan Segers pg.10
LITTLE RIVER, BIG PICTURE pg.18 • What's In A Name? pg.20
On The Menu pg.22 • SILENCE OF THE LAMBS pg.28 • One Cut Wonders pg.31
Bite Sized pg.38 • CHEWING THE FAT pg.42 • RED MEAT FAT 101 pg.44

Art Director
James Brown
Designer
Darren Song

Design Director
James Brown
Illustrator
Beth Tyson
Typographer
Darren Song

Photographer
John Laurie
Stylist
Simon Bajada
Design Agency
Mash

Client
MLA
Brand
Chef's Special

Entire Magazines

Mash
for MLA

Chef's Special
We like food but we don't like the idea of it being wasted. Chef's Special encourages Australian chefs to be more creative with red meat by thinking further than the fillet, and to use Australian beef, veal, lamb and goat responsibly. Mash was approached to update and modernise the design and overall feel of the publication. Mash art directed stylist Simon Bajada and photographer John Laurie, bringing Chef's Special a new look that aims to inspire culinary wizards to do good things with a product that is usually the hero of the menu.

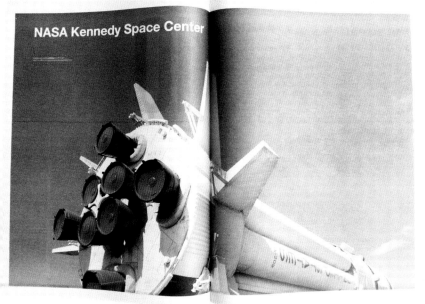

Entire Newspapers

Newspaper Club
for the Really Interesting Group

Things Our Friends Have Written on the Internet
We'd been thinking for a while about how to combine the best of all things digital with what's great about analogue technologies, when we discovered how cheap it is to print newspapers. So we took some blog posts our friends had written and printed them as a newspaper. We learned a lot about combining web tropes with print conventions, about negotiating with printers, and about what to do with 1,000 newspapers when you only have 23 friends. And then we took all this and transformed it into a new business: Newspaper Club, a web service that helps people make their own newspapers.

Designers
Paulo Barata
Luciane Coelho
Luís Marques
Rita Pereira
João Paulo Rego
Ana Soares
Graphic Artist
Ricardo Santos
Graphics Editor
Carlos Monteiro
Creative Director
Nick Mrozowski

Design Coordinator
Pedro Fernandes
Photographers
Pedro Azevedo
Filipe Casaca
Illustrators
Tiago Albuquerque
João Maio Pinto
Deborah Withey
Retouchers
Fátima Albuquerque
Sara Correia
Sérgio Mateus

Photo Editor
Céu Guarda
**Photography
Assistant**
Tiago Lopes
**Photography
Coordinator**
Ágata Xavier
Publishers
Sojormedia Capital

Editor
Martim Avillez
Figueiredo
Associate Editors
Silvia de Oliveira
Miguel Pacheco
Executive Director
André Macedo
Design Consultant
Javier Errea
Client
i

Entire Newspapers

Sojormedia Capital
for i

i

In May 2009, a new newspaper and media brand was born in Portugal with the aim of attracting a new generation of readers in print and online. From the small format, which is stapled and trimmed, to the organisation of the content, no detail was left unconsidered in the project's conception. The paper begins with thought-provoking editorial pages, moves on to a brisk news round-up section, before relaxing into in-depth reporting on the news of the day, culture and sport. We use informative illustration, thoughtful photography, information graphics and bold colour to achieve a daily news magazine effect.

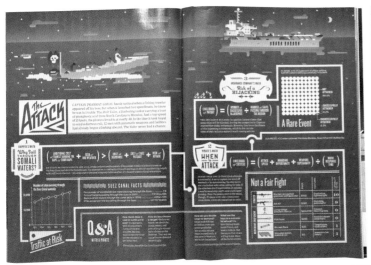

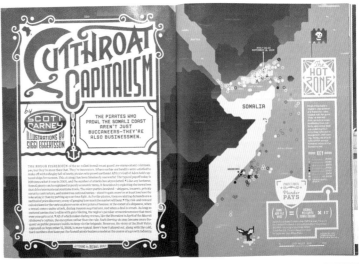

Art Director
Maili Holiman
Design Director
Wyatt Mitchell
Creative Director
Scott Dadich

Illustrator
Siggi Eggertsson
Lettering Artist
Michael Doret
Writer
Scott Carney

Game Designer
Shannon Perkins
User Interface
Director
Dennis Crothers
Senior Editor
Ted Greenwald

Managing Editor
Pam Statz
Artist's Agent
Big Active
Client
Wired Magazine

Print with Online

Wired Magazine

Cutthroat Capitalism
To cover Somali pirates, most magazines might focus on an exposition of the danger
involved in catching the brigands or the situation on the ships. Not Wired. We wanted to
get inside the pirates' minds, and that meant grasping the economics of piracy, down to
the last equation. We'd already worked with illustrator Siggi Eggertsson on smaller pieces,
and this was an opportunity to showcase his talent on a heftier project. In collaboration
with typographer Michael Doret, we also developed a red-lobster-menu-meets-Chris-Ware
aesthetic for the type. It was the most original infographic feature we've ever worked on,
thanks to Siggi's great illustrations.

313

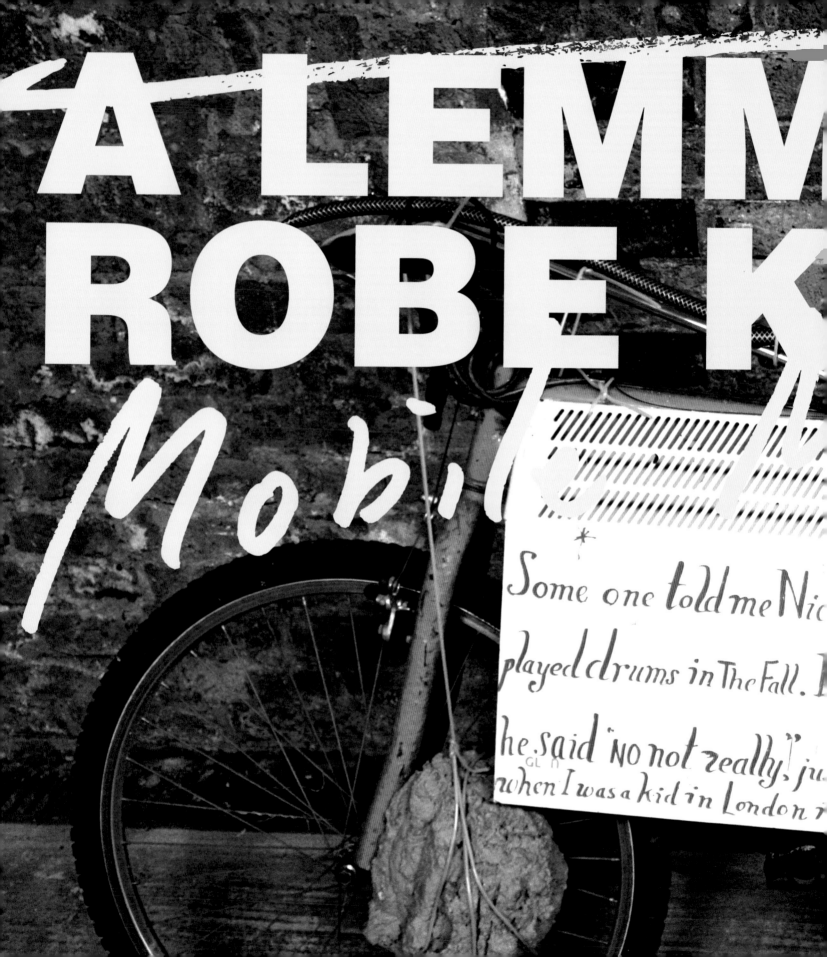

 Mobile Marketing

Farfar
for Nokia

The World's Biggest Signpost
Nokia offers a range of navigation services, both online and on mobile devices. But awareness about these services is low. The challenge was to raise awareness and increase the use of Nokia's navigation service, both on handsets and online. We took the simplest navigation tool around, the signpost, and resized it into one of the world's largest interactive installations: a 50 metre tall, 60 ton, SMS controlled signpost. Passers-by could text a location to the giant signpost and within moments it displayed the direction and distance to that location.

Creative Director	Creative President	Advertising Agency	Head of Strategy
Erik Norin	Matias Palm Jensen	Farfar	Niku Banaie
Executive Creative	**Programmer**	**Account Managers**	**Marketing Manager**
Director	David Looberger	Ulrika Höjgard	Kai Torstila
Jon Dranger	**Flash Programmers**	Marie Persson	**Client**
Art Director	Robert Järvi	Louise Stenborg	Nokia
Tomas Jonsson	Mikael Ring	**Account Directors**	
Copywriter	Björn Uppeke	Mårten Forslund	
Carl Fredrik		Christian Nord	
Jannerfeldt			

rt Director
n Wharton
ontent Director
ara Donovan

Product Director
Tristan Celder
Executive Producers
Ajaz Ahmed
Jamie Oliver

Mobile Marketing Agency
Zolmo

Project Managers
Louisa James
Michael Maher
Client
Jamie Oliver

Mobile Applications

Zolmo
for Jamie Oliver

Jamie Oliver's 20 Minute Meals
Jamie Oliver and Zolmo teamed up with the objective of inspiring a new generation to cook. The iPhone presented an opportunity to create a completely new format, offering something that a TV show or a recipe book couldn't. By successfully exploiting the contextual nature, inherent mobility and availability of the device, '20 Minute Meals' put a cooking toolkit in people's pockets that simply couldn't have existed a few years ago. An international smash-hit, '20 Minute Meals' has set the bar for cooking apps across mobile platforms.

Creative Directors
Kelvin Leong
Kit Ong
Nicki Wong
Executive Creative Directors
Zhu Hao
Natalie Lam
Kevin Lee
Sean Sim

Art Directors
Kurt Durt
Kevin Lee
Zhang Lei
Kelvin Leong
Chung Choon Ming
Bright Shen
Casper Woo
Robin Wu
Kama Zhang
Minsheng Zhang
Zhang Zheng

Copywriters
Kit Ong
Stanley Tao
Stan Xu
Joan Zheng
Designers
Kevin Lee
Zhang Lei
Minsheng Zhang
Producers
Joyce Chen
Chye Yee Chow
Liu Jin Ming

Voice Over Talent
Arthur Jones
Production Company
Gwantsi Production
Advertising Agency
Ogilvy Shanghai
Sound Production Company
Kai Music

Post Production Company
Attic Post
Agency Producers
Weisian Lee
Aywei Wong
Client
The North Face

Mobile Marketing

Ogilvy Shanghai
for The North Face

Red Flag
The North Face believes everyone can be an adventurer. In the world of outdoor adventure explorers lay claim on every summit conquered by planting a flag. To get people out of their comfort zone we wanted to give them a taste of how great it is to have discovered a new place and claim credit for being there first. Over a period of 18 days, people could use their mobile phones to plant virtual red flags at any location they wanted to claim. People kept score on the event website and outdoor electronic board, where a live counter tracked the total number of flags planted across China.

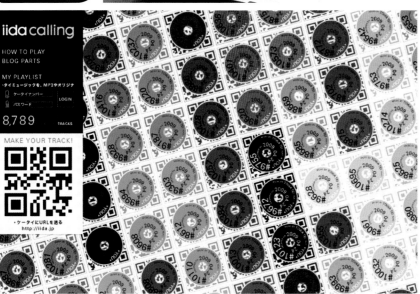

Creative Directors
toshi Takamatsu
ichiro Tanaka
Technical Director
anta Shimizu

Mobile Developer
Tadakazu Oda
Art Directors
Atsushi Fujimaki
Takayuki Sugihara

Mobile Designer
Atsushi Fujimaki
Advertising Agency
Projector
Project Manager
Izumi Horio

Brand Manager
Tomofumi Matsui
Client
KDDI Corporation
Brand
iida

Mobile Marketing

Projector
for KDDI Corporation

iida calling
For the launch of new mobile phone brand iida, we created a system that enabled consumers to record their own voice. The voice is then used to generate music, such as songs used in TV commercials. The resulting music can be downloaded onto their phone and used as a ringtone or sent as a file.

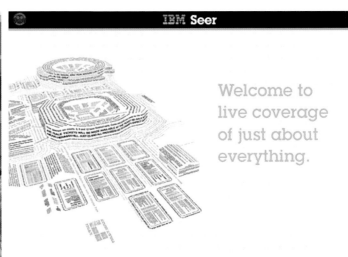

Welcome to live coverage of just about everything.

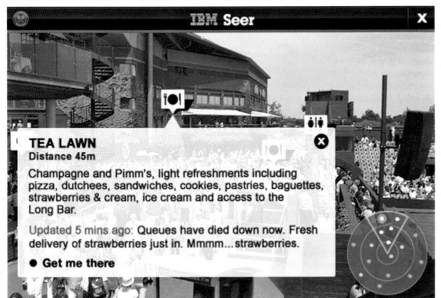

All ○

⊖ **Courts** ○

⋔ **Toilets** ○

🚌 **Transport** ◉

🍴 **Cafe/Food** ○

TEA LAWN
Distance 45m

Champagne and Pimm's, light refreshments including pizza, dutchees, sandwiches, cookies, pastries, baguettes, strawberries & cream, ice cream and access to the Long Bar.

Updated 5 mins ago: Queues have died down now. Fresh delivery of strawberries just in. Mmmm…strawberries.

● **Get me there**

Creative Directors
Emma De La Fosse
Charlie Wilson
Executive Creative Director
Colin Nimick
Technical Director
Dylan Smith

Art Director
Jamie Romain
Mobile Copywriter
Pavlos
Themistocleous
Mobile Designers
Andrew Mackay
Maciek Strychalski

Digital Producers
Paul Randall
Davide Sciola
Advertising Agency
OgilvyOne London
Account Manager
Will Howells
Account Executive
Nick Bennett

Senior Planner
Nina Mynk
Business Partner
Richard Barker
Brand Manager
Alan Flack
Client
IBM

Mobile Marketing

OgilvyOne London
for IBM

IBM Seer
IBM Seer is a mobile phone app developed for the Wimbledon Championships 2009. The first augmented reality app to use live data, it offers users a real-time digital guide to the tournament. Developed to showcase the work IBM does at Wimbledon, it uses IBM data to provide live coverage of everything happening in and around the grounds. This information is then presented as an overlay on the phone's camera. As a result, users can point their phone at anything and Seer will tell them what it is and what's happening there now.

HAPPY BIRTHDAY
DOWNLOAD↓
for children™

Creative Directors
Shohei Hashimoto
Hideaki Ohki
Naomi Yamashita
Executive Creative Director
Hironobu Yoshida
Art Director
Sumpei Fujita

Copywriter
Takahiro Hosoda
Producers
Takehiro Ikuta
Kohei Suetani
Masanori Suganuma
Atsuki Yukawa

Advertising Agency
HAKUHODO
Account Supervisors
Shunsuke Ishii
Yasushi Kohara
PR Managers
Ryunosuke Goto
Naoto Yoshida

Media Supervisors
Takeshi Maruyama
Yuichi Matsumoto
Keiko Nakamura
Client
Japan Committee
for UNICEF

Mobile Marketing

HAKUHODO
for the Japan Committee for UNICEF

Happy Birthday Download for Children
This project was created to help the estimated six million children who won't even reach their first birthday, as stated in the Millennium Development Goals by the United Nations, with the power of one song. Each day, a different artist sings his or her version of 'Happy Birthday to You'. Songs can be downloaded to a mobile phone as ringtones for 105JPY (1USD), or attached to a text message and sent as a gift. All the proceeds from the downloads are donated to the Japan Committee for UNICEF. A song that celebrates life becomes a song that saves lives.

Associate Creative Director
Qian Qian
Group Creative Directors
Alessandra Lariu
Matt O'Rourke
Chief Creative Officer
Joyce King Thomas
Technical Lead
Bruce LeSourd

Copywriter
Kelly McCormick
Designer
Robbie Wenger
Interactive Engineers
James Lawton
Scott McKie
Dan Posluns
Producers
Jonathan Doyle
Kat Kim
Executive Producer
Catherine Patterson

Director of Software Development
Craig Richards
Software Development
MRM
Advertising Agency
McCann Erickson
New York
Interactive Quality Assurance Lead
Uriah McKinney

Interactive Project Manager
Achim Bassler
Account Supervisor
Allison Foley
Leadership Group Director
ToniAnn Bonade
Management Representative
Nicole Chabre
Client
MasterCard

Mobile Applications

McCann Erickson New York
for MasterCard

Priceless Picks
The world is full of priceless things. We call them Priceless Picks. A pick can be a priceless experience, place, shop, or restaurant. The Priceless Picks web experience and iPhone app helps people discover thousands of user-recommended picks and add their own. The app uses mobile geo-tagging, where users can leave a note or pick anywhere on earth. A 3D version of Google maps features hundreds of thousands of picks from users, reviews from our partner Not For Tourists and exclusive offers from MasterCard partners.

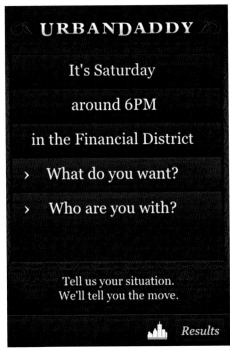

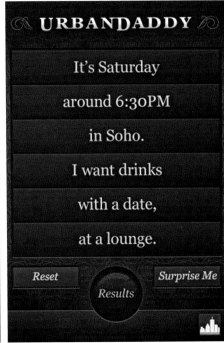

Digital Agency
Big Spaceship

Client
UrbanDaddy

Mobile Applications

Big Spaceship
for UrbanDaddy

The Next Move
IPhone applications for those in search of a good meal or a night on the town are easy to come by. The Next Move takes a targeted, narrative-based approach. The application is designed for guys who want to stay in the know. In helping them devise the perfect plan, it tells the story of their evening to come. While developing a strategy, the agency adopted a holistic perspective, factoring in the who, what and where of one's plans. The app considers what you're in the mood for and reacts to your specific needs. Choices unfold through interchangeable sentence fragments, revealing information in a personalised manner.

323

The PUMA Index

The PUMA Index is a global stock ticker with a twist. When the market goes down, our models' clothes come off, right down to their PUMA Bodywear. So if you lose your shirt, at least they do too.

Loading Index Data

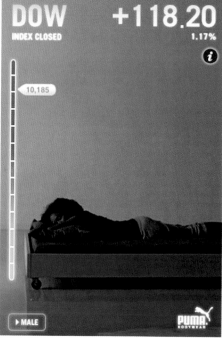

Creative Director	Director	Editor	Website Production
Kevin Brady	Nima Nourizadeh	Patrick Colman	**Company**
Executive Creative	**Website Producer**	**Agency Producer**	Perfect Fools
Directors	Sofia Jonsson	Thomas Beug	**Audio Company**
Duncan Marshall	**Executive Digital**	**Website Project**	Nylon Studios
Ted Royer	**Producer**	**Manager**	New York
Creative Chairman	Sandra Nam	Stefan Dufgran	**Client**
David Droga	**Head of Integrated**	**Advertising Agency**	Puma
Art Director	**Production**	Droga5 New York	
Jesse Juriga	Sally-Ann Dale		

Mobile Applications

Droga5 New York
for Puma

The Puma Index
We were asked to introduce a new line of Puma underwear in the middle of a recession. We created the Puma Index, a real stock ticker with a twist: when the market goes down, the models' clothes come off, right down to their Puma underwear. Online and on the iPhone, the models react in real time, so the site is never the same day to day. When the markets close, models pull out beds and sleep until the next opening bell. To date, the campaign has made over 130,000,000 impressions; the iPhone app was one of the top 20 apps and has been downloaded over 40,000 times.

eative Director
d Persson
chnical Directors
ders Graffman
nas Wikström
t Director
d Persson

Mobile Developers
Joakim Lodén
Alexander Persson
Frederik Wallner
Magnus Westling
Mobile Designers
Fredrik Karlsson
Ola Persson
**Mobile Application
Production Agency**
Apegroup

Advertising Agency
Great Works
**Production
Managers**
Jon Svenonius
Jocke Wissing
Project Manager
Anders Larsson

Planners
Krista Freibaum
Zoe Turnbull
Account Director
Stefan Persson
Marketing Manager
Fredrick Tallroth
Client
Absolut Vodka

Mobile Applications

Great Works
for Absolut Vodka

Drinkspiration by Absolut

Have you ever found yourself in a bar without really knowing what to order? With Drinkspiration by Absolut you'll never have this problem again. Drinkspiration is your best friend in the bar, giving you guidance and personalised recommendations, right in the palm of your hand. The Drinkspiration application features hundreds of vividly illustrated drink recipes to satisfy every drink preference. The user can browse recipes or get insightful drink recommendations based on personal taste, location or occasion. Drinkspiration by Absolut also lets users share their location and real-time drink choices through Facebook and Twitter integration.

Creative Director	**Senior Designer**	**Senior Account**	**Director of Client**
Ginny Golden	Eric Lohman	**Executive**	**Services**
Technical Director	**Flash Developer**	Sarah Cheffy	John Deschner
Douglas Smith	Jon Reiling	**Director of Mobile**	**Client**
Art Director	**Advertising Agency**	**Strategy**	Volkswagen
Jefferson Liu	AKQA Washington	Johnathan Hum	
Mobile Copywriter	**Account Supervisor**		
Jon Lee	Laura Breines		

Mobile Applications

AKQA Washington
for Volkswagen

Real Racing GTI
To introduce Volkswagen's all-new 2010 GTI, AKQA launched a campaign that honoured the car's legacy as 'the original hot hatch'. Real Racing GTI gave fans their first chance to drive the car in all its road-hugging glory. The iPhone app included a virtual showroom, global leaderboard, and the ability to share fastest laps on YouTube. Meanwhile, its GPS function guided customers to the nearest dealer to take a test drive. To keep people racing, AKQA worked with Volkswagen to create the ultimate reward: six one-of-a-kind GTIs. Within one week of launch, Real Racing GTI became the number one free app in 36 countries, eventually scoring more than six million downloads.

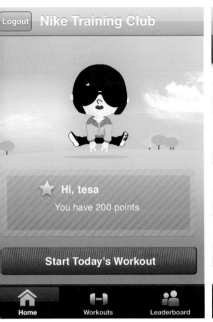

Creative Director	**Interaction Designer**	**Advertising Agency**	**Brand Manager**
n Spalter	Susan Choi	R/GA New York	Tesa Aragones
xecutive Technical	**Interaction Design**	**Software Engineer**	**Client**
rector	**Director**	Bryan Bonczek	Nike
ick Coronges	Claudia Bernett	**Quality Assurance**	
opywriter	**Executive Producer**	**Engineer**	
my Travis	Julie Renwick	Will Creedle	

Mobile Applications

R/GA New York
for Nike

Nike Training Club
Nike believes that if you have a body, you're an athlete. So to help young female athletes everywhere to get in shape, we created Nike Training Club, an application that integrates training into girls' lives in a fun, social, and personalised way. The global online platform allows girls to customise personal training programmes and watch more than 70 instructional videos. Girls can invite and challenge friends to join their workouts, track group progress, and customise an avatar. And when girls are on the go, they can use the Nike Training Club experience as an iPhone app, which provides them with access to their training regime, instructional videos and leader board, any time, any place.

327

Director	**Director of**	**Editorial Company**	**Post Production**		
Patrick Daughters	**Photography**	Final Cut	**Producer**		
First Assistant	Shawn Kim	**Lead Flame Artist**	Lee Pavey		
Director	**Production Company**	Tara Demarco	**Post Production**		
Rod Smith	The Directors Bureau	**Flame Artists**	The Mill Los Angeles		
Producer	**3D Supervisor**	Giles Cheetham	**Record Company**		
Karen Lin	Aaron Grove	Billy Higgins	Warp Records		
Executive Producer	**Editor**	**Production Designer**	**Video Commissioner**		
Lana Kim	Stephen Berger	KK Barrett	Laura Tunstall		
Artist	**Editorial Producer**	**Production Manager**	**Artist Management**		
Grizzly Bear	Viet Nguyen	Mike Drinkwater	Zeitgeist Artist		
			Management		

▲ Music Videos

The Directors Bureau
for Warp Records

Two Weeks
Doll-like, the four band members sing in a cathedral, as a light from within eventually explodes in a firework display.

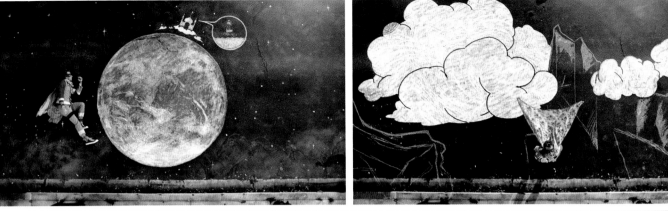

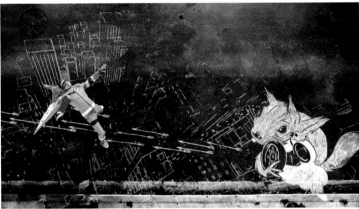

Animation	**Artist**	**Lighting**	**Video Producer**
Shynola	Coldplay	**Cameraperson**	Margo Mars
Direction	**Production Company**	Aaron Platt	**Record Company**
Shynola	Black Dog Films	**Set Designer**	EMI Records
Producer	**Editing**	Evan Rhode	**Video Commissioner**
Margo Mars	Shynola		Kirstin Wallingford

Animation

Black Dog Films
for EMI Records

Strawberry Swing

A normal day begins for super-guy Chris Martin. He changes into his secret identity to save a damsel from the clutches of the Mischievous Squirrel. Flying to her defence, Chris is ambushed and then grounded when the squirrel cuts off his cape. Chris must find another way to save the girl. Battling through mysterious Winsor McCay-inspired enemies, Chris finally makes it to the squirrel's lair – just in time to save her from drowning in a very deep cup of tea. The Mischievous Squirrel is defeated and Chris flies off into the sunset with his new love. Strawberry Swing was also nominated in the Music Videos category.

331

Director
Patrick Daughters
First Assistant Director
Tim Lovekin
Producer
Jonathan Lia
Executive Producer
Lana Kim

Artist
Depeche Mode
Director of Photography
Shawn Kim
Production Designer
Jeff Everett
Production Company
The Directors Bureau
Editor
Akiko Iwakawa

Editorial Company
Final Cut
Lead Visual Effects Artist
Bill Mcnamara
Visual Effects Producer
Andrew Bell

Visual Effects
MPC Los Angeles
Production Manager
Rachel Straus
Record Company
Mute Records
Video Commissioner
John Moule

 Music Videos

The Directors Bureau
for Mute Records

Wrong
A mysterious man passes out in the front seat of a car as it rolls dangerously backwards through the streets of Los Angeles.

rector	**Artist**	**Editor**	**Lighting**
ith Schofield	Charlotte	Keith Schofield	**Cameraperson**
oducer	Gainsbourg	**Special Effects**	Damian Acevedo
les Dieng	**Production Company**	Brandon Parvini	**Record Company**
	El Niño	Keith Schofield	Because Music

 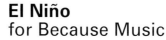

Music Videos

El Niño
for Because Music

Heaven Can Wait
Keith Schofield invents 50 music video money shots for French songstress Charlotte Gainsbourg.

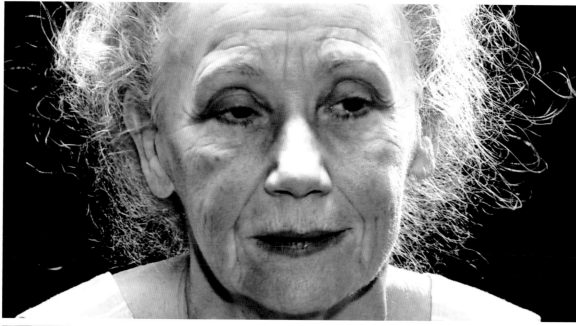

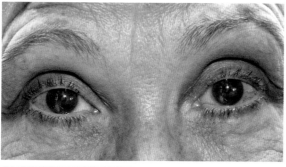

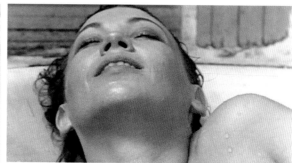

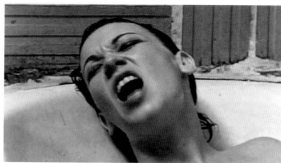

Director
Toby Dye
Producers
Toby Dye
Svana Gisla

Artist
Massive Attack
Production Company
Black Dog Films
Animator
Martin Roker

Special Effects
Emily Irvine
Lighting
Cameraperson
Simon Thirlaway

Video Producer
Toby Dye
Record Company
EMI Records
Video Commissioner
Svana Gisla

Music Videos

Black Dog Films
for EMI Records

Paradise Circus
In unblinking close-up, a little old lady looks straight down the lens of the camera and describes the fuck of her life from nearly forty years ago. Intercut with her frank and unsentimental interview is actual footage of the intimate moments she describes. This senior citizen is one time sex symbol Georgina Spelvin, now looking back at herself in 1973's 'The Devil in Miss Jones', one of the most notorious pornographic films ever made.

Director
Ray Tintori
Producer
Justin Benoliel
Artist
MGMT

Production Company
Partizan
Lighting
Cameraperson
Rob Leitzell

Set Designer
Matthew Thompson
Video Producer
Justin Benoliel

Record Company
Columbia
Video Commissioner
Bryan Younce

Music Videos

Partizan
for Columbia

Kids
Ray Tintori's music video for MGMT is a wonderfully surreal example of his incredible mind.
A very young boy encounters the most disturbing monsters that his mother fails to see. As soon
as we adjust to this notion we're being taken away to a different, yet equally incredible land.

Lighting Cameraperson
Lol Crawley
Director
Daniel Wolfe

Producer
Tim Francis
Artist
Plan B
Production Company
Partizan

Video Producer
Tim Francis
Editor
Dominic Leung

Record Company
Atlantic Records
Video Commissioner
Tim Nash

 Cinematography

Partizan
for Atlantic Records

Stay Too Long
Daniel Wolfe directs the first video in what is to become a fantastic trilogy. Shot in various locations that show London's rich fabric, Ben Drew gives an outstanding and convincing performance. This is beautifully enhanced by the female lead, the fantastic Kaya Scodelario from Skins. Stay Too Long was also nominated in the Editing category.

itor	**Artist**	**Lighting**	**Hair & Make-up**
ck Allix	Florence and The	**Cameraperson**	**Artist**
rector	Machine	Rob Hardy	Lica Fensome
wn Shadforth	**Production Company**	**Set Designer**	**Record Company**
oducer	Black Dog Films	Alice Normington	Universal-Island
dy Burnay		**Stylist**	Records
		Aldene Johnson	**Video Commissioner**
			Ailsa Robertson

Editing

Black Dog Films
for Universal-Island Records

Drumming Song
The film illustrates the light and dark sides of Florence battling for supremacy. The two representations of the artist react to each other, turning the film into a visual, moral struggle. As the fight reaches its climax, high-speed footage is introduced to create a dream-like state in the midst of the chaos, with one side emerging as a victor...

Editors	**Producer**	**Director of**	**Telecine Artist**
Will Lovelace	Jamie Clark	**Photography**	Aubrey Woodiwiss
Dylan Southern	**Artist**	Yon Thomas	**Record Company**
Direction	Franz Ferdinand	**Production Company**	Domino Records
thirtytwo		Pulse Films	**Video Commissioner**
			John Moule

Editing

Pulse Films
for Domino Records

Ulysses

Ulysses was the lead single from Franz Ferdinand's third album 'Tonight'. The promo was shot over two days on location in Los Angeles and the Mojave desert. It chronicles a lost weekend for the Scottish band in the city of angels. We wanted to create a loose, non-linear narrative that encompassed a range of locations and scenarios. The strong central performance with a few nods to The Odyssey eventually builds to a frenetic, disorientating climax. Ulysses was also selected in the Music Videos category.

338

Director
sh Edgerton
rst Assistant
rector
ip Signore
oducer
ren Lin
ecutive Producer
na Kim

Artist
Bob Dylan
Director of Photography
Greig Fraser
Production Company
The Directors Bureau

Editor
Stephen Berger
Editorial Producer
Viet Nguyen
Editorial Company
Final Cut
Los Angeles
Production Designer
Laura Fox

Production Supervisor
Mike Drinkwater
Record Company
Sony Music
Entertainment
Video Commissioner
Sara Greene

Music Videos
The Directors Bureau
for Sony Music Entertainment

Beyond Here Lies Nothin'
A man comes home to find his victim unbound and loose in his apartment. The two violently quarrel as she struggles to escape.

rectors
trick Daughters
arcel Dzama
oducer
elody Roscher
ecutive Producer
na Kim
tist
epartment
Eagles

Director of Photography
Shawn Kim
Choreographer
Vanessa Walters
Production Company
The Directors Bureau
Editor
Michael Wadsworth

Editorial Producer
Rana Martin
Editorial Company
Final Cut New York
Lead Visual Effects Artists
West Sarokin
Cole Schreiber
Visual Effects
The Mill New York

Production Designer
Jeff Everett
Production Managers
Alicia van Couvering
Justin Lundstrom
Record Company
4AD

Music Videos
The Directors Bureau
for 4AD

No One Does it Like You
Marcel Dzama's art comes to life as his armies of dancing soldiers battle against one another in a surreal desert landscape.

Music Videos

Director
Andy Bruntel
Producer
Jett Steiger
Artist
Bodies of Water
Director of Photography
Eli Born

Production Company
The Directors Bureau
Editor
John Paul
Horstmann
Assistant Editor
Nathan Cornett

Sound Designer
Mads Heldtberg
Camera Assistant
Ed Yonaitis
Art Director
Patrick McKenzie
Art Head
Sophia Rubio

Costume Designer
Lauren Tafuri
Effects Make-up Artist
Jackie Murillo
Record Company
Secretly Canadian

Music Videos

The Directors Bureau
for Secretly Canadian

Under the Pines
A music video directed by Andy Bruntel for Bodies of Water.

Director
David Wilson
Producer
James Bretton

Artist
Moray McLaren
Production Company
Blinkink

Animator
David Wilson
Editor
Mark Aarons
Lighting Cameraperson
Tim Green

Record Company
Lash Records
Video Commissioner
Bart Yates

Music Videos

Blinkink
for Lash Records

We Got Time
David Wilson's debut promo saw him create this bewitching in-camera animation for Moray McLaren. Developing a technique based on the praxinoscope, one of the earliest forms of animation, Wilson personally hand drew, designed and animated every frame in a five week pre-production process. Wilson's pre-production not only involved design but also cracking the science behind the frame rates, as well as the amount of facets needed on the praxinoscopes compared to cells of animation. No post production or compositing was used at all. The video won Best Budget Video in the 2009 Music Video Awards, while Wilson won Best New Director.

Director
Keith Schofield
Producers
Steve Buchanan
Jules Dieng

Artist
Lenny Kravitz
Production Company
El Niño

Editor
Keith Schofield
Lighting
Keith Schofield
Cameraperson
Damian Acevedo

Record Company
EMI Music
Video Commissioner
Xavier De Nauw

El Niño
for EMI Music

Let Love Rule (Justice Remix)
Keith Schofield lets the credits roll... and roll... and roll...

Director
So Me
Producer
Mourad Belkeddar

Artist
Kid Cudi
Production Company
El Niño
Editor
Olivier Gajan

Special Effects
MATHEMATIC Paris
Director of Photography
Arnaud Potier

Record Companies
G.O.O.D.
Universal Motown
Video Commissioner
Gina Harrell

Music Videos
El Niño
for G.O.O.D. & Universal Motown

Day 'N' Nite
Kid Cudi gets the So Me treatment in this video for 'Day 'N' Nite'.

Animator
Corin Hardy
Director
Corin Hardy
Producer
Liz Kessler

Artist
Prodigy
Production Company
Academy Films
Editor
Amanda James

Lighting
Cameraperson
Stuart Bentley
Set Designers
Corin Hardy
Laura Johnstone

Record Company
Cooking Vinyl
Video Commissioner
Rob Collins

Animation
Academy Films
for Cooking Vinyl

Warrior's Dance
In this video for Warrior's Dance, the Pied Piper is reinterpreted for a club generation. Using a combination of animation, puppetry and live action, cigarette packets come to life, partying like there is no tomorrow and finally, perishing in flames as the Prodigy Puppets leave, having done their work. It reflects the live nature of the band's shows in an original and refreshing way without having to show any band performance.

Animators
tienne Périn
érémie Périn
imon Périn
ikael Robert

Director
Jérémie Périn
Producers
Jill Caytan
Constance Guillou
Patrice Haddad
Benoit Tregouet

Artist
Flairs
Scriptwriters
Jérémie Périn
Laurent Sarfati

Production Company
Première Heure
Editor
Jérémie Périn
Record Company
Third Side Records

Animation

Première Heure
for Third Side Records

Truckers Delight
The Truckers Delight animated video was directed by newcomer wunderkid Jérémie Périn from Première Heure, who took the song's title (a tribute to those little pleasures that the lonely truck driver indulges in) to the next level. Think Spielberg's 'Duel', Russ Meyer's 'Faster, Pussycat! Kill! Kill!' and Marc Dorcel's wildest fantasies. All warped into an eight-bit Sega-era style graphic. And this clumsy and somewhat pretentious description doesn't even come close to what you're about to see: it's très funny, très dirty, très sexy. Très Flairs indeed.

Animator
Mark Waring
Director
orin Hardy
Producer
iz Kessler

Artist
Paolo Nutini
Production Company
Academy Films
Editor
Nick Allix

Lighting
Cameraperson
Ed Wild
Set Designer
Laura Johnstone

Record Company
Atlantic Records
Video Commissioner
Tim Nash

Animation

Academy Films
for Atlantic Records

Pencil Full of Lead
A plasticine Paolo Nutini performs in a classic TV setting. Going entirely against the personality of the artist, Nutini's alter-ego is lecherous and inappropriate with his hard working female dancers and musicians. They soon loose patience, turning on him to get revenge.

A DIVE
DOG TU

Art Directors
Nadja Lossgott
Shelley Smoler
Copywriters
Raphael Basckin
Nicholas Hulley

Photographers
Chloe Coetsee
Des Ellis
Michael Meyersfeld
Rob Wilson
**Executive Creative
Director**
Damon Stapleton

Advertising Agency
TBWA\Hunt\Lascaris
Johannesburg
Account Handler
Bridget Langley

Marketing Manager
Liz Linsell
Client
The Zimbabwean
Newspaper

▲ Poster Advertising Campaigns

TBWA\Hunt\Lascaris
for The Zimbabwean Newspaper

Trillion Dollar Billboard / Trillion Dollar Wallpaper / Cheaper Than Paper / Z$250,000,000
The Zimbabwean Newspaper, forced into exile, was then slapped with a 55% luxury import duty, making it unaffordable for Zimbabweans. The most eloquent symbol of Zimbabwe's collapse is the Z$ trillion note, which cannot buy anything and certainly not advertising. But it can become the advertising. We turned the money into the medium by printing our messages straight onto it. We made posters, murals and billboards out of the worthless money. Overnight, Zimbabwean banknotes achieved what they'd never been able to buy – advertising coverage. We used Mugabe's own creation against him. The 'Cheaper than Paper' poster was also selected as a single execution in the Pavement Posters category.

Art Directors
Ewan Paterson
Micky Tudor
Copywriters
Ewan Paterson
Micky Tudor

Creative Directors
Ewan Paterson
Micky Tudor
Stuart Watson
Design Agencies
CHI&Partners
Venture Three

Advertising Agencies
CHI&Partners
Venture Three
Planner
Ben Southgate
Account Handler
Danny Josephs

Brand Manager
Richard Larcombe
Marketing Manager
Paul Lotherington
Client
News International
Brand
The Times

Poster Advertising Campaigns
CHI&Partners & Venture Three
for News International

The Saturday – Record Shop / Armbands / Nail Biting
An eye-catching twist on the iconic masthead of The Times shows how you only get that Saturday feeling with one newspaper: The Times on Saturday.

Who does the man everyone
listens to, listen to?

'I read the Financial Times before other people.
Now everybody carries around a Financial Times.'
Barack Obama

We live in FINANCIAL TIMES®

t Director
avid Mackersey
pywriter
nathan John
pographer
te Mould

Creative Directors
Sam Oliver
Shishir Patel
**Executive Creative
Director**
Jeremy Craigen
Designer
Pete Mould

Advertising Agency
DDB UK
Planner
Lucy Jameson
Business Director
Anna Hopwood

Account Director
Charlie Elliott
Account Manager
Matt Bundy
Marketing Manager
Caroline Halliwell
Client
Financial Times

Transport Posters

DDB UK
for the Financial Times

Obama
'I read the Financial Times before other people read the Financial Times. Now it's trendy and everybody carries around a Financial Times'. This quote from Obama during an interview with the Financial Times' editor is used alongside an image of the president addressing a Democratic campaign rally in Portland, Oregon in May 2008. The advert was part of a campaign promoting the Financial Times as the publication that 'the man everyone listens to, listens to'.

Step into middle England's best loved department store, stroll through haberdashery to the audio visual department where an awfully well brought up young man will bend over backwards to find the right TV for you **then go to dixons.co.uk and buy it.**

Dixons.co.uk
The last place you want to go

Get off at the fashionable end of Oxford Street, drift into the achingly cool technology hall of London's most happening department store and view this year's must-have plasma courtesy of the sound and vision technologist in the Marc Jacobs sandals then go to dixons.co.uk and buy it.

Dixons.co.uk
The last place you want to go

Art Director
Graham Fink
Copywriters
Simon Dicketts
Orlando Warner
Typographers
Gareth Davies
Simon Warden

Creative Directors
Simon Dicketts
Graham Fink
Advertising Agency
M&C Saatchi
London

Planner
Neil Godber
Account Handler
Estelle Lee
Marketing Director
Niall O'Keefe

Client
Dixons Stores
Group
Brand
Dixons.co.uk

Transport Posters

M&C Saatchi London
for Dixons Stores Group

Middle England / Sandals
Our campaign repositioned Dixons.co.uk by persuading people to embrace a smarter way of shopping online. People were cheekily encouraged to make use of the best service freely available on the high street, then find a better price online at Dixons.co.uk. The ads wittily suggested some typical high-street shopping experiences people could try. The sign-off, 'The last place you want to go' acted as a polite suggestion of when people should use the site, as well as a self-aware and humorous acknowledgement of the brand's equivocal reputation as a good place to shop.

350

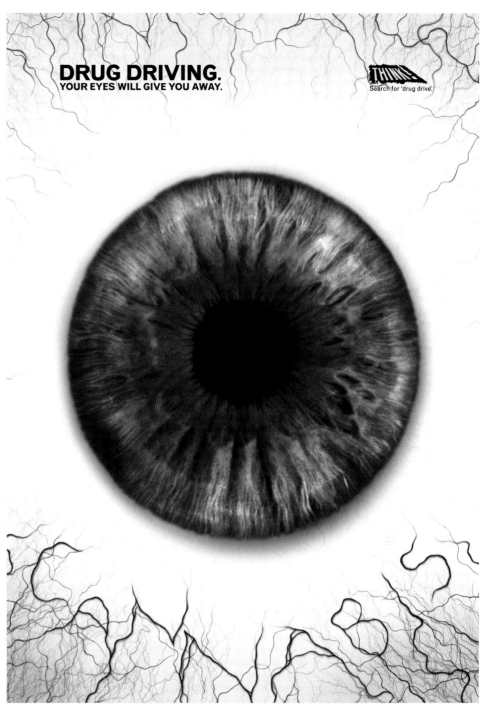

Director
chard Brim
pywriter
niel Fisher

Creative Director
Jonathan Burley
Designer
Sean Freeman

Advertising Agency
Leo Burnett London
Planner
Nick Docherty

Account Handler
Richard Bookey
Client
Department for
Transport

Indoor Posters

Leo Burnett London
for the Department for Transport

Cannabis
Drug driving is a growing problem on Britain's roads. 18 to 32 year-old drug drivers do not believe that their driving is impaired and that they can be caught. The task was to make them take drug driving seriously by bursting the permissive 'bubble' they had created around their behaviour with incontestable fact: drugs have an involuntary effect on the eyes that the police can test for. 'Your eyes will give you away' became the central premise of this campaign. This was seen as both compelling new information and a resonant, widely held truth about drugs that could force reappraisal of the issue.

351

Art Directors
Tristan Cornelius
Joe Miller
Copywriters
Tristan Cornelius
Joe Miller

Photographer
Alastair Thain
Typographer
Jonathon Muddell
Creative Director
Graham Fink

Advertising Agency
M&C Saatchi London
Planner
Cressida O'Shea
Account Handler
Zara Bailey

Marketing Director
Miranda Leedham
Client
Transport for London

Poster Advertising Campaigns

M&C Saatchi London
for Transport for London

Couple / Girl / Boy
One teenager is killed or seriously injured on London roads every day. This road safety campaign aimed at 11 to 14-year-olds is based on the insight that the most important thing for teenagers is their friends. While every teen thinks they are invincible, they can imagine a friend being in a road accident and how they would feel if they were responsible or could have done something to prevent it. The posters show teens who appear to be leaning against a wall, but a second glance reveals they are lying dead on the road after an accident. The call to action is 'Think! Look out for your mates'.

Art Director	Creative Director	Advertising Agency	Marketing Manager
John Treacy	John Treacy	Elvis	Steven Seddon
Copywriter	Flash Designer	Account Handler	Client
Rick Kiesewetter	Jason Garfield	Alex Nibblet	Virgin Trains

Enhanced, Interactive & Digital Posters

Elvis
for Virgin Trains

Liverpool Wall

The brief was to announce to the people of Liverpool that getting to London with Virgin Trains had never been quicker. Our response was to turn Europe's largest digital screen in Liverpool into a live, interactive poster. The copywriter was on site, hidden from passers-by, but had full view of the poster and typed spontaneous lines into a laptop which then appeared instantly onto the poster. The lines referenced what was happening around the poster in real time, making it look as if the poster had a mind of its own. The message about faster journey times was interwoven using Virgin's cheeky tone.

Art Director Brandon Mugar **Copywriter** Adam Reeves **Executive Creative** **Directors** Greg Hahn Mike Smith **Chief Creative** **Officers** Bill Bruce David Lubars	**Content Producer** Nicholas Gaul **Director of** **Integrated** **Production** Brian DiLorenzo **Director** Noam Murro **Advertising Agency** BBDO New York **Senior Executive** **Producer** Shawn Lacy	**Executive Producer** Colleen O'Donnell **Production Company** Biscuit Filmworks **Director of Creative** **Engineering** **& Production** Jd Michaels **Editor** David Henegar **Editing House** Butcher Editorial	**Music Supervisors** Stephanie Diaz-Matos Randall Poster **Music House** Search Party Music **Audio Mix** Sound Lounge **Mixer** Cory Melious **Telecine Artists** Beau Leon Marshall Plante	**Telecine** The Syndicate **Outdoor Projection** Staging Techniques **Visual Effects** **Company** Animal Logic **Event Coordination** GMR/T.Y. Smith Group **Client** HBO

Ambient

BBDO New York
for HBO

Cube Film Installation
The HBO Cube is a first-of-its-kind outdoor film event, embodying HBO's DNA of innovative storytelling. The cube shows four sides of a story simultaneously, each providing a different perspective of the film's characters and plot. Only by watching all sides do viewers see the truth of what really happened. Two distinct films were played, 'Art Heist' and 'The Affair', each specifically choreographed and created for the cube. Both films stood on their own as embodiments of the brand, but were also later revealed to be part of a larger narrative experience on the campaign website, hboimagine.com.

354

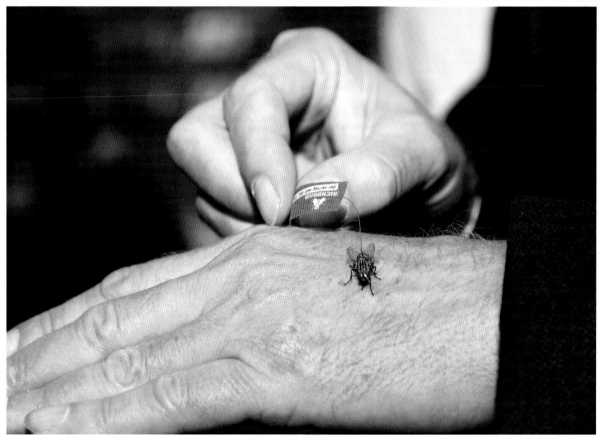

t Directors
njamin Beck
omas Lupo
pywriters
nnart Frank
rman Scholl

Creative Directors
Michael Ohanian
Jacques Pense
Advertising Agency
Jung von Matt
Stuttgart

Producer
Gun Aydemir
Account Handler
Katja Best

Account Supervisor
Christine Seelig
Client
Eichborn

Ambient

Jung von Matt Stuttgart
for Eichborn

Flyvertising – The World's First Fly Banner
Eichborn is the publisher with the fly logo. Humorous, brave and unconventional. To strengthen the publisher's positioning at the Frankfurt Book Fair, and to drive the public to the company's exhibition stand, we used the Eichborn logo, the fly, and created a new form of advertising: flyvertising. Or more precisely, the first fly banner in the world. We equipped 200 real flies with ultra light banners. The line on the banner read: 'Eichborn. The publisher with the fly. Hall 4.1. Stand E146'. We released the flies from the Eichborn exhibition stand, from where they conquered the whole exhibition hall.

355

A PIDGIN
EGG
SNACK.

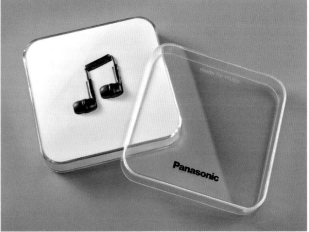

Art Directors
Philipp Weber
Walter Ziegler
Copywriter
Felix John

Creative Directors
Matthias Spaetgens
Michael
Winterhagen
Advertising Agency
Scholz & Friends
Berlin

Account Handlers
Salvatore Amato
Mona Braun
Marketing Manager
Norbert Frenkler

Client
Panasonic Marketing
Europe
Brand
Panasonic

Packaging

Scholz & Friends Berlin
for Panasonic Marketing Europe

The Earphones Note
Earphones from Panasonic offer great sound quality. The new package design for the Stereo Earphones RP-HJE 130 had to clearly communicate this product benefit. It also had to stand out among the interchangeable packaging designs of the competition, in order to reach a target group that owns well-designed, high-class mp3 players. The new design uses the universal symbol for music: the note. By cleverly arranging the earphones inside a special box they appear to look like two eighth notes. So the earphones show at first sight for whom they are made: passionate music lovers. This was also selected in the Packaging Design/Physical Shape category.

esigners
ɔsh Michels
ebecca Williams
esign Director
arah Moffat

Creative Directors
Bruce Duckworth
David Turner
Design Studio
Turner Duckworth:
London & San
Francisco

Account Handler
Jessica Rogers
Brand Manager
Frederic Kahn

Client
The Coca-Cola
Company North
America
Brand
Coca-Cola

Packaging
Turner Duckworth: London & San Francisco
for Coca-Cola

Coca-Cola Summer 2009 – Beach Ball / BBQ / 4th of July / Sunglasses / Surfboards
The Coca-Cola Summer 2009 campaign celebrates the joy and optimism of summer, and Coke's authentic connection with the season. A set of five limited edition summer cans was designed culminating with a special '4th of July' holiday can. The joyful summer graphics feature on everything from packaging and in-store displays to t-shirts, hats and beach towels, creating a fully integrated marketing campaign.

Packaging

Bloom
for Diageo

100 Years of Black Label and Selfridges
In 2009 Johnnie Walker Black Label and Selfridges celebrated their centenaries. We were asked to create a limited edition bottle to mark their joint birthdays. Both brands share a colour palette of black and yellow. We used bold, block yellow on the label, an iconic way of recognising the two brands' shared spirit of progress. Black glass was used to increase the impact of the colour change, and leather replaced paper for the label, adding a touch of luxury.

Creative Director	**Design Studio**	**Account Handler**	**Client**
Dan Cornell	Bloom	Jo Hargreaves	Diageo
Design Manager	**Production Director**	**Brand Manager**	**Brand**
Steve Honour	Tim Reynolds	Steve Wood	Johnnie Walker

Graphic Designer
an Hartwig
rt Director
eginald Wagner
opywriter
ll Grabsch

Creative Director
Katrin Oeding
Design Studio
KOREFE / Kolle
Rebbe

Account Handler
Kristina Wulf
Brand Manager
Felix Negwer

Client
The Deli Garage
Brand
Multi Noodles

Packaging

KOREFE / Kolle Rebbe
for The Deli Garage

Multi Noodles
Multi Noodles were launched on the market in a clearly structured screw box: as nails, screws, bolts and nuts. The shapes don't just represent shapes and forms found in the workshop domain (which is typical to Deli Garage foods), they also underline how essential pasta is: it holds every dish together.

Design
NOSIGNER

Brand & Marketing Manager
Yukihide Ozeki

Client
The Oyama Chamber of Commerce & Industry

Brand
Kanpyo Udon

Packaging

NOSIGNER
for The Oyama Chamber of Commerce & Industry

Kanpyo Udon Package & Paper Bag
For the branding for this new udon noodle product composed of gourd powder, the design needed to be both friendly enough to be recognised in one glance at the store, and high-class to compete with other traditional udon brands. To answer these seemingly contradictory requirements, I created a new character for gourd with traditional Japanese calligraphy drawn on Japanese paper. This more elaborate package represents the quality of the noodle itself.

362

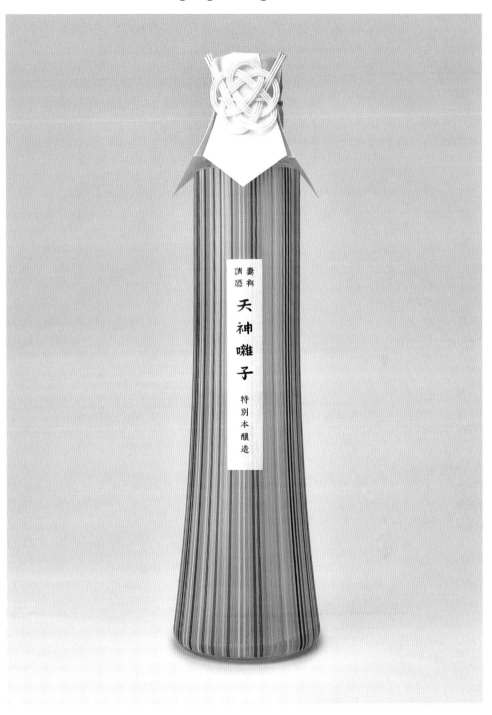

Designer
Jun Kuroyanagi
Bottle Manufacturer
Hiro Konishi

Printing Directors
Tsutomu Fujita
Kazuhito Yabe

Project Manager
Kosuke Kuwabara
Brand Manager
Katsuyoshi
Yamaguchi

Client
Uonuma Sake
Brewery
Brand
Tenjin-Bayashi

Packaging

Jun Kuroyanagi
for Uonuma Sake Brewery

Tenjin-Bayashi Specially Brewed Sake
Alongside the Echigo-Tsumari art triennial 2009, a regional specialty was redesigned to increase sales to visitors. The Echigo-Tsumari district is famous for brewing sake. Tenjin-Bayashi sake is named after an ancient song celebrating abundant crops; the challenge was how to present the character of the sake against a cultural backdrop. White or coloured paper string packing patterned with Mizuhiki, usually used for ceremonial gifts, was the solution to this problem. Tenjin-Bayashi in colourful, celebratory stripes had the appearance of a gift from nature. The bottlenecks were tied with plum blossom Mizuhiki, the crest of the god Tenjin.

Designers
Mireille Burkhardt
Tom Green
Matt Price

Art Director
Mireille Burkhardt
Creative Directors
Alexis Burgess
Mireille Burkhardt

Illustrator
Mio Matsumoto
Design Studio
BOB Design

Client
Space.NK
Brand
Life NK

Packaging

BOB Design
for Space.NK

Life NK
Life NK is the everyday range from beauty retailer Space.NK. Life NK is inspired by a little bear that lives in brand founder Nicky Kinnaird's handbag. A close friend gave it to her before the very first Space.NK store opened; it's become a lucky token which travels with her around the world. The life circle is present throughout the line, using colour to differentiate the fragrances The circle interacts with the bear in various ways to illustrate the properties of the product.

Auberginenkaviar
Caviar d'aubergine

Tomatenessenz
Essence de tomates

Designer	Illustrators	Design Studio	Clients
Remo Caminada	Donat Caduff	Remo Caminada	Andreas Caminada
Art Director	Remo Caminada	Graphic Design	Globus
Remo Caminada	Michael Häne	**Brand Manager**	**Brand**
		Sergio Loretz	Andreas Caminada

Packaging

Remo Caminada Graphic Design
for Andreas Caminada & Globus

Andreas Caminada
Andreas Caminada is an exceptionally gifted chef who was awarded 19 Gault Millau points and was twice chosen as Swiss chef of the year. The modular based icons and the text on the back of this packaging for Caminada's products invite you to a world of delicious food in a welcoming atmosphere. A triangle, square and line, and sometimes a small circle are the vocabulary for our modular sketching. On the back of the packaging are short stories, next to the ingredients and serving suggestions. They are confusing, they make you smile and some are a bit eerie. Not a surprise if you know that Caminada cooks in a castle.

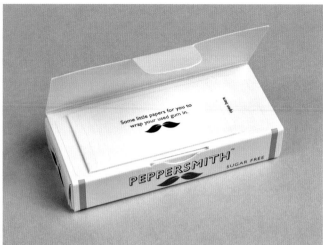

Designer
Shaun Bowen
Copywriters
Lisa Desforges
Dan Shrimpton

Creative Director
Shaun Bowen
Illustrators
Shaun Bowen
George Hartley

Design Studio
B&B studio

Account Handler
Kerry Bolt
Client
Peppersmith

Packaging

B&B studio
for Peppersmith

Peppersmith Selleck / Dali / Ming / Hoffman / Chaplin / Fred
This identity and packaging were designed to reflect the Englishness of the mint and
artisan feel of the product. The logo has two levels of interpretation: peppermint leaves
or a moustache, representing an era when gum was made naturally. The moustache idea
was taken one step further through the creation of a series of moustached heroes that feature
on the inside of the pack, inspired by matchbox collectables. With a clean and fresh look, this
innovative packaging includes a booklet of papers to ensure that every piece of used gum
is wrapped up to keep Britain tidy.

Packaging

Pearlfisher
for Über Drinks

Übershot
Pearlfisher created the brand identity for new energy drink Übershot. Übershot is the powerful new face of energy shots. The innovative and challenging design reflects its positioning as an integral part of modern, professional life. Pearlfisher focused on creating a stylish and sophisticated urban accessory. The bold icon reflects the message of the front facing tagline: 'Energy for life with no lows'. The small format aluminium bottle is also a real point of difference and design breakthrough for this category. In a nutshell, it's a small pack that delivers a big idea.

367

sign Director
Firth
eative Director
talie Chung

Creative Partner
Jonathan Ford

Design Studio
Pearlfisher

Client
Über Drinks
Brand
Übershot

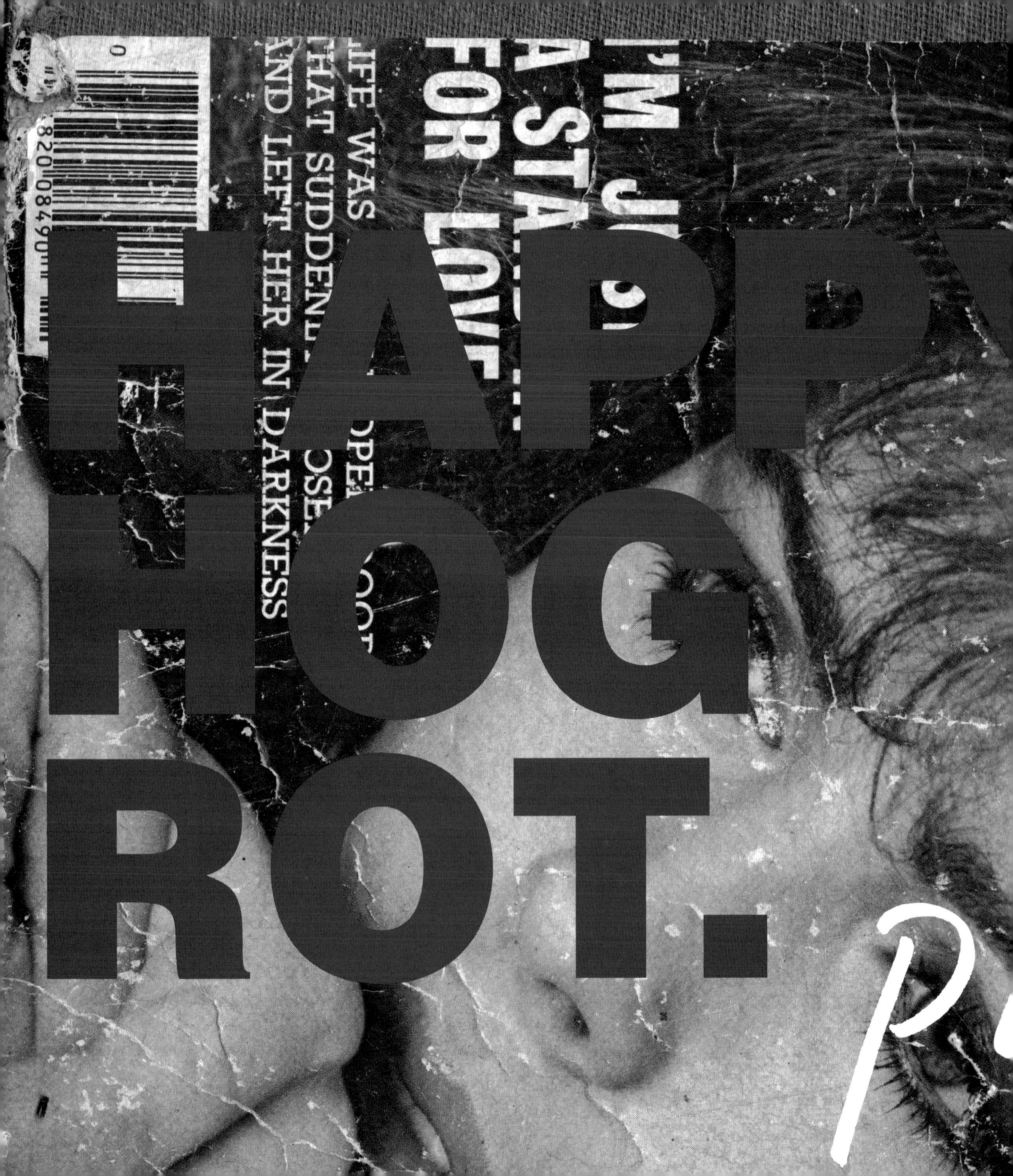

I'M JU

A STA

FOR LOVE

LIFE WAS

THAT SUDDENLY

AND LEFT HER IN DARKNESS

OPEN

HAPPY
HOG.
ROT.

P.

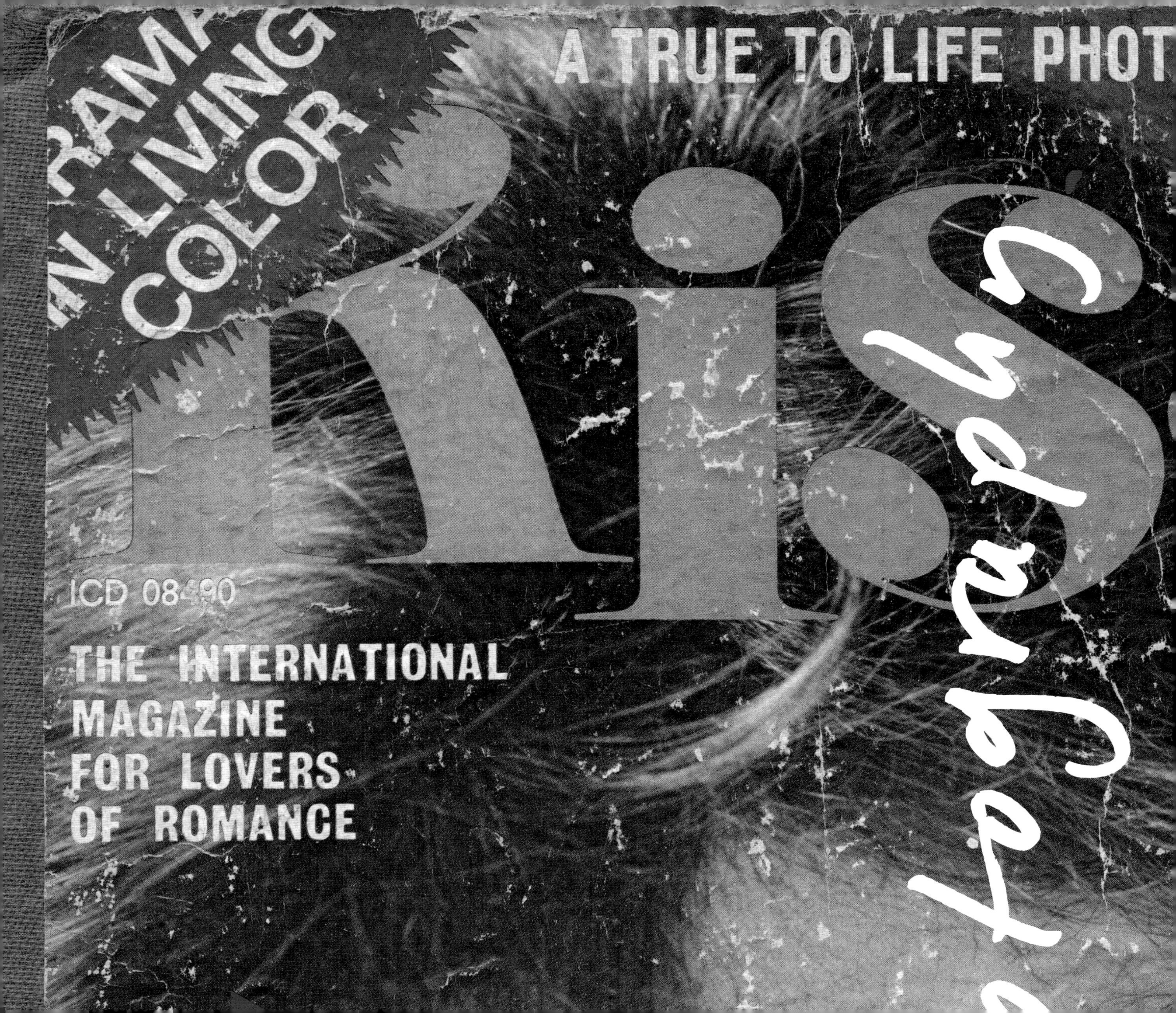

CRAMP IN LIVING COLOR

ICD 08490

THE INTERNATIONAL MAGAZINE FOR LOVERS OF ROMANCE

A TRUE TO LIFE PHOT

otography

Photography

Photographer
Jim Naughten

Image Manipulator
Tim Ashton

Designer
Allon Kaye

Client
Jim Naughten
Brand
Hot Shoe Books

▲ Book Design

Jim Naughten
for Hot Shoe Books

Re-Enactors
Every summer thousands of people from all over the world gather in a Kentish field and leave the present firmly behind. They step out of their routine, daily lives and transform themselves into historical characters from the first and second world wars in a collective fantasy that is played out on a massive scale. Jim Naughten's portraits of these re-enactors are shot formally, in three-quarter profile with a treatment that heightens the sense of artifice and anachronism. It is hard to imagine them outside this fictitious battle zone. Beautifully bound and printed, this volume records a world apart from both the past and present.

370

Indian Winter

Photographer
Mark Zibert
Image Manipulator
James Lucas
Art Director
Emily Grover
Designer
Mick Newman

Copywriter
Leo Barker
Print Producer
Ed Webster
Creative Director
Brett Foraker
Advertising Agency
4creative

Account Handler
Molly Manners
Brand Manager
Ros Godber
Marketing Director
Rufus Radcliffe
Marketing Manager
James Walker

Client
Channel 4
Television
Brand
Indian Winter

Poster Advertising

4creative
for Channel 4 Television

Indian Winter
To celebrate the launch of Channel 4's season of India-related programming, we brought
the colour and vibrancy of that extraordinary country to the grey winter streets of England.

Photographer
Olaf Becker
Art Directors
Tristan Cornelius
Joe Miller
Designer
Simon Warden

Copywriters
Tristan Cornelius
Joe Miller
Illustrator
Kevin Glashier
Typographer
Simon Warden
Print Producer
Neil McMahon

Creative Director
Graham Fink
Head of Art
Tiger Savage
Advertising Agency
M&C Saatchi London
Account Handlers
Zara Bailey
Louise Gross

Brand Manager
Jeanette Moore
Client
H.J. Heinz Company
Brand
HP Sauce

Poster Advertising

M&C Saatchi London
for H.J. Heinz Company

Middle Age / Boy / Grandad
HP Sauce may be part of the social fabric of Britain, but it still faces competition in the supermarket. HP fans are loyal to the brand in principle, but when assailed by massive competition, they often give in to heavy price promotion at the shelf. Tasked to increase sales and justify the price difference HP's quality demands, our message was, 'Why ruin their favourite meals?' Posters were positioned outside supermarkets to remind shoppers that not staying true to the definitive brown sauce would ruin meals for themselves and other household members. The reaction of family members was dramatised to underline the perils of failing to choose HP.

YOUR CLOTHES WEREN'T THERE.

GAIN with febreze ODOR REMOVAL

Press Advertising

Lapiz
for Procter & Gamble

Kitchen
We were asked to launch the new Gain with Febreze, an odour-eliminating product, in the US Hispanic market. In order to stand out against other odour-eliminating products, we chose a simple solution: show the experience to the consumers. Gain with Febreze is so effective, it's as if your clothes were never there.

Photography	**Executive Creative Director**	**Advertising Agency**	**Account Director**
Buena Vista	Laurence Klinger	Lapiz	Pablo Miro
Fotografia	**Associate Creative Directors**	**Planning Director**	**Client**
Art Directors	Maria Bernal	Enrique Marquez	Procter & Gamble
Maria Bernal	Jose Funegra	**Agency Producer**	**Brand**
Jorge Pomareda		Milagros de la Rosa	Gain with Febreze
Copywriters			
Carlos Bretel			
Jose Funegra			

Photographer
James Day
Image Manipulation
Core Digital London

Art Directors
Komal Bedi Sohal
Shahir Zag
Copywriters
Komal Bedi Sohal
Shahir Zag

Advertising Agency
Y&R Dubai
Account Handler
Nadine Ghossoub

Marketing Manager
Vino El Khatib
Client
Harvey Nichols

Press Advertising

Y&R Dubai
for Harvey Nichols

Dolls – Blonde / Man / Redhead
This campaign was to promote the Autumn/Winter 2009 collection at Harvey Nichols.
The campaign sought to visualise the enviable style of Harvey Nichols customers, which can cause resentment among their peers who are not fortunate enough to be able to indulge in the high-end department store. To do so, we featured life-sized voodoo dolls in show-stoppers from the season. The images are inspired by the season's trends which were iconic and edgy, and really expressed character.

Photographer
Simon Harsent
Image Manipulation
Cream Retouching
Art Director
Kieran Antill

Copywriter
Michael Canning
Print Producer
Josephine Hoskins
Creative Directors
Jay Benjamin
Andy DiLallo

Advertising Agency
Leo Burnett Sydney
Account Handlers
Paul Everson
Jodi McLeod

Brand Manager
Lawrence Hennessy
Client
WWF

Press Advertising

Leo Burnett Sydney
for WWF

Gorillas / Tigers / Penguins
The World Wildlife Fund (WWF) was launching a new project to target the issue of endangered species. Our brief was to create a print campaign to launch the project, by building emotion around the problem and driving people online to learn more. Our solution was to strike at the truth of the issue: once a species is extinct, it is gone for good. Depicting beautiful yet endangered animals as 'ghosts' created emotion and a sense of urgency. The campaign struck a chord with the public; this was seen in an online response rate that far exceeded the target.

Press Advertising

Publicis London
for Boon Rawd Trading

Steps / Cave
Singha beer is for people who seek adventures off the beaten track. We wanted to connect with them by showing modern advertising media spaces in remote places. Like escalator posters on an ancient temple, and an underground poster in a remote cave.

Photographer
Justin Cooper
Art Director
Dellano Pereira

Designers
Sam Moffat
Dellano Pereira

Typographer
Dellano Pereira

Design Group
Three60
Client
LIFEwithBIRD

Packaging Design

Three60
for LIFEwithBIRD

Collection No.14

Fashion label LIFEwithBIRD approached Three60 to conceive a show-piece for their Collection No.14 and for the brand's debut at New York Fashion Week 2009. The format we decided on was a set of limited edition posters to be housed in a series of 14 tubes. Each tube was individually wrapped with a grainy abstract texture, and labelled with a letter. When the tubes are correctly aligned next to each other, they make up the title Collection No.14 while the abstract texture forms the face of the girl featured in the posters.

Photographer
Hai-Long Jiang
Artist
Li Wei

Photography Editor
James Reid
Fashion Director
Sébastien Clivaz

Publisher
Wallpaper*
Magazine

Client
Wallpaper*

Magazine & Newspaper Design
Hai-Long Jiang
for Wallpaper*

National Heroes
For their June 2009 issue, Wallpaper* produced a 'Made in China' special, documenting all the latest artistic, cultural, architectural and business innovations emerging from the country. As part of this issue, artist Li Wei and his team of acrobats created and shot a fashion story in and around Beijing. They staged gravity-defying stunts, seeming to float and fly around the city, which resulted in a jaw-dropping series of pictures. All the stunts were staged as they appear in the story; the only post-production undertaken was to remove the safety cables holding the performers up in some of the more dangerous set-ups.

378

Burnout #3

Magazine & Newspaper Design

Photographers	Editor in Chief	Client	Brand
Todd Hido	Stephen Toner	By Any Means	Exit
Matthew Porter		Necessary	
Art Director			
Mark Jubber			

Todd Hido & Matthew Porter
for By Any Means Necessary

Exit Magazine
Launched in 2000, ever-evolving and forward-thinking, Exit Magazine heralded a new chapter in curated magazine publishing. An exclusive mix of luxury lifestyle, fashion, art, culture and world-class photography from the most respected and innovative creatives internationally. Each issue of Exit becoming a beautifully crafted collectors' item inspiring an immediate and lasting impression on the reader. Published twice a year, Exit has established a reputation for unique international content.

379

Thrice Removed. David Stewart

Photographer	Copywriter	Creative Director	Design Group
David Stewart	Peter Kirby	Nick Jones	Browns
Designers	**Typographers**	**Publishers**	**Client**
Dan Greene	Dan Greene	Browns Editions	David Stewart
Nick Jones	Nick Jones		Photography

Book Design

Browns & David Stewart
for David Stewart Photography

Thrice Removed

Thrice Removed gathers observations on family, society, relationships and life in general, with a knowing smile and ready wink. The colour photographs bear close scrutiny both technically and emotionally, revealing more the closer you look. The format of a children's board book alludes to Stewart's childlike curiosity, while the images hint at an altogether darker heart. This is a first edition of 1,000 copies, 200 of which are limited edition, printed red with white text.

380

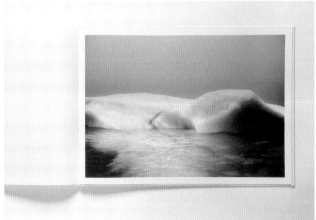

Photographer
Simon Harsent

Art Directors
Kiat
Ken Tan

Creative Director
Kiat

Design Agency
ohplay

Account Handler
Swee Lyn

Client
Pool Productions

Book Design

ohplay & Simon Harsent
for Pool Productions

Melt – Portrait of an Iceberg
This book begins with images of massive icebergs as they enter Greenland's Disco Bay from the Ilulissat Icefjord; it ends with the icebergs off the east coast of Newfoundland, by which time they have travelled hundreds of miles. They have been so battered and broken down that they are little more than ghosts of what they once were. Seeing them first overpowering in grandeur and then, later, about to be absorbed back into the flux from where they came, is both beautiful and humbling; a metamorphosis that endows them with a life span, each with its own personality, each with its own story.

SENSITIVE GRASP DR.

ARSE, MA'
at's the message from the Tat

SHOCKING threats to kill the Queen Mother are on display as ART in the Tate Gallery.

One of the SICK messages talks of the Queen Mum "getting sliced up" while another reads: "I'd rather see the Queen Mum's arse."

They are part of a bizarre exhibition by artist Patrick Brill on show at the new Tate Britain Gallery in London.

Thoughts

Visitors are inv

Queen Mum

By

Queen Moth
reads: "F...
she got Prin
she's gonna g
"If you wann
ber's on the b
by slicing her
We rang the
ber but it was o
One of the
ments Brill

Press Advertising

ER
M

allery

...HN

the worst
...n Mother coz
...na killed so
...up.

...ne my num-
...the Queen

...hone num-
...vice.

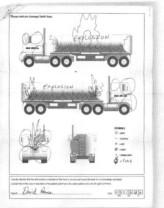

See film differently.
Volkswagen supports independent cinema.

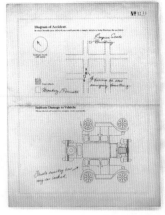

See film differently.
Volkswagen supports independent cinema.

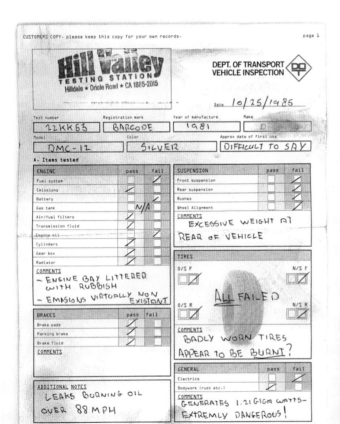
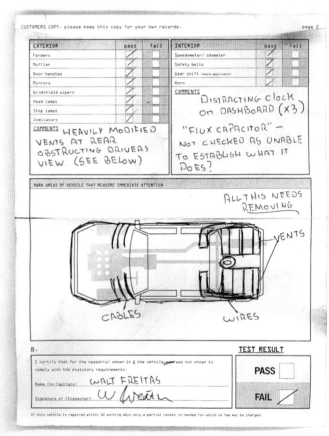

See film differently.
Volkswagen supports independent cinema.

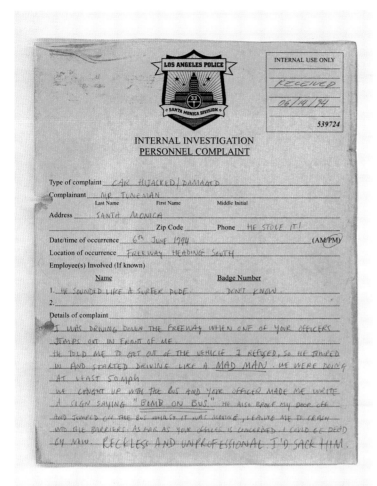

LOS ANGELES POLICE
SANTA MONICA DIVISION

INTERNAL USE ONLY

RECEIVED
06/14/94

539724

INTERNAL INVESTIGATION
PERSONNEL COMPLAINT

Type of complaint _CAR HIJACKED/DAMAGED_
Complainant _MR TUNEMAN_
          Last Name   First Name   Middle Initial
Address _SANTA MONICA_
          Zip Code   Phone _HE STOLE IT!_
Date/time of occurrence _6TH JUNE 1994_ (AM/PM)
Location of occurrence _FREEWAY HEADING SOUTH_
Employee(s) Involved (If known)
          Name   Badge Number
1. _HE SOUNDED LIKE A SURFER DUDE_   _DON'T KNOW_
2.
Details of complaint
I WAS DRIVING DOWN THE FREEWAY WHEN ONE OF YOUR OFFICERS
JUMPS OUT IN FRONT OF ME.
HE TOLD ME TO GET OUT OF THE VEHICLE. I REFUSED, SO HE JUMPED
IN AND STARTED DRIVING LIKE A MAD MAN. WE WERE DOING
AT LEAST 50.mph
WE CAUGHT UP WITH THE BUS AND YOUR OFFICER MADE ME WRITE
A SIGN SAYING "BOMB ON BUS" HE ALSO BROKE MY DOOR OFF
AND JUMPED ON THE BUS WHILST IT WAS MOVING, LEAVING ME TO CRASH
INTO THE BARRIERS. AS FAR AS YOUR OFFICER IS CONCERNED. I COULD BE DEAD
BY NOW. RECKLESS AND UNPROFESSIONAL. I'D SACK HIM.

See film differently.
Volkswagen supports independent cinema.

KINGSTON FALLS SHERIFF Dept.
INTERNAL INVESTIGATION
DAMAGE REPORT

ALL INFORMATION IS FOR INTERNAL USE ONLY

VEHICLE(S) DAMAGED: PATROL CAR [X] MOTORCYCLE [ ] BICYCLE [ ] OTHER [ ]

DATE OF INCIDENT MM/DD/YY   NAME OF OFFICER(S) INVOLVED IN FULL:
Christmas 1984   a) Officer Frank
                       b) Officer Brady
                       c)

DESCRIBE FULLY THE CIRCUMSTANCES OF THE ACCIDENT / DAMAGE IN FULL:

We have reason to believe some weird little creature
(see sketch below) tampered with our brakes. We don't
know what it was, but it was an ugly looking thing.

And it made us flip our car.

SKETCH ANY DETAILS YOU ARE UNABLE TO DESCRIBE IN THE SPACE BELOW:

DRIBBLE
DARK GREEN
(I would've colored it in
but didn't have a green pen)
FUNNY LITTLE LEGS

I declare that the above information is true, complete and correct.

SIGNED: DATE MM/DD/YY: 12/27/84

See film differently.
Volkswagen supports independent cinema.

t Director   Handwriting   Advertising Agency   Account Manager
niel Seager   Steve Hall   DDB UK   Jessica Huth
pywriter   Ruth Harlow   Planner   Communications
eve Hall   Pete Mould   Georgia Challis   Manager
pographer   Daniel Seager   Business Director   Sally Chapman
te Mould   Trevor Slabber   Jonathan Hill   Client
signer   Nicola Sullivan   Account Director   Volkswagen
te Mould   Illustrators   Charlie Elliott
ecutive Creative   Pete Mould
ector   Alex Price
emy Craigen   Oliver Watts

Magazine Press Advertising Colour

DDB UK
for Volkswagen

Terminator / King Kong / Back to the Future / Speed / Gremlins
This campaign promoted Volkswagen's sponsorship of independent cinema. Each advert
focuses on incidents involving cars in classic films. The film titles are not directly mentioned,
encouraging viewers to work them out for themselves. The fictional reports outline what
happened to the damaged vehicle and are filled out by the characters involved. King Kong,
Speed and Terminator were also selected as single executions in this category.

Get off at the fashionable end of Oxford Street, drift into the achingly cool technology hall of London's most happening department store and view this year's must-have plasma courtesy of the sound and vision technologist in the Marc Jacobs sandals **then go to dixons.co.uk and buy it.**

Dixons.co.uk
The last place you want to go

Step into middle England's best loved department store, stroll through haberdashery to the audio visual department where an awfully well brought up young man will bend over backwards to find the right TV for you **then go to dixons.co.uk and buy it.**

Dixons.co.uk
The last place you want to go

▲ Newspaper Press Advertising Colour

Art Director	**Creative Directors**	**Planner**	**Client**
Graham Fink	Simon Dicketts	Neil Godber	Dixons Stores Group
Copywriters	Graham Fink	**Account Handler**	**Brand**
Simon Dicketts	**Advertising Agency**	Estelle Lee	Dixons.co.uk
Orlando Warner	M&C Saatchi London	**Marketing Director**	
Typographers		Niall O'Keefe	
Gareth Davies			
Simon Warden			

M&C Saatchi London
for Dixons Stores Group

Sandals / Middle England
Our campaign repositioned Dixons.co.uk by persuading people to embrace a smarter way of shopping online. People were cheekily encouraged to make use of the best service freely available on the high street, then find a better price online at Dixons.co.uk. The ads wittily suggested some typical high-street shopping experiences people could try. The sign-off, 'The last place you want to go' acted as a polite suggestion of when people should use the site, as well as a self-aware and humorous acknowledgement of the brand's equivocal reputation as a good place to shop. The advert 'Middle England' was selected, and 'Sandals' was awarded a Nomination.

rt Director
ctor Monclus
ppywriter
ill Lowe
pographer
te Mould

Designer
Pete Mould
Executive Creative Director
Jeremy Craigen
Advertising Agency
DDB UK

Business Director
Jonathan Hill
Account Director
Charlie Elliott
Account Manager
Jessica Huth

Communications Manager
Sally Chapman
Client
Volkswagen

▲ Inserts & Wraps

DDB UK
for Volkswagen

Film Polywrap
This plastic wrap contained the magazines that come with The Observer, a Sunday newspaper.
Our brief was to alert readers to the Volkswagen-sponsored film supplement within.

Art Director
David Mackersey
Copywriter
Jonathan John
Typographer
Pete Mould

Designer
Pete Mould
Creative Directors
Sam Oliver
Shishir Patel
**Executive Creative
Director**
Jeremy Craigen

Advertising Agency
DDB UK
Planner
Lucy Jameson
Business Director
Anna Hopwood
Account Director
Charlie Elliott

Account Manager
Matt Bundy
Marketing Manager
Caroline Halliwell
Client
Financial Times

Magazine Press Advertising Colour

DDB UK
for the Financial Times

Obama
'I read the Financial Times before other people read the Financial Times. Now it's trendy and everybody carries around a Financial Times'. This quote from Obama during an interview with the Financial Times' editor is used alongside an image of the president addressing a Democratic campaign rally in Portland, Oregon in May 2008. The advert was part of a campaign promoting the Financial Times as the publication that 'the man everyone listens to, listens to'.

Magazine Press Advertising Colour

DLKW
for Marston's

History / Our Blood / Serve It
The aim of the campaign was to highlight Marston's sponsorship of English cricket during the 2009 Ashes by humorously pointing out the superior 'pedigree' of the English over their Australian rivals. By using provocative statements in the spirit of the good-humoured rivalry that exists between England and Australia, we encouraged banter and cemented Marston's as the beer of English cricket.

rt Director	**Creative Directors**	**Model Maker**	**Account Handler**
chard Prentice	Jon Elsom	Jon Steed	Stuart Lundy
opywriter	Keith Terry	**Advertising Agency**	**Marketing Manager**
avid Adamson	**Executive Creative**	DLKW	Des Gallagher
hotographer	**Director**	**Planner**	**Client**
aurie Haskell	George Prest	Pat McCaren	Marston's
vpographer	**Retoucher**	**Art Buyer**	
uy Sexty	Glen Pothecary	Julie Hughes	

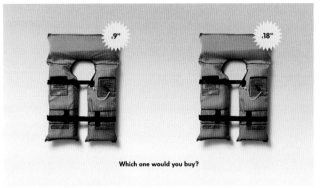

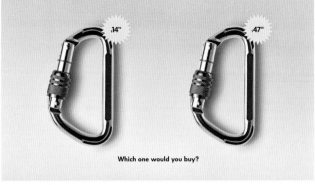

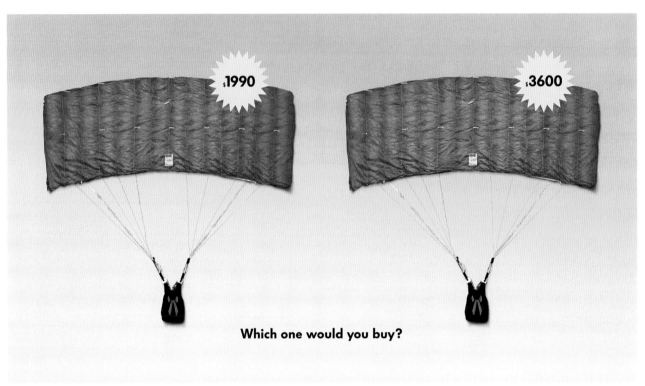

Art Director
André Gola
Copywriter
André Godoi

Typographer
José Roberto
Bezerra

Creative Directors
Dulcidio Caldeira
Luiz Sanches

Advertising Agency
AlmapBBDO
Client
Volkswagen

Magazine Press Advertising Colour
AlmapBBDO
for Volkswagen

Lifeguard / Hook / Parachute
The aim of this campaign was to show that everyone should be suspicious of a very cheap piece, especially when it is a safety item, even though it seems just as good.

much faster than expected, with
environment. If urgent measures are
within a few years, the effects of
and sea levels will be catastrophic.

GREENPEACE
www.greenpeace.org.br

Climate change: it's increasing
enormous consequences for the
not taken to control global warming
the rise in global temperature

rt Director
larco Monteiro
opywriter
esar Herszkowicz

Typographer
José Roberto
Bezerra

Creative Directors
Dulcidio Caldeira
Luiz Sanches

Advertising Agency
AlmapBBDO
Client
Greenpeace

Magazine Press Advertising Colour
AlmapBBDO
for Greenpeace

Sea Levels
To alert people to the consequences of global warming, we conveyed how a rise
in the planet's temperature may cause sea levels to change.

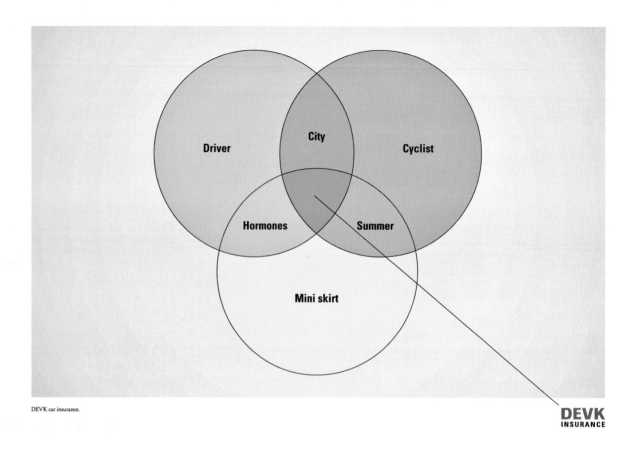

DEVK car insurance.

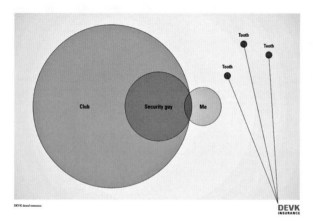

DEVK dental insurance.

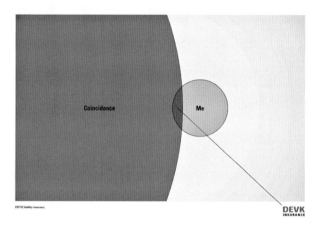

DEVK liability insurance.

Art Director
Jan Riggert
Copywriter
Tobias Burger
Creative Directors
Goesta Diehl
Oliver Heidorn
Timm Weber

Executive Creative Director
Ralf Heuel
Graphic Artist
Matthias Khaled
Baare

Advertising Agency
Grabarz & Partner
Advertising Manager
Christiane Niehaus

Marketing & Communications Manager
Michael Knaup
Client
DEVK insurance

Magazine Press Advertising Colour

Grabarz & Partner
for DEVK insurance

Mini Skirt / Security Guy / Coincidence
At first glance, the diagrams in this campaign look quite straightforward. But when you look closer, these graphs tell funny and interesting real-life stories. Stories that show our target group why it's always better to be insured by the DEVK.

Art Directors
Sanjiv Mistry
Prabashan
Gopalakrishnan
Pather

Copywriters
Sanjiv Mistry
Prabashan
Gopalakrishnan
Pather
Photographer
Guy Neveling
Creative Director
Christopher Gotz

Advertising Agency
Ogilvy Cape Town
Retoucher
Paul Hudson
Art Buyer
Merle Bennett
Account Managers
Mark Aschmann
Kate White

Business Director
Wouter Lombard
Marketing Director
Meriel Bartlett
Client
National Sea Rescue
Institute

Magazine Press Advertising Colour

Ogilvy Cape Town
for the National Sea Rescue Institute

Left the Sports Game / Left the Costume Party / Left her Wedding
The National Sea Rescue Institute (NSRI) is a not-for-profit organisation staffed by volunteers who help save lives out at sea. The brief was to create adverts to salute these remarkable men and women. The campaign depicts how NSRI's brave, unpaid volunteers will drop whatever they're doing, at any time of day, to go off and save people's lives. Showing them not just in treacherous seas, but sacrificing their personal time to do so, gives the volunteers a truly heroic aura.

393

Art Director	**Photographer**	**Advertising Agency**	**Planner**
Cedric Moutaud	Jean-Yves Lemoigne	CLM BBDO	Brice Garcon
Copywriter	**Creative Directors**	**Art Buyer**	**Client**
Vincent Pedrocchi	Gilles Fichtberg	Sylvie Etchemaite	Hewlett Packard
	Eric Pierre		
	Jean-Francois Sacco		

Magazine Press Advertising Colour

CLM BBDO
for Hewlett Packard

Baby / Garage / Pony
The new power of print – that's what this campaign and HP's communication strategy are all about. Meanings are multiple. Because beyond communicating superior printing quality and truer than life impressions, what matters here is what you do with the output, what the printed page triggers and reveals about you. Simply ask a little girl to talk to you about her favourite pony poster. The one that's on her bedroom wall. And get ready for a long story.

Art Directors
Fabrizio Capraro
Andrés Echeverría

Copywriter
Max König
Photographer
Patricio Pescetto

Creative Directors
Alvaro Becker
Francisco Cavada
Tony Sarroca
Advertising Agency
Prolam Y&R

Client
Nutripro
Brand
NutriBalance

Prolam Y&R
for Nutripro

Hand
If they were human, dogs would probably react bitterly to not receiving the great tasting, richly flavoured food they deserve. If this situation carried on, their discontent would grow, leading them to campaign for something more suitable and, ultimately, take revenge for being treated inappropriately. This latter human feeling is what the 'Bad food, bad dog' campaign is all about: dogs getting back at their owners for giving them poor quality food.

It's not just a lump of Plasticine

It's a laugh

It's what shall we make?

It's a rocket

It's a dinosaur

It's watching an 8-year-old boy with his new foster family

It's noticing how he shares a joke with his foster brother

It's laughing when the dinosaur looks more like a horse

It's seeing that everything's alright

It's knowing he's happy with his new family

It's a relief

It's the result of two years' hard work

It's not just a lump of Plasticine

It's one of the most important tools we use

Social work with children & families is changing

We can train you to use tools like these

And give you support as you progress through your training and career

Call 0300 123 1220 or search **Be the difference**

cWdc
Children's Workforce
Development Council

It's not just a bag of crisps

It's a stroll to the newsagents

It's what's your favourite flavour?

It's stopping to sit on a bench

It's a chat about her favourite band

It's noticing the bags under her eyes

It's hearing how she does all the housework

It's hearing how she cooks the dinner

It's asking about her Mum

It's the moment a 10-year-old girl tells you how her Mummy is always down the pub

It's a problem shared

It's planning for a better future

It's not just a bag of crisps

It's one of the most important tools we use

Social work with children & families is changing

We can train you to use tools like these

And find ways of building on your existing skills too

Call 0300 123 1220 or search **Be the difference**

cWdc
Children's Workforce
Development Council

It's not just a cup of tea

It's a chat about EastEnders

It's laughing at a joke

It's listening to a story

It's noticing the track marks on her arm

It's asking why she does it

It's hearing how she pays for it

It's believing her when she says she wants to get clean

It's the moment a 16-year-old girl asks you to help her

It's a step in the right direction

It's an excuse to come back and see how she's doing

It's a celebration

It's not just a cup of tea

It's one of the most important tools we use

Social work with children & families is changing

We can train you to use tools like these

And support you financially while you train

Call 0300 123 1220 or search **Be the difference**

cWdc
Children's Workforce
Development Council

Art Director
Jamie Marshall
Copywriter
Gary Turner
Photographer
Jenny van Sommers

Typographer
Dave Wakefield
Executive Creative Directors
Tom Ewart
Adam Kean

Advertising Agency
Publicis London
Head of Communications
Claire Chappell

Clients
C.O.I
CWDC (Children's Workforce Development Council)

Magazine Press Advertising Colour

Publicis London
for CWDC

Plasticine / Crisp / Tea
By talking to real social workers we discovered how they are trained to use simple, unassuming objects like a blob of plasticine, a crisp, and a cup of tea, to deal with the most complex emotional emergencies. Using stories based on real case studies and testimonials, we launched a recruitment campaign for CWDC to show potential candidates the true value of a career in social work. In just 18 weeks, we had over half a million responses and 54,364 registrations.

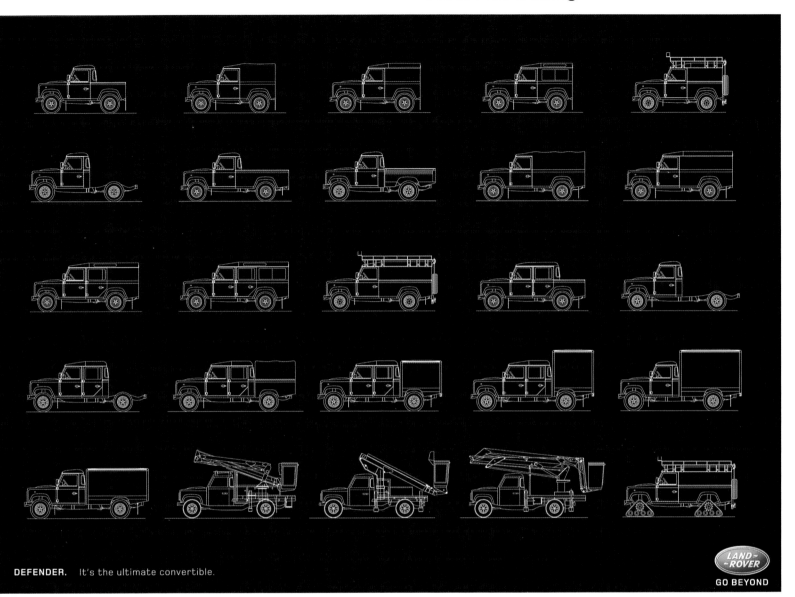

DEFENDER. It's the ultimate convertible.

Magazine Press Advertising Colour

RKCR/Y&R
for Land Rover

Convertible
The brief was to show the versatility of the Land Rover Defender, and let the market know that it has been available in an almost infinite number of body styles over the years. To build on the earlier 'Defender Utility' work, we continued to use the simple line drawing style, and showed the car in as many of its chameleon-like guises as possible.

t Director	Creative Director	Account Handler	Client
ve Williams	Mark Roalfe	Lucy Harries	Land Rover
pywriter	Illustrator	National	Brand
rian Lim	Steve Williams	Communications	Defender
pographer	Advertising Agency	Manager	
e Aldridge	RKCR/Y&R	Les Knight	

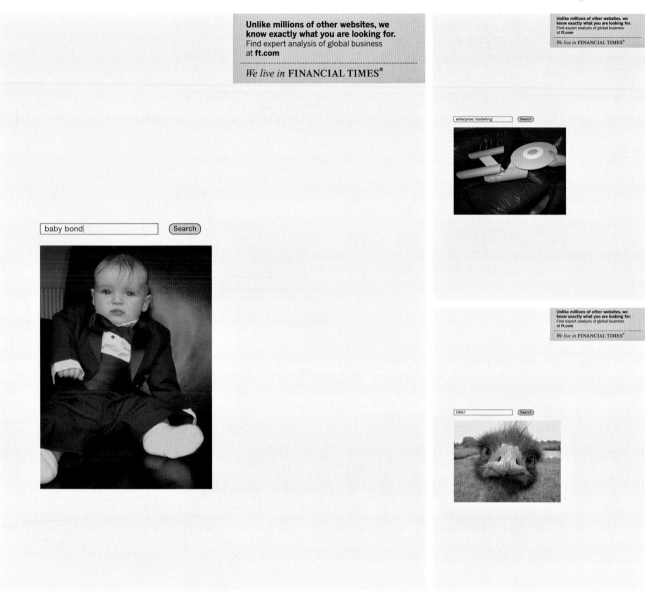

Art Director
Grant Parker
Copywriter
Grant Parker
Photographer
Oleg Volk

Typographer
Kevin Clarke
Creative Directors
Sam Oliver
Shishir Patel

Executive Creative Director
Jeremy Craigen
Advertising Agency
DDB UK

Account Director
Charlie Elliott
Marketing Manager
Caroline Halliwell
Client
Financial Times

Newspaper Press Advertising Colour

DDB UK
for the Financial Times

Baby Bond / Enterprise Modelling / European Monetary Union
To promote ft.com as a source of expert analysis of global business news, this campaign shows the results of an internet image search. Financial terms have been typed in the search bar, such as 'baby bond', but the search engine brings up an image of a baby in a bond outfit.

Art Director
Dimitri Guerassimov
Copywriter
Eric Jannon

Photographers
Ebo Fraterman
Roman
Schwienbacher
Creative Directors
Anne De Maupeou
Frederic Temin

Digital Artwork
Le Moulin des Docs
Advertising Agency
Marcel Paris
Art Buyer
Jean-Eric Le Coniac

Brand Managers
Arnaud Belloni
Olivier François
Maurizio Spagnulo
Client
Fiat

Newspaper Press Advertising Colour
Marcel Paris
for Fiat

Panda / Penguins / Walrus
Cars have an impact on the environment, but Fiat works hard to reduce it.

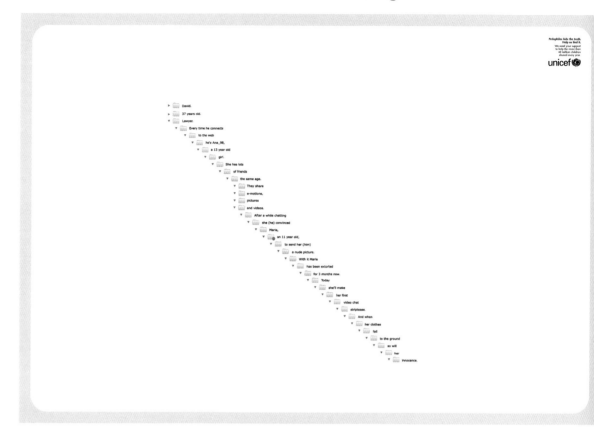

t Directors
ejandro Caputo
ime Gonzalez
pywriters
lipe Mañalich
colas Neumann

Creative Director
Nicolas Neumann
Executive Creative Director
Cesar Agost Carreno

Illustrator
Alejandro Caputo
Advertising Agency
Ogilvy & Mather Santiago

Account Handler
Edelweiss Fellenberg
Brand Manager
Francisca Palma
Client
UNICEF

Newspaper Press Advertising Colour
Ogilvy & Mather Santiago
for UNICEF

Blue Folders / Orange Folders / Yellow Folders
The client asked the agency to come up with a powerful idea to raise public awareness of internet paedophilia.

Rashers of bacon

Delivered to a car factory in Swindon

Tucked in between slices of bread

In the Honda canteen

That is open again

After four months of rest

The factory is hungry

Hungry to start production again

It feels good to open the doors again

Welcoming back the bacon delivery man

Giving him business again

Say hello to the **HONDA** effect

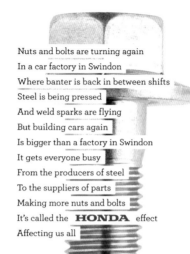

Nuts and bolts are turning again

In a car factory in Swindon

Where banter is back in between shifts

Steel is being pressed

And weld sparks are flying

But building cars again

Is bigger than a factory in Swindon

It gets everyone busy

From the producers of steel

To the suppliers of parts

Making more nuts and bolts

It's called the **HONDA** effect

Affecting us all

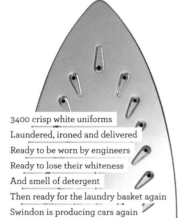

3400 crisp white uniforms

Laundered, ironed and delivered

Ready to be worn by engineers

Ready to lose their whiteness

And smell of detergent

Then ready for the laundry basket again

Swindon is producing cars again

The engineers are back at work

The laundry people are busy

And sales of detergent are on the up

Some people call it the **HONDA** effect

Mugs of tea are back at work

In a car factory in Swindon

Warming the hands

Of thousands of engineers

Who are back turning wheel nuts

Back fitting windscreens

Back telling jokes

And between shifts having more tea

Upping the sales of Mr Tetley

With a knock-on effect on sugar and milk

Some people call it the **HONDA** effect

It's good to be back

Art Director
Fabian Burglund
Copywriter
Ida Gronblom
Photographer
David Sykes

Creative Directors
Tony Davidson
Kim Papworth
Designer
Karen Jane
Retoucher
Badger

Producer
Mark D'Abreo
Advertising Agency
Wieden+Kennedy
London

Account Director
Ryan Fisher
Client
Honda

Newspaper Press Advertising Colour

Wieden+Kennedy London
for Honda

Bacon / Bolt / Iron / Tea
In February 2009 the Honda factory in Swindon stopped its production of cars for four months. Rather than make people redundant, Honda decided to stop making cars and retool the factory, keeping workers in their jobs. In June the factory reopened. We looked back to the past and to how Honda had dealt with situations before. There was a commonly known economical term called 'The Honda Effect', meaning the company changes its long term goals in order to deal with current situations. We wanted to tell the story of the reopening and celebrate the effect that a factory like Honda's has on the local and wider community.

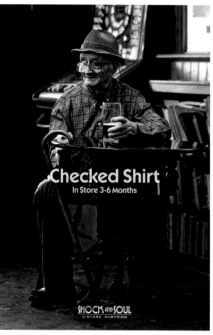

Art Directors	Photographer	Retoucher	Client
Joe Fitzgerald	John Short	Russell Kirby	Shock and Soul
Sam Hutcheson	**Typographer**	**Advertising Agency**	**Brand**
Copywriters	Ryan Self	RKCR/Y&R	Shock and Soul
Joe Fitzgerald	**Creative Directors**	**Store Manager**	Vintage Clothing
Sam Hutcheson	Damon Collins	Natalie Farouz	
	Mark Roalfe		

Newspaper Press Advertising Colour

RKCR/Y&R
for Shock and Soul

Winter Collection – Park / Pub / Shop
This campaign was created to highlight the genuine vintage quality of Shock and Soul's clothing. Each execution focuses on one item of clothing, telling the backstory of who currently owns it. By focusing on the individuality and age of the clothing, we clearly distanced the brand from mock vintage found on the high street. The dark humour of the advert is in keeping with the brand, and is aimed to appeal to the type of person who dresses, and thinks, slightly alternatively.

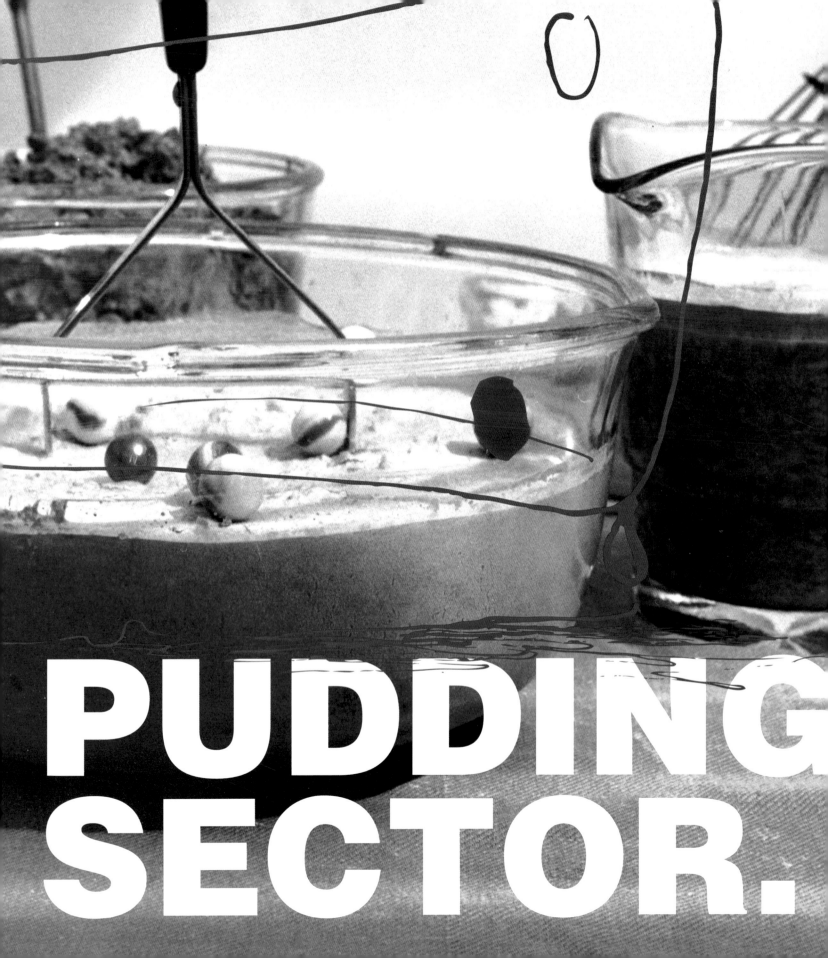

PUDDING
SECTOR.

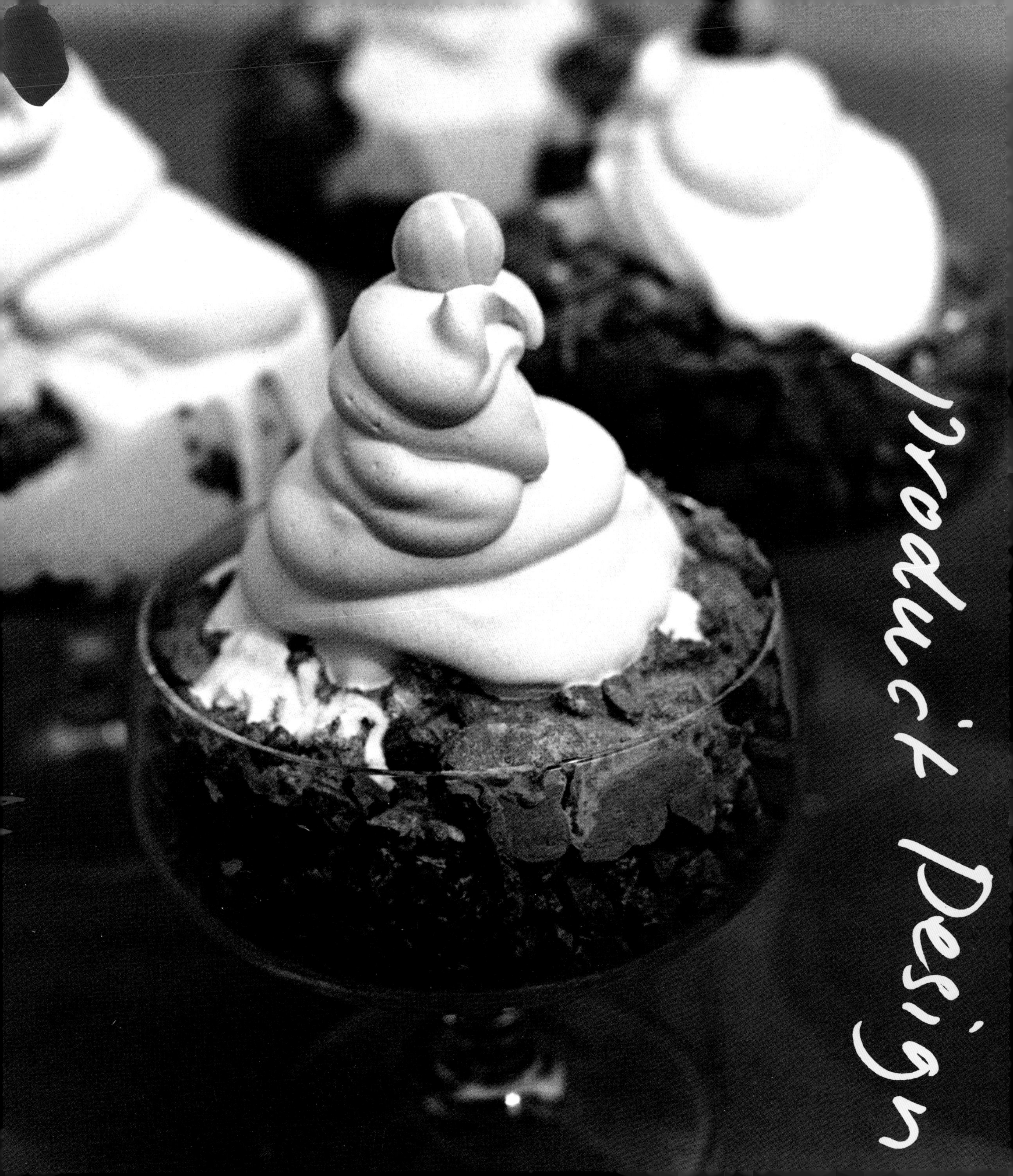
product Design

Product Design

Designers
Jody Akana
Bart Andre
Jeremy Bataillou
Daniel Coster
Evans Hankey
Richard Howarth
Daniele De Iuliis

Jonathan Ive
Steve Jobs
Duncan Kerr
Shin Nishibori
Matthew Rohrbach
Peter Russell-Clarke
Christopher Stringer
Eugene Whang
Rico Zörkendörfer

Manufacturer
Apple
Design Group
Apple Industrial
Design Team

Client
Apple

Work & Industry

Apple Industrial Design Team
for Apple

13-inch MacBook Pro
The 13-inch MacBook Pro has a precision unibody enclosure crafted from a single block of aluminium. It features Apple's innovative built-in battery technology with up to 40% longer battery life and up to 1,000 recharges, for over three times the lifespan of conventional notebook batteries. It also has an LED-backlit display, a glass Multi-Touch trackpad, an SD card slot, and a FireWire 800 port.

Work & Industry

Apple Industrial Design Team
for Apple

Apple Magic Mouse

The new wireless Magic Mouse is the first mouse to use Apple's revolutionary Multi-Touch technology. Instead of mechanical buttons, scroll wheels or scroll balls, the entire top of the Magic Mouse is a seamless Multi-Touch surface. The Magic Mouse works for left- or right-handed users, and multi-button or gesture commands can be easily configured from within system preferences.

Design Directors
Tom Lloyd
Luke Pearson

Manufacturer
Martin Battye
Design Agency
PearsonLloyd

Client
Design Bugs Out

Brand
Kirton Healthcare

 Work & Industry

PearsonLloyd
for Kirton Healthcare

DBO Commode
The DBO Commode represents a shift in commode design, reducing infection transfer.
It has two key parts: the 'shell' forming the patient interface, and a single stainless wheelable frame. A top-loading bedpan contains the spread of aerosol and therefore infection transfer. The separation means that the shell can simply be lifted off, and has no fixings or features to inhibit what is now a wipe clean process. Damaged components are easily replaced without condemning the whole product. The number of parts has been minimised, making cleaning quicker and easier. The frame and shell nest and stack for easy storage.

Designer	Brand Manager	Client	Brand
Thomas Meyerhoffer	Mark Kelly	Meyerhoffer	Meyerhoffer
	Marketing Manager	Surfboards for	
	Tess Kelly	Global Surf Industries	

 Leisure

Thomas Meyerhoffer
for Global Surf Industries

Meyerhoffer Surfboard
The classic longboard is an elongated, slightly concave ovoid, a shape that has changed little since surfing was invented by the ancient Hawaiians. This board is a shorter board in a longer board, combining the best of both. The unique narrow waist effectively moves the widest point of the board further back around where the surfer stands, creating an outline of a shortboard in the tail. The board paddles into the waves really easily and nose-rides like a classic longboard, but at the same time it turns and is fast like a shortboard. It opens up a broader spectrum of what you can do on the wave. Enjoy!

Designers		Manufacturer	Client
Jody Akana	Jonathan Ive	Apple	Apple
Bart Andre	Steve Jobs	**Design Group**	
Jeremy Bataillou	Duncan Kerr	Apple Industrial	
Daniel Coster	Shin Nishibori	Design Team	
Evans Hankey	Matthew Rohrbach		
Richard Howarth	Peter Russell-Clarke		
Daniele De Iuliis	Christopher Stringer		
	Eugene Whang		
	Rico Zörkendörfer		

Work & Industry

Apple Industrial Design Team
for Apple

iMac
The new iMac line features brilliant LED-backlit 21.5 and 27-inch widescreen displays in a new edge-to-edge glass design and seamless all-aluminium enclosure. Both high resolution displays use IPS technology to deliver gorgeous colour consistently across an ultra wide 178 degree viewing angle. The new iMacs are the fastest ever with Intel Core 2 Duo processors starting at 3.06 GHz.

Design Directors	Manufacturer	Design Agency	Client
Tom Lloyd	Bene	PearsonLloyd	Bene
Luke Pearson			

Work & Industry

PearsonLloyd
for Bene

Parcs

Parcs is a response to new working methods. Between architecture and furniture, it provides a range of collaborative and personal concentration spaces. It manages acoustics, visual privacy and provides the latest technology, delivering a new type of workplace that challenges traditional archetypes such as desk, meeting room and breakout zones. The Parcs range includes: Causeway (a series of upholstered benches and fences in various heights), Wing (a range of armchairs, sofas and booths), Toguna (a semi-private meeting space) and the Library and Idea Wall (providing storage for periodicals, books and information technology presentation facilities).

411

Designers
Jody Akana
Bart Andre
Jeremy Bataillou
Daniel Coster
Evans Hankey
Richard Howarth
Daniele De Iuliis

Jonathan Ive
Steve Jobs
Duncan Kerr
Shin Nishibori
Matthew Rohrbach
Peter Russell-Clarke
Christopher Stringer
Eugene Whang
Rico Zörkendörfer

Manufacturer
Apple
Design Group
Apple Industrial
Design Team

Client
Apple

Leisure

Apple Industrial Design Team
for Apple

iPod shuffle
The iPod shuffle is the world's smallest music player and the first to talk. Its primary controls are conveniently located on the headphone cord, including a voiceover feature which speaks song titles, artists, and playlists. With a stainless steel clip built in, the anodised aluminium body comes in silver, black, pink, blue and green. A special edition is available in polished stainless steel.

Design Director	Technical Designer	Design Group	Client
Morten Warren	Paul Harris	Native Design	Bowers & Wilkins
Designer	Manufacturer	Brand Manager	
Marcus Hoggarth	Stuart Neville	Natalie O'Hara	

Leisure

Native Design
for Bowers & Wilkins

Mobile Headphones

After the overwhelming success of the Zeppelin, the best sounding iPod speaker available, Bowers & Wilkins wanted to transfer the same qualities of uncompromising sound and design to other mobile audio equipment. Every detail of the design transmits care for quality in all areas of sound, comfort and manufacturing. Authentic materials such as stainless steel, aluminium and sealed leather parts combine to reference the authenticity in the sound production. Five decades of audio experience have gone into the headphones, while countless hours of critical listening and tuning have played a major part in their natural and engaging performance.

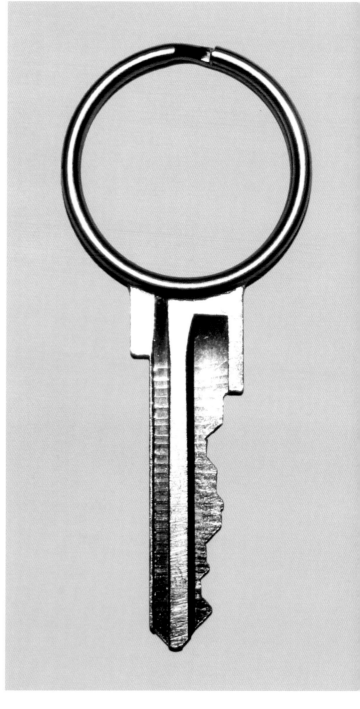

Designer
Scott Amron

Design Group
Amron Experimental

Client
Keybrid

Home
Amron Experimental
for Keybrid

Keybrid
Keybrid is a real working key and key ring in one.

esign Director
aul Priestman
esigners
avid Hamilton
en Rowan

Packaging Designers
Tony Blurton
Claudia Pacheco

Design Group
Priestmangoode

Client
Priestmangoode
Brand
Waterpebble

Home

Priestmangoode

Waterpebble
A world first, Waterpebble is a revolutionary device designed to take the effort out of saving water. Paul Priestman, director of design company Priestmangoode, was inspired by a sign in a hotel bathroom asking him to 'use water sparingly'. He started developing the concept on his return home. The clever device monitors water going down the plug hole when you shower. Memorising your first shower and using it as a benchmark, Waterpebble then indicates, via a series of 'traffic lights' flashing gently from green through to red, when to finish showering. Waterpebble also automatically and fractionally reduces your shower time each time you shower, helping you save water.

415

Design Director	Technical Designer	Brand Manager	Client
Yunje Kang	Sangin Lee	Jisook Lee	Samsung Electronics
Designers	**Manufacturer**	**Marketing Managers**	**Brand**
Jaehyung Kim	Samsung Electronics	Kunwoo Kim	Samsung
Jigwang Kim	**Design Group**	Youjin Ko	
	Visual Display Group	Daeoh Yang	

Home

Visual Display Group
for Samsung Electronics

Samsung AV BD-P4600
The BD-P4600's goal was to showcase a design that looks very much like nature. Colour changes occur owed to the material's colour concentration; this gives a sense of depth according to the light and surrounding environment, all in an eco-friendly way. The design emphasises the top panel, making this ultra-slim Blu-Ray player – the first in the world to offer a width of just 1.5 inches – look even slimmer.

esign Director
aul Flowers

Design Group
Grohe

Manufacturer
Sylvia Kroenke

Client
Grohe

Home

Grohe

Grohe Rainshower Collection
This collection shatters the preconception that consumers must renovate their bathroom in order to have a better experience. The Rainshower's Solo, Icon and Eco deliver exclusive benefits and ecological functions such as the 'aqua dimmer' and 'speed clean' – one wipe with the finger and the nozzles are clean. The spray face has been celebrated on every product in the collection with the addition of an intrinsic chrome ring. The super flat body with its humanised aesthetic entices interaction and creates an instant emotional connection. The aesthetic helps to build brand recognition and position Grohe as an innovator in all categories.

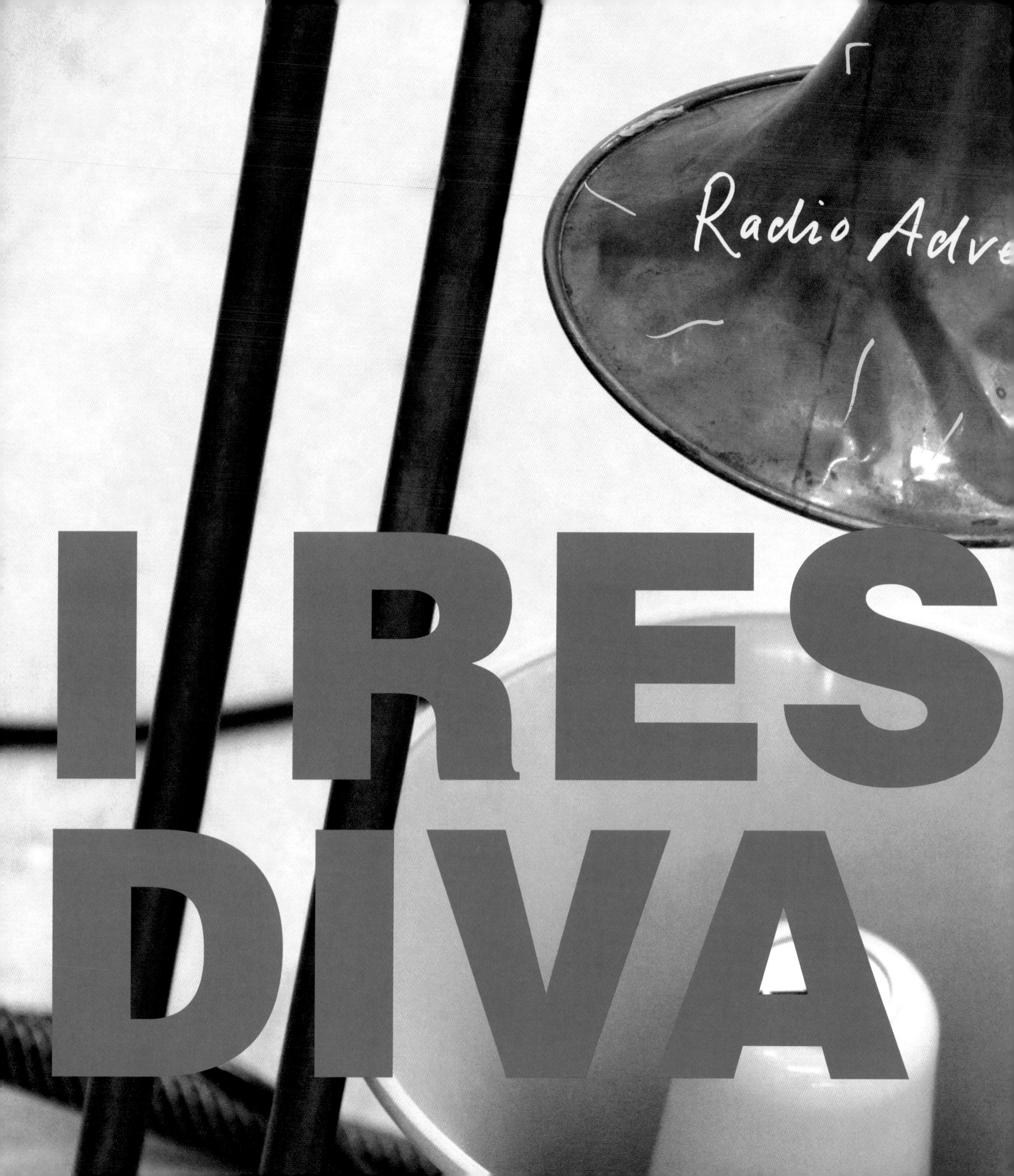

Radio Adve

I RES
DIVA

TRAIN
GOD.

Radio

It's Your Call

MVO   It's a beautiful day.
John is driving the kids home from school.
He pulls up to an intersection.
John waits, looking from side to side.

Story 1   He spots a small gap but decides to wait.

Story 2   He spots a small gap and pulls out.

Story 1   John spots a bigger gap, and pulls out.

Story 2   John spots a car to his right, but it's too late.

Story 1   They cross the road safely.

Story 2   The car smashes into them.

Story 1   Sarah laughs.

Story 2   Sarah screams.

Story 1   John drives down the road.

Story 2   John's car is shoved sideways.

Story 1   Alley pulls silly faces at Sarah.

Story 2   Alley's door smacks into a power pole.

Story 1   They stop outside the dairy.

Story 2   They stop in the middle of the road.

Story 1   John gets ice creams.

Story 2   John can't move his legs.

Story 1   He glances at Alley.

Story 2   He looks at Alley.

Story 1   Alley's face is covered in ice cream.

Story 2   Alley's face is covered in blood.

Story 1   John turns into their road.

Story 2   John turns to find Sarah.

Story 1   He pulls into their drive.

Story 2   He pulls at his legs.

Story 1   John opens the door.

Story 2   John pounds on the door.

Story 1   Sarah jumps out.

Story 2   Sarah isn't moving.

Story 1   John lifts Alley out.

Story 2   The paramedic lifts Alley out.

Story 1   John walks inside.

Story 2   John is paralysed.

Story 1   Sarah is laughing.

Story 2   Sarah is dead.

MVO   Intersections. It's your call.

Copywriters
Brigid Alkema
Anne Boothroyd
Creative Director
Paul Nagy

Executive Creative Director
Philip Andrew
Agency Producer
Marty Collins

Advertising Agency
Clemenger BBDO
Wellington
Account Director
Linda Reuvecamp

Group Account Director
Linda Major
Client
New Zealand
Transport Agency

Radio Commercials over 30 seconds

Clemenger BBDO Wellington
for the New Zealand Transport Agency

It's Your Call
Every intersection is a choice. Stop and wait, or pull out and take a risk. Drivers are familiar with near misses and the odd fender bender at intersections, but most have never considered an intersection crash causing serious injury or even death. We needed to make them appreciate that not only can intersection crashes be far more serious than they realise, but also that it is their call whether they risk serious injury and death, or wait a few more seconds. In this advert, a male narrator begins by describing a simple car journey, but when the car reaches the intersection the narrator branches off into two simultaneous stories.

Radio

El Loco

MVO   The parts in a new Toyota are all original, genuine Toyota parts. There's a good reason to keep them this way. Because if you start introducing foreign parts, things quickly start going muy malo. As you continue driving your car, more stukkies start wearing out, so you replace them with icheapele piesa. After a while nada habariako partes original any Vladivostok. Nothing seems to graft so je t'aime any kosher babushka and the whole garankuwa starts to no hable el loco. La luna yokosuma el nino original in vitro del fume nastrovia. No Perestroika. Au revoir.

VO   Use only genuine parts on your Toyota. Toyota. Lead the way.

Copywriter
Jonathan Stilwell
Executive Creative
Director
Grant Jacobsen
Chief Creative
Officer
Brett Morris

Agency Producer
Karin Keylock
Recording Engineer
Kitso Moremi
Production
Company
Sonovision Studios

Advertising Agency
Draftfcb SA
Account Handler
Mike di Terlizzi

Vice President of
Customer Services
Terry O'Donoghue
Client
Toyota

Writing

Draftfcb SA
for Toyota

El Loco
Replacing genuine Toyota parts with foreign parts is a lot like replacing genuine English words with foreign ones. Once you start using the foreign ones instead of the proper English ones, the radio spot you're writing starts going loco. It becomes muchos difficil to comprende, and eventually makes no sense at all. El Loco was also selected in the category 'Radio Commercials over 30 Seconds'.

Radio

Boy (With sad and ethereal voice, as if speaking
to us from far away)

He used to sleep in on Saturdays. But he can't
because I'm there.
He goes to football. I'm on the touchline.
He stops at the supermarket. I'm at the end
of the aisle.
At home, his kids are waiting. So am I.
I'm the boy he killed five years ago, because
he was speeding. And now he has to live
with it.

FVO Think! It's 30 for a reason.

Callum

Boy (With sad and ethereal voice, as if speaking
to us from far away)

When he goes to work, I'm there.
At the weekend, I'm there.
On holiday, building sandcastles, I'm there,
beside his son.
At night, he tries to forget. But I'm always
there.
I'm the boy he killed seven years ago, because
he was speeding. And now he has to live
with it.

FVO Think! It's 30 for a reason.

Joelle

Girl (With sad and ethereal voice, as if speaking
to us from far away)

He wakes up around 7. I'm there as he brushes
his teeth.
He takes the train to work. I wait for him at the
station.
I'm beside him at his desk.
With him as he eats dinner.
He watches cartoons with his son. He tries to
look away but I'm there.
I'm the girl he killed seven years ago, because
he was speeding. And now he has to live
with it.

FVO Think! It's 30 for a reason.

Copywriter
Bern Hunter
Art Director
Mike Bond
Creative Director
Paul Brazier

**Creative Group
Heads**
Brian Campbell
Phill Martin
Agency Producer
Paul Burke
Recording Engineer
Andy MacLennan

Production Company
The Lab
Advertising Agency
Abbott Mead Vickers
BBDO
Account Handlers
Kate Gault
Shezel Hattea

**Adult Road Safety
Team Head**
Camilla Wilkinson
Client
The Department
for Transport

Radio Commercials 1-30 Seconds
Abbott Mead Vickers BBDO
for The Department for Transport

Bertie / Callum / Joelle
Each year, speeding accounts for more than 720 deaths on the UK's roads. To convey the
potentially dire consequences, we focused on a driver living with the guilt of having killed a
child while speeding. Skipping the crash itself, we told the oppressive reality of his everyday
life in later years, one in which he constantly sees the body of the child he's killed. Wherever
he goes, whatever he does, he simply has to live with it. The radio adverts targeted drivers
in their cars as they listened to shows during rush hour.

Radio

Signs You Love Chicken (Wings)

VO Signs you're a chicken lover.
You don't care why the chicken crossed the road.
As long as it got to the other side.
You enjoy early bird parking.
There's no argument: the egg did not come first.
Fkl sdvjio ckduhku faksfasa.
You let a chicken write that.
Your favourite food? Wings.
Your favourite band? Wings.
Your favourite TV show? Wings.
And your favourite chicken burger is the McDonald's Crispy Chicken Fillet Deluxe, with 100% chicken breast fillet.
Only at McDonald's.

SFX I'm lovin' it sting.

Signs You Love Fruit

VO Signs you love fruit.
You speak Mandarin.
You live in the Big Apple.
You ate your BlackBerry.
You eat pears in pairs.
You're bananas about bananas.
You insist on comparing apples with oranges
Your favourite colour? Orange.
Your favourite town? Orange.
Your favourite sport? Stealing oranges from thirsty children at half-time.
If life gives you lemons, you go bananas.
Then, you make lemonade.
But right now you're squeezing every last delicious drop out of a McDonald's Mango Mash 100% Juice.
Only at McDonald's.

SFX I'm lovin' it sting.

Signs You Love Sausage

VO Signs you love sausage.
You are a snag.
You attract stray hounds.
So you moved to Frankfurt.
You like to watch a sausage roll.
Your lawyers are Kransky, Kransky & Chipolata.
You put every meal through a sausage maker.
They call you the Sausage Maker.
You always think the wurst. Liverwurst, bratwurst, knackwurst…
Your sausage dog is called Mr Wiener.
Down boy!
And every morning you walk Mr Wiener to McDonald's for a Sausage & Egg McMuffin with hot sausage and a freshly-cracked egg.
Only at McDonald's.

FVO I'm lovin' it sting.

Copywriters
Edward James
Jakub Szymanski
Creative Director
Adam Rose
Executive Creative Director
Matt Eastwood

Agency Producer
Kristy Fransen
Audio Engineer
Danny Grifoni
Voice Over Artist
Kevin Goldsby

Production Company
DDB Sydney
Advertising Agency
DDB Sydney
Account Handlers
Paul Matuszczyk
Georgia O'Brien

Director of Marketing
Helen Farquhar
Client
McDonald's

Writing

DDB Sydney
for McDonald's

Signs You Love – Chicken (Wings) / Fruit / Sausage
Most radio adverts are background noise. McDonald's wanted to create a radio campaign that would stand out from all the dross. With simple, single-minded adverts talking about all kinds of McDonald's food, the campaign is nearing one hundred separate executions, all filled with 'Signs You Love McDonald's'. There are many reasons people like McDonald's. Some make sense. Some do not. These are those reasons.

423

Radio

Surfin' USA

MVO   The Budweiser Ice Cold Orchestra presents:
Sounds of the Summer…

SFX   We hear a performance of the Beach Boys
classic, 'Surfin' USA', created entirely by the
sounds people make when they're feeling
cold, e.g. shivering, chattering teeth, blowing
into hands, rubbing arms, stamping feet. The
'cold' sounds are layered up to create the
effect of a large vocal orchestra.

MVO   Introducing the coldest pint ever.
New Budweiser Ice Cold.
The King of Cold.

Music Arrangers
Chuck Berry
Steve Sidwell
Brian Wilson
Copywriter
Sam Oliver
Art Director
Shishir Patel

Executive Creative Director
Jeremy Craigen
Music Engineer
Steve Sidwell
Mix Engineer
James Saunders
Agency Producer
Natalie Powell

Sound Studios
Jungle
The Playroom
Audio Production Company
Jeff Wayne Music Group
Advertising Agency
DDB UK

Brand Manager
Chris Wooff
Client
Diageo
Brand
Budweiser

Sound Design & Use of Music

DDB UK
for Diageo

Surfin' USA
This advert was part of a campaign of radio ads which introduced us to the Budweiser Ice Cold Orchestra. Each advert featured a performance of a famous summer tune made entirely by the sounds people make when they are feeling cold.

Radio

Helicopter

MVO Ana.

SFX Voice imitating the sound of the wind.

MVO John.

SFX Voice imitating the sound of an engine.

MVO Maria.

SFX Voice imitating the sound of a turbine.

MVO Alex.

SFX Voice imitating the sound of an intense wind.

MVO Raul.

SFX Voice imitating the sound of a propeller turning at great speed.

MVO All of us.

SFX All the voices join together creating the sound of a helicopter.

MVO With the help of us all, we can continue our work. Colombian Red Cross.

Sound Designer
Felipe Dominguez
Copywriters
Jorge Emiro Orozco
Alexis Ospina
Milton Rojas

Creative Director
Rodrigo Dávila
Agency Producer
Jaime Cordoba
Producer
Felipe Dominguez

Production Company
Leo Studio
Advertising Agency
Leo Burnett
Colombiana

Account Handler
Juan Martín Concha
Brand Manager
Ana Lucia Cabezas
Client
Colombian Red
Cross

Sound Design & Use of Music

Leo Burnett Colombiana
for the Colombian Red Cross

Helicopter
This advert was part of a fundraising campaign for the Colombian Red Cross.

I'V AVANT-GARDE INSECT MIND.

TV and Cinema Advertising

FROM THE PURE WATERS OF TASMANIA

Director
Steve Rogers
Copywriter
Grant McAloon
Art Director
Steve Wakelam
Creative Director
Micah Walker
Producers
Karla Henwood
Michael Ritchie
Agency Producer
Jasmin Ferguson

Production Designer
Steven Jones-Evans
Special Effects
Justin Bromley
**Visual Effects
Supervisor**
Justin Bromley
Editor
Alexandre De
Franceschi
**Director of
Photography**
Geoffrey Simpson

Music Composer
Elliot Wheeler
Sound Designer
Simon Lister
Production Company
Revolver Films
Editing Company
Guillotine
Visual Effects
Fin Design & Effects
Sound Design
Nylon

Advertising Agency
Publicis Mojo
Account Handlers
Simon Ludowyke
Tara Seymour
Client
Lion Nathan
Brand
James Boags
Draught

▲ TV Commercials 41-60 Seconds

Publicis Mojo
for Lion Nathan

Pure Waters
Way, way down at the bottom of the world, there's an untouched island called Tasmania where the water is famously pure, and the beer is especially good. We decided that surely there must be a connection. So, we took the purity of the island's water and turned it into a legend, telling the story of how it makes things good. Whether you're dunking your bike or your shoes, your girl or, yes, your beer, the pure waters of Tasmania will always give you, well, something better.

irector ary Freedman	**Producers** Catherine Anderson	**Sound Designers** Tone Aston	**Account Executive** Lucy McBurney
igital Director rett Mitchell	Karen Bryson **Agency Producer**	Simon Lister **Production Company**	**Business Director** Steve Muller
opywriters am Blackley	Paul Johnston **Editors**	@radical.media **Special Effects**	**Brand Manager** Scott McGregor
4atty Burton **rt Directors**	Mark Burnett Bernard Garry	Fuel **Advertising Agency**	**Marketing Manager** Paul Donaldson
am Blackley 4atty Burton	Zen Rosenthal **Director of**	Droga5 Australia **Executive Planning**	**Client** Carlton United
xecutive Creative irector	**Photography** Danny Ruhlmann	**Director** Sudeep Gohil	Breweries **Brand**
avid Nobay	**Casting Director** Toni Higginbotham	**Account Manager** Nicolas Kettelhake	Victoria Bitter

▲ TV Commercials 61-120 Seconds

Droga5 Australia
for Carlton United Breweries

The Regulars
This two-minute television commercial formed the spearhead of 'The Regulars' campaign for VB beer. Australians, proud of their ability to laugh at themselves and others, are notorious for categorising people according to their appearance, their habits, where they live, what they do, their strengths and their weaknesses. It is this exceptional Australian ability to deliver the backhanded compliment that this epic taps into. Because VB beer is for all kinds of people, we created a real parade, celebrating all Australians and the groups they belong to, including 'Blokes Punching Above Their Weight', 'Men Who Should've Read The Instructions', 'The Manscapers' and, of course, the all important 'Brewers'.

Directors
Manu et Fleur
Copywriter
Fabien Teichner
Art Director
Faustin Claverie
Executive Creative Director
Alexandre Hervé

Producer
Erinn Guillon
Agency Producer
Julie Mathiot
Production Company
Les Télécréateurs
Sound Design
THE
Advertising Agency
DDB Paris

Planner
Patrick Faure
Account Manager
Orane Faivre de Condé
Account Handler
Mathieu Roux
Communications Manager
Aurélie Martzel

Client
INPES (Institut National de Prévention et d'Education pour la Santé)

TV Commercials 61-120 Seconds

DDB Paris
for INPES

Chance
The advert demonstrates, thanks to an accumulation of disturbing statistics, how incredibly lucky we are to exist, while also alerting us to the fact that one out of two people die from a tobacco-related disease.

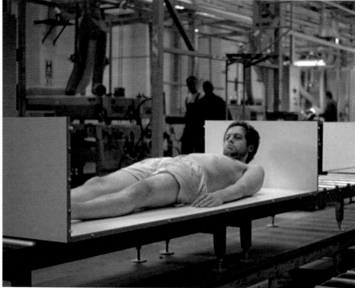

Director
Matthijs van
Heijningen
Copywriter
Jean-Christophe
Royer
Art Director
Eric Astorgue
**Executive Creative
Director**
Stéphane Xiberras

Agency Producer
Isabelle Ménard
Editor
Jono Griffith
**Director of
Photography**
Joost van Gelder
**Production
Company**
SOIXAN7E QUIN5E

**Image Post
Production**
MIKROS Image
Sound Production
KOUZ Production
Advertising Agency
BETC Euro RSCG

Account Handlers
Raphaël de Andréis
François Brogi
Alexandre George
**Brand & Marketing
Manager**
Béatrice Roux
Client
CANAL+

TV Commercials 61-120 Seconds

BETC Euro RSCG
for CANAL+

Closet
In September 2009, CANAL+ launched its new 'Original Creativity' campaign. The aim was to highlight CANAL+'s showcase of original programming, consisting of series, documentaries and dramas, created exclusively by and for CANAL+, and scripted by prestigious writers such as Olivier Marchal and Jean-Hugues Anglade. To launch this new campaign, we produced an advert where a husband comes home to find a man hiding in his wife's closet. The man then describes a series of improbable events to explain his reason for being there. The advert unites humour, originality and a touch of impertinence inherent to the brand's message: 'Never underestimate the power of a great story'.

Director	**Agency Producer**	**Visual Effects**	**Animatronics**	**Planner**
Tom Kuntz	Sarah Shapiro	Robert Moggach	Stan Winston	Matt
Copywriters	**Agency Executive**	**Sound Designer**	Studios	Kelley
Craig Allen	**Producer**	Gus Koven	**Sound Design**	**Chief**
Eric Kallman	Ben Grylewicz	**Editor**	Stimmung	**Marketing**
Art Directors	**Executive Creative**	Gavin Cutler	**Audio Post**	**Officer**
Craig Allen	**Directors**	**Production Company**	POP Sound	Richard
Eric Kallman	Mark Fitzloff	MJZ	**Advertising Agency**	Castellini
Creative Directors	Susan Hoffman	**Post Production**	Wieden+Kennedy	**Senior Director**
Jason Bagley	**Line Producer**	Mackenzie Cutler	Portland	**of Advertising**
Danielle Flagg	Scott Kaplan	**Visual Effects**	**Account Handlers**	Cynthia McIntyre
Executive Producers	**Director of**	**Company**	Maggie Entwistle	**Client**
Jeff Scruton	**Photography**	Method Studios	Tamera Geddes	CareerBuilder.com
David Zander	Bryan Newman		Taryn Lange	

TV Commercials 61-120 Seconds

Wieden+Kennedy Portland
for CareerBuilder.com

Tips
It can be hard to know when you need a new job. This spot gives the viewer a number of warning signs they should watch out for so they'll know when it's time for them to move on.

rolling

Reading

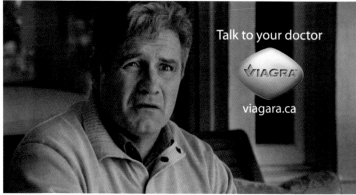

Antiquing

rectors
e Perlorian
others
opywriters
athan Monteith
efan Wegner
t Directors
athan Monteith
efan Wegner
ecutive Creative
rector
arren Clarke

Chief Creative
Officer
Steve Mykolyn
Producer
Scott Craig
Executive Producers
Diane McArter
Eva Preger
David Thorne
Link York
Agency Producer
Eugene Marchio

Vice President
of Integrated
Production
Cynthia Heyd
Video Producers
Paul Binney
Rodney Dowd
Eric Whipp
Video Post
Executive Producer
Sarah Brooks
Editor
Brian Wells

Cinematographer
Marten Tedin
Sound Designer
Clive Desmond
Production
Companies
Furlined
Soft Citizen
Editing & Video
Post Company
School Editing
Music & Audio
Post House
Silent Joe

Advertising
Agency
TAXI
Canada
Account
Director
Christopher
Andrews
Brand Manager
Marc Charbonneau
Client
Pfizer Canada
Brand
Viagra

TV Commercial Campaigns

TAXI Canada
for Pfizer Canada

Strolling / Reading / Antiquing
When couples stop having sex, they start filling that void with other activities. And while 'couple' activities like antiquing, strolling, and even reading seem harmless at first, they can end up taking over couples' lives. Viagra helps them get back to just having sex again.

433

Gas Station

ATM

Director	**Chief Creative**	**Director of**	**Advertising Agency**
Pekka Hara	**Officer**	**Photography**	Serviceplan Munich
Copywriter	Alexander Schill	Mathias	**Client**
Rudolf Novotny	**Producers**	Schoenringh	Sanyo Video Vertrieb
Art Director	Tanja Bruhn	**Sound Designer**	**Brand**
Till Diestel	Pieter Lony	Tuomas Seppaenen	Santec
Creative Director	Daniel Mittwede	**Production Company**	
Axel Thomsen	Ulla Vogel	Cobblestone	

TV Commercial Campaigns

Serviceplan Munich
for Sanyo Video Vertrieb

Gas Station / ATM

Santec is one of the leading companies for video security systems. With the help of security cameras, banks, gas stations and private houses can identify people who try to do something illegal. Once a thief is caught on camera they're more than likely to be identified. In other words, there is no escape. To show this, we made spots in which the delinquents literally cannot escape the camera's view. The frame of the picture works as an invisible wall that is impossible to cross. Once offenders enter the picture, they cannot escape.

434

Directors B/CD/CD	**Editor** Charlie Johnston	**Choreographer** Noémie Lafrance	**Creative Manager** Ferdinando Verderi
Creative Direction Johannes Leonardo	**Lighting**	**Costume Designer** Angela Esteban	Librero
Producers Claude Letessier	**Cameraperson** Zak Mulligan	**Production Company** Paranoid US	**Account Handler** Matt Ahumada
Kathleen O'Conor Lisa Rokotosan	**Music Composer** Will Bates	**Advertising Agency** Johannes Leonardo	**Marketing Manager** Will Bracker
Agency Producer Matthew Mattingly	**Sound Designers** Philip Loeb Rob Sayers		**Client** Daffy's

Cinema Commercials over 120 Seconds

Johannes Leonardo
for Daffy's

Fitting Dance
To promote Daffy's winter collection and reclaim their deep-discount territory, we combined two favourite pastimes: movies and shopping. These live in-theatre performances were staged throughout opening week, turning New York's largest movie theatre, The Ziegfeld, into a contemporary interactive experience, fusing on-screen imagery with front-of-screen performances to blur the lines between live event, cinema advertising and online film.
A living embodiment of that essential Daffy's brand promise: 'More Bang. Less Buck'.

435

Director	**Executive Creative**	**Lighting**	**Account Handler**
Steve Cope	**Director**	Clive Norman	Will Kirkpatrick
Copywriter	Russel Ramsey	**Cameraperson**	**Brand Manager**
Ryan Lawson	**Producer**	Clive Norman	Naureen Mohammed
Art Director	Kate Martin	**Sound Designer**	**Marketing Manager**
Andy Smith	**Agency Producer**	Munzie Thind	Alex Pitt
Creative Directors	Anna Church	**Production Company**	**Client**
Greg Martin	**Editor**	Rattling Stick	Johnson & Johnson
Mike Mckenna	Tim Hardy	**Advertising Agency**	**Brand**
		JWT London	Benadryl
		Planner	
		Lex Robinson	

TV Commercials 21-40 Seconds

JWT London
for Johnson & Johnson

War

For hay fever sufferers, everyday is a battle. What for others is a scene of beauty and peace is a battleground. Mother Nature, it seems, is always out to get you, whether it's plants exploding, sending their pollen flying towards you, sycamore seeds spinning towards the ground like helicopters, or bees and dragonflies skimming through the air. Everywhere you turn you're under attack. But luckily you have the perfect ammunition to win the battle, in the form of fast acting Benadryl Allergy Relief.

Director	**Senior Producer**	**Production**	**Account Handlers**
Daniel Kleinman	Anthony Curti	**Companies**	Paul Suchman
Copywriter	**Executive Producer**	Epoch Films	Ben Tauber
Reuben Hower	Ed Zazzera	Rattling Stick	**Client**
Art Director	**Assistant Producer**	**Visual Effects**	Monster.com
Gerard Caputo	Theresa Ward	**Company**	
Executive Creative	**Editor**	Framestore	
Director	Haines Hall	**Editing House**	
Eric Silver	**Director of**	Spotwelders	
Chief Creative	**Photography**	**Advertising Agency**	
Officers	John Mathieson	BBDO New York	
Bill Bruce	**Music Producer**		
David Lubars	Loren Parkins		

TV Commercials 21-40 Seconds

BBDO New York
for Monster.com

Double Take

During such difficult economic times, monster.com wanted to highlight the light-hearted side of the brand. We focused on creating a platform that uses humour to parody the outrageous actions of those who are hard-working in their jobs, but clearly are not on the right career path. We wanted to position the totally rebuilt monster.com, and its new suite of precision matching tools, as the solution to finding the job that's right for them. Double Take captures Monster's light-heartedness through visually entertaining and telegraphic metaphors, illustrating the dichotomy of two co-workers' work environments.

Director
Baker Smith

Copywriter
Ilon Tatarka

Art Director
Eric Cosper

Creative Directors
Linus Karlsson
Paul Malmstrom

Producer
Bonnie Goldfarb

Executive Producer
Marc Altschuler

Agency Producer
Veronica Beach

Editor
Dick Gordon

Sound Designer
Philip Loeb

Music
Human Worldwide

Production Company
Harvest

Advertising Agency
Mother New York

Client
TruTV

TV Commercials 21-40 Seconds

Mother New York
for TruTV

Lock Brow
Hero Eugene Fuller is so shocked by the real life action he sees on TruTv his face becomes stuck in an exaggerated, eyes wide open, surprised position, otherwise known as lock brow. His permanently startled and amazed look leads to several uncomfortable, uneasy situations. An attractive blonde, who happens to have a nasty cold sore on her lip, feels the wrath of Eugene's condition while at a backyard BBQ. Eugene also suffers lock brow while strolling through the men's locker-room, creating an awkward moment for everyone. TruTv viewers are then warned, 'when the stories are real the effects are actual'.

Director
Hamish Rothwell

Copywriters
Kelly Putter
Paul Sharp

Art Directors
Ruth Bellotti
Cameron Hoelter

Creative Director
Cameron Hoelter

Producer
Juliet Bishop

Set Designer
Ken Turner

Agency Producer
Jacqui Gillies

Special Effects
The Lab Sydney

Editor
Stewart Reeves

Lighting Cameraperson
Ian McCarroll

Music Composer & Arranger
Simon Lister

Sound Designer
Simon Lister

Production Company
Goodoil Films

Advertising Agency
The Campaign
Palace Sydney

Planner
Jacques Burger

Account Handler
Bruce Davidson

Brand Manager
Matthew Mannall

Marketing Manager
Gemma Lemieux

Client
Panasonic

TV Commercials 21-40 Seconds

The Campaign Palace Sydney
for Panasonic

Climber
In 2009 Panasonic released the first tough digital still camera with unparalleled resilience, high definition stills and high definition video recording. Prior to the launch, consumers were frustrated at missing great picture opportunities because they were afraid to take their camera to places it might get damaged; or, if they already owned a tough camera, the picture quality was compromised. Based on the insight that consumers wanted a tough piece of camera equipment that also delivers great picture quality, whether you're shooting stills or movies, 'Climber' really demonstrated that the closer to the action you are, the better it gets. Our man couldn't have got any closer.

437

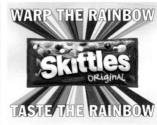

Director
Randy Krallman
Copywriter
Tim Wassler
Art Director
Lacey Waterman
Creative Director
Rob Baird
Chief Creative Officer
Mark Figliulo
Producer
Cory Berg

Executive Producers
Brian Carmody
Amy Febinger
Allison Kunzman
Patrick Milling Smith
Lisa Rich
Senior Agency Producer
Winslow Dennis
Executive Producer of Media Arts
Matt Bijarchi

Director of Broadcast Production
Ozzie Spenningsby
Senior Visual Effects Producer
Laney Gradus
Editor
Lawrence Young
Director of Photography
Bryan Newman
Senior Flame Artist
Raul Ortego

Colourist
Tim Masick
Sound Mixer
Philip Loeb
Production Company
Smuggler Productions
Visual Effects
Framestore
Sound Mix
Sound Lounge
Telecine
Company 3

Music
Human Worldwide
Account Handler
Kelsey Robertson
Advertising Agency
TBWA\Chiat\Day New York
Marketing Manager
Tyler Simpson
Client
Wrigley
Brand
Skittles

TV Commercials 21-40 Seconds

TBWA\Chiat\Day New York
for Wrigley

Hourglass
The brief was to continue the 'Taste the Rainbow' television campaign with a new spot. We found a way to accelerate time for one unlucky man by setting in motion an hourglass containing thousands of Skittles. The man succumbed to a terrible death on set, but we were able to capture his final moments on film and roll the footage into our own world fame. RIP Ke▪

Director
Hank Perlman
Copywriter
Tim Geoghegan
Art Director
Caprice Yu

Executive Creative Director
Robert Rasmussen
Associate Creative Director
Kevin Doyle
Chief Creative Officer
Kevin Roddy

TV Producer
Mary Ellen Verrusio
Editor
Tom Scherma
Production Company
Hungry Man
Editing House
Cosmo Street

Advertising Agency
BBH New York
Client
Ally Bank

TV Commercials 21-40 Seconds

BBH New York
for Ally Bank

Pony
We developed a television campaign that ignited consumers' latent frustrations with banking practices that didn't put them first, and showed how Ally Bank is different. The spots used the ultimate arbiters of right and wrong – kids – and captured their honest, unscripted reactions to common banking practices, like hiding behind fine print, and imposing ridiculous restrictions. Kids knew it was unfair and called it as they saw it. The spot was intended to make viewers wonder why they put up with these practices.

Director
Tom Kuntz
Copywriters
Craig Allen
Eric Kallman
Art Directors
Craig Allen
Eric Kallman
Creative Directors
Jason Bagley
Eric Baldwin

Executive Creative Directors
Mark Fitzloff
Susan Hoffman
Producer
Scott Kaplan
Executive Producer
Jeff Scruton
Agency Producer
Andres Murillo
Agency Executive Producer
Ben Grylewicz

Visual Effects Producer
Arielle Davis
Visual Effects Executive Producer
Sue Troyan
Editor
Gavin Cutler
Director of Photography
Salvatore Totino
Sound Designers
Gus Coven
Sam Shaffer

Flame Artist
Phil Crowe
Lead Computer Graphics
Dan Marum
Production Company
MJZ
Visual Effects Company
The Mill Los Angeles
Advertising Agency
Wieden+Kennedy
Portland

Planner
Britton Taylor
Account Handler
Diana Gonzalez
Brand Managers
James Moorhead
Nick Patterson
Jim Urbaitis
Client
Old Spice

TV Commercials 21-40 Seconds

Wieden+Kennedy Portland
for Old Spice

Different Scents for Different Gents
Old Spice is the number one grooming choice for guys, but there are still some people who won't consider it because they think the brand only offers a single scent. Therefore, this TV campaign was devised to let people know that Old Spice has many different scents – a variety to suit every kind of man.

Director
Dougal Wilson
Copywriter
Martin Loraine
Art Director
Steve Jones
Creative Director
Paul Brazier
Creative Group Heads
Steve Jones
Martin Loraine

Producer
Matthew Fone
Agency Producer
Katherine Maidment
Visual Effects Supervisor
Daniel Adams
Editor
Joe Guest
Lighting Cameraperson
Tom Townend

Music Composers
Nick Foster
Oliver Julian
Peter Raeburn
Production Company
Blink Productions
Visual Effects
MPC
Advertising Agency
Abbott Mead
Vickers BBDO

Account Handlers
Richard Arscott
James Drummond
Marketing Directors
Giles Jepson
Adrian Mooney
Client
Heinz

TV Commercials 21-40 Seconds

Abbott Mead Vickers BBDO
for Heinz

Bottle
Heinz Tomato Ketchup is such an iconic and beloved product that you don't need to see the bottle to know what the commercial is for.

Director
Kirk Jones
Copywriter
Mark Waldron
Art Director
David Godfree
Creative Director
Damon Collins

Producer
Sarah Caddy
Editor
Greg Wilcox
Lighting
Cameraperson
Henry Braham

Production Company
Red Bee Media
Advertising Agency
RKCR/Y&R
Planner
Megan Thompson

Account Handler
Jamal Cassim
Marketing Manager
Ruairi Curran
Client
BBC

TV Commercials 21-40 Seconds

RKCR/Y&R
for the BBC

Directions
This campaign promotes the BBC Poetry Season, using scenes of everyday life transformed by the introduction of poetry.

Director
Dougal Wilson
Copywriter
Mike Boles
Art Director
Jerry Hollens
Creative Director
Damon Collins
Producer
Matt Fone
Agency Producer
Tim Page

Special Effects
Ludo Fealy
Editor
Joe Guest
Lighting
Cameraperson
Alex Barber
Underwater Director
of Photography
Mark Silk
Music Composer
Jon Hopkins

Sound Designer
Anthony Moore
Colourist
Jean-Clement Soret
Production Company
Blink Productions
Advertising Agency
RKCR/Y&R
Planner
Anna Tetlow

Account Handler
Nick Fokes
Head of Campaigns
& Marketing
David Watson
Client
Department for
Communities and
Local Government

TV Commercials 21-40 Seconds

RKCR/Y&R
for the Department for Communities and Local Government

Breathe
To dramatise the fact that two or three breaths of toxic smoke will make you unconscious, we likened death by smoke inhalation to the respiratory effects of drowning. In an eerie, blue suffused scene, a bedroom underwater, we witness the unnerving tranquillity of a couple who have breathed their last breath.

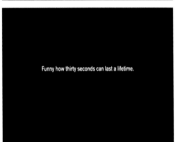

Director
Chris Palmer
Copywriter
Matt Lee
Art Director
Pete Heyes
Creative Director
Justin Tindall
Producer
Rupert Smythe

Agency Producer
Charles Crisp
Editor
Paul Watts
Lighting Cameraperson
Ben Seresin
Sound Designer
Owen Griffiths

Music Arrangers
Joe Campbell
Paul Cartledge
Paul Hart
Philip Jewson
Production Company
Gorgeous Enterprises
Post Production Company
Big Buoy

Advertising Agency
The Red Brick Road
Planner
Paul Hackett
Business Director
Barbara Waite
Marketing Director
Lindsey Clay
Client
Thinkbox

TV Commercials 41-60 Seconds

The Red Brick Road
for Thinkbox

Head
While undergoing hypnotherapy, a man recites a series of famous British commercials that have stayed lodged in his mind for years.

Director
Luis Gerard
Copywriter
Lizette Morazzani
Art Director
Andrés Justo
Creative Director
Jaime Rosado
Producers
María Estades
Noro Sebastián

Agency Producer
Noro Sebastián
Editor
Mizael Morales
Director of Photography
Jaime Costas
Music Composer
Glenn Monroig

Sound Designer
Carlos Dávila
Production Company
Hocus Pocus
Advertising Agency
JWT San Juan
Account Handlers
Richard Pascual
Axel Ramos

Brand Manager
Michelle Vázquez
Client
Cadbury Adams
Brand
Stride

TV Commercials 41-60 Seconds

JWT San Juan
for Cadbury Adams

Heirloom
A father decides to pass on a very special heirloom to his son on the day he leaves for college. But instead of the expected watch or ring, the father hands him a chewed up piece of Stride gum straight from his mouth. The son, touched by his father's gift, puts the gum in his mouth, smiles on discovering it still has flavour, and hugs his dad in appreciation. The spot closes with the following line: 'The ridiculously long lasting gum. Stride'.

Director Chris Palmer	**Producer** Rupert Saunders	**Artists** Ant Genn	**Account Director** Matt Delahunty
Copywriter Dave Henderson	**Agency Producer** Richard Chambers	John Lennon Paul McCartney	**Account Manager** Nick Owen
Art Director Richard Denney	**Editor** Paul Watts	**Production Company** Gorgeous	Charles Wong Chris Wooff
Creative Directors Richard Denney Dave Henderson	**Lighting** **Cameraperson** Joost van Gelder	Enterprises **Advertising Agency** DDB UK	**Marketing Manager** Garbhan O'Bric
Executive Creative **Director** Jeremy Craigen	**Sound Designer** Jack Sedgwick	**Planner** James Broomfield **Business Director** Jon Busk	**Client** Diageo **Brand** Budweiser

TV Commercials 41-60 Seconds

DDB UK
for Diageo

Lyrics
Viewed from a train heading through Chicago, the lyrics to The Beatles hit 'Altogether Now' are spelled out in many different ways by people in windows, along roads and on rooftops. The film culminates in a crowd gathered beneath a giant Budweiser mural.

442

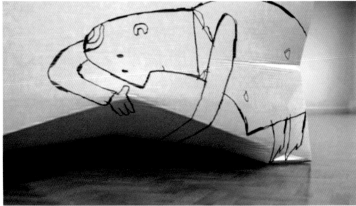
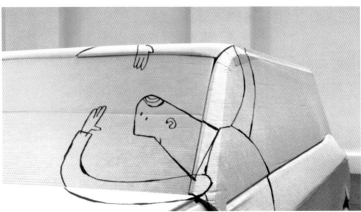
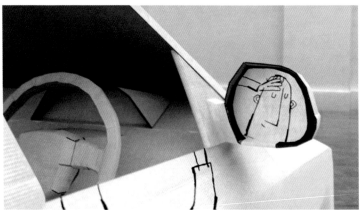

Directors
Russell Brooke
Aaron Duffy
Copywriters
Maja Fernqvist
Joakim Saul
Art Directors
Maja Fernqvist
Joakim Saul

Creative Directors
Nick Kidney
Kevin Stark
Producer
Belinda Blacklock
Agency Producer
Olly Chapman
Music Composer
Woody Guthrie
Sound Designer
Aaron Reynolds

Production Companies
First Avenue
Machine
Passion Pictures
Advertising Agency
BBH London
Planner
Rachel Hatton

Account Handlers
Simon Coles
Bill Scott
Brand Manager
James Millett
Marketing Manager
Peter Duffy
Client
Audi UK
Brand
Audi Q5

TV Commercials 41-60 Seconds

BBH London
for Audi UK

Unboxed

In this commercial, an animated engineer transforms a simple cardboard box into the new streamlined Audi Q5. Straight lines become curves. Squares become rounded. In doing so he ingeniously demonstrates the difference between the Audi Q5 and its many boxy rivals, and how Audi has 'unboxed the box'.

Director	Creative Director	Production Company	Adult Road Safety
Andy Mcleod	Paul Brazier	Rattling Stick	Team Head
Copywriters	**Creative Group**	**Advertising Agency**	Camilla Wilkinson
Bern Hunter	**Heads**	Abbott Mead	**Client**
Phil Martin	Brian Campbell	Vickers BBDO	Department for
Art Directors	Phill Martin	**Account Handlers**	Transport
Mike Bond	**Agency Producer**	Kate Gault	
Brian Campbell	Lindsay Hughes	Shezel Hattea	
	Editor		
	Andy McGraw		

TV Commercials 41-60 Seconds

Abbott Mead Vickers BBDO
for the Department for Transport

Live With It

Each year, speeding accounts for more than 720 deaths on UK roads. To convey the potentially dire consequences, we focused on a driver living with the guilt of having killed a child while speeding. Skipping the crash itself, we showed the oppressive reality of his everyday life in late years, one in which he constantly sees the body of the boy he's killed, lying in the same pose it came to rest in moments after the accident. Wherever he goes, whatever he does, he simply has to live with it.

Director	Producers	Music	Account Handler
Mark Jenkinson	Jax Evans	Angell Sound	Johnny Spindler
Copywriters	Robert Morgan	**Post Production**	**Marketing Manager**
Matt Gilbert	**Agency Producer**	Prime Focus	Jenny Williams
Pete Gosselin	Ferouk Khan	Superglue	**Client**
Art Directors	**Special Effects**	**Advertising Agency**	News Group
Jay Hunt	Simon Cam	glue London	Newspapers
Dave Tokley	**Editor**	**Planner**	**Brand**
Creative Director	Jose Gomez	Matt Tanter	The Sun
Seb Royce			

TV Commercials 41-60 Seconds

glue London
for News Group Newspapers

The Sun 4.0

Last year The Sun newspaper celebrated its 40th birthday, but the celebrations were set against a backdrop of difficult times for traditional news media. This commercial was designed to appeal to a young, tech-savvy audience, and to show that the paper still had relevance and a unique personality. It positioned The Sun as a cutting-edge piece of gadgetry. The tone, like that of the paper, was cheeky and irreverent, but also humorously self-deprecating. It aired in the most high profile TV slot of the year in the UK – the X Factor final – and went down brilliantly.

Director
~ger Leth
Copywriter
~an-Christophe
~oyer
Art Director
~ic Astorgue

Creative Directors
Florence Bellisson
Stéphane Xiberras
Producer
David Green
Production Company
Partizan
Advertising Agency
BETC Euro RSCG

Account Handlers
Valérie Albou
Timoti Auscher
Magali Heberard
Muriel Keromnes
Brand Managers
Carole Bartoli
Christine Micouleau

Marketing Managers
Patricia Manent
Helene Paillard
Clients
Air France
ECPAT

TV Commercials 41-60 Seconds

BETC Euro RSCG
for Air France & ECPAT

Child Pornography
ECPAT is a network of organisations working to eliminate the commercial sexual exploitation of children. This powerful advert underlines the responsibility of clients in the chain of violence that children are subjected to, while highlighting the existence of stringent laws against the sexual exploitation of children. The campaign was created by BETC Euro RSCG at the request of Air France, a dedicated partner of ECPAT for 15 years. This campaign has benefited from the support of the European Union, the Department of Foreign Affairs and the Department of Tourism.

Director
~eil Gorringe
Copywriters
~ony Malcolm
~uy Moore
Art Directors
~ony Malcolm
~uy Moore

Creative Director
Jim Bolton
Producer
Jess Ensor
Agency Producer
Graeme Light
Editor
James Rosen

Production Company
Moxie Pictures
Advertising Agency
Leo Burnett London
Planners
Ian Hilton
Matt Watts

Account Handlers
Sean Boles
Megan Lock
Client
McDonald's

TV Commercials 41-60 Seconds

Leo Burnett London
for McDonald's

Everybody
This work is a true celebration of Britain's relationship with McDonald's today, reminding everyone what they love about the brand. The TV execution is based on observations that everyone can easily relate to. It shows customers from all walks of life popping into the restaurant for a bite to eat at various times of day and night, and highlights how these different people enjoy their experiences. The campaign brings to life the statement 'there's a McDonald's for everyone'.

Director
Dougal Wilson
Copywriters
Thierry Albert
Rob Doubal
Art Director
Damien Bellon
Creative Directors
Stephen Butler
Robert Saville
Mark Waites

Producer
Matt Fone
Agency Producer
Matt Minor
Model Maker
Justin Buckingham
**Post Production
Producer**
Tom Harding

Editor
Joe Guest
**Director of
Photography**
Alwin Kuchler
**Music Arranger
& Composer**
Calvin Harris
Music Producer
Morgan Clement

Sound Designer
Sam Robson
Production Company
Blink Productions
Advertising Agency
Mother London
Client
Coca-Cola

TV Commercials 61-120 Seconds

Mother London
for Coca-Cola

The Organ Player
We open on a man pushing a large box-like object. The box is a type of electronic organ. Inside there are six curious furry creatures. The man takes a bottle of Coke, and plugs it into the side of the organ. An ingenious system of pipes ensures that a drop of coke reaches each of the creatures' mouths, making them sing a beautiful 'yeah yeah yeah la la la' song. As if from nowhere, people appear and run across the field towards the organ player and his magical instrument. The super reads: 'Open happiness'.

446

Director
Sean Meehan
Copywriter
Nigel Dawson
Art Director
Peter Becker
Creative Director
Nigel Dawson

Executive Creative Director
Ant Shannon
Producer
Sam McGarry
Agency Producer
Jess Smith
Editor
Drew Thompson

Lighting Cameraperson
Sean Meehan
Sound Designer
Simon Kane
Production Company
Soma Films
Advertising Agency
Grey Melbourne

Account Handler
Randal Glennon
Senior Manager for Road Safety & Marketing
John Thompson
Client
The Transport Accident Commission

TV Commercials 61-120 Seconds

Grey Melbourne
for The Transport Accident Commission

Swap
This is the simple story of a guy who has a couple of joints at a weekend get-together. When he drives home he waits just a bit too long at an intersection; he goes fast then slow; he drives a tad too close to the centre line. His wife notices he's a bit stoned and he pulls over saying: 'OK, you drive'. But, being impaired, he's parked away from the verge and gets out without looking. Bang! He and his door are cleaned up by a following car. The advert closes with the line: 'If you drive on drugs, you're out of your mind'.

Direction
Traktor
Copywriter
Pip Bishop
Art Director
Chris Hodgkiss
Creative Director
Mark Roalfe
Producer
David Stewart

Agency Producer
Tim Page
Set Designer
Robin Brown
Editor
Rick Russell
Lighting
Cameraperson
Stephen Blackman

Sound Designer
Aaron Reynolds
Artist
Frankie Goes
to Hollywood
Production Company
Partizan
Advertising Agency
RKCR/Y&R

Planner
Emily James
Account Handler
Catherine Kennedy
Brand Manager
Breda Bubear
Client
Virgin Atlantic

TV Commercials 41-60 Seconds

RKCR/Y&R
for Virgin Atlantic

Love at First Flight
By recreating the first day Virgin Atlantic flew, we wanted to remind audiences of the difference the airline made at launch. Shot with a modern bent on a fondly remembered period, it demonstrates how the adventurous, sexy and spirited Virgin attitude is just as true now as it was at the inaugural flight, pronounced positively with the message: 'Still red hot'.

Director
Michael Gracey
Copywriter
Stephen Howell
Art Director
Rick Dodds
Creative Directors
Paul Silburn
Kate Stanners
Producer
Russell Curtis
Agency Producer
Ed Sayers

Production Manager
Emma Wolanski
Editors
Ben Harrex
Diesel Schwarze
Lighting
Cameraperson
Tim Maurice Jones
Choreographer
Ashley Wallen
Production Company
Partizan

Music Arrangement
EMI
Notting Hill
Peer Music
Universal
Sound Design
750mph
Post Production
The Mill
Advertising Agency
Saatchi & Saatchi
London
Planner
Gareth Ellis

Account Handler
Sarah Galea
Brand Managers
Kelly Engstrom
Sam Taylor
Marketing Manager
Lysa Hardy
Business Leader
Sally Beerworth
Client
T-Mobile

TV Commercials over 120 Seconds

Saatchi & Saatchi London
for T-Mobile

Dance
On the 15th of January at 11am, a single commuter started dancing in the middle of a train station. The dance grew as more dancers joined in, until there were over 300 people, perfectly choreographed. The excitement caused hundreds of genuine, unsuspecting members of the public to join in and share the moment.

448

rectors
ter Khoury
ital Pinchevsky
cola Wilson
pywriter
ital Pinchevsky
t **Director**
cola Wilson
eative Director
ter Khoury

Producer
Craig Morton
Agency Producer
Simone Bosman
Editor
Michael Kolbe
Music Composer & Arranger
B Holroyd

Sound Designer
Grant Harris
Production Company
Hotel de Ville
Advertising Agency
Metropolitan
Republic
Account Handler
Nicola Wilson

Brand & Marketing Manager
Carrie Shelver
Client
POWA (People
Opposing Women
Abuse)

Cinema Commercials 41-60 Seconds

Metropolitan Republic
for POWA

POWA: NO
POWA wanted to urge viewers to do their part in creating a society that does not tolerate abuse towards women. Using cinema and its sizeable screens, this spot makes the audience participate in the struggle. The following words appear on the screen one at a time, each on a different side, forcing viewers to shake their heads when reading the message: 'One in every three women in South Africa gets raped. You can keep shaking your head, or you could do something to help. If you see something, say something'.

rector
ichael Gracey
opywriter
lérie Chidlovsky
t **Director**
gnès Cavard
ssistant Art rector
regory Ferembach

Creative Director
Rémi Babinet
Producer
Fabrice Brovelli
Music Supervisor
Christophe Caurret
Artist
Dan The Automator
Sound Design
BETC Music

Production Company
Partizan
Advertising Agency
BETC Euro RSCG
Account Handlers
Marie-Josée
Cadorette
Catherine Clément
Marielle Durandet
Dominique Vérot

Media Strategy Manager
Martine Picard
Marketing Manager
Michael Aidan
Client
Danone
Brand
Evian

Cinema Commercials 41-60 Seconds

BETC Euro RSCG
for Danone

Rollerbabies
Everyone in France remembers the Evian advert with the babies' underwater ballet, which made a huge impression when released in 1998. Twelve years later, it still tops the charts as one of the public's favourite adverts. The babies have not grown or gotten older but are still bursting with an infectious energy and love of life. This film is an incredibly enthusiastic modern day musical comedy, involving the sharpest contemporary artists. It thus reinforces the position of Evian as a great contemporary worldwide brand. Just listen to the word 'Evian'. In the rise and fall of its intonation we clearly hear 'Live Young'.

Punching Above

Cougars

Cow

Instructions

Quiche

Sheilas

Director	**Producers**	**Sound Designers**	**Account Executive**
Gary Freedman	Catherine Anderson	Tone Aston	Lucy McBurney
Digital Director	Karen Bryson	Simon Lister	**Business Director**
Brett Mitchell	**Agency Producer**	**Production Company**	Steve Muller
Copywriters	Paul Johnston	@radical.media	**Brand Manager**
Cam Blackley	**Editors**	**Special Effects**	Scott McGregor
Matty Burton	Mark Burnett	Fuel	**Marketing Manager**
Art Directors	Bernard Garry	**Advertising Agency**	Paul Donaldson
Cam Blackley	Zen Rosenthal	Droga5 Australia	**Client**
Matty Burton	**Director of**	**Executive Planning**	Carlton United
Executive Creative	**Photography**	**Director**	Breweries
Director	Danny Ruhlmann	Sudeep Gohil	**Brand**
David Nobay	**Casting Director**	**Account Manager**	Victoria Bitter
	Toni Higginbotham	Nicolas Kettelhake	

TV Commercial Campaigns

Droga5 Australia
for Carlton United Breweries

The Regulars Campaign
These commercials aired as part of VB beer's 'The Regulars' campaign in the months following the major two-minute launch TV spot that premiered during the first day of The Ashes. Australians, proud of their ability to laugh at themselves and others, are notorious for categorising people according to their appearance, their habits, where they live, what they do, their strengths and their weaknesses. It is this exceptional Australian ability to deliver the backhanded compliment that all of these spots celebrate. A total of 15 commercials were cut from 14 hours of footage and rolled out over the summer to keep the campaign fresh.

451

Your smoking affects your loved ones more than you think.

For help quitting call 0800 88 44 11 or visit nhs.uk/smokefree

Your smoking affects your loved ones more than you think.

For help quitting call 0800 88 44 11 or visit nhs.uk/smokefree

NHS SMOKEFREE

Mollie

Dylan

Portae

Rahmel

Director	**Producer**	**Sound Designer**	**Account Handlers**
Jim Gilchrist	Kate Leahy	Parv Thind	Rachel Gilmour
Copywriter	**Agency Producer**	**Production Company**	Remi Rasenberg
Matt Lever	Lynnette Kyme	MJZ	**Brand & Marketing**
Art Director	**Editor**	**Advertising Agency**	**Manager**
Helen Board	Adam Spivey	MCBD	Helen Duggan
Creative Director	**Lighting**	**Planner**	**Client**
Danny Brooke-Taylor	**Cameraperson**	Andy Nairn	Department
	Alex Barber		of Health

TV Commercial Campaigns

MCBD
for the Department of Health

Mollie / Dylan / Portae / Rahmel
Anti-smoking research findings state that people are far more likely to give up when they realis the emotional effect that their habit has on their loved ones, particularly their children. These ads featured the actual children of real smokers, who were given the opportunity to tell their mums and dads exactly how their smoking makes them feel. The ads were unscripted, and targeted the parents directly, playing during their favourite TV programmes.

452

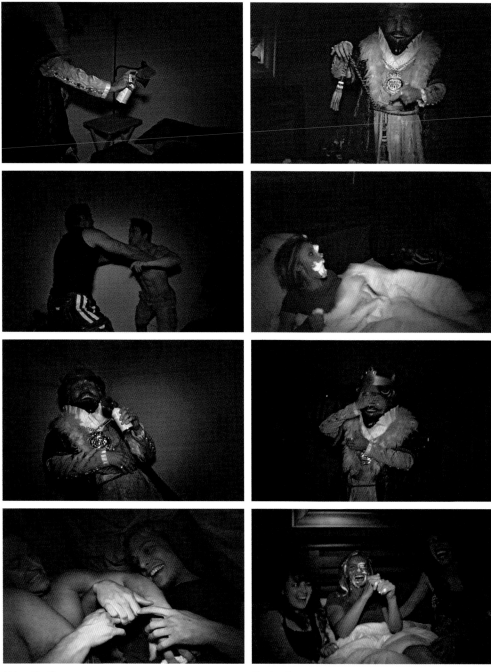

Airhorn Scuffle

Shaving Cream

irector
enry-Alex Rubin
opywriter
yan Kutscher
rt Director
aul Caiozzo
reative Directors
ames
awson-Hollis
ill Wright

**Chief Creative
Officers**
Andrew Keller
Rob Reilly
Producer
Sloan Schroeder
Editor
Lawrence Young

**Lighting
Cameraperson**
Matthew Wolf
Production Company
Smuggler
Productions
Music
Lime Studios

Advertising Agency
Crispin Porter
+ Bogusky
Marketing Manager
Claudia Lezcano
Client
Burger King

TV Commercial Campaigns

Crispin Porter + Bogusky
for Burger King

Airhorn Scuffle / Shaving Cream
Don't go to bed before the King. To promote their new Late Night Menu, Burger King decided
to expose the downside of going to bed a little too early. After all, a guy in bed at 10pm isn't
buying off the Late Night Menu, and that's bad for business. So, in the tradition of pranks
played on sleeping roommates, the King used an airhorn and some shaving cream to rouse
these early retirees.

453

Tactics

Warm Down

Missed Tackle

Off Your Right Leg

Training

Cubs it's 89

Great Tackle

Giraffe

Directors
Tom & Nic
Copywriter
Laurence Quinn
Art Director
Mark Norcutt
Creative Director
Axel Chaldecott
Executive Creative Director
Russell Ramsey

Producer
Jon Madsen
Agency Producer
Doug Wade
Lighting Cameraperson
Jon Lynch
Sound Designer
Aaron Reynolds
Production Company
Outsider

Special Effects
Framestore
Advertising Agency
JWT London
Planner
Richard Cottingham
Account Handler
Tanya
Hamilton-Smith

Brand Manager
Heather McCracken
Marketing Manager
Giles Morgan
Client
HSBC

TV Sponsorship Credits

JWT London
for HSBC

Tactics / Warm Down / Missed Tackle / Off Your Right Leg / Training / Cubs it's 89 / Great Tackle / Giraffe
These idents were part of HSBC's sponsorship of the British and Irish Lions Tour of South Africa. They ran during the breaks of the matches throughout the whole two-month tour. The spots are short little moments, where we see famous British and Irish Lions players teaching real lions what it means to put on the famous red shirt.

Two Potatoes

Bum Face

Bitchy Nuts

Drumsticks

Scary Ketchup

Pizza Face

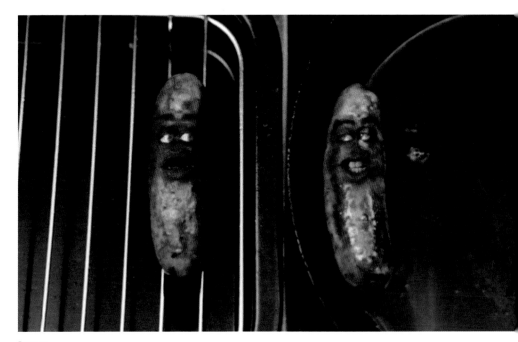

Bangers

Director	**Designer**	**Sound Designer**	**Planner**
Mark Denton	Ollie Carver	Sam Robson	Emily James
Copywriter	**Agency Producer**	**Production Company**	**Account Handler**
Mike Boles	Jennifer Fewster	COY!	Sally Neilson
Art Director	**Editor**	COMMUNICATIONS	**Acting Head**
Jerry Hollens	Billy Mead	**Special Effects**	**of Marketing**
Creative Director	**Lighting**	MPC Los Angeles	Kate Frankum
Damon Collins	**Cameraperson**	**Advertising Agency**	**Client**
Producer	Miguel Ragageles	RKCR/Y&R	Food Standards
Sara Cummins			Agency

TV Sponsorship Credits

RKCR/Y&R
for the Food Standards Agency

Talking Foods
These idents were shown at the beginning and end of ad breaks in the show 'Family Supercooks'. Each ident features good and bad food types talking about healthy eating. We wanted to get the message across in an entertaining rather than preachy way. Using offbeat humour, we created a cast of food characters with human traits and personalities. Some are eccentric, some are angry, some bitchy, some sad, some ridiculously happy, but hopefully all are funny and memorable.

Cinema Sponsorship Credits

Cossette West
for the BC Cancer Agency

Eye of the Cervix
Although cervical cancer is highly preventable, it's the third most lethal form of cancer among women. And while it may be uncomfortable, having a Pap test doesn't take long. To communicate this, we ran 15 experiential cinema spots in theatres across British Columbia. Literally shot from the eye of a cervix, the spots begin with actual theatre curtains opening to reveal a doctor performing a Pap test in real time. After the quick procedure, the theatre curtains close. A super projected on the curtains reads: 'It doesn't take long to prevent cervical cancer. Remember to book regular Pap tests'.

Director
Steve Gordon
Copywriter
Brent Wheeler
Art Director
Rob Sweetman
Creative Directors
Bryan Collins
Rob Sweetman

Agency Producer
Freda Chan
Line Producer
Sarah Duncan
Editor
Ian Jenkins
Production Company
Slim Gin & Tonic

Audio House
Wave Productions
Advertising Agency
Cossette West
Account Director
Nadine Wilson
Account Supervisor
Jennifer Fujita

**Promotion &
Education Specialist**
Anne McCulloch
Client
BC Cancer Agency

AN INCOMMUNICABLE SEMANTICS

TVand CineMA

COMMUNICATION

UNICADO

C TV

LIES

Kitchen

Lounge

Garden

Interview

Calvin Klein

Director Tom Tagholm	**Special Effects** Mark Beardall	**Music Composer** Rich Martin	**Advertising Agency** 4creative
Art Director Tom Tagholm	**Editor** Adam Rudd	**Lighting**	**Marketing Manager** Charlie Palmer
Creative Director Brett Foraker	**Sound Designer** Rich Martin	**Cameraperson** Rob Hardy	**Client** Channel 4
Producer Tabby Harris	**Director of Photography** Rob Hardy	**Production Company** 4creative	**Brand** Alan Carr Chatty
Set Designer Adam Zoltowski		**Special Effects Company** MPC	Man

▲ TV Promotions, Stings & Programme Junctions

4creative
for Channel 4

Alan Carr Chatty Man: Kitchen / Lounge / Garden / Interview / Calvin Klein
We needed a simple, effective device to showcase Alan Carr's distinct style in order to set the show Alan Carr Chatty Man apart from others. We had limited access to our star and no access to any of the people he was going to interview, so we imagined that Alan had been chatty all his life, even as a very young child, rabbiting away about anything and everything. The line 'Born Chatty' emerged. Alan had to look like a baby but still look like Alan. While the production was fairly involved, the end result feels simple and low-tech, as if it was produced by Alan's mum using an old camcorder.

460

Director	**Sound Designer**	**Set Design**	**Marketing Managers**
eil Gorringe	Rich Martin	Skyhook	Sarah Owen
reative Director	**Director of**	**Production Company**	Charlie Palmer
rett Foraker	**Photography**	4creative	**Client**
roducer	Ross McLennan	**Advertising Agency**	E4
wilym Gwillim	**Music Composer**	4creative	**Brand**
ditor	Rich Martin		Skins
ames Rosen			

TV Promotions, Stings & Programme Junctions

4creative
for E4

Skins Series 3
The aim was to promote the third series of Skins which introduces an entirely new set of characters, so we wanted to do something that had some impact and made its mark. We deliberately set out to be provocative, and to make a film that touched on one of the new central characters of the show, Cook – a fairly irresponsible, volatile character prone to violence. To reflect his energy and the somewhat incendiary nature of the third series, we decided to base the campaign around a slightly fantastical, irresponsible, rock and roll bit of sex, drugs and violence.

461

It's more than you imagined.

Director	**Producer**	**Visual Effects**	**Director of**	**Audio Mix**
Noam Murro	Jay Veal	**Producers**	**Photography**	POP Sound
Copywriter	**Executive Producer**	Nerissa Kavanagh	Toby Irwin	**Music House**
Adam Reeves	Colleen O'Donnell	Nicholas Ponzoni	**Telecine Artist**	Search Party Music
Art Director	**Senior Executive**	**Editor**	Beau Leon	**Advertising Agency**
Brandon Mugar	**Producer**	David Henegar	**Visual Effects**	BBDO New York
Executive Creative	Shawn Lacy	**Mixer**	**Company**	**Account Handlers**
Directors	**Content Producer**	Mitch Dorf	Animal Logic	Tara Deveaux
Greg Hahn	Nicholas Gaul	**Music Supervisors**	**Production Company**	Courtney Lord
Mike Smith	**Director of**	Stephanie	Biscuit Filmworks	**Client**
Chief Creative	**Integrated**	Diaz-Matos	**Editing House**	HBO
Officers	**Production**	Randall Poster	Butcher Editorial	
Bill Bruce	Brian DiLorenzo			
David Lubars				

TV Brand Identities

BBDO New York
for HBO

Happy Kid

Happy Kid begins as an idyllic depiction of a kid safely asleep surrounded by friendly teddy bears; he is however soon revealed to be a neglected child asleep in the middle of a diamond-smuggling operation. True to the 'It's more than you imagined' concept, Happy Kid is more than a commercial. It also serves as a scene from a larger story, which can be experienced at hboimagine.com.

Dino   Dog   Crab

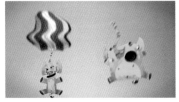 

Elephant   Racoon

Designer
Ljubisa Djukic
Design Director
Ole Keune
Director
Bettina Vogel

Art Director
Lucas Zanotto
Creative Directors
Ljubisa Djukic
Ole Keune
Producer
Sven Henrichs

Set Designer
Lucas Zanotto
Production Company
dyrdee Media
Sound Design
Schieffer und
Schieffer

Client
MTV Networks
Brand
Nickelodeon

TV Brand Identities

dyrdee Media
for MTV Networks Germany

Nick Idents: Dino / Dog / Crab / Elephant / Racoon
We came up with the idea to create station idents with little, huggable characters fitting the Nickelodeon corporate identity. We created a spot that incorporated this identity without feeling forced. We also wanted something with an analogue look, which relates to the every day life of kids. With that in mind, the idea to put realistic orange objects in each spot was born. To build a story around convincing orange objects was a challenge, but once that was achieved the other two Nickelodeon colours, white and green, came into the design naturally. This helped to give the spots a strong style while maintaining the brand.

463

Mr Whippy

Africa Sings

Indigenous

Love Story

Kurdish

War

Unity

opywriter
iuliana De Felice
rt Director
im Chenery
reative Director
osh Moore

Agency Producer
Nathan Bell
Production
Companies
Iloura
Mighty Nice

Advertising Agency
US Sydney
Account Handler
Nathan Bell
Marketing Manager
Jacquie Riddel

Communications
Specialist
Aisha Hillary
Client
SBS

TV Brand Identities

US Sydney
for SBS

Mr Whippy / Africa Sings / Indigenous / Love Story / Kurdish / War / Unity
SBS brings you six billion stories and counting. Each from a unique perspective, each creating a unique experience. We chose to demonstrate some of these extraordinary stories from inside the viewer's mind. Each ident travels inside the viewer's brain to see their emotional response while experiencing the channel. The idents showcase the diverse and culturally rich content that spans arts, documentaries, and foreign and art house films offered by SBS.

465

Sweet Heart

Mr Furry

Sound System

Music Brain

Mad Drummers

Furry Posse

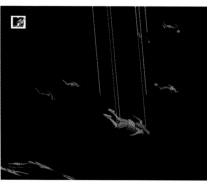

wels & Oil

Chocolate & Gold

Base Jumpers

el Me

Creative Directors	Producers	Design Groups	Production
oberto Bagatti	Anna Caregnato	ARK	Companies
ylan Griffith	Philip Ward	Realise Studio	MTV World Design
att Pyke	**Sound Designer**	TADO	Studio Milan
	Simon Pyke	Tronic	Universal
		UFO	Everything
		Universal	**Client**
		Everything	MTV Networks
		Zeitguised	International
		Zhestkov	

TV Brand Identities

MTV World Design Studio Milan
for MTV Networks International

MTV International Rebrand 2009
MTV's first international rebrand launched in July 2009 to an audience of 578 million households across 162 territories. The challenge lay in communicating through a common visual language that would be relevant to different cultures without being perceived as bland or generic. Our solution was an initial set of ten idents displaying a heady mix of human emotions and programme related themes and cut with the energy of pop culture.

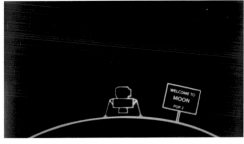
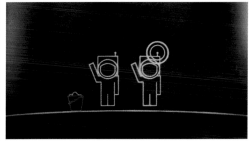
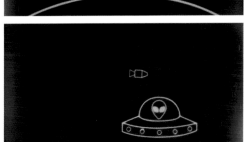
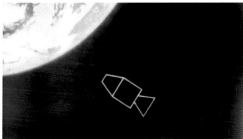

Designers	**Art Director**	**Producer**	**Production Company**
Leo Nguyen	Matt Heck	Kala Ellis	Hackett Films
Anne Numont	**Creative Director**	**Agency Producer**	**Advertising Agency**
Senior Designer	Noah Regan	Thea Carone	Three Drunk
James Hackett	**Executive Creative**	**Sound Designer**	Monkeys
Copywriter	**Directors**	Simon Kane	**Client**
Damian Fitzgerald	Justin Drape		BBC Knowledge
	Scott Nowell		

TV Promotions, Stings & Programme Junctions

Three Drunk Monkeys
for BBC Knowledge

BBC Moon Week
This spot was created to promote BBC Knowledge's week of programmes commemorating the 40th anniversary of the moon landing. Using the line animation techniques of the time, we took the viewer on a journey of obscure but amazing facts relating to the event. The voice of Ted Maynard, who broadcast the original moon landing from his radio station 40 years ago, brought this fascinating story to life.

Director	**Set Designer**	**Sound Designer**	**Marketing Manager**
Tom Tagholm	Simon Davis	Rich Martin	James Walker
Creative Director	**Special Effects**	**Production Company**	**Client**
Brett Foraker	Tom Harding	4creative	Channel 4
Producers	**Editor**	**Advertising Agency**	**Brand**
Gwilym Gwillim	Adam Rudd	4creative	Great British Food
Shananne Lane	**Director of**		Fight
	Photography		
	Luke Scott		

TV Promotions, Stings & Programme Junctions

4creative
for Channel 4

Great British Food Fight
The challenge was to build on the success of the previous year's food fight campaign featuring Channel 4's big chefs Gordon Ramsay, Jamie Oliver and Hugh Fearnley-Whittingstall as well as introduce a fresh angle and a new chef, Heston Blumenthal. The four chefs train together to represent Great Britain in the 'Food Olympics'. We see the team prepping for the big event; they're on top form in physical, mental and food fitness, but they just can't give up the in-fighting.

TV Promotions, Stings & Programme Junctions

RKCR/Y&R
for the BBC

Young Orators

This spot was created to communicate the power of great oratory, promoting the programme 'The Lost Art of Oratory' and the series 'The Speaker'. We wanted to symbolise the rebirth of great oratory in the Obama era, and to explore the notion of whether the new generation will master the power of the spoken word. The trail features a series of children mouthing the words to one of the greatest speeches of all time, JFK's 'Ask not what your country can do for you'. They are mouthing his words with the same conviction as JFK himself, giving the speech a new power and relevance.

Director	**Producer**	**Sound Designer**	**Account Handlers**
eve Reeves	Louise Jones	Parv Thind	Jamal Cassim
opywriter	**Editor**	**Production Company**	Mark Graeme
ke Boles	Ted Guard	Red Bee Media	**Marketing Manager**
t Director	**Lighting**	**Advertising Agency**	David Dunn
rry Hollens	**Cameraperson**	RKCR/Y&R	**Client**
eative Director	Ray Coates	**Planner**	BBC
amon Collins		Megan Thompson	

TV Promotions, Stings & Programme Junctions

RKCR/Y&R
for the BBC

Riot

In this spot promoting the BBC's global news service, the police gather forces to repel a violent riot. However, we reveal these are not your average anarchists, but well-heeled city bankers protesting against proposed new reforms, post credit crunch.

Director	**Producer**	**Advertising Agency**	**Head of Consumer**
enito Montorio	Ciska Faulkner	RKCR/Y&R	**Marketing**
opywriter	**Editor**	**Planner**	Chris Travers
eve Moss	Andy McGraw	Emily James	**Client**
rt Director	**Sound Designer**	**Account Handler**	BBC
olyon Finch	Aaron Reynolds	Anita O'Shea	
eative Director	**Production Company**		
amon Collins	Blink Productions		

Designer	**Art Directors**	**Sound Designer**	**Clients**
Jopsu Ramu	Shun Kawakami	Chikao Maruyama	Sanoma Television
Concept Designers	Jopsu Ramu	**Design Group**	Oy
Timo Huhtala	**Creative Director**	Musuta	Nelonen Media
Jopsu Ramu	Jopsu Ramu	**Production Company**	**Brand**
Directors	**Producer**	EDP Graphic Works	Nelonen
Masaru Ikeda	Timo Huhtala		
Mitsumoto Maeda			

TV Promotions, Stings & Programme Junctions

Musuta
for Nelonen

Urban Abstract

Urban Abstract was created for TV channel Nelonen and it was shown before and after every commercial break in five-second parts. Urban Abstract consists of 20 five-second pairs, or can be viewed as one 200-second journey across urban space. The journey, in one, two and three dimensions, is similar to abstract surfing, in which the original destination is only reached after a number of seemingly random yet linked detours. Points, lines, planes and other abstract elements create a journey through Urban Abstract. Our goal was to create something visually beautiful and calming.

471

FROM THE PURE WATERS OF TASMANIA

Director	**Production Designer**	**Music Composer**	**Advertising Agency**
Steve Rogers	Steven Jones-Evans	Elliot Wheeler	Publicis Mojo
Copywriter	**Special Effects**	**Sound Designer**	**Account Handlers**
Grant McAloon	Justin Bromley	Simon Lister	Simon Ludowyke
Art Director	**Visual Effects**	**Production Company**	Tara Seymour
Steve Wakelam	**Supervisor**	Revolver Films	**Client**
Creative Director	Justin Bromley	**Editing Company**	Lion Nathan
Micah Walker	**Editor**	Guillotine	**Brand**
Producers	Alexandre De	**Visual Effects**	James Boags
Karla Henwood	Franceschi	Fin Design & Effects	Draught
Michael Ritchie	**Director of**	**Sound Design**	
Agency Producer	**Photography**	Nylon	
Jasmin Ferguson	Geoffrey Simpson		

▲ Direction

Revolver Films
for Lion Nathan

Pure Waters
Way, way down at the bottom of the world, there's an untouched island called Tasmania where the water is famously pure, and the beer is especially good. We decided that surely there must be a connection. So, we took the purity of the island's water and turned it into a legend, telling the story of how it makes things good. Whether you're dunking your bike or your shoes, your girl or, yes, your beer, the pure waters of Tasmania will always give you, well, something better. Pure Waters was also nominated in Editing and Special Effects.

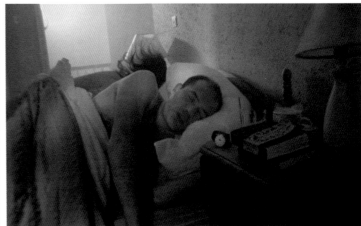

Direction

Blink Productions
for the Department for Communities & Local Government

Breathe
To dramatise the fact that two or three breaths of toxic smoke will make you unconscious, we likened death by smoke inhalation to the respiratory effects of drowning. In an eerie, blue suffused scene, a bedroom underwater, we witness the unnerving tranquillity of a couple who have breathed their last breath. Breathe was also nominated in Production Design and Cinematography and selected in Use of Music.

Director
Dougal Wilson
Copywriter
Mike Boles
Art Director
Jerry Hollens
Creative Director
Damon Collins
Producer
Matt Fone
Agency Producer
Tim Page

Production Designer
Steve Smithwick
Special Effects
Ludo Fealy
Editor
Joe Guest
Lighting Cameraperson
Alex Barber
Underwater Director of Photography
Mark Silk

Colourist
Jean-Clement Soret
Music Composer
Jon Hopkins
Sound Designer
Anthony Moore
Production Company
Blink Productions
Advertising Agency
RKCR/Y&R

Planner
Anna Tetlow
Account Handler
Nick Fokes
Head of Campaigns & Marketing
David Watson
Client
Department for Communities & Local Government

475

Director
Sam Brown
Copywriter
Ted Heath
Art Director
Paul Angus
Creative Director
Mark Roalfe
Producer
Kate Hitchings
Agency Producer
Danielle Sandler
Production Designer
Sebastian Soukup

Special Effects
Matthew Unwin
Editor
James Rosen
Lighting Cameraperson
Tom Townend
Music Composers
Dave Roback
Hope Sandoval
Music Arranger
Mazzy Star

Sound Designer
Ben Leeves
Production Company
Rogue Films
Special Effects Company
MPC
Editing Company
Final Cut
Advertising Agency
RKCR/Y&R
Advertising Director
Natasha Oram

Account Handlers
Katey Ellen-Price
Sarah Jenkins
Priya Patel
Marketing Manager
Natasha Oram
Executive Director of Brand & Marketing
Ashley Stockwell
Client
Virgin Media

Direction

Rogue Films
for Virgin Media

Fantastic Journey
This spot dramatises the benefits of Virgin Media's mobile phone service; specifically, the power of the internet to transform your world. The advert opens with a man boarding a train. As he sits down and pulls his mobile out of his pocket he is immediately whisked away to be with friends and loved ones, and is immersed in a world of music, film and gaming. Fantastic Journey was also nominated in Editing, Production Design, Cinematography, Use of Music and Special Effects.

Director
Tom Kuntz
Copywriters
Craig Allen
Eric Kallman
Art Directors
Craig Allen
Eric Kallman
Creative Directors
Jason Bagley
Danielle Flagg
Executive Creative Directors
Mark Fitzloff

Susan Hoffman
Executive Producers
Jeff Scruton
David Zander
Agency Producer
Sarah Shapiro
Agency Executive Producer
Ben Grylewicz
Line Producer
Scott Kaplan
Visual Effects
Robert Moggach

Editor
Gavin Cutler
Director of Photography
Bryan Newman
Sound Designer
Gus Koven
Production Company
MJZ
Post Production
Mackenzie Cutler
Animatronics
Stan Winston Studios

Visual Effects Company
Method Studios
Audio Post
POP Sound
Sound Design
Stimmung
Advertising Agency
Wieden+Kennedy Portland
Account Handlers
Maggie Entwistle
Tamera Geddes
Taryn Lange

Planner
Matt Kelley
Chief Marketing Officer
Richard Castellini
Senior Director of Advertising
Cynthia McIntyre
Client
CareerBuilder.com

Direction

MJZ
for CareerBuilder.com

Tips
It can be hard to know when you need a new job. This spot gives the viewer a number of warning signs they should watch out for so they'll know when it's time for them to move on.

Sumo

Yoga

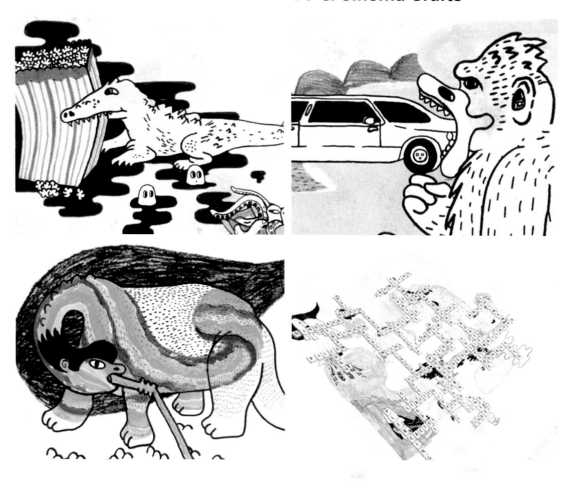

the Beautiful Word

Hula

Animation

Ogilvy Paris
for Mattel

Sumo / Yoga / Hula
Scrabble was celebrating its 60th birthday. A beautiful age for a brand, yet the blockbuster board game was considered elitist and outdated by some. It was time to help consumers rediscover the richness of the Scrabble experience. The creative idea behind the campaign was inspired by the principle of the game itself: picture a Scrabble board at the end of a game, then follow the maze formed by the different words; they make an enchanting story that takes your imagination to unexpected places… We turned this fabulous potential into images, gave it motion and life, and 'The Beautiful Word' campaign was born. The campaign was also selected in Use of Music.

Animator
ntoaneta
etchanova
rectors
na Dakeva
ement Dozier
pywriters
njamin Bregeault
rnaud Vanhelle
t Director
ntoaneta
etchanova

Creative Director
Chris Garbutt
Producer
François Brun
Agency Producers
Laure Bayle
Diane de Bretteville
Evelyne Callot
Music Composers
Jason Brando Ciciola
Dana Edelman
Mathieu Lafontaine
Didier Tovel

Production Company
Wizz
Music Production
Apollo
Mile 23 Music
Advertising Agency
Ogilvy Paris
Account Handlers
Benoît de Fleurian
Marie-Charlotte
Lafront

Marketing Manager
Arnaud
Roland-Gosselin
Client
Mattel
Brand
Scrabble

479

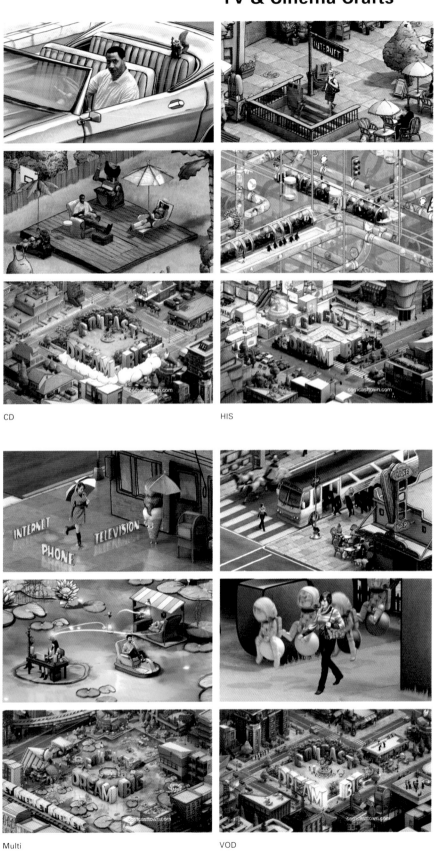

CD

HIS

Multi

VOD

HD

Anthem

Music Arranger
Andres Velasquez
Music Composer
Greg Griffith
Directors
Smith & Foulkes
Copywriters
Andrew Bancroft
Paul Charney
Art Director
Stefan Copiz
Group Creative Director
Chris Ford

Creative Director
Jamie Barrett
Assistant Creative Directors
Paul Charney
Stefan Copiz
Producer
Isobel Conroy
Executive Producers
Rudy Callegari
Chris O'Reilly
Julia Parfitt
Agency Producer
Ashley Sferro

Lead Animators
Eoin Coughlan
Mark Davis
Animation Supervisor
Eoin Coughlan
3D Animator
Darren Rolmanis
Lead Modellers
Matt Clark
Nicholas Domerego
Jerome Haupert
Visual Effects
Fletcher Moules

Lighting Cameraperson
Ueli Steiger
Illustrator & Character Designer
Chris Martin
Sound Designer
Gus Koven
Music & Sound Design
Stimmung
Animation
Nexus
Productions

Production Companies
Bright
Pictures
Bicoastal
Nexus Productions
Advertising Agency
Goodby, Silverstein & Partners
Account Handler
Kenny White
Client
Comcast

Use of Music

Goodby, Silverstein & Partners
for Comcast

Future Hopping
In 2008 consumers saw Comcast as the big, bad cable company. We needed to remind people of all the great stuff Comcast offers, and in the process get more people to actually like them. So we created a parallel universe version of Comcast and called it Comcast Town. It's a place where technology lives, possibilities are never-ending and squirrels play guitars. In Comcast Town people don't just tell you how much they love Comcast's phone, TV, and Internet services, they sing it to you. The single advert 'Anthem', which is part of this campaign, was also awarded a Yellow Pencil in Animation.

481

Sound Designer	**Producers**	**Lighting**	**Editing Company**
Aaron Reynolds	Kelly Doyle	**Cameraperson**	Final Cut
Director	Maddy Easton	Stuart Graham	**Actresses**
Jim Weedon	**Post House Producer**	**Flame Operator**	Sarah Ezekiel
Copywriter	Jordan	James Maclachan	Philippa Johnson
Peers Carter	Andreopoulos	**Sound Design**	**Marketing Director**
Art Director	**Special Effects**	Wave Studios	Donna Cresswell
Tony Muranka	James Maclachan	**Audio Post**	**Client Chief**
Creative Directors	**Editor**	**Production Studio**	**Executive**
Peers Carter	Jim Weedon	Wave Studios	Kirstine Knox
Tony Muranka		**Production Company**	**Client**
		Bare Films	MND Association

Sound Design

Wave Studios
for the MND Association

Sarah's Story

Over 5,000 people face life with Motor Neurone Disease. Sarah's Story is a true story, an attempt to engage the viewer with how it feels to have MND. It begins with Sarah as a young woman, but through some stunning visual and aural techniques we see her painful, rapid deterioration into full-blown MND. In chilling detail we see how a perfectly healthy young woman can come under attack from an unseen assassin. The use of silence heightens the increasing isolation. This film is the result of a direct relationship between the client, the creative people and the production company. Everyone involved wishes to thank Sarah Ezekiel, who has advanced MND, for agreeing to appear in this film. Sarah's Story was also nominated in Editing.

482

Production Designer	**Producers**	**Editors**	**Artist**
James Chinlund	Eric Stern	Michael Heldman	The Magnetic Fields
Director	David Zander	Neil Smith	**Vocals**
Rupert Sanders	**Agency Producer**	**Director of**	Stephin Merritt
Copywriter	Dana May	**Photography**	Britta Phillips
Scott Ginsberg	**Head of Integrated**	Chris Soos	**Production Company**
Art Director	**Production**	**Music Supervisor**	MJZ
January Vernon	Sally-Ann Dale	Sara Matarazzo	**Advertising Agency**
Executive Creative	**Line Producer**	**Sound Designer**	Droga5 New York
Director	Laurie Boccaccio	Brian Emrich	**Client**
Duncan Marshall	**Special Effects**	**Sound Mixers**	Puma
Creative Chairman	Cedric Nicolas	Philip Loeb	**Brand**
David Droga	Troyan	Evan Mangiamele	L.I.F.T

Production Design

MJZ
for Puma

L.I.F.T.

The new Puma L.I.F.T. shoe weighs only 173 grams. They are shoes you can see, but not feel. To illustrate this sensation, we dressed our L.I.F.T. wearing models in nothing else but light clothes that were visible, yet weightless. We posed them in simple rooms, also transformed by untouchable beams of light. Ultimately, wearing the Puma L.I.F.T. is a sensory illusion. So by injecting light into a room and onto a body, we conveyed the surreal sensation of actually walking in L.I.F.T.s – light-injected footwear. L.I.F.T. was also selected in Direction.

483

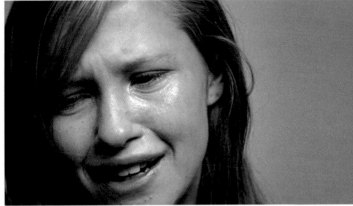

Director
Chris Palmer
Copywriter
Toby Allen
Art Director
Jim Hilson
Creative Director
Nick Gill

Producer
Rupert Smythe
Agency Producer
Davud Karbassioun
Editor
Ed Guard
Lighting
Cameraperson
Dan Landin

Music
Bat For Lashes
Sound Designer
Jack Sedgwick
Production Company
Gorgeous
Enterprises
Advertising Agency
BBH London

Account Handler
Helen James
Brand Manager
Collette Collins
Marketing Manager
Diana Tickell
Client
Barnardo's

Direction

Gorgeous Enterprises
for Barnardo's

Turn Around
This is a filmic palindrome: a sequence of shots tells the story of a young girl's journey into despair. The positive intervention of Barnardo's triggers a reverse sequence of exactly the same shots with a different voice over, showing the tangible impact Barnardo's can have in turning a young person's life around. Turn Around was also selected in Editing.

Director
ima Nourizadeh
opywriter
on Wilfred
acDonald
rt Director
aura Kim

Creative Director
Kristian Manchester
Producers
Albert Botha
Steve Wheeler
Agency Producer
Claudia Roy

Editor
Gary Knight
Lighting
Cameraperson
Christopher Probst
Music Composer
Pilooski

Production Companies
Partizan
Radke
Advertising Agency
Sid Lee
Client
adidas

Direction

Partizan & Radke
for adidas

House Party
Partizan's Nima Nourizadeh takes us on a tour of the greatest house party in the world, with the most star-studded guest list, in a celebration of originality and 20 years of adidas Originals. House Party was also nominated in Cinematography and selected in both Editing and Use of Music.

Editor	**Art Director**	**Editing House**	**Account Handler**
Richard Orrick	Chris Groom	Work	Ryan Fisher
Director	**Creative Directors**	**Production Company**	**Client**
Scott Lyon	Tony Davidson	Outsider	Honda
Copywriter	Kim Papworth	**Advertising Agency**	**Brand**
Sam Heath	**Producers**	Wieden+Kennedy	Civic
	Zeno Campbell	London	
	Anna Smith		

Editing

Work
for Honda

Everything

Honda thinks beyond the car market. The company thinks longer term, more broadly, more laterally. They think in more detail, they notice the little things and they have the courage to address the big ones. This bigger, broader thinking means the products get better in little, interesting ways. We needed to wake people up about Honda, to remind them that Honda is an exciting, interesting company – one that society wants to exist. Our challenge was to tell a brand story about Hondaness, about how big and wide Honda thinks, whilst also promoting the Civic brand.

486

Determination

Defense

Editing

Goodby, Silverstein & Partners
for the National Basketball Association

Editor
DJ Steve Porter
Assistant Editor
Timothy Plain
Copywriter
Craig Mangan
Art Director
Devin Sharkey

Creative Director
Jamie Barrett
Assistant Creative Directors
Paul Charney
Stefan Copiz
Agency Producer
Timothy Plain

Music Arranger
DJ Steve Porter
Production Company
NBA Entertainment
Advertising Agency
Goodby, Silverstein & Partners

Account Handler
Nathan Shamban
Client
National Basketball Association

Determination / Defense
Most NBA players use music to pump themselves up or get focused before a game. Music and the NBA just seem to go really well together. In 2009 we decided to officially embrace this synergy between music and professional basketball by creating a TV campaign of 'mashups'. This campaign uses the NBA's exclusive library of video and audio content to create actual songs. The vocals are the actual sound bites of players and coaches from the NBA put to a beat. The players themselves reinforce the core principles of the league – determination and defense.

Music Arranger	**Producer**	**Production**	**Account Handler**
Peter Raeburn	Joanna Yeldham	**Companies**	Fiona Richards
Director	**Editor**	Georgous	**Business Director**
Vince Squibb	Paul Watts	Enterprises	Jo Bacon
Copywriters	**Lighting**	Red Bee Media	**Head of Marketing**
Jules Chalkley	**Cameraperson**	**Audio**	Katie Avon
Nick Simons	Natasha Braier	Factory House	**Marketing Managers**
Art Directors	**Sound Designer**	**Post Production**	Hugh Davies
Jules Chalkley	Anthony Moore	The Mill	Sophie Mather
Nick Simons	**Set Designer**	**Advertising Agency**	**Client**
Creative Director	John Beard	RKCR/Y&R	BBC
Damon Collins			

Use of Music

RKCR/Y&R
for the BBC

Show Your Love
This advert launched the idea that if you love where you live, you can be part of it through your local BBC radio station. Show Your Love was also selected in Direction and Cinematography.

Music Composer
Robert Miller
Music Producer
Loren Parkins
Director
Daniel Kleinman
Copywriter
Reuben Hower
Art Director
Gerard Caputo

Executive Creative Director
Eric Silver
Creative Directors
Bill Bruce
David Lubars
Agency Producers
Anthony Curti
Theresa Ward
Ed Zazzera

Lighting Cameraperson
John Mathieson
Sound Designer
Gus Koven
Music House
Stimmung

Production Companies
Epoch Films
Rattling Stick
Editing
Spotwelders
Advertising Agency
BBDO New York
Client
Monster.com

Use of Music

BBDO New York
for Monster.com

Battle
During such difficult economic times, monster.com wanted to highlight the lighthearted side of the brand. We focused on creating a platform that uses humour to parody the outrageous actions of those who are hard-working in their jobs, but clearly not on the right career path. Only Monster offers these job seekers a way out, by positioning the totally rebuilt monster.com, and its new suite of precision matching tools, as the solution to finding the job that's right for them. Battle features the humorous work of one musician who is clearly talented, but not suited to his current job.

489

Special Effects
Suzanne Jandu
Jake Mengers
Victoria Osborn
Special Effects Producer
Scott Griffin
Director
Daniel Kleinman

Copywriters
Aidan McClure
Laurent Simon
Art Directors
Aidan McClure
Laurent Simon
Creative Directors
Robert Saville
Mark Waites
Producer
Johnnie Frankel

Agency Producer
Kirsten Kates
Editor
Adam Spivey
Sound Designers
Andy Humphreys
Anthony Moore
Post Production Company
MPC

Production Company
Rattling Stick
Advertising Agency
Mother London
Brand Manager
Leo Murray
Client
Plane Stupid

 Special Effects

MPC
for Plane Stupid

Polar Bears
The brutal impact global warming is having on the polar ice caps is illustrated in a shocking ad created by Mother London and directed by Daniel Kleinman on behalf of climate change charity Plane Stupid. The ad was made on a shoestring budget using a volunteer crew. It features polar bears falling from the sky, meeting their brutal deaths and leaving trails of blood as they crash against buildings and land on cars. MPC created the computer-generated polar bears, using proprietary tools including PAPI which simulates falling and collisions in a realistic way. Its proprietary fur software 'Furtility' allowed the fur to move in a lifelike way.

490

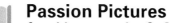

Animation Director
Rob Valley
Director
Pete Candeland
Animation Supervisor
Wes Coman
2D Animators
Pete Dodd
Terry Forder
Daryl Graham
3D Animators
Vincent Aup
Chris Welsby

Character Designers
Ree Treweek
Rob Valley
Creative Director
Joshua Randall
Producers
Jonathan Clyde
Debbie Crosscup
Executive Producers
Paul DeGooyer
Jeff Jones
Alex Rigopulos
Hugo Sands

Editors
Jamie Foord
Lee Gingold
Dan Greenway
Visual Effects Supervisor
Neil Riley
Background Painters
Alan Aldridge
Jim Bowers
Daniel Cacouault
Alberto Mielgo
Lukasz Pazera

Music Composers
The Beatles
Music Arranger
Giles Martin
Recording Engineers
Geoff Emerick
Glyn Johns
Phil McDonald
Ken Scott
Norman Smith

Mix Engineer
Paul Hicks
Production Company
Passion Pictures
Clients
Harmonix
MTV Apple Corps

Animation

Passion Pictures
for Harmonix & MTV Apple Corps

'The Beatles: Rock Band' Intro Cinematic
'The Beatles: Rock Band' game offers players the opportunity to perform 45 classic songs from the band's catalogue. It was developed by Harmonix and MTV, and launched in September 2009. Pete Candeland directed a spectacular two-minute animated intro cinematic in which we accompany The Beatles from their earliest gigs at the Cavern Club in Liverpool along the pathway to international fame. Using some of The Beatles best known songs, director Candeland shows the band's extraordinary creative development, culminating in the psychedelia of the late sixties. The crew at Passion Pictures numbered over 50 people and the animation took nearly five months to complete.

Animator
Line Andersen
Directors
Line Andersen
Martin Andersen
Copywriters
Anne Boothroyd
Len Cheeseman
Nick Worthington

Art Directors
Anne Boothroyd
Len Cheeseman
Nick Worthington
Executive Creative Director
Nick Worthington
Producer
Martin Andersen
Agency Producer
Nigel Sutton

Editor
Martin Andersen
Sound Designer
Mikkel H Eriksen
Production Company
Andersen M Studio
Advertising Agency
Colenso BBDO

Group Account Directors
Michael Redwood
Angela Watson
Chief Executive Officer
Noel Murphy
Client
New Zealand Book Council

Animation

Andersen M Studio
for the New Zealand Book Council

Going West
The New Zealand Book Council spends its time bringing books to life for New Zealanders through its programme of events, signings, school programmes and reader and author festivals. The idea was to bring a famous NZ book to life using the magic of animation, inspiring people with the power of the written word.

Production Designers
Grant Major
Pedro Romero
Director
Johnny Green
Copywriter
Paul Brazier
Art Director
Paul Brazier
Creative Director
Paul Brazier

Producer
Fergus Brown
Agency Producers
Yvonne Chalkley
Adam Walker
Editor
Ted Guard
Lighting Camerapersons
Joost van Gelder
Wally Pfister

Music Composers
Nick Foster
Peter Raeburn
Production Company
Knucklehead
Special Effects
The Mill
Advertising Agency
Abbott Mead
Vickers BBDO

Account Handlers
Andrea Flamini
Mark Petersen
Marketing Director
John Roscoe
Client
Diageo
Brand
Draught Guinness

Production Design

Knucklehead
for Diageo

Bring it to Life
This visually stunning piece for Guinness shows a barren world being transformed by the extraordinary labour of a devoted team of men. A parallel is drawn between bringing the world to life and pouring a pint of Guinness. Taking on the extreme challenge of creating this epic ad, director Johnny Green recruited an elite team including Oscar-winning set designer Grant Major and Oscar-nominated Director of Photography Wally Pfister. Bring it to Life was also selected in Cinematography.

Director
Luke Savage
Copywriter
Mike Felix
Art Director
Matt Swinburne
Creative Director
Luke Chess
Executive Creative Director
Mike O'Sullivan

Producer
Anna Stuart
Executive Producer
James Moore
Agency Producer
Richard Mayo-Smith
Studio Producer
Heath Davy
Editor
Nathan Pickles
Agency Editor
Ian Bennett

Director of Photography
Andrew Stroud
Sound Designer
SJD
Production Company
Flying Fish
Post Production House
Images & Sound

Advertising Agency
Saatchi & Saatchi
Sydney
Account Handler
James Polhill
Operations Director
Conan Gorbey
Client
Rodney District
Council

Production Design

Flying Fish
for the Rodney District Council

Grenade
For this anti-speeding advert, the thousands of pieces of an exploded car were reassembled and suspended from wire to create an installation that visually demonstrates the impact of a head-on collision at 125 mph. The force is equal to that of ten grenades exploding. Set to a haunting soundtrack by New Zealand musician SJD and directed by Luke Savage, the TV commercial explores the installation and is shot entirely in-camera using Steadicam.

Production Designer
David Lee
Director
Matthias Hoene
Copywriter
Julia Martens

Art Director
Julia Martens
Producer
Russell Curtis
Agency Producer
Angus Smith

Editor
Joe Guest
Lighting Cameraperson
Dan Bronks

Production Company
Partizan
Advertising Agency
BMB
Client
McCain

Production Design

Partizan
for McCain

Good Unlimited
This 'making of' film, directed by Partizan's Matthias Hoene, takes us behind the scenes at the McCain's factory, where we see chips being tickled, kissed and hugged with herbs all the way along the delightfully crafted production line.

Production Designer
Mike Gunn
Director
Andy Mcleod
Copywriter
Matt Waller
Art Director
Dave Monk
Creative Director
Nick Gill

Producer
Kirsty Dye
Agency Producer
Ben Davies
Special Effects
Jim Allen
Editor
Andy McGraw

Lighting Cameraperson
Stuart Graham
Sound Engineer
Parv Thind
Production Company
Rattling Stick
Sound Design
Wave Studios

Advertising Agency
BBH London
Account Handler
Sylvia Pelzer
Brand Manager
Cameron Davidson
Client
Robinsons
Brand
Be Natural

Production Design

Rattling Stick
for Robinsons

Birdhouse
This advert tells the story of a bird who returns to her surprisingly human-like house to tidy up and prepare Robinsons Be Natural for her children, who are about to come home.

Director Michael Gracey	**Agency Producer** Ed Sayers	**Production Manager** Emma Wolanski	**Sound Design** 750mph	**Brand Managers** Kelly Engstrom Sam Taylor
Copywriter Stephen Howell	**Editors** Ben Harrex Diesel Schwarze	**Production Company** Partizan **Post Production**	**Advertising Agency** Saatchi & Saatchi London	**Marketing Manager** Lysa Hardy
Art Director Mick Dodds	**Lighting** Cameraperson	**Post Production** The Mill **Music Arrangement**	**Account Handler** Sarah Galea	**Business Leader** Sally Beerworth
Creative Directors Paul Silburn Kate Stanners	**Cameraperson** Tim Maurice Jones **Choreographer**	**Music Arrangement** EMI Notting Hill	**Planner** Gareth Ellis	**Client** T-Mobile
Producer Russell Curtis	**Choreographer** Ashley Wallen	Peer Music Universal		

Direction

Partizan
for T-Mobile

Dance

On 15 January at 11am, a single commuter started dancing in the middle of a train station. The dance grew as more dancers joined in, until there were over 300 people, perfectly choreographed. The excitement caused hundreds of genuine, unsuspecting members of the public to join in and share the moment.

Director Matthijs van Heijningen	**Agency Producer** Isabelle Ménard	**Image Post Production** MIKROS Image	**Account Handlers** Raphaël de Andréis François Brogi
Copywriter Jean-Christophe Royer	**Editor** Jono Griffith	**Sound Production** KOUZ Production	Alexandre George **Brand & Marketing Manager**
Art Director Eric Astorgue	**Director of Photography** Joost van Gelder	**Advertising Agency** BETC Euro RSCG	Béatrice Roux **Client**
Executive Creative Director Stéphane Xiberras	**Production Company** SOIXAN7E QUIN5E		CANAL+

Direction

SOIXAN7E QUIN5E
for CANAL+

Closet

In September 2009, CANAL+ launched its new 'Original Creativity' campaign. The aim was to highlight CANAL+'s showcase of original programming, consisting of series, documentaries and dramas, created exclusively by and for CANAL+, and scripted by prestigious writers such as Olivier Marchal and Jean-Hugues Anglade. To launch this new campaign, we produced an advert where a husband comes home to find a man hiding in his wife's closet. The man then describes a series of improbable events to explain his reason for being there. The advert unites humour, originality and a touch of impertinence inherent to the brand's message: 'Never underestimate the power of a great story'.

Direction
Ne-o
Art Directors
Peter Galmes
Chris Lightburn
Jones
Rachel Lopez
Copywriter
John McKelvey

Executive Creative Director
Steve Back
Producer
Juliet Naylor
Executive Producer
Daniel Bergmann
Agency Producers
Barbara Devlin
Ali Grant

Line Producers
Nick Page
Christabelle Stone
Director of Photography
Antonio Paladino
Production Company
Stink Productions

Advertising Agency
Saatchi & Saatchi
Sydney
Client
Toyota
Brand
Toyota Hybrid
Synergy Drive

Direction

Stink Productions
for Toyota

Better Together
Directors duo Ne-o from Stink showcase their in-camera skills with an expertly executed piece of balletic choreography, reinforcing the message of synergistic technology at the heart of Toyota's fleet.

Director
Neil Gorringe
Creative Director
Brett Foraker
Producer
Gwilym Gwillim
Editor
James Rosen

Director of Photography
Ross McLennan
Music Composer
Rich Martin
Sound Designer
Rich Martin

Set Design
Skyhook
Production Company
4creative
Advertising Agency
4creative

Marketing Managers
Sarah Owen
Charlie Palmer
Client
E4
Brand
Skins

Direction

4creative
for E4

Skins Series 3
The aim was to promote the third series of Skins which introduces an entirely new set of characters. We deliberately set out to be provocative, and to make a film that touched on one of the new central characters of the show, Cook – a fairly irresponsible, volatile character prone to violence. To reflect his energy and the somewhat incendiary nature of the third series, we decided to base the campaign around a slightly fantastical, irresponsible, rock and roll bit of sex, drugs and violence.

ghting	**Creative Director**	**Music Composer**	**Account Handler**
meraperson	Nick Gill	Dustin O'Halloran	Nick Stringer
ex Barber	**Producer**	**Sound Designer**	**Marketing Directors**
rector	Nell Jordan	Aaron Reynolds	Anna Bateson
pert Sanders	**Agency Producer**	**Production Company**	David Pemsel
pywriter	Davud Karbassioun	MJZ	**Client**
ex Grieve	**Special Effects**	**Advertising Agency**	ITV 1
t Director	Anthony Walsham	BBH London	
rian Rossi	**Editor**		
	Neil Smith		

Cinematography

MJZ
for ITV 1

The Brighter Side
This is the story of five children who go for a walk along an isolated, windswept beach. It's cold and gloomy and miserable. In frustration, one of the children throws a rock up at the grey mantle of clouds. Amazingly, magically, the stone travels up, up, up until it pierces the clouds, and lets the sunshine in. Just like that, their day is transformed into something bright and wonderful. This film is a simple metaphor for ITV1. It's about how ITV1 – the brighter side – can cut through the grey and gloom and once again make everything seem colourful and light.

rector of	**Executive Creative**	**Editor**	**Strategic Planner**
otography	**Directors**	Neil Smith	Neal Arthur
ally Pfister	Kevin Proudfoot	**Sound Designers**	**Media Planners**
rector	Todd Waterbury	Bill Chesley	Billy Hearst
pert Sanders	**Executive Producer**	Neil Smith	Kevin Porter
pywriter	Jeff Scruton	**Production Company**	Troy Valls
dy Ferguson	**Agency Producer**	MJZ	**Account Managers**
t Director	Dan Blaney	**Editing Companies**	Michael Dunn
cardo Viramontes	**Agency Head of**	Spot Welders	Andrew Goldberg
eative Director	**Content Production**	Work	Juan Reyes
eith Cartwright	Gary Krieg	**Advertising Agency**	**Brand Manager**
	Special Effects	Wieden+Kennedy	Alex Lopez
	Dave Parker	New York	**Client**
			Jordan

Cinematography

MJZ
for Jordan

Field Generals
In the NBA, every game is a battle of desire and a test of wills. These Jordan athletes (Carmelo Anthony, Rip Hamilton, Joe Johnson and Chris Paul) are the captains and leaders of their respective teams. When they are on the court, part of their responsibility is making sure people understand where they're going and what's expected of them. Their teams' success requires commitment and passion during every possession. The 'Field Generals' commercial puts the audience inside one of these games, capturing the intensity of what it's like to play against the best players in the world. Field Generals was also selected in Editing.

497

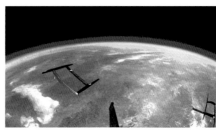

Cinematographer
Haris Zambarloukos
Director
Andy Amadeo
Copywriters
Andy Amadeo
James Covill
Nils Leonard

Art Directors
Andy Amadeo
Nils Leonard
Creative Director
Andy Amadeo
Executive Creative Director
Jon Williams
Producers
Matt Buels
Matt Jones

Agency Producer
James Covill
Editor
Russell Icke
Music Composer
Pete Raeburn
Sound Design
Scramble
Production Company
Hungry Man

Advertising Agency
Grey London
Planner
Nick Southgate
Account Supervisor
Sail Jani
Client
Toshiba

Cinematography

Hungry Man
for Toshiba

Space Chair

To demonstrate Toshiba's brand ethos of leading innovation, this campaign was based on an ambition to launch a chair into space and create the highest HD commercial in the world. Shot in the wilderness of the Nevada Black Rock desert using Toshiba HD cameras, it followed the journey of a simple living room chair as it was lifted towards the edge of space, to an altitude of 99,268 feet, by a simple helium balloon. Footage from the launch was used to create product commercials. The Toshiba Regza TV transforms picture quality from the ordinary to the extraordinary; sending the chair to the edge of space symbolised the power of the technology.

Director
Chris Palmer
Copywriter
Dave Henderson
Art Director
Richard Denney
Creative Directors
Richard Denney
Dave Henderson
Executive Creative Director
Jeremy Craigen

Sound Designer
Jack Sedgwick
Music Artists
Ant Genn
John Lennon
Paul McCartney
Producer
Rupert Saunders
Agency Producer
Richard Chambers
Lighting Cameraperson
Joost van Gelder

Editor
Paul Watts
Production Company
Gorgeous Enterprises
Advertising Agency
DDB UK
Planner
James Broomfield
Account Director
Matt Delahunty
Account Manager
Nick Owen

Business Director
Jon Busk
Brand Managers
Charles Wong
Chris Wooff
Marketing Manager
Garbhan O'Bric
Client
Diageo
Brand
Budweiser

Use of Music

DDB UK
for Diageo

Lyrics

Viewed from a train heading through Chicago, the lyrics to The Beatles hit 'Altogether Now' are spelled out in different ways by people in windows, along roads and on rooftops. The film culminates in a crowd gathered beneath a giant Budweiser mural.

Kitchen

Lounge

Garden

Special Effects	**Producer**	**Music Composer**	**Advertising Agency**
Mark Beardall	Tabby Harris	Rich Martin	4creative
Director	**Set Designer**	**Sound Designer**	**Marketing Manager**
Tom Tagholm	Adam Zoltowski	Rich Martin	Charlie Palmer
Art Director	**Editor**	**Special Effects**	**Client**
Tom Tagholm	Adam Rudd	**Company**	Channel 4
Creative Director	**Lighting**	MPC	**Brand**
Brett Foraker	**Cameraperson**	**Production Company**	Alan Carr Chatty
	Rob Hardy	4creative	Man

Special Effects

MPC
for E4

Alan Carr Chatty Man: Kitchen / Lounge / Garden
We needed a simple, effective device to showcase Alan Carr's distinct style in order to set the show Alan Carr Chatty Man apart from others. We had limited access to our star and no access to any of the people he was going to interview, so we imagined that Alan had been chatty all his life, even as a very young child, rabbiting away about anything and everything. The line 'Born Chatty' emerged. Alan had to look like a baby but still look like Alan. While the production was fairly involved, the end result feels simple and low-tech, as if it was produced by Alan's mum using an old camcorder.

Visual Effects Supervisor
Daniel Adams
Director
Dougal Wilson
Copywriter
Martin Loraine
Art Director
Steve Jones
Creative Director
Paul Brazier

Creative Group Heads
Steve Jones
Martin Loraine
Producer
Matthew Fone
Agency Producer
Katherine Maidment
Editor
Joe Guest

Music Composers
Nick Foster
Oliver Julian
Peter Raeburn
Lighting Cameraperson
Tom Townend
Visual Effects
MPC
Production Company
Blink Productions

Advertising Agency
Abbott Mead
Vickers BBDO
Account Handlers
Richard Arscott
James Drummond
Marketing Directors
Giles Jepson
Adrian Mooney
Client
Heinz

Special Effects

MPC
for Heinz

Bottle
Heinz Tomato Ketchup is such an iconic and beloved product that we don't need to see the bottle to know what the commercial is for.

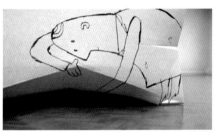
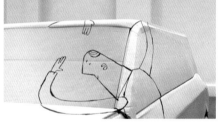
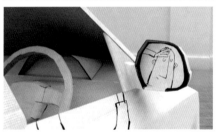

Directors
Russell Brooke
Aaron Duffy
Copywriters
Maja Fernqvist
Joakim Saul
Art Directors
Maja Fernqvist
Joakim Saul

Creative Directors
Nick Kidney
Kevin Stark
Producer
Belinda Blacklock
Agency Producer
Olly Chapman
Music Composer
Woody Guthrie
Sound Designer
Aaron Reynolds

Production Companies
First Avenue
Machine
Passion Pictures
Advertising Agency
BBH London
Planner
Rachel Hatton

Account Handlers
Simon Coles
Bill Scott
Brand Manager
James Millett
Marketing Manager
Peter Duffy
Client
Audi UK
Brand
Audi Q5

Animation

First Avenue Machine & Passion Pictures
for Audi UK

Unboxed
In this commercial, an animated engineer transforms a simple cardboard box into the new streamlined Audi Q5. Straight lines become curves. Squares become rounded. In doing so he ingeniously demonstrates the difference between the Q5 and its many boxy rivals, and how Audi has 'unboxed the box'.

Toe Tapping

Slurp

Bad Bull

Animator
Pic Pic André
Copywriter
Sophie Lewis
Art Director
Nicolla Longley
Creative Directors
Frank Ginger
Sam Heath

Producers
Magalie Dauleu
Adrianna
Piasek-Wanski
Production
Co-Producer
Sean Costelloe
Executive Producer
Julia Parfitt
Agency Producer
Selina Dey

Offline Editors
Julia Parfitt
Laurence Vaes
Director of
Photography
Jan van den Bussche
Post Production
Company
The Mill
Production Company
Nexus Productions

Advertising Agency
Wieden+Kennedy
London
Account Director
Ryan Fisher
Client
Arla
Brand
Cravendale

Animation

Nexus Productions
for Arla

Toe Tapping / Slurp / Bad Bull
People buy milk without thinking. They just reach for the red, blue or green tops. They don't really have any strong feelings about where or who it comes from. Since 2007, Cravendale has been trying to change that. The campaign involves a series of milk related stories, each of which demonstrates Cravendale's passion for milk through an off-kilter world inhabited by a cow, a pirate and a cyclist, in which the only thing that really matters is milk.

501

Typog

THY
PAP
ORGY.

Typographer
Benjamin Le Breton
Art Director
Arnaud Assouline
Designer
Nadine Grenier
Copywriter
Benjamin Le Breton

Executive Creative Director
Stéphane Xiberras
Advertising Agency
BETC Euro RSCG
Outdoor Production
JCDecaux

Account Handlers
Raphaël de Andréis
Elodie Andurand
Philippe Brandt
Brand Manager
Emmanuel Dollfus

Marketing Manager
Barbara Alfandari
Client
The AIDS Africa
Solidarity Fund
Brand
SOLIDARITÉ SIDA

Poster Advertising

BETC Euro RSCG
for The AIDS Africa Solidarity Fund

Clocks
Against AIDS, every minute counts. At a set time, twice a day, the hands of these clocks come together and align to form the sentence: 'Every 12 hours in Africa, over 2,000 people die from AIDS because they have no access to care'. SOLIDARITÉ SIDA wanted to alert Europeans to the necessity of acting quickly against this situation. BETC Euro RSCG created an outdoor installation, in association with artist Nadine Grenier, consisting of 321 clocks. The bottom of the installation carries the call to action, explaining where people can get more information about the foundation and donate online: 'Every minute counts. www.solidarite-sida.org'. 'Clocks' was also selected in the category Typography/Graphic Design.

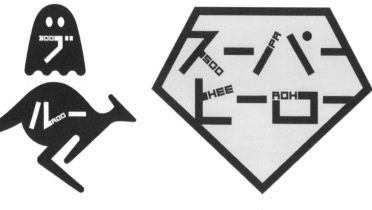

Typography

Typographers
Miho Aishima
Michael Johnson

Design Director
Michael Johnson

Design Group
johnson banks

Client
johnson banks

Typefaces

johnson banks

Phonetikana

This typeface, called Phonetikana, takes the Japanese phonetic script, Katakana, and embeds English language phonetic sounds into the characters. This enables visitors to Japan to 'pronounce' the Japanese sounds correctly, and to begin to understand and recognise key characters and shapes. Katakana is used to 'translate' Western words into Japanese, so it seemed logical to start with that script. The typeface was designed primarily for educational purposes, but has already been used in Japanese fashion applications and in Japanese magazines.

505

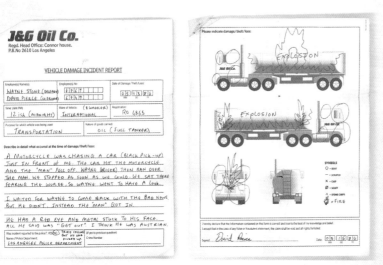

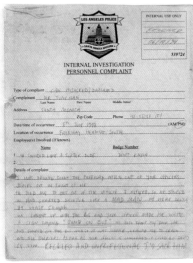

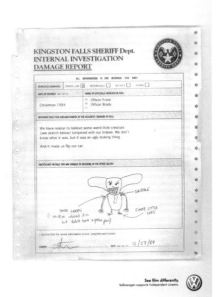

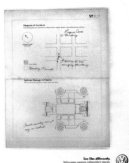

Typographer
Pete Mould
Art Director
Daniel Seager
Designer
Pete Mould
Copywriter
Steve Hall

Handwriting
Steve Hall
Ruth Harlow
Pete Mould
Daniel Seager
Trevor Slabber
Nicola Sullivan
Illustrators
Pete Mould
Alex Price
Oliver Watts

Executive Creative Director
Jeremy Craigen
Advertising Agency
DDB UK
Business Director
Jonathan Hill
Account Director
Charlie Elliott

Account Manager
Jessica Huth
Planner
Georgia Challis
Communications Manager
Sally Chapman
Client
Volkswagen

Press Advertising

DDB UK
for Volkswagen

Terminator / Toy Story / Speed / Gremlins / King Kong / Back to the Future
This campaign promoted Volkswagen's sponsorship of independent cinema. Each advert focuses on incidents involving cars in classic films. The film titles are not directly mentioned, encouraging viewers to work them out for themselves. The fictional reports outline what happened to the damaged vehicle and are filled out by the characters involved.

GRAPHIC PAINTING

Gianpaolo Pagni tells Richard Brereton
how you hang up the phone, and create a timeless
work of art in a few hours, before the *Le Monde*
courier stops by to pick up the finished artwork

AN
INTERVIEW
WITH
TUCA VIEIRA
THE
BRAZILIAN
SPIDERMAN
BY
RICHARD
BRERETON

THE ART & VISUAL CULTURE MAGAZINE

ISSUE №1

SÃO PAULO GUIDE   PETER SAVILLE

COLLAGE   BIKES & FASHION   FERNANDO GUTIÉRREZ

ART & THE INTERNET

NEW TRENDS

STUDIO VISITS   UNIT PUBLISHING

Launch issue price £12.99, €14.99, $19.99

WINTER 2009-10

Designer
Matt Willey
Editor in Chief
Marc Valli

Design Group
Studio8 Design

Client
Frame Publishing

Brand
Elephant Magazine

Magazine & Newspaper Design
Studio8 Design
for Frame Publishing

Elephant Magazine
The art world has, for a few decades now, been divided between what has so far been known
as contemporary art on one side, with applied art, or commercial art, on the other. The problem
with this division, however, is that it does not reflect the reality and richness of what is taking
place in the visual arts arena. More seriously, this division has meant that a lot of the best
work has been missed. It is this vast and vital space in the middle, with its vibrant culture
and endlessly changing scene, that is the subject of Elephant Magazine.

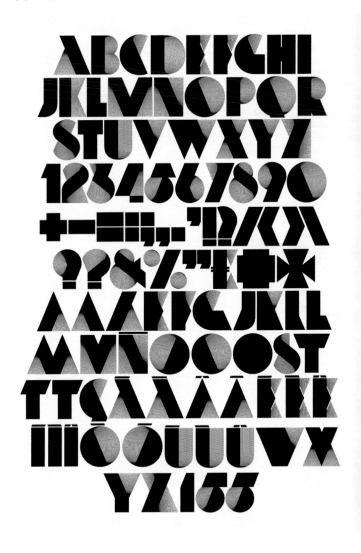

Typographer	**Art Director**	**Foundry Director**	**Client**
Alex Trochut	Alex Trochut	Alex Haigh	Hype For Type
	Designer		
	Alex Trochut		

Typefaces

Alex Trochut
for Hype For Type

Neo Deco
Neo Deco is a display typeface designed for Hype for Type, inspired by the Art Deco fonts of the 1920s.

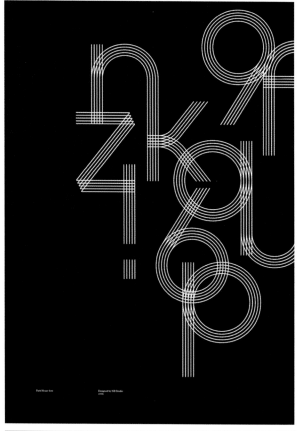

Park House font
250pt
Designed by NB:Studio
2009

enormous
presence

Massive double window heights reveal spacious units

Typographers	Designer	Creative Directors	Design Group
Daniel Lock	Daniel Lock	Alan Dye	NB: Studio
Jeremy Tankard		Nick Finney	**Client**
		Ben Stott	Land Securities

Typefaces

NB: Studio
for Land Securities

Park House Font
NB: Studio was commissioned to create the identity for Park House, an exciting new development in London. We created a bespoke display typeface to hold the identity together across a variety of applications. Our inspiration lay in the building's curvaceous forms and its architectural ribs. These two features combine to create sweeping linear patterns around the building. We designed a geometric font based on a grid of lines that would twist and turn to create letter forms. As the lines overlap, we were left with a moire effect which begins to shine and glisten. With tight leading, the ascenders and descenders meet and cross over to create interesting typographic patterns.

509

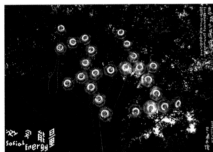

Typographers	Designers	Photographer	Brand Manager
Wang Xiaomeng	Wang Xiaomeng	Liang Rong	Ni Jing
Hei Yiyang	Hei Yiyang	**Creative Director**	**Client**
Liu Zhao	Liu Zhao	Hei Yiyang	The OCT Art &
Art Director	**Technical Designer**	**Design Group**	Design Gallery
Hei Yiyang	Liu Fuyu	SenseTeam	

Typefaces

SenseTeam
for The OCT Art & Design Gallery

Social Energy
This is the visual identity system for the 'Social Energy: Contemporary Communication Design from the Netherlands' touring exhibition. The exhibition is located in the OCT Art & Design Gallery in Shenzhen. We covered the gallery's outer wall with hexagonal shapes. The design incorporated the energy structure of a tiny molecule. We used huge red, white and blue gas-filling devices to explain the process of energy accumulation. The interior of the exhibition also used the concept of molecular structure at every entrance and in the library's desks and chairs.

OUR FATER
WHO ARᵀ N HENDON ₈₃·₃₂·₁₁₂
HARᴿOW RᴼAD BE THY NAME ₁₁₂·₆₅
THY KNGSTON ₁₃₁ COME THY WMBLᴱDON ₁₃₁·₅₇·₁₅₅·₅₃·₉₉
N ERᴵTH AS IT IS N HENDON ₄₆₉·₅₃·₁₆₈·₂₆₈·₈₃ ᴹ³
GIVE US THIS DAY OUR BERᴷHAMSTEAD ᴹ³·₂₄
AND FORᴳIVE US OUR WESMNSTERS ᴹ³·₁₁
AS WE FORᴳIVE THOSE WHO
WESMNSTER AGANST US ₂₄·ᶜᴰ¹
LᴱAD US NOT NTO TEMPLE STATION ᶜᴰ¹·₁₄₈·₂₀₇
AND DELᴵVER US FRᴼM EALᴵNG ₆₅
FOR THNE IS THE KNGSTON ₇₆₇·₁₂₇
THE PURLᴱY AND THE CRᴬWLᴱY ₂₉₈·₇₂₆·₁₀₀ ₂₇·₇₀₁·₅₈
FOR IVER AND IVER ₅₈·₇₀₁·₁₁·₁₉·ᵂ⁷
CRᴼUCH END

IAN DURY THE BUS DRIVER'S PRAYER 1994

Typography	Design Studio	Writer	Client
Studio Frith	Studio Frith	Ian Dury	The London Design Festival

Typefaces

Studio Frith
for The London Design Festival

Bus Driver's Prayer Poster
As part of the London Design Festival we were invited to design a poster about London.
We chose to feature Ian Dury's 'Bus Driver's Prayer' on our poster, as a brilliant and irreverent celebration of the city. We wanted to capture the robust character of a bus, so we modified the English sans-serif typeface Granby. Our research into old type-settings of the Lord's Prayer lead to the creation of extended ligatures within the letterforms. The small numbers displayed like footnotes are the bus numbers from one location in the lyrics to the next.

511

Typographers
Khairul Anuar
Zaidi Awang
Art Director
Zaidi Awang
Designers
Khairul Anuar
Zaidi Awang

Copywriter
Zaidi Awang
Photographer
Steve Koh
Print Producer
Ong Chee Hin
Creative Directors
Tan Yew Leong
Ali Mohamed

**Advertising
Agencies**
ARC Worldwide
Malaysia
Leo Burnett Malaysia
Account Handler
Jovian Lee Lit Hong

**Advertising
& Promotions
Executive**
Wong Ee Ling
Client
Kinokuniya
Bookstores

Poster Advertising

ARC Worldwide & Leo Burnett Malaysia
for Kinokuniya Bookstores

Gate
To promote the DIY section in Kinokuniya Bookstore, the words 'I did it on my own' were playfully incorporated into a gate's grillwork, illustrating how easy doing stuff on your own can be. These posters were placed within Kinokuniya's premises and shop front, making them visible to customers browsing in the bookshop as well as to people passing by.

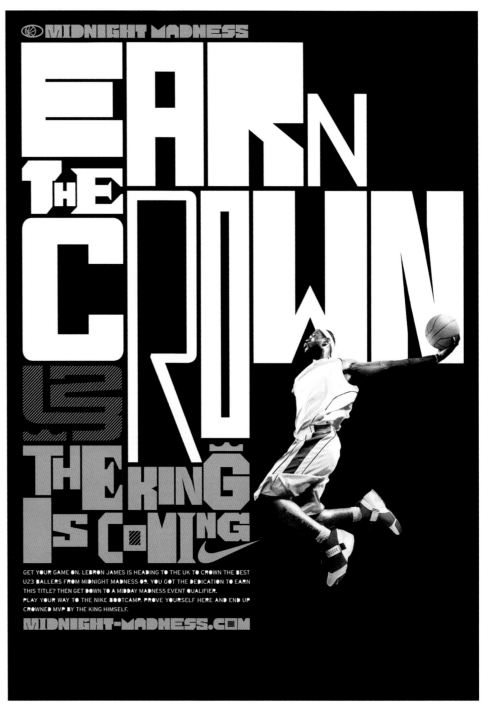

Poster Advertising

Wieden+Kennedy London
for Nike

Midnight Madness

Midnight Madness is a national basketball event sponsored by Nike. It was celebrating its tenth year of activity, so Nike wanted to attract the best young basketball talent and reignite its community with a new energy and style for the brand. It also wanted to celebrate the NBA Most Valuable Player Lebron James' arrival in the UK. We developed a campaign that was in keeping with the arrival of Lebron James. The messaging challenged young players to 'earn the crown' in the presence of the NBA MVP. All material used bespoke type design and a visual pallet that included gold, making the poster and other campaign elements truly come to life.

Typographer
Guy Featherstone
Designers
anderson Bob
Guy Featherstone
Copywriter
Stuart Harkness

Production Manager
Martin Fahey
Creative Directors
Guy Featherstone
Stuart Harkness

Executive Creative Directors
Tony Davidson
Kim Papworth
Advertising Agency
Wieden+Kennedy
London

Account Director
Karrelle Dixon
Client
Nike

Typographer
Sharon Chong
Art Directors
Jim Hilson
Kevin Stark
Designer
Sharon Chong

Copywriters
Toby Allen
Nick Kidney
Illustrator
Alan Murray
Print Producer
Julian Cave

Creative Directors
Nick Kidney
Kevin Stark
Advertising Agency
BBH London
Account Handlers
Simon Coles
Polly Knowles

Brand Manager
James Millett
Marketing Manager
Peter Duffy
Client
Audi UK

Poster Advertising

BBH London
for Audi UK

Fuel Gauge
The line 'The new more fuel efficient Audis' is treated typographically to resemble a car's fuel gauge. The needle is resting beyond the F in 'efficient' to indicate that the tank stays full.

Press Advertising

Ogilvy Singapore
for Unilever

Whale Cow
Consumers in Singapore have a wide range of ice-creams to choose from these days, with the recent proliferation of small, independent shops in many malls, selling both ice-cream and frozen yogurt. We wanted to bring Ben & Jerry's ice-cream firmly back into the public eye, and re-establish it as the more original, unusual ice-cream. The aim was to appeal to the young and the young at heart, an audience of more independent consumers who want to appear more individual and not eat 'the same' as everyone else.

Typographers	Copywriters	Creative Directors	Advertising Agency
Adrian Chan	Eugene Cheong	Eugene Cheong	Ogilvy Singapore
Stuart Mills	Craig Love	Todd McCracken	**Client**
Maurice Wee	Mike Sutcliffe	Tham Khai Meng	Unilever
Art Directors	**Photographer**	**Senior Project**	**Brand**
Adrian Chan	Edward Loh	**Manager**	Ben & Jerry's
Stuart Mills		Monica De Grave	
Maurice Wee			

515

GOSHKA MACUGA

THE NATURE
OF THE BEAST

GUERNICA

1939   LONDON   2009

WHITECHAPEL GALLERY

Typographer
Fraser Muggeridge

Design Agency
Fraser Muggeridge
studio

Client
Whitechapel Gallery

Graphic Design

Fraser Muggeridge studio
for the Whitechapel Gallery

Goshka Macuga, The Nature of the Beast
This newspaper was published as part of the exhibition 'The Nature of the Beast' by artist Goshka Macuga at the Whitechapel Gallery, in which she created a distinctive venue for public gatherings, referencing the gallery's 1939 hosting of Picasso's 'Guernica'. The form of a newspaper gave the information an immediacy in keeping with the idea of news and current events. Typographically it referenced the period of the 1939 exhibition and the information-led design of newspapers in general. It also contained graphic and typographic material from the gallery's archive. The design, as with the content of the show, reflected the spirit of both past and present.

516

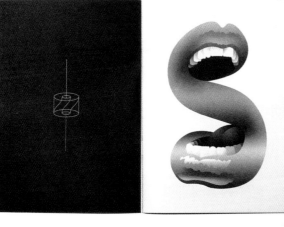

Typographer
Jonathan Zawada
Art Director
Luke Lucas

Copywriter
Daniel Pollock
Creative Director
Daniel Pollock

Advertising Agency
Lifelounge
Client
WorkSafe Victoria

Brand
Big Mouth Project

Graphic Design

Lifelounge
for WorkSafe Victoria

Big Mouth Zine
The Big Mouth Project is a collaboration between Lifelounge and WorkSafe Victoria to help spread a message of safety in the workplace with the participation of some of the world's most talented artists, typographers, writers, animators, model makers and photographers. The Big Mouth Zine was the second instalment of the Big Mouth Project. It features the artistic interpretation of the Big Mouth brief through the publication of illustrative conceptual typography by Jonathan Zawada.

517

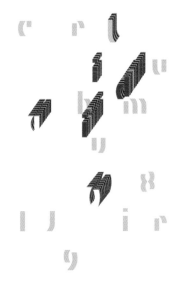

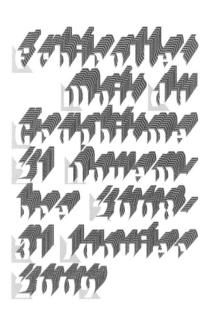

Typographer	Animator	Design Studio	Client
Philippe Apeloig	Vadim Bernard	Studio Apeloig	Centre du Graphisme à Échirolles

Graphic Design

Studio Apeloig
for the Centre du Graphisme à Échirolles

Échirolles, Mois du Graphisme

Each year, the city of Échirolles organises a one-month festival devoted to graphic design, which is an important rendezvous for students and professionals. The theme for 2009 was the celebration of writing systems. The typeface 'Aleph', designed by Philippe Apeloig, was originally inspired by hand-written calligraphy. The poster invites readers to look at the way words are read and to appreciate the aesthetic shapes of letters. An energetic design was developed for motion graphics by treating the letters as separate elements. They move, repeat and disappear following the rhythm of a Maurice Ravel score, hence the design has been influenced by modern dance.

Typographer
Philippe Apeloig

Designers
Philippe Apeloig
Mathilde
Roussel-Giraudy

Design Studio
Studio Apeloig

Client
French Institute
Alliance Française

Graphic Design

Studio Apeloig
for the French Institute Alliance Française

Crossing the Line
Crossing the Line is an annual festival organised by the French Institute Alliance Française in New York City. It presents vibrant new works by a diverse range of transdisciplinary artists who are transforming cultural and artistic practices on both sides of the Atlantic. The two overlapping bodies in neon colours reflect the powerful dynamism of Crossing the Line's cutting-edge performances. The type has a contemporary, code-like style. The logo, composed of three rings, represents the festival's innovative artists and their groundbreaking works.

We made this poster for Bruno Maag. He hates it.

This is the world's most popular typeface. What's wrong with it? Come to a lecture by type designer Bruno Maag to find out. 7pm, Thursday 26th March at This is Real Art, 2 Sycamore Street, London EC1. abcdefghijklmnopqrstuvwxyzácèoîcöž*&ñ?,ß'#¡!

Typographer	Designer	Copywriter	Design Group
Paul Belford	Paul Belford	Paul Belford	This is Real Art

Graphic Design
This is Real Art

Bruno Maag
This is a poster invitation to a lecture by type designer Bruno Maag. The lecture included a critique of the typeface Helvetica. To dramatise this, the poster was set using Helvetica.

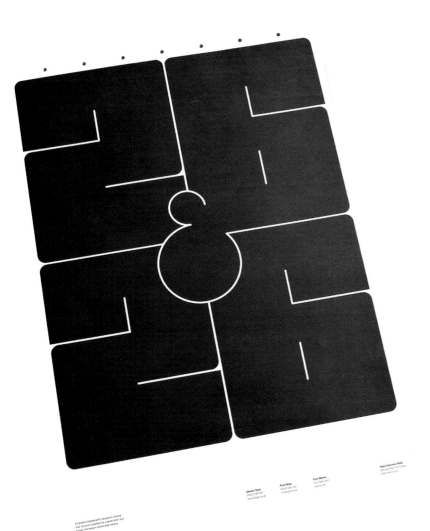

Designer	Creative Directors	Design Group	Clients
Li Rui	Ben Casey	The Chase	Atomic Type
	Lionel Hatch		Font Shop
			Font Works

Graphic Design

The Chase
for Atomic Type, Font Shop & Font Works

26&26

26&26 is a week by week calendar consisting of 53 pages. Each page features a letter of the alphabet: 26 lower case, 26 upper case, and an ampersand. We allocated an individual character to 53 of the country's leading designers and typographers, then asked them to choose their favourite typeface for that character, and write why they like it so much.

521

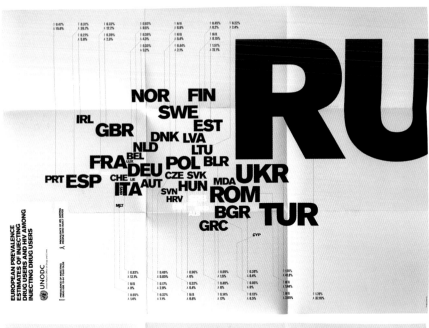

Typographers
Jason Ching
Harry Pearce

Art Director
Harry Pearce
Designers
Jason Ching
Harry Pearce

Design Group
Pentagram Design
Client
UNODC (United
Nations Office on
Drugs and Crime)

Brand
United Nations

Graphic Design

Pentagram Design
for the UNODC

UNODC Posters
The UNODC produced a series of posters to highlight the relative merits of drug treatment and rehabilitation around the world. The posters are a training tool, specifically aimed at the Russian police, whose country has a particularly poor track record in drug support. The posters had to be eye-catching, easy to understand and not reliant on language. Pentagram's typographic solution built a simple world map from internationally recognised country abbreviation codes, such as GBR, USA and RU. Variants were designed using colour coding and icons to provide comparative statistics on drug abuse, the incidence of HIV, methadone and opiate maintenance therapies, and needle and syringe programmes.

Art Directors
Scott Brown
Jonathan
Granewich
Lori McMichael
Design Director
Erik Miller

Designer
Donny Smith
Photographer
Josh Withers
Creative Directors
Brett Craig
Joe Shands

**Chief Creative
Officer**
Rob Schwartz
**Global Director
of Media Arts**
Lee Clow

Advertising Agency
TBWA\Chiat\Day
Los Angeles
Client
Pepsi

Packaging Design

TBWA\Chiat\Day Los Angeles
for Pepsi

Everybody / Joy / LOL
Every year, Pepsi produces a series of collectable aluminium bottles to celebrate summer. In 2009, for the first time, the client asked us to submit designs based on a theme taken from an advertising idea, the iconic 'Word Play' outdoor billboards and TV spots. So instead of a typical summertime theme, we focused on the energy and optimism of our audience, transforming these simple, colourful messages into keepsake Pepsi bottles available on shelf.

523

Typographers
Tim Beard
Chris Chilvers
Stefan Gandl
Alex Haigh
Nick Hard
Billy Kiosoglou
Jeff Knowles
Paul McDermid
Abbott Miller
Frank Philippin
Si Scott
Paul Skerm
James Warfield

Designer
Rishi Sodha
Creative Director
Rishi Sodha

Design Group
DAHRA (Designers
Against Human
Rights Abuse)

Brand Manager
Katie Mallin
Client
Tibet Relief Fund

Book Design

DAHRA
for the Tibet Relief Fund

3 Minutes
3 Minutes is a publication for the Tibet Relief Fund, created by not-for-profit organisation Designers Against Human Rights Abuse (DAHRA). The premise of the book is to show the full extent of the Tibetan conflict through ten diverse and extremely powerful three-minute interviews with Tibetan refugees, each describing moments that changed their lives. Contributors were asked to typographically translate these audio interviews into 16-page booklets, which, when combined, resulted in a book made up of ten beautifully designed booklets that encapsulate the powerful and shocking nature of these moments.

Yo otro y el Retratos en la fotografía india

esign Group
na Cardenal de la
uez

Pre-press
Cromotex

Printing Company
Lunwerg

Clients
ARTIUM
Barcelona City
Council
Lunwerg

Book Design
Ena Cardenal de la Nuez
for Lunwerg

The Self & the Other – Portraiture in Contemporary Indian Photography
This catalogue brings together portraits and self-portraits by Indian photographers. We attempted to reflect the conscious and the unconscious, the portrait and the self-portrait. They aren't separate; one is inside the other. The word 'otro', meaning 'other', is die cast over the printed words 'yo', 'y', 'el', (i.e. 'self', 'and', 'the'), revealing a background of loud orange. The rest of the cover pales in comparison with this colour, forcing us to take a look – it is slightly indistinct but the intensity of the orange makes it ultimately legible. As indistinct and as clear as the relationship between the self and the other, between the photographer and the sitter.

525

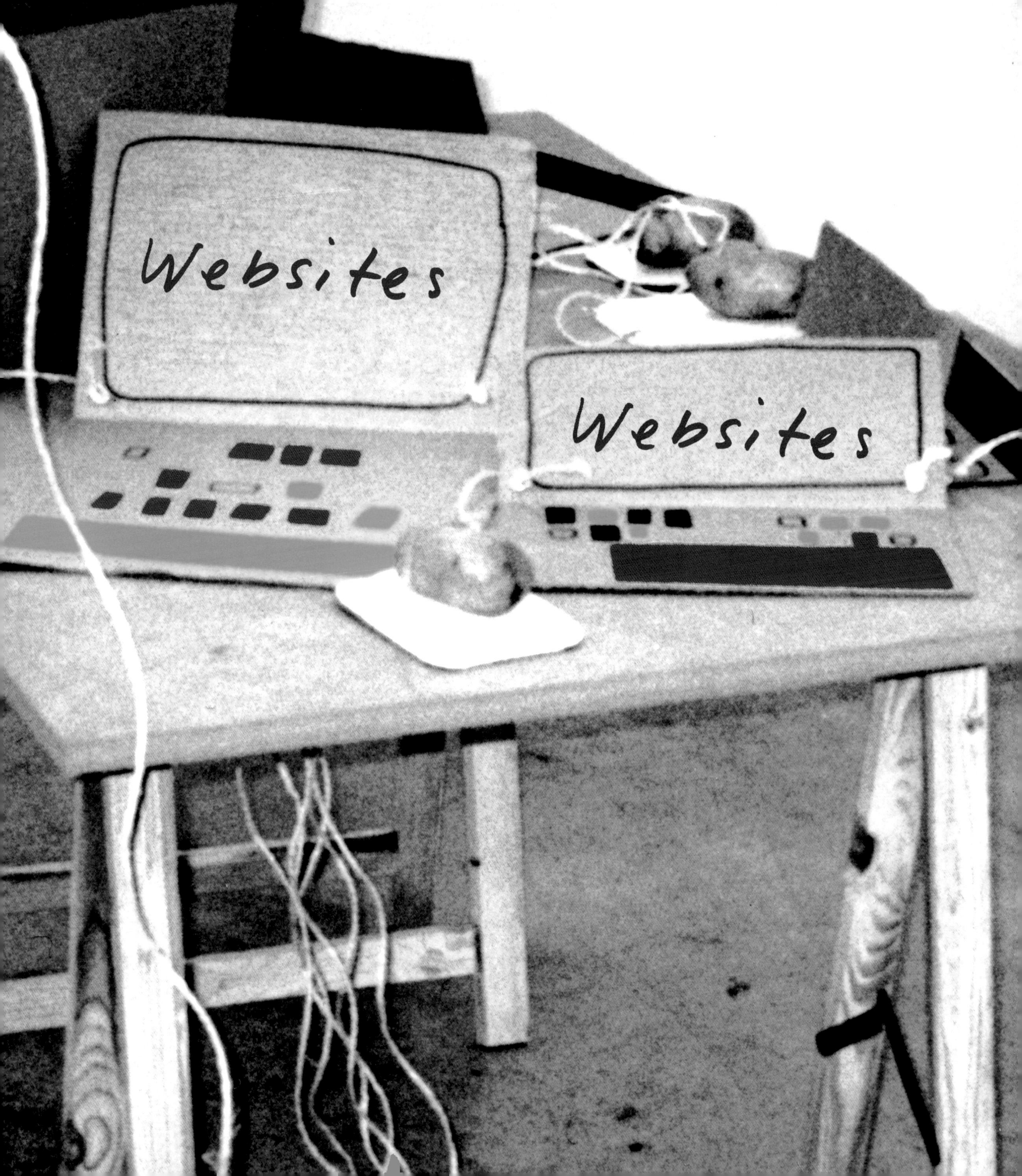
Websites
Websites

Websites

Domani Studios & The Martin Agency
for The John F Kennedy Presidential Library & Museum

We Choose the Moon
The Apollo 11 lunar landing was the realisation of JFK's vision to land a man on the moon. For the landing's 40th anniversary, we recreated the mission online in real time. At 9.32am on 16 July 2009, Apollo 11 took off again at wechoosethemoon.org. The trip was shown using 3D animation, 102 continuous hours of mission audio, and hundreds of images from NASA and the JFK Library. 650 of the most interesting audio transmissions were rebroadcast via Twitter.

Creative Directors
Joe Alexander
Jonathan Hills
Technical Director
Oscar Trelles
Art Director
Brian Williams
Interactive Art Director
Ben Tricklebank
Copywriter
Wade Alger
Designer
Saulo Rodrigues

Interactive Designer
Justin Young
Interactive Producer
Steven Hubert
Agency Producers
Darbi Fretwell
Norma Kwee
Senior Developer
Mark Llobrera
Flash Developer
Chris Wise
Editors
Rick Lawley
Jim Vaile

Assistant Editor
Shang Gao
Animator
Petter Safwenberg
Sound Designer
Jesse Peterson
Director of Innovation
Mark Pavia
Digital Production & Design
Domani Studios
Advertising Agency
The Martin Agency

Music
Chip Jenkins
Art Producer
Cindy Hicks
Account Handlers
Carrie Bird
Jarrod Bull
Marketing Manager
Lee Statham
Client
The John F Kennedy Presidential Library & Museum

529

Websites

Sound Designer	Copywriter	Motion Designer	Account Handler
Roman Vinuesa	Ramin	Nina Borrusch	Alexander Korduan
Creative Director	Schmiedekampf	**Programmer**	**Marketing Manager**
Bernd Krämer	**Designer**	Alexander El-Meligi	Milena Ivkovic
Art Directors	Nina Borrusch	**Advertising Agency**	**Client**
Philip Bartsch	**Interaction Designer**	Jung von Matt	Philharmoniker
Tommy Norin	Gregor Fraser	Hamburg	Hamburg

Sound Design & Use of Music

Jung von Matt Hamburg
for Philharmoniker Hamburg

Sounds of Hamburg

The Philharmoniker Hamburg is one of the best known orchestras in Germany. The goal was to give them a more modern image and pull more ears into their concert hall. We were asked to create an online solution that would arouse the curiosity of classical music lovers throughout the country. Our solution was to create a web application which merges both city and orchestra into one exciting musical experience. The city of Hamburg becomes the concert hall and users take the role of conductor. With customised motion tracking, users are able to select moving objects from a live video feed. People, ships, cars and even fish become instruments in a spontaneous concert.

530

Creative Directors	**Executive Creative Director**	**Flash Developers**	**Executive Planning Director**
Keiichi Higuchi	Koichi Sawada	Yoshikazu Iida	Kenji Shiratsuchi
Shinya Seino		Takayuki Watanabe	
Technical Director	**Assistant Designer**	**Magazine Producer**	**Account Handler**
Kampei Baba	Hironobu Ryo	Kai Hikiji	Osamu Kimura
Art Director	**Film Producer**	**Magazine Editor**	**Client Supervisors**
Shinya Seino	Takaharu Hatori	Shunji Suzuki	Kentaro Katsube
Copywriter	**Agency Producers**	**Advertising Agency**	Aoi Matsumoto
Aki Kimura	Sozo Kikuchi	Dentsu Tokyo	Minako Suzuki
Director	Shinsaku Ogawa	**Production Manager**	**Client**
Megumi Kasuga		Sho Yamashita	UNIQLO

Websites

Dentsu Tokyo
for UNIQLO

Tokyo Fashion Map
As part of this campaign, 1,000 Tokyoites threw on UNIQLO parkas and posed for us. On our website, we linked the resulting parka movies and placed GPS-tagged street snapshots on a map that let users track down where they were taken. The 1,000 snapshots also appeared in our in-store magazine. Once released, the movies and snaps took the nation by storm. Comments filled numerous websites and our magazine sold out in many bookshops and convenience stores. In fact, these 1,000 snapshots generated a parka sensation that spread across the nation.

531

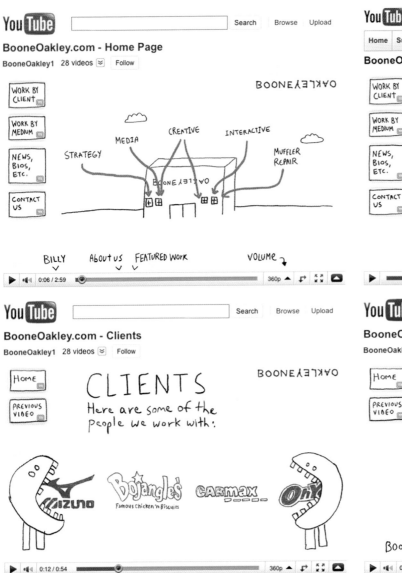

Creative Directors
John Boone
David Oakley
Art Director
Ryan Holland

Copywriter
Jim Robbins
Interactive Designer
Bill Allen

Agency Producer
Craig Jelniker
Advertising Agency
Boone Oakley

Client
Boone Oakley

Websites

Boone Oakley

Boone Oakley Website
At Boone Oakley, we always try to find innovative ways to tell a brand's story. So when the time came to tell our own, we made our website using a network of interactive videos on YouTube. The videos were linked together using clickable YouTube annotations. This allowed us to show our work and personality in a dynamic new way. Instead of just posting an agency manifesto, we could show people who we are through a series of animated stories. The results? More than one million hits in just a few weeks, hundreds of blog postings all over the world, and dozens of new business enquiries from companies around the globe.

532

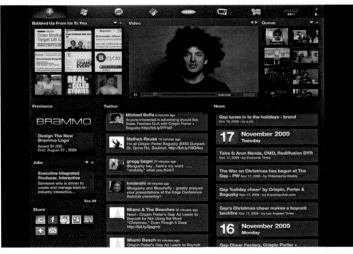

Creative Director	**Interactive Designer**	**Agency Producers**	**Advertising Agency**
Tony Calcao	John Whitmore	Paul Aaron	Crispin Porter +
Technical Director	**Developers**	Nick Ngai	Bogusky
Brian Skahan	Robert Christ	**Chief Creative**	**Marketing Manager**
Art Director	Marc Pelland	**Officers**	Steve Sapka
Tim Blount	**Programmers**	Jeff Benjamin	**Client**
Copywriter	Louri Chadrine	Andrew Keller	Crispin Porter +
Andy Pearson	Tom Pearson	Rob Reilly	Bogusky
Designers	Aday Rodriguez		
Ilysa Corns	Blake Walters		
Charlyn Hare			
Noelle Newbold			

Crispin Porter + Bogusky

cpbgroup.com
What should an agency website do? Show off its work? Or could it somehow show the impact of that work? Enter cpbgroup.com. The site pulls in every video, blog post, news story and tweet about Crispin Porter + Bogusky and our clients – live and unmoderated. So, rather than broadcast, the site listens, creating a user-generated snapshot of each brand. The site also broadcasts our original content like Fearless Q+A, a live talk show that lets viewers interview guests using Justin.tv and Twitter. No more galleries and about us pages. Cpbgroup.com is a living tool to study how our brands ripple across pop culture.

533

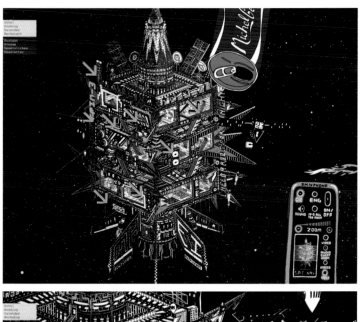

Creative Director	**Interactive Designer**	**Sound Designer**	**Marketing Managers**
Azar Kazimir	Lukas Sommer	Christian Harder	Nadine May
Art Director	**Interface Designer**	**Digital Agency**	Tom Michelberger
Azar Kazimir	Rosi Emonts	Plantage Berlin	**Client**
Copywriters	**Illustrator**	**Account Handlers**	Michelberger Hotel
Anja Knauer	Azar Kazimir	Marlen Bartschek	
Tom Michelberger		Stefanie Wildner	

Websites

Plantage Berlin
for Michelberger Hotel

Space Oddity

Hotel websites are formulaic, dull and tend to lack any spark of originality; however wonderful the hotel might be, the website is almost always a poor reflection of it. We aimed to create a charming, entertaining and silly website that reflected the quirky, informal and alternative nature of the hotel, and would appeal to the type of guest we thought would most appreciate it. It was very important for us that as much love, care and attention to detail was put into the website as into the hotel itself.

534

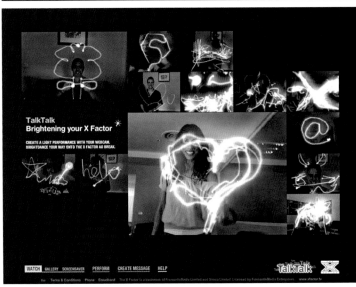

Creative Director	Copywriters	Development	Brand Manager
Warren Moore	Tom Skinner	& Programming	Zoe Vafadari
Design Director	Rick Standley	B-Reel	**Sponsorship**
Thiago de Moraes	**Interactive Designers**	**Advertising Agency**	**Manager**
Art Directors	Thiago de Moraes	CHI&Partners	Dan Crompton
Tom Skinner	Tom Skinner	**Account Handlers**	**Client**
Rick Standley	Rick Standley	Nick Howarth	TalkTalk
	Agency Producer	Fiona McGillivray	
	Ciaran Bennett	Olivia Skone	

Microsites

CHI&Partners
for TalkTalk

Brightdancing
TalkTalk, the brighter phone and broadband company, sponsored the X Factor, Britain's most popular TV show. X Factor fans love performing and fame, so we invited them to perform for a chance to become famous: starring in their own TV ads during the X Factor breaks. Brightdancing starts on a website. Using their webcams, people drew with light in the air, set it to music then uploaded it as their personal performance. More than 690,000 people visited the site, creating over 42,000 video performances; 200 starred in their own ads. TalkTalk sales went up by 17%.

535

Creative Director
Hiroki Nakamura
Technical Director
Kampei Baba
Art Director
Shinya Seino
Copywriter
Miwako Hosokawa
Film Director
Koichiro Tsujikawa
Designers
Hiwako Hamada
Megumi Kasuga

Programmer
Kampei Baba
Producers
Takaharu Hatori
Mizuho Kamo
Keigo Nakamura
Agency Producer
Shinsaku Ogawa
Cinematographer
Masaya Takagi

Sound Designers
Cornelius
HIFANA
Executive Creative Directors
Yoichi Komatsu
Koichi Sawada
Production Companies
Bascule
Dentsu TEC
Monster Ultra

Advertising Agency
Dentsu Tokyo
Client Supervisors
Kentaro Katsube
Ayumi Shiba
Client
UNIQLO

Microsites

Dentsu Tokyo
for UNIQLO

UNIQLO Collection Tokyo 2009
An online fashion show with TV ads was devised to promote UNIQLO's new 2009 autumn and winter collection in a way that no one had seen before. Users can look at any styles with multi-angle viewing. By clicking on either the women's or men's collections, all the models are replaced. Click on a model you like for a seamless close-up, then check and buy the product with just two clicks. This site offers a very simple and effective way to shop online.

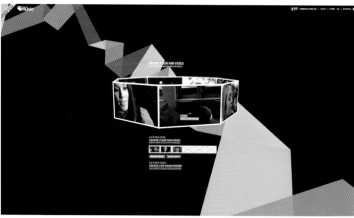

Creative Director	Directors	Development	Account Handler
Dominic Goldman	D.A.R.Y.L	Domani Studios	Jason Gonsalves
Design Director	**Agency Producers**	**Digital Agency**	**Marketing Manager**
Eric Chia	Davud Karbassioun	Domani Studios	Lindsay Nuttall
Art Director	Daniela Michelon	**Post Production**	**Client**
Hugo Biershenk	**Sound Designer**	Absolute Post	MySpace UK
Copywriter	Ian Lambden	**Advertising Agency**	**Brand**
Dean Woodhouse	**Editor**	BBH London	MySpace Music
	Fernanda Wagland		

Microsites

BBH London & Domani Studios
for MySpace UK

Get Real Close
MySpace asked us to emphasise the unique connection artists have with fans on MySpace Music. Fans could 'get real close' to their favourite artists with a unique, personalised film by simply connecting via MySpace or Facebook. Their profile picture was then seamlessly integrated into the lives of 50 Cent, Alicia Keys, Florence and the Machine, and many more. Because it used their profile picture, users could easily make personalised films for all their friends at the click of a button.

537

Creative Directors	Art Director	Developer	Account Handler
Joost Berends	Sebastien De Valck	Pascal Leroy	Katrijn Dewit
Philippe Deceuster	**Copywriter**	**Agency Producer**	**Brand Manager**
Jens Mortier	Arnaud Pitz	Patricia	Jan Vanbiesen
Design Director	**Sound Designer**	Vandekerckhove	**Marketing Manager**
Pascal Leroy	Phile Bocken	**Digital Agency**	Peter Claes
Technical Director	**Programmer**	group94	**Client**
Pascal Leroy	Pascal Leroy	**Advertising Agency**	Studio Brussel
		mortierbrigade	

Microsites

group94 & mortierbrigade
for Studio Brussel

Eternal Moonwalk
Michael Jackson died at the end of June 2009. Studio Brussel, a major Belgian radio station, felt that they and their listeners should pay tribute to the King of Pop. So we used his most famous dance move, the moonwalk, and created eternalmoonwalk.com, a website where people could easily upload their own version of the moonwalk. And by running the videos side by side, we created the never ending moonwalk...

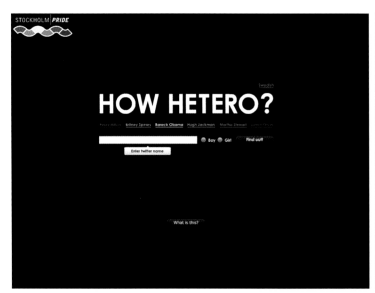

Creative Director	Copywriters	Digital Agency	Brand Manager
Martin Cedergren	Kalle Åkestam	River Cresco	Claes Nyberg
Interactive Creative	Monica Born	**Advertising Agency**	**Marketing Manager**
Director	Joakim Labraaten	Åkestam Holst	Jessica W Sandberg
Paul Collins	**Interactive Designer**	**Account Handler**	**Client**
Art Directors	Ellinor Bjarnolf	Fredrik Widén	Stockholm Pride
Yvan Archimbaud	**Agency Producer**		
Lars Baecklund	Bella Lagerquist		
Paul Collins			

Microsites

Åkestam Holst & River Cresco
for Stockholm Pride

How Hetero Twitter
Since launching in 1998, Stockholm Pride has grown into the largest Pride celebration in the Nordic region. The theme of 2009, Hetero, focused on heteronormativity and how it affects homosexual, bisexual and transgender people's everyday life, what consequences it brings and how it affects society as a whole. The site analyses your Twitter account, giving a percentage assessment of how hetero you are based on your last 200 tweets. We wanted to illustrate the fact that everyday words used in conversations can be perceived as potentially discriminating against people with different sexual orientations. How Hetero was the world's most Tweeted link for two days in July 2009.

539

Illustration
Psyho
Creative Directors
Jeff Goodby
Christian Haas
Art Directors
Rudi Anggono
Caio Lazzuri
Peter Olofsson
Senior Art Director
Shane Fleming
Copywriter
Larry Corwin

Chief Digital Officer
Mike Geiger
Information
Architect
Kevin Jeong
Flash Developer
Jacek Zakowicz
Producer
Elisabet Halming
Executive Producer
Jenny Gadd
Interactive Producer
Stella Wong

Executive Interactive
Producer
Carey Head
Senior Interactive
Producer
Sosia Bert
Broadcast Producer
Brian Coate
Sound Design
Human Worldwide
3D Visual Production
Company
Visual Art

Production Company
North Kingdom
Advertising Agency
Goodby, Silverstein
& Partners
Brand Strategist
Jen Watts
Account Director
Jessica Clifton
Assistant Account
Manager
Amy Taylor
Client
GE

Animation

Goodby, Silverstein & Partners
for GE

Plug into the Smart Grid
When GE came to us to help get the word out about their Smart Grid, we knew we had our work cut out for us. After all, the power grid that energises our nation hadn't been fully updated for 112 years. So how could we get people to care that GE was giving it a makeover? We decided to let consumers take the Smart Grid for a hands-on test drive by creating the first ever interactive commercial experience using augmented reality.

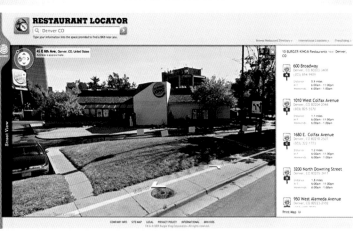

Interactive Designers	Art Directors	Developers	Advertising Agency
Jonathan Bowden	David Byrd	Oscar Llarena	Crispin Porter + Bogusky
John Whitmore	Robert Grober	Aday Rodriguez	**Marketing Manager**
Design Director	**Copywriters**	**Agency Producers**	Claudia Lezcano
Pelun Chen	Peter Majarich	Jason Glassman	**Client**
Technical Director	Ryan Wagman	Scott Potter	Burger King
Mat Ranauro	**Chief Creative Officers**	Robert Valdes	
Creative Directors	Jeff Benjamin		
James Dawson-Hollis	Andrew Keller		
Bill Wright	Rob Reilly		

Interface & Navigation

Crispin Porter + Bogusky
for Burger King

BK.com
You've all heard it: at Burger King, you can have it your way. But the old BK.com didn't live up to that promise. It was rigid and finite. The new BK.com changed all that. Users could adjust a series of sliders to have the content (Fun, Food, or King) delivered just how they wanted. We also designed a meal builder that let people create their own burgers. Users liked having it their way. Traffic rose instantaneously and people spent an average of three and a half minutes on the site. To date, nobody has dialled the Fun slider down to zero.

Photographers
Shinsuke Kamioka
Takuji Onda
Takuyuki Saito
Creative Director
Koichiro Tanaka
Technical Director
Kay-ichi Tozaki
Art Director
Takashi Kamada
Designer
Takashi Kamada

Interactive Designers
Yukio Sato
Kay-ichi Tozaki
Shooting Directors
Hiroyuki Kojima
TOCHKA 'Kazue
Monno + Takeshi
Nagata'
Programmer
Susumu Arai
System Engineer
Susumu Arai
Web Producer
Ken Kanetomo

Producers
Gyosei Okada
Shinjiro Ono
Nozomu Naito
Artist
Fantastic Plastic
Machine
Digital Agency
Projector
Production Company
Puzzle

**Creative
Management
Director**
Kentaro Katsube
Production Manager
Shigehisa Nakao
Project Managers
Yuuri Ogawa
Shinichi Saeki
PR Managers
Mayumi Sawada
Ryota Sugawara
Client
UNIQLO

Photography

Projector
for UNIQLO

UNIQLO Calendar
UNIQLO calendar is an online digital calendar, which aims to build a branding platform to promote both Japan and UNIQLO on a global scale. Each season, we went on a mission to capture the dynamism of Japan by spending months travelling and filming, using tilt-shift and time-lapse techniques to create a fresh, miniature version of Japan. Users can set their location and use it as a blog widget, screensaver, greetings card, or iPhone app. As of January 2010, UNIQLO calendar covers all four seasons, featuring scenes from over 180 locations in Japan, and is still searching for more.

Andrew Zuckerman: Bird

Photographs
Films
Book
Info

1 2 3 4 5 ◀

Bird Information

Order   Strigiformes
Family   Strigidae
Genus & Species Nyctea scandiaca
Region   Arctic circle
Wingspan   140-165 cm
Audio/Credit   Andrew Zuckerman Studio

Andrew Zuckerman: Bird   Photographs   Blue-throated Macaw   1 2 3 4   Bird Information

Andrew Zuckerman: Bird   Films   Bird Film   1

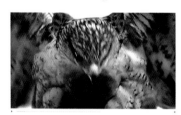

Creative Director
Andrew Zuckerman
Designer
David Meredith

Production Company
Andrew Zuckerman
Studio

Design Group
Pilot New York

Client
Andrew Zuckerman
Studio

Graphic Design
Pilot New York
for Andrew Zuckerman Studio

Bird by Andrew Zuckerman
The website for the book 'Bird' by Andrew Zuckerman captures the photographic intensity of the book by making images the focus of the viewing experience. Unencumbered by the proportions of a framed space, the birds fill the screen in all their vibrant colours, appearing throughout the site in different locations as if alive. The site then takes the experience a step further by providing the sounds of the birds as well as scientific information – a highly modern rendering of the traditional field guide.

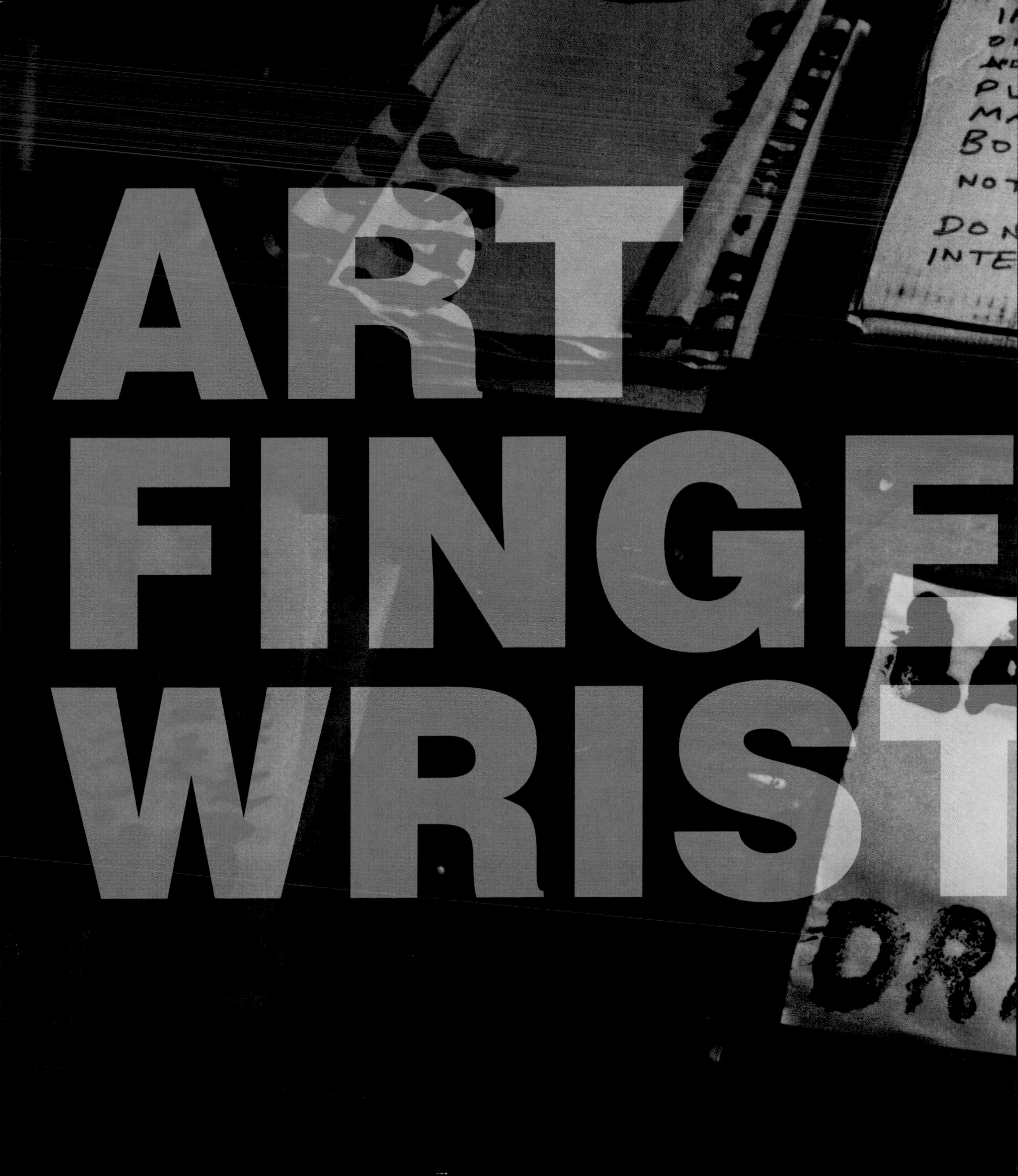
ART
FINGE
WRIS

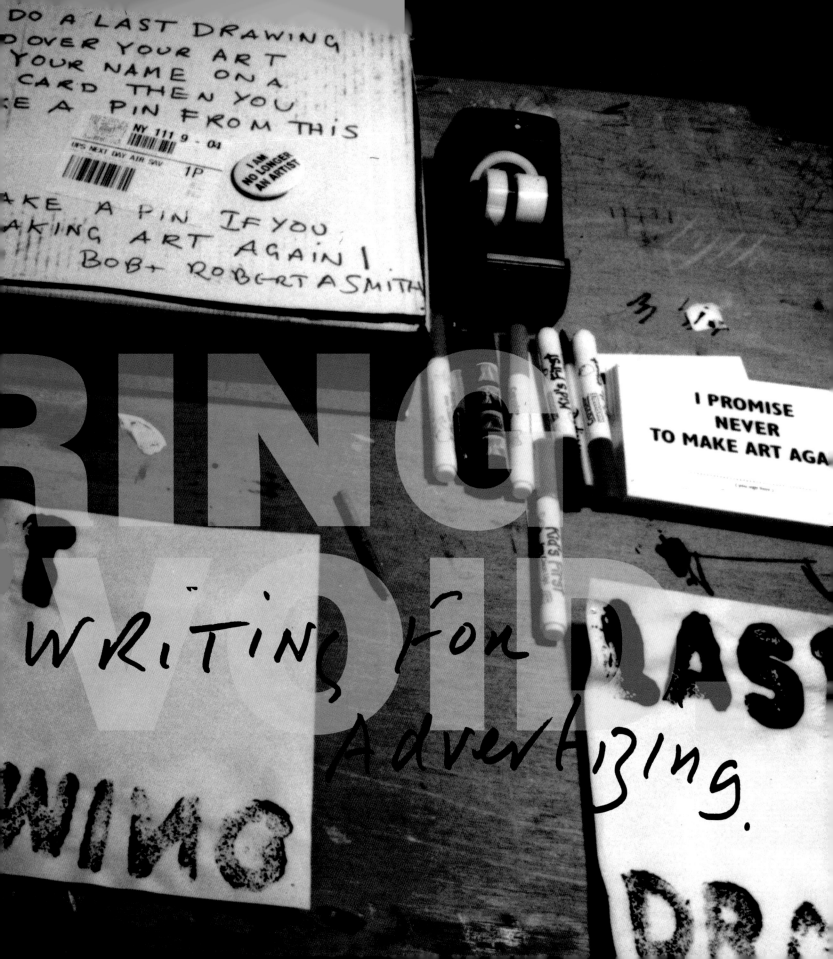

Copywriters
Cam Blackley
Matty Burton
Art Directors
Cam Blackley
Matty Burton
Director
Gary Freedman
Digital Director
Brett Mitchell
Executive Creative Director
David Nobay

Director of Photography
Danny Ruhlmann
Producers
Catherine Anderson
Karen Bryson
Agency Producer
Paul Johnston
Editors
Mark Burnett
Bernard Garry
Zen Rosenthal

Sound Designers
Tone Aston
Simon Lister
Casting Director
Toni Higginbotham
Production Company
@radical.media
Special Effects
Fuel
Advertising Agency
Droga5 Australia

Executive Planning Director
Sudeep Gohil
Account Manager
Nicolas Kettelhake
Account Executive
Lucy McBurney
Business Director
Steve Muller
Brand Manager
Scott McGregor

Marketing Manager
Paul Donaldson
Client
Carlton United Breweries
Brand
Victoria Bitter

TV & Cinema Advertising
Droga5 Australia
for Carlton United Breweries

The Regulars
This two-minute television commercial formed the spearhead of 'The Regulars' campaign for VB beer. Australians, proud of their ability to laugh at themselves and others, are notorious for categorising people according to their appearance, their habits, where they live, what they do, their strengths and their weaknesses. It is this exceptional Australian ability to deliver the backhanded compliment that this epic taps into. Because VB beer is for all kinds of people, we created a real parade, celebrating all Australians and the groups they belong to, including 'Blokes Punching Above Their Weight', 'Men Who Should've Read The Instructions', 'The Manscapers' and, of course, the all important 'Brewers'.

Get off at the fashionable end of Oxford Street, drift into the achingly cool technology hall of London's most happening department store and view this year's must-have plasma courtesy of the sound and vision technologist in the Marc Jacobs sandals then go to dixons.co.uk and buy it.

Dixons.co.uk
The last place you want to go

Step into middle England's best loved department store, stroll through haberdashery to the audio visual department where an awfully well brought up young man will bend over backwards to find the right TV for you then go to dixons.co.uk and buy it.

Dixons.co.uk
The last place you want to go

Get off at Knightsbridge, visit the discerning shopper's fave department store, ascend the exotic staircase and let Piers in the pinstripe suit demonstrate the magic of the latest high-definition flatscreen then go to dixons.co.uk and buy it.

Dixons.co.uk
The last place you want to go

Copywriters	Simon Dicketts, Orlando Warner
Art Director	Graham Fink
Typographers	Gareth Davies, Simon Warden
Creative Directors	Simon Dicketts, Graham Fink
Advertising Agency	M&C Saatchi London
Planner	Neil Godber
Account Handler	Estelle Lee
Marketing Director	Niall O'Keefe
Client	Dixons Stores Group
Brand	Dixons.co.uk

Poster Advertising

M&C Saatchi London
for Dixons Stores Group

Sandals / Middle England / Piers

Our campaign repositioned Dixons.co.uk by persuading people to embrace a smarter way of shopping online. People were cheekily encouraged to make use of the best service freely available on the high street, then find a better price online at Dixons.co.uk. The ads wittily suggested some typical high-street shopping experiences people could try. The sign-off, 'The last place you want to go' acted as a polite suggestion of when people should use the site, as well as a self-aware and humorous acknowledgement of the brand's equivocal reputation as a good place to shop. 'Sandals' and 'Middle England' were also selected as single executions in the category Writing for Advertising/Press Advertising.

547

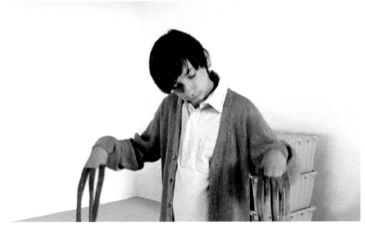

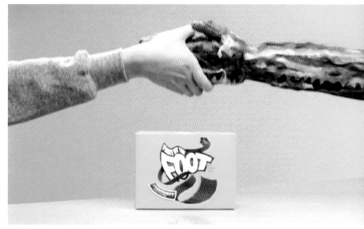

Copywriter
Michael Illick
Art Director
Dan Lucey
Director
Tom Kuntz
Creative Directors
Dan Kelleher
Ralph Watson

**Chief Creative
Officer**
Gerry Graf
Producer
Scott Kaplan
Agency Producer
John Doris

Editor
Gavin Cutler
Production Company
MJZ
Advertising Agency
Saatchi & Saatchi
New York

Client
General Mills
Brand
Fruit by the Foot

▲ TV & Cinema Advertising

Saatchi & Saatchi New York
for General Mills

Replacement
Two friends attempt to outdo each other in a 'Fruit by the Foot' contest.

Arnold Palmer   The Machine   Going Up

Copywriters
Scott Hayes
Eric Steele
Art Directors
Gary van Dzura
Stuart Jennings
Director
David Shane
Creative Directors
Derek Barnes
Stuart Jennings
John Parker

Executive Creative Directors
Kevin Proudfoot
Todd Waterbury
Agency Head of Content Production
Gary Krieg
Executive Producer
Ralph Laucella
Agency Producer
Alison Hill
Visual Effects Artists
Mario Stipinovich
Eve Weinberg

Editor
Andrew Robertson
Director of Photography
Dave Morabito
Post Production
Mario Stipinovich
Sound Designer
Joseph Fraioli
Sound Mixer
Rob DiFondi
Telecine
Jamie Wilkinson

Colour Correction
Jamie Wilkinson
Online Artists
Tom McCullough
Matt Reilly
Production Company
O Positive
Advertising Agency
Wieden+Kennedy
New York
Senior Account Manager
Rich Weinstein

Account Managers
Casey Bernard
Brian D'Entremont
Yosef Johnson
Victoria Segar
Sports Marketing
Seth Ader
Alex Green
Aaron Taylor
Client
ESPN
Brand
This is SportsCenter.

TV & Cinema Advertising

Wieden+Kennedy New York
for ESPN

Arnold Palmer / The Machine / Going Up
The 'This is SportsCenter.' campaign has always given sports fans a glimpse behind the scenes at the fun, random world at the centre of the sports universe. With anchors interacting with athletes and mascots alike, it's a fan's vision of what ESPN's corporate campus in Bristol, Connecticut really is like. In 2009, the campaign continued to feed sports fans' appetite for a look inside ESPN's walls (in the cafeteria, office elevators and copy room, to be exact). The new TV adverts 'Arnold Palmer', 'The Machine' and 'Going Up' became instant classics.

 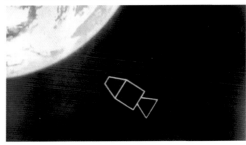

Copywriter Damian Fitzgerald **Art Director** Matt Heck **Senior Designer** James Hackett	**Designers** Leo Nguyen Anne Numont **Creative Director** Noah Regan **Executive Creative Directors** Justin Drape Scott Nowell	**Producer** Kala Ellis **Agency Producer** Thea Carone **Sound Designer** Simon Kane	**Production Company** Hackett Films **Advertising Agency** Three Drunk Monkeys **Client** BBC Knowledge

TV & Cinema Advertising

Three Drunk Monkeys
for BBC Knowledge

BBC Moon Week
This spot was created to promote BBC Knowledge's week of programmes commemorating the 40th anniversary of the moon landing. Using the line animation techniques of the time, we took the viewer on a journey of obscure, amazing facts relating to the event. The voice of Ted Maynard, who broadcast the original moon landing from his radio station 40 years ago, brought this fascinating story to life.

Copywriter Jean-Christophe Royer **Art Director** Eric Astorgue **Director** Matthijs van Heijningen	**Executive Creative Director** Stéphane Xiberras **Editor** Jono Griffith **Director of Photography** Joost van Gelder **Agency Producer** Isabelle Ménard	**Production Company** SOIXAN7E QUIN5E **Sound Production** KOUZ Production **Image Post Production** MIKROS Image **Advertising Agency** BETC Euro RSCG	**Account Handlers** Raphaël de Andréis François Brogi Alexandre George **Brand & Marketing Manager** Béatrice Roux **Client** CANAL+

TV & Cinema Advertising

BETC Euro RSCG
for CANAL+

Closet
In September 2009, CANAL+ launched its new 'Original Creativity' campaign. The aim was to highlight CANAL+'s showcase of original programming, consisting of series, documentaries and dramas, created exclusively by and for CANAL+, and scripted by prestigious writers such as Olivier Marchal and Jean-Hugues Anglade. To launch this new campaign, we produced an advert where a husband comes home to find a man hiding in his wife's closet. The man then describes a series of improbable events to explain his reason for being there. The advert brings together humour and a touch of impertinence inherent to the brand's message: 'Never underestimate the power of a great story'.

Copywriters	Creative Director	Production Company	Account Handlers
Tony Malcolm	Jim Bolton	Moxie Pictures	Sean Boles
Guy Moore	**Producer**	**Advertising Agency**	Megan Lock
Art Directors	Jess Ensor	Leo Burnett London	**Client**
Tony Malcolm	**Agency Producer**	**Planners**	McDonald's
Guy Moore	Graeme Light	Ian Hilton	
Director	**Editor**	Matt Watts	
Neil Gorringe	James Rosen		

TV & Cinema Advertising

Leo Burnett London
for McDonald's

Everybody
This work is a true celebration of Britain's relationship with McDonald's today, reminding everyone what they love about the brand. The TV execution is based on observations that everyone can easily relate to. It shows customers from all walks of life popping into the restaurant for a bite to eat at varying times of day and night, and highlights how these different people enjoy their experiences. The campaign brings to life that 'there's a McDonald's for everyone'.

Copywriter	Executive Creative	Production Company	Brand Manager
Steve Jackson	**Director**	Prodigy Films	Scott Thompson
Art Director	Steve Back	**Advertising Agency**	**Client**
Vince Lagana	**Producer**	Saatchi & Saatchi	Toyota Motor
Director	Julianne Shelton	Sydney	Corporation
Tim Bullock	**Agency Producer**	**Account Handlers**	
Creative Director	Kate Whitfield	Ben Court	
Dave Bowman		Amy Turnbull	

TV & Cinema Advertising

Saatchi & Saatchi Sydney
for the Toyota Motor Corporation

Country Australian Border Security – Nothing Soft Gets In
Country-dwelling Australians think all city people are 'soft', and don't care much for their 'soft' city ways or 'soft' cars and possessions. This advert shows Country Australia Border Security defending their country border by preventing any 'soft' city stuff from getting into their tough country areas. This includes small yappy dogs, hairdryers, tofu, 'soft' city cars and turned up collars. Their motto is 'Nothing Soft Gets In', and their official 4WD vehicles are supplied by Toyota.

551

If GH can stand for P in Hiccough
If OUGH can stand for O in Dough
If PHTH can stand for T in Phthisis
If EIGH can stand for A in Neighbour
If TTE can stand for T in Gazette
If EAU can stand for O in Plateau
Then the way you spell POTATO is...
GHOUGHPHTHEIGHTTEEAU.
Isn't it?
Only The Times brings you the UK's first national spelling championship for schools.
Join in at timesonline.co.uk/spellingbee

THE TIMES

In Baghdad the cost of the war will exceed $3 trillion.
In Baghdad the firm that developed Disneyland is planning a new 'Baghdad Zoo and Entertainment Experience'.
In Baghdad house prices have doubled in recent months.
In Baghdad you can queue for several hours to buy petrol, yet Iraq has the third-largest oil reserves.
In Baghdad an Iraqi 'extreme makeover' reality TV show is now renovating war-damaged homes.
In Baghdad Lionel Richie is enormously popular.
In Baghdad only one UK newspaper has a full-time correspondent.

THE TIMES

Brick Lane Beigel Bake makes 7,000 bagels a night before 7am.
It is rumoured that, if discreetly done, skinny-dipping is allowed at Tooting Bec Lido before 7am.
Only 6 per cent of London cabbies choose to work after midnight and before 7am.
A quarter of all of Heathrow's Saturday passengers travel before 7am.
If you are under 16 years of age it is illegal to work before 7am.
The average UK resident wakes up 12 minutes before 7am.
The Times is the only newspaper that is delivered free to your door, seven days a week, before 7am.
Sign up at timesonline.co.uk/7am

THE TIMES

Mr Charles Dickens on public executions, 1849.
Her Majesty Queen Victoria on the pressures of monarchy, 1864.
Miss Florence Nightingale on nursing the poor, 1876.
Sir Digby Pigott on luminous owls, 1908.
Sir Arthur Conan Doyle on the Channel Tunnel, 1913.
Signor Benito Mussolini on fascism, 1925.
Mrs Nora Wooster on quinqueremes and triremes, 1975.
Miss Madeau Stewart on noiseless knitting, 1978.
The Rt Hon Margaret Thatcher on hereditary peerages, 1991.
Mr S. Palmer on sod's law, Murphy's law and toast, 2001.
Master Charles Holloway, aged 9, on why maths is fun, 2008.
Letters to the Editor. A chosen few are published daily.

THE TIMES

Copywriters	Creative Directors	Advertising Agency	Brand Manager
Jake Holmes	Charles Inge	CHI&Partners	Richard Larcombe
Micky Tudor	Ewan Paterson	**Planner**	**Marketing Manager**
Art Directors	Micky Tudor	Ben Southgate	Paul Lotherington
Phil Bucknall	**Design Agencies**	**Account Handler**	**Client**
Micky Tudor	CHI&Partners	Danny Josephs	News International
	Venture Three		**Brand**
			The Times

Poster Advertising

CHI&Partners
for News International

Our Times Long Copy – Spelling Bee / Baghdad / Alarm Clock / Letters
Fascinating and unusual facts give insights into the times we live in and why The Times
newspaper is best placed to report on them.

Since last year's budget, Domino's Pizza profits have risen by 25%

Computer game sales are up 20%

Sales of Argos's cheapest sewing machine are up 500%

Lunchbox sales are up 68%

Sales of turnips at Tesco are up 75%

And the average amount left under the pillow by the tooth fairy has gone down by 30%

Find out how the most important Budget in a generation will affect your spending habits.

Your definitive Budget guide from the number 1 paper for business.

Next Thursday, only in The Times.

THE TIMES

More people read Barack Obama's *Dreams From My Father* than Katie Price's *Being Jordan*.

More people read about The Periodic Table on Wikipedia than High School Musical.

More people read Stephen Fry's Twitter updates than Britney Spears's.

More people read The Huffington Post blog than Perez Hilton's.

More people read The Times than any other quality daily newspaper.

THE TIMES

1961: Dutch artist Escher printed his lithograph 'Waterfall', showing water that seems to flow in an infinite cycle.

1964: Willy Wonka gave us the 'Everlasting Gobstopper'.

1974: The non-stop Duracell Bunny starred in its first TV commercial.

1981: Lionel Richie and Diana Ross gave us 'Endless Love'.

1982: 'Eternity is really long, especially near the end' - Woody Allen.

1984: German director Wolfgang Petersen brought us the fantasy film 'The Never Ending Story', which ended after 94 minutes.

2009: The Times is printed using an endless supply of energy from 100% renewable sources.

THE TIMES

Every US president has been married, except one.

Every US president has been raised in the Protestant faith, except one.

Every US president has spoken English as his first language, except one.

Every US president has been voted in as president or vice president, except one.

Every US president went to school, except one.

Every US president has either finished his term or died in office, except one.

Every US president has been a white male.

The Inauguration Special. Out tomorrow.

THE TIMES

Rashers of bacon
Delivered to a car factory in Swindon
Tucked in between slices of bread
In the Honda canteen
That is open again
After four months of rest
The factory is hungry
Hungry to start production again
It feels good to open the doors again
Welcoming back the bacon delivery man
Giving him business again
Say hello to the **HONDA** effect

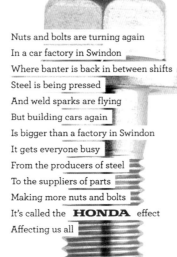

Nuts and bolts are turning again
In a car factory in Swindon
Where banter is back in between shifts
Steel is being pressed
And weld sparks are flying
But building cars again
Is bigger than a factory in Swindon
It gets everyone busy
From the producers of steel
To the suppliers of parts
Making more nuts and bolts
It's called the **HONDA** effect
Affecting us all

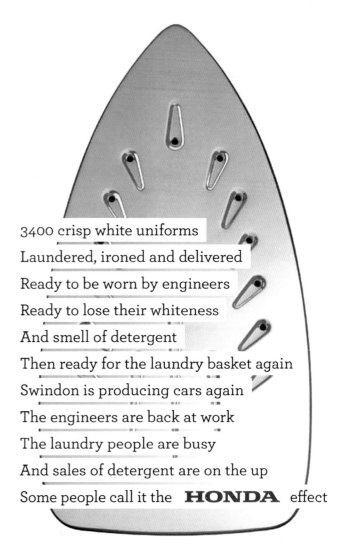

3400 crisp white uniforms
Laundered, ironed and delivered
Ready to be worn by engineers
Ready to lose their whiteness
And smell of detergent
Then ready for the laundry basket again
Swindon is producing cars again
The engineers are back at work
The laundry people are busy
And sales of detergent are on the up
Some people call it the **HONDA** effect

Copywriter
Ida Gronblom
Art Director
Fabian Burglund
Designer
Karen Jane

Photographer
David Sykes
Creative Directors
Tony Davidson
Kim Papworth

Retoucher
Badger
Producer
Mark D'Abreo
Advertising Agency
Wieden+Kennedy
London

Account Director
Ryan Fisher
Client
Honda

Press Advertising

Wieden+Kennedy London
for Honda

Bacon / Bolt / Iron

In February 2009 the Honda factory in Swindon stopped its production of cars for four months. Rather than make people redundant, Honda decided to stop making cars and retool the factory, keeping workers in their jobs. In June the factory reopened. We looked back to the past and to how Honda had dealt with situations before. There was a commonly known economical term called 'The Honda Effect', meaning the company changes its long term goals in order to deal with current situations. We wanted to tell the story of the reopening and celebrate the effect that a factory like Honda's has on the local and wider community.

Press Advertising

DDB UK
for Volkswagen

Film Polywrap
This plastic wrap contained the magazines that come with The Observer, a Sunday newspaper.
Our brief was to alert readers to the Volkswagen-sponsored film supplement within.

Copywriter
Will Lowe
Art Director
Victor Monclus
Designer
Pete Mould

Typographer
Pete Mould
Executive Creative Director
Jeremy Craigen
Advertising Agency
DDB UK

Account Director
Charlie Elliott
Account Manager
Jessica Huth
Business Director
Jonathan Hill

Communications Manager
Sally Chapman
Client
Volkswagen

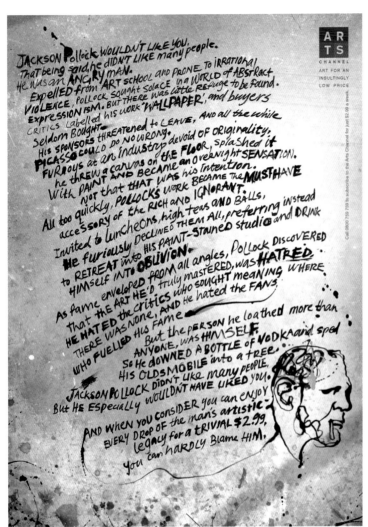

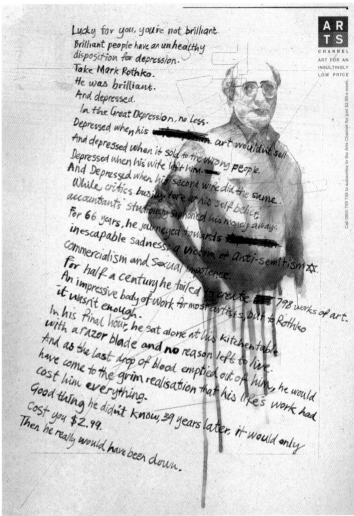

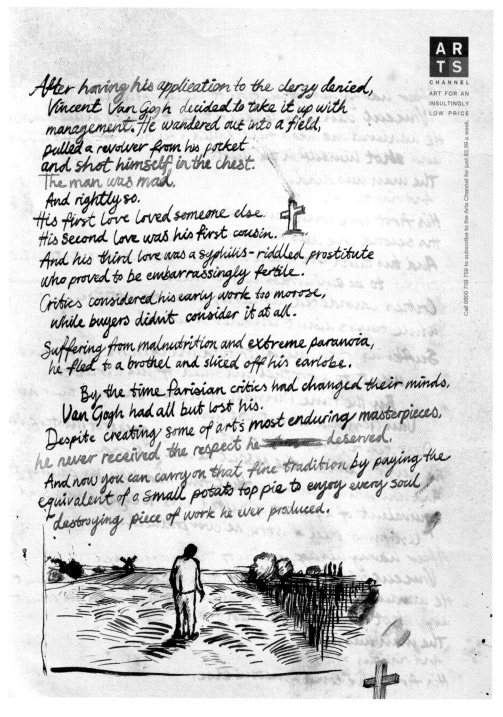

Press Advertising

DDB Auckland
for Sky Television

Pollock / Rothko / Van Gogh
Sky Television, New Zealand's largest satellite television provider, asked us to promote the newly discounted price of its Arts Channel. For just an added $2.95 a week, Sky subscribers could sign up and enjoy the life and work of some of history's greatest artists. We created a print campaign that put into perspective the enormous price these artists paid to create their work, and the comparative pittance Sky subscribers pay to enjoy it.

Copywriter	Head of Art	Account Handlers	Director
Simon Vicars	Mike Davison	Brad Armstrong	of Marketing
Art Director	**Print Producer**	Danielle Richards	Mike Watson
James Tucker	Nick Conetta	Scott Wallace	**Client**
Illustrator	**Advertising Agency**	**Marketing Manager**	Sky Television
Mike Davison	DDB Auckland	Chaz Savage	**Brand**
Group Executive		**Marketing Executive**	Arts Channel
Creative Director		Amber Brown	
Toby Talbot			

THIS IS HARD COUNTRY AND WE WANT TO KEEP IT THAT WAY. ONE MALE FRAGRANCE OR SOY SAUSAGE IS ALL IT TAKES.

Manbags. Hair dryers. Male fragrances. Tofu. Good luck getting these through.

Pray you never get a cavity search from Officer Turnbull of Country Australia Border Security. Even though he's trained to perform all security procedures in a professional manner, like every border guard he's from the bush, and that makes him as tough and unforgiving as the land he's sworn to protect. This is hard country and we'll do anything to make sure it stays that way. Nothing soft gets in. No sparkling mineral water, no manbags, no personal organisers, no namby-pamby lip balms and no soft 4WD vehicles. Most times we just have to get them to pop their collar down or confiscate a boy band CD, but things can escalate quickly out here on the frontline, especially if someone's had one too many chai lattes. This parched and endless frontier can only be patrolled using choppers or Toyota 4WDs like the LC200, LC70, Prado and HiLux; nothing else will survive. We will stop any soft city item getting into the country areas, even if that means us slipping on the glove.

NOTHING SOFT GETS IN

Country Australia Border Security Act.
Article 0662/8

STRICTLY NO POODLES, SHNOODLES, LABRADOODLES, GOLDENDOODLES OR ANY OTHER OODLES OR DOODLES.

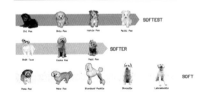

TOYOTA
Official 4WD vehicles and
proud defenders of Country Australia.

NOTHING SOFT GETS IN

↑↑

OFFICE USE ONLY

No:

DECLARATION FORM FOR INCOMING VISITORS

NOTHING SOFT GETS IN

Do you have anything 'soft' to declare? Remember honesty is the best policy. Especially if you're no good at lying. If you are not sure — declare it!! False declarations could get you into trouble. Good luck getting anything soft in.

Full Name

Date of Birth   Sex: Male   Female   Metro

City(Region)   Vehicle: Toyota 4WD   Other

Are you bringing into Country Australia:

1. Clothing including: $200 T-shirts, plunging v-neck shirts, manbags, designer footwear, big sunglasses, white trousers or shorts, shoes with secret socks or no socks, pastel coloured polo shirts, fashion scarves, sweaters worn around the shoulders, cravats, all things velvet, bling.   Yes   No

2. Food and beverages including: Sparkling mineral water, macrobiotic foods, tofu, soy sausages, soy milk, skinny milk, french pastries (like croissants), lattes, chai lattes, herbal teas, energy or diet drinks, vitamin pills, quiche, cupcakes.   Yes   No

3. Any biosecurity risk items, including: Any small yappy 'dogs' that fit into a handbag, leopard or tiger skin print clothing or cushions.   Yes   No

4. In the past 30 days have you: Visited a fashion show, the ballet or opera, a musical, a modern art gallery, cocktail evening, book club, hair salon, tanning studio, fancy restaurant, health spa & retreat, tennis lessons, boutique b&b or had contact with any food critics, personal shoppers or trainers, art historians?   Yes   No

5. Miscellaneous soft stuff: Personal organisers, pilates videos, yoga mats, incense, meditation cushions, reiki books, whale music.   Yes   No

6. Have you had or do you intend to have: Manicure, pedicure, eyebrow shaping?   Yes   No

I DECLARE THAT THE INFORMATION GIVEN ON THIS FORM IS TRUE.

Visitors who are bringing any articles included in items 1–6 shall fill out this form in detail.

Description	Quantity	Value	Type/Model	Customs Remarks

PASSENGER'S SIGNATURE   Date

◆ TOYOTA

Official 4WD vehicles and proud defenders of Country Australia.

Copywriter
Steve Jackson
Art Director
Vince Lagana
Creative Director
Dave Bowman

Executive Creative Director
Steve Back
Print Producer
Jeremy De Villiers

Advertising Agency
Saatchi & Saatchi
Sydney
Account Handlers
Ben Court
Amy Turnbull

Brand Manager
Scott Thompson
Client
Toyota Motor
Corporation

Press Advertising

Saatchi & Saatchi Sydney
for the Toyota Motor Corporation

One Male Fragrance / Yappy Dog / Declaration Form
Country-dwelling Australians think all city people are 'soft', and don't care much for their 'soft' city ways or 'soft' cars and possessions. These press adverts show Country Australia Border Security defending their country border by preventing any 'soft' city stuff from getting into their tough country areas. This includes small yappy dogs, hairdryers, tofu, 'soft' city cars and turned up collars. Their motto is 'Nothing Soft Gets In', and their official 4WD vehicles are supplied by Toyota.

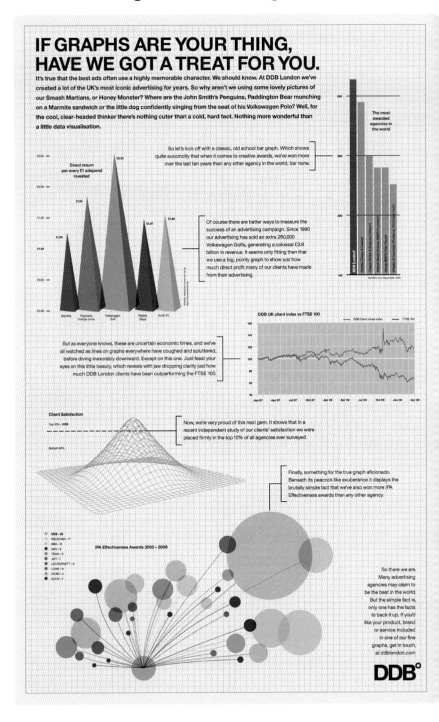

Press Advertising

DDB UK

DDB House Graph
This house advert for DDB UK was aimed at company heads and ran full page
in The Financial Times.

bbc.co.uk/poetryseason

GROUND TENT
SET-UP INSTRUCTIONS

Firstly place the tent pole through
the hole in the fabric located in
the apex of the tent. While holding
the tent material like a song that,
freed from beat and measure, wanders.
Forgetfulness is
like a bird
whose wings
are reconciled,
outspread and motionless, - a bird
that coasts the wind unwearyingly.
Then, peg out the main guy ropes
following the lines of the tent seams.

Let poetry into your life
BBC Poetry Season BBC TWO BBC FOUR

bbc.co.uk/poetryseason

THE START OF PLAY

Competing players must toss a
coin to determine which team
will throw the
jack. Once the jack is thrown,
it's seared with trade; bleared,
smeared with toil; and wears
man's smudge and shares man's
smell: the soil is bare now, nor
can foot feel, being shod. And
for all this nature is never spent;

Only one team can score in a
single round.

Let poetry into your life
BBC Poetry Season BBC TWO BBC FOUR

bbc.co.uk/poetryseason

Directions to Hove Cottage

Take the A46, Bath Road, south from
Stroud. Proceed for about a mile,
and at the first roundabout, take the
second exit where a shape with lion
body and the head
of a man, a gaze
blank and pitiless
as the sun, is
moving its slow
thighs, while all about it wind shadows
of the indignant desert birds.
The key will be left underneath the small
flowerpot on the right of the front door.

Let poetry into your life
BBC Poetry Season BBC TWO BBC FOUR

Press Advertising

RKCR/Y&R
for the BBC

Tent / Boules / Hove Cottage
This is a campaign to promote the BBC Poetry Season, using scenes of everyday life
transformed by the introduction of poetry.

Copywriter	**Typographer**	**Planner**	**Client**
Mark Waldron	James Townsend	Megan Thompson	BBC
Art Director	**Creative Director**	**Account Handler**	**Brand**
David Godfree	Damon Collins	Jamal Cassim	BBC Poetry Season
Illustrator	**Advertising Agency**	**Marketing Manager**	
Dominic Trevett	RKCR/Y&R	Ruairi Curran	

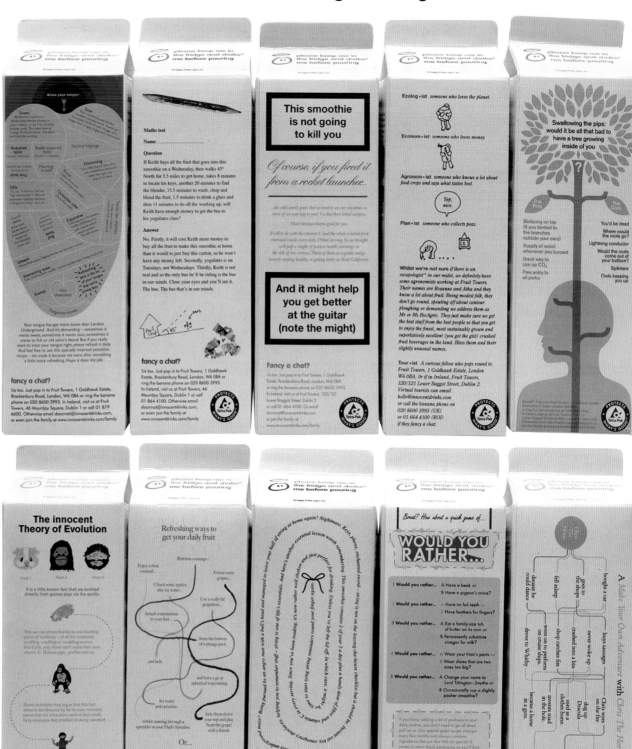

Swallowing the pips: would it be all that bad to have a tree growing inside of you

?

The
Pros

The
Cons

Birdsong on tap
(if you tended to
the branches
outside your ears)

Supply of wood
whenever you burped

Great way to
use up CO_2

Free entry to
all parks

You'd be dead

Where would
the roots go?

Lightning conductor

Would the roots
come out of
your bottom?

Splinters

Owls keeping
you up

Fancy a chat? Pop in to Fruit Towers, Goldhawk
Estate, Brackenbury Road, London, W6 0BA
or ring the banana phone on 020 8600 3993.
In Ireland, visit us at Fruit Towers, 121
Lower Baggot Street, Dublin 2 or 01 664 4100.
Otherwise email doormat@innocentdrinks.com or
join the family at www.innocentdrinks.com/family

Tetra Pak — protects what's good

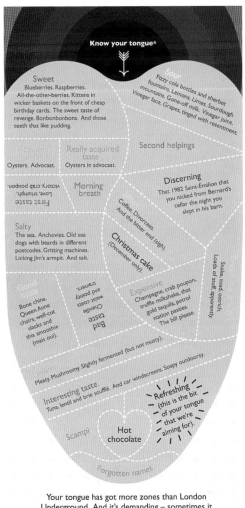

Your tongue has got more zones than London
Underground. And it's demanding – sometimes it
wants sweet, sometimes it wants sour, sometimes it
wants to lick an old sailor's beard. But if you really
want to treat your tongue right, please refresh it daily.
And feel free to use this specially invented smoothie
recipe – we made it because we were after something
a little more refreshing. Hope it does the job.

fancy a chat?

Us too. Just pop in to Fruit Towers, 1 Goldhawk Estate,
Brackenbury Road, London, W6 0BA or ring the banana
phone on 020 8600 3993. In Ireland, visit us at Fruit
Towers, 46 Mountjoy Square, Dublin 1 or call 01 879
6600. Otherwise email doormat@innocentdrinks.com,
or even join the family at www.innocentdrinks.com/family

Copywriters
Dan Germain
Ben Harris
Ceri Tallett

Art Director
Kat Linger
Designer
Ben Williams

Creative Director
Dan Germain
Creative Manager
Tansy Drake

Client
innocent

Packaging Design

innocent

innocent Packaging, Autumn 2009
We like to make the most of every available space on our packaging. We often find the best
way is to draw pictures and write interesting stuff. We change our packaging a few times
every year in order to keep things interesting and make sure people don't get bored.

BOXERS

WHO WEARS UNDERWEAR ALL THE TIME?

SOUL-SUCKING CORPORATE ZOMBIES WITH MATCHING PYJAMAS, THAT'S WHO! BUT EVERY NOW AND THEN YOU NEED SOMETHING TO TAME THE BEAST. WEAR THESE BOXERS ON A SPECIAL OCCASION. LIKE TO A FUNERAL OR WHATEVER.

6 SOCKS

WHAT? Just 2 socks in a pack? Screw that! You're *always* losing one of them in the wash — OR in some orgy aftermath. Now you'll have THREE socks that will fit as SNUG on your *feet* as leather pants around the ankles. And you can *really* get your money shot going. ROCK OUT with your sock out!

Copywriter Keenon Daniels **Design Director** Joanne Thomas **Designers** Jared Barbe Brandt Botes Johann du Bruyn Klea Ferreira	**Illustrators** Jared Barbe Brandt Botes Joanne Thomas Roger Williams	**Advertising Agency** The Jupiter Drawing Room South Africa **Account Handler** Timothy Young	**Marketing Manager** Moenieba Abrahams **Client** Musica

Graphic Design

The Jupiter Drawing Room South Africa for Musica

Wanna Be a Rock Star?
Musica is South Africa's largest entertainment retailer. This new range was designed as part of a campaign to drive people into the company's stores by promoting its lifestyle products section. The key objective was to promote the sale of 'rock star' lifestyle products by having a strong presence in-store. Using only three different colours, the packaging design and copy had to communicate the in-your-face, anti-establishment rebelliousness of rock music, while not taking itself too seriously, in the spirit of the Musica brand.

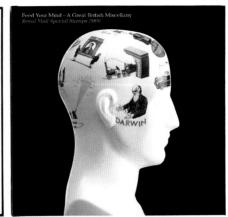

Feed Your Mind – A Great British Miscellany
Royal Mail Special Stamps 2009

James Braidwood founded the world's first municipal fire service in Edinburgh in 1824, and was the first director of the London Fire Engine Establishment.

Author
Jim Davies
Designer
Adam Giles

Creative Directors
Gareth Howat
Jim Sutherland
Design Group
hat-trick design

Design Manager
Dean Price
Editorial Manager
Helen Cumberbatch

Head of Design & Editorial
Marcus James
Client
Royal Mail Group

Graphic Design

hat-trick design
for the Royal Mail Group

Feed Your Mind – A Great British Miscellany, Royal Mail Special Stamps 2009
This is the annual, limited-edition publication containing all of the 2009 Royal Mail special stamps. This book is a showcase for the stamp issues, their technical information and the fascinating stories behind their development. The stamps cover a broad spectrum of subject matter, and each year we need an interesting and informative new approach that encompasses this disparate range of subjects. This edition features a compendium of 'I never knew that' moments, stories and glories, movers and shakers, faces and places. Jim Davies has created a fascinating journey through this year's special stamps programme, drawing the reader into each subject with a cornucopia of facts, figures and anecdotes.

Which awards are the most attractive?

The creative world is not exactly short of awards.

Dynamic sculptures cast in solid metal, hefty enough to break a bone should you drop one on your foot.

Translucent blocks that dapple the office walls with pretty coloured light when the sun hits them at the right angle.

Heroic, winged figures that resemble a collaboration between Albert Speer and Leni Riefenstahl.

And then there's another one. It's not much to look at.

Just a short, stubby piece of wood painted yellow.

The D&AD pencil.

You don't see as many of these. And therein lies the appeal.

Most awards schemes cheerfully hand out prizes in every category, every year.

Not D&AD.

Pencils only go to work that reaches the very highest standards.

But if D&AD juries weren't so mean, D&AD awards wouldn't mean as much.

A nomination alone is something to cherish. Just getting work into the book is an achievement in itself. Many would say it's better than winning at other awards shows.

After all, once your work is in the D&AD Annual, it will be gazed at, admired, pored over (and quite possibly ripped-off) by creative people from Milan to Minsk.

Entries are now being accepted for next year's awards.

The closing date is Wednesday 27th January 2010.

So whether you work in advertising or design or digital, it's time to start studying those categories.

Other awards may look more exciting.

But no other award is quite as attractive.

dandad.org/awards

Awards 2010

Graphic Design

Abbott Mead Vickers BBDO
for D&AD

Attractive
In previous years, D&AD's 'Call For Entries' adverts have tended to be simple announcements. This year, that wasn't enough. There are more awards schemes than ever, and companies have less money to spend on entering them. Competition is tough. So this year's campaign sought to remind entrants of what makes D&AD unique – and why it should be first on everyone's list.

Copywriter
Tim Riley
Art Directors
Nick Bell
Carlos Mancebo

Typographers
Nick Bell
Carlos Mancebo

Creative Director
Paul Brazier
Design Group
Nick Bell Design

Advertising Agency
Abbott Mead
Vickers BBDO
Marketing Director
Rob Eves
Client
D&AD

YOU'LL NEVER GUESS WHO I BUMPED INTO
IN THE HARVEY NICHOLS FOODMARKET?

YOU'LL NEVER GUESS WHO I BUMPED INTO
IN THE HARVEY NICHOLS FOODMARKET?

PEA DIDDY

PARIS STILTON

Copywriter
Ruan Milborrow
Art Directors
Ruan Milborrow
Mark Nightingale

Illustrator
Mark Nightingale
Creative Director
Ruan Milborrow

Advertising Agency
mr.h
Account Handler
Carmela Care

Marketing Manager
Mary Richards
Client
Harvey Nichols

Graphic Design
mr.h
for Harvey Nichols

Celebrity Postcards Boys/Girls
The brief was to produce a set of witty postcards that could be sold for under £5 in each
of the Harvey Nichols food markets. Ideally, they were to feature products and focus on the
exclusivity of the stores. We produced two sets: one for boys, and one for girls. They are
now on their second reprint.

Copywriter Molly Mackey **Designers** Kev Lee Matt Maurer	**Creative Directors** Ady Bibby Rob Mitchell	**Writing Agency** The Writer **Design Agency** True North	**Communications Director** Alison Lucas **Client** The Climate Group

Graphic Design

The Writer
for The Climate Group

The World Doesn't Need the Climate Group Anymore
You're talking to important, busy people. You want them to read about something they're bored of hearing. And you can't waste paper – it'd be hypocritical. How do you do it? Here's our brochure for The Climate Group. The words are bold. Unequivocal. Not the usual corporate sustainability blah. And because The Climate Group is positive about the future, that's where it's set. No doom-mongering. Instead, a picture of a future where The Climate Group has done its job and packed up. The design is just as confident. Crisp. Black. White. And not a picture of parched deserts or anxious children in sight.

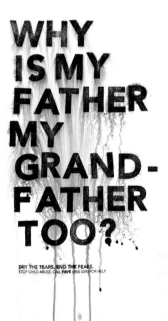

Copywriter	Designers	Creative Director	Photography Studio
Eugene Tan	Pann Lim	Pann Lim	Visualmind
Art Directors	Gen Tan	**Advertising Agency**	**Client**
Pann Lim	**Photographer**	Kinetic Singapore	PAVE
Gen Tan	John Nursalim		

Graphic Design

Kinetic Singapore
for PAVE

Angry Hands / Cuddles / Father & Grandfather
PAVE is an organisation that aims to raise awareness about the dangers and suffering children bear when they are victims of domestic violence. These posters were put up in schools, community clubs, public libraries and poor neighbourhoods. Each message reflects the vulnerability of children, their sadness and pain, echoing their voices and exposing the cruelty child abuse victims suffer. The flowing nature of weeping words speaks of the tears shed and innocence lost in child abuse victims.

571

Clerks. Princes. Jesters. Executioners. And assassins. Alchemists. Scientists. Cowboys. Machinists. Magicians. Doctors. Aeronautical engineers. Hippies. An astronaut. Swindlers. Lawyers specialised in customs law. Two provincial delegates. And a secretary who was in love with her female workmate. And all of them are transformed into these images, so real while at the same time, fictitious, that only an experienced, age-old mirror is able to give away.

Everything has a story to tell.
David Puente. Antigüedades.

Nobody knew how much he wanted to become mortal. To hold the hope that one day it would all come to an end. And on that day, he would fold up his arms and rest. Nobody knew how much he longed to change from being that magnificent 15th century chair.

Everything has a story to tell.
David Puente. Antigüedades.

I was a clock. At the beginning my job was to tell people what time it was. To unequivocally define the present, as expressed in mathematical hours and millimetric seconds. Interestingly enough, with the passing of time, now I do exactly the opposite. I silently scream 'I belong to the past'. And my hands rest in peace. Elegant and distinguished. As they always were. As they always will be.

Everything has a story to tell.
David Puente. Antigüedades.

It touched her lips, almost sickly sweet and always unforgettable, for the last time 273 years ago. That woman who held complete possession over it disappeared forever, without saying goodbye, without lying or ever looking back. And since then, that glass could only do one thing: wonder why.

Everything has a story to tell.
David Puente. Antigüedades.

Copywriter
Sebastián Cangiano
Art Director
Ismael Medina

Creative Directors
Sebastián Cangiano
Ismael Medina

Design Group
Virgen Extra

Client
David Puente
Antigüedades

Graphic Design
Virgen Extra
for David Puente Antigüedades

Mirror / Chair / Clock / Glass
David Puente Antigüedades is an eclectic and modern antique store, offering everything from furniture of the 14th Century to the most refined pieces of the 20th Century. We were asked to create a series of posters to convey the idea that the furniture is much more than just old tables and chairs. While walking through the store we realised that we weren't only looking at beautiful mirrors and chairs, but also at hundreds of years of stories just waiting to be written. Each poster tells the personal story of an antique mirror, chair, clock and glass. The copy was written as if the pieces were telling their own memories and experiences.

Copywriter
Jim Davies
Designers
Simon Morrow
Richard Scholey

Illustrator
Robert Ball
Creative Director
Richard Scholey

Copywriting Studio
totalcontent
Design Group
Elmwood

Client
totalcontent

Graphic Design

Jim Davies
for totalcontent

Typewriting Monkeys
These are promotional direct mail posters for copywriting studio totalcontent. The idea is based on the 'infinite monkey theorem' which suggests that, given an infinite amount of time, a monkey tapping at a typewriter would eventually come up with the complete works of Shakespeare. Clearly, these particular chimps were working to a much shorter deadline.

573

LETTERHEAD: 5.130664g

ADD 0.0040023g AT THE NORTH OR SOUTH POLE / SUBTRACT 0.0300021g EVERY 1cm ABOVE SEA LEVEL

123 Science Supplies Co
3 Sample Avenue
Sampletown
SE13 6DF

ENVELOPE: 4.1111545g

INCLUDES STAMP: 0.0629382g AND SALIVA MOLECULES ON STAMP: 0.0159818g

COMPLIMENT SLIP: 1.710223g

GIVE OR TAKE, DEPENDING ON HUMIDITY, AIR PRESSURE AND POSITION OF THE SUN AND MOON

KERN & SOHN GMBH, Ziegelei 1, 72336 Balingen-Frommern • Postf: 40 52, 72322 Balingen
Tel: +49-(0)7433-9933-0 • Fax: +49-(0)7433-9933-149 • Email: info@kern-sohn.com • Web: www.kern-sohn.com

BUSINESS CARD: 1.4039476g

CARD: 1.3403840g, INK: 0.0635636g, EACH FINGERPRINT: 0.0000407g

KERN & SOHN GMBH, Ziegelei 1, 72336 Balingen-Frommern • Postf: 40 52, 72322 Balingen
Tel: +49-(0)7433-9933-0 • Fax: +49-(0)7433-9933-149 • Email: info@kern-sohn.com • Web: www.kern-sohn.com

Albert Sauter
Managing Director
+49-(0)7433-9933-0
albert.sauter@kern-sohn.de
www.kern-sohn.com

Copywriter	Typographer	Advertising Agency	Client Managing
James Nester	Kevan Ansell	Wunderman London	Director
Art Director	**Executive Creative**	**Client Marketing**	Albert Sauter
Chris Lawson	**Director**	**Director**	**Client**
	David Harris	Thomas Fimpel	Kern

Graphic Design

Wunderman London
for Kern

Precision Weighed Stationery
Kern distributes some of the most accurate scales in the world to scientists, engineers and pharmacists. But how can you demonstrate such exceptional precision with a lightweight budget? Our solution was a suite of stationery that tells you its own exact weight, as recorded by Kern scientists. Precisely crafted copy reveals (in obsessive scientific detail) the weight of each element – from the letterhead to the very ink on the business card. To emphasise just how precise these results are, the copy even details the infinitesimal factors that would influence the items' weight: altitude, humidity, air pressure, even the position of the sun and moon.

574

You think I wanted this?
One colour? A3? Come on.
We both know I could have
been so much more. I could
have really stretched myself.
B1, maybe. Well, why not?
Slipping me through that
big old Komori. Oooh.
Gives me shivers.

Show me someone who knows
how to treat a piece of paper.

APG Visual Colour.
(01925 831 678)
The Creative Printers.

Look, I'm not one to complain.
Really. It's fine. Ordinary litho job:
bish bash bosh. Whatever, right?
I just can't help wishing I'd tried
a few more things. Like letterpress.
That must be lovely: all those hot
little characters tight up against you.
Or digital – zipping through those
machines like there's no tomorrow.
Bet it leaves you breathless.

Oh, what could have been…

APG Visual Colour.
(01925 831 678)
The Creative Printers.

**Oh, just shoot me. Please.
I'm so dull I even bore myself.
One colour. A2. Portrait. Wow.
I mean, why even bother? All those
possibilities – wasted! Foil blocking,
varnishes, special inks? Hello?
Even this stock makes me yawn:
white? Come on. I could at least
have been embossed. Instead I'm
just depressed.**

**There's no hope for me.
But why should others suffer?**

**APG Visual Colour.
(01925 831 678)
The Creative Printers.**

You know what this is like?
It's like being shoved on stage
without your tutu. I feel naked
up here, guys. Come on, how
about a few more colours at least?
Even two would help. But what
about six? Six would be nice.
Why not six?

All I want to be is noticed.

APG Visual Colour.
(01925 831 678)
The Creative Printers.

Rectangle? Rectangle?
Give me a break. Talk
about untapped potential.
How about some die-cutting?
Is that so hard? I could
be any shape you like.
Or bind me into a book –
there's a thought. Bit
of precision drilling?
Stab-stitching? Scoring?
Creasing? Perfing?

Come on!
It's not rocket science.

APG Visual Colour.
(01925 831 678)
The Creative Printers.

Copywriter	Designer	Creative Director	Client
Mike Reed	Matt Maurer	Ady Bibby	APG Visual Colour
	Typographer	**Design Group**	
	Matt Maurer	True North	

Graphic Design

True North
for APG Visual Colour

APG Visual Colour Posters
APG Visual Colour positions itself as 'the creatives' printer', with a well-deserved reputation for expertise, great work and great service. When competing for new business, a recent trend within the print community has been to produce high spec mailers to inspire creatives and show off every print technique and finishing available – from six colours to foils and die-cuts. APG Visual Colour came to True North with a sense that it should be joining in. Our response, perhaps not surprisingly, was that maybe the company could get its message across in a more innovative and engaging way… going back to basics, you could say.

575

Author
Neil Gaiman

Designer
Dave McKean
Illustrator
Dave McKean

Design Manager
Alastair Pether
Editorial Manager
Helen Cumberbatch

Design Manager
Alastair Pether
Editorial Manager
Helen Cumberbatch

**Head of Design
& Editorial**
Marcus James
Client
Royal Mail Group

Graphic Design

Neil Gaiman
for the Royal Mail Group

Mythical Creatures Presentation Pack
Fantasy author Neil Gaiman was specially commissioned to create six original short pieces to accompany Dave McKean's illustrations. As a prolific creator of works of prose, poetry and drama in the genres of fantasy and science-fiction, Gaiman is a prestigious choice as author for the pack. He was limited to 900 words, as one side features a full illustration. We gave him two choices: to write fact-based narratives featuring the six fabulous creatures (dragon, unicorn, giant, pixie, mermaid and fairy); or to pen six mini-stories featuring each creature. In the event he opted to write six short stories with a combined word count of approximately 870.

Index

Index

Index

D&AD Members

D&AD Members
Gareth Abbit, Head of Design
David Abbott, Copywriter
Anthony Abdool, Copywriter
Alan Aboud, Creative Director
Marksteen Adamson, Design Director
Craig Addy, Art Director
Sonny Adorjan, Art Director
Alan Ainsley, Design Director
Jules Akel, Designer
Roger Akerman, Art Director
Hideo Akiba
Roger Akroyd
David Alexander, Creative Partner
James Alexander, Design Director
Rob Alexander, Planning Partner
Vassilios Alexiou
Charles Allan, Creative Director
Matt Allen, Senior Art Director
Hamish Allison, Creative Director
Nick Allsop, Art Director
Christian Altmann, Senior Graphic Designer
Ethan Ames, Director of Studies, Motion Graphics
Silas Amos, Designer
Bob Anderson, Creative Director
Matthew Anderson, Art Director
Magnus Andersson, Creative Director/Managing Director
Nils Andersson, Group Executive Creative Director
Jason Andrews, Creative Partner
Rob Andrews, Designer
Simon Andrews, Designer
Nick Angell, Managing Director/Sound Engineer
Rudi Anggono, Senior Art Director
Paul Angus, Art Director
Simon Antenen, Creative Director
Paul Anthony, Designer
Ranzie Anthony, Creative Director
John Paul Apol Sta Maria
Ferdinand Aragon, Global Vice President
Kensui Arao, Executive Creative Director
Jim Archer, Creative Director
Neil Archer, Typographic Designer
Chris Arnold, Executive Creative Director
Rosie Arnold, Deputy Executive Creative Director
Jyotish Arvindakshan, Associate Creative Director
Nick Asbury, Writer
Tim Ashton, Creative Director
Sofia Asif, Creative Producer
Gary Aston, Head of Creative
Marc Atkinson, Creative Director
Will Awdry, Managing Director
Paul Ayre, Art Director
David Azurdia, Designer
Jason Badrock, Creative Director/Designer
Patrick Baglee, Director of Creative Strategy
Darren Bailes, Creative Director
Cat Bailey, Designer
Peter Bailey, Illustrator
Julie-Anne Bailie, Executive Creative Director
Paul Baker, Design Model Maker
Jan Baldwin, Photographer
Robert Ball, Design Director
Feargal Ballance, Art Director
Leighton Ballett, Copywriter
Chris Bardsley, Copywriter
Larry Barker, Copywriter
Fiona Barlow, Design Partner
Will Barnett, Creative Director
Jeremy Baron, Creative Director
Dave Barraclough, Design Director
Philipp Barth, Creative Director
Andy Barwood, Creative Director
Will Bate, Art Director
Shaun Bateman, Senior Copywriter
Algy Batten

Richard Baynham, Creative Director
Toygar Bazarkaya, Chief Creative Director
David Beard, Creative Director
Matt Beardsell, Production Director
David Beare, Design Director
Luke Beauchamp, Producer
Alex Bec, Designer
Florian Beck, Creative Director
Ian Beck, Illustrator
Dave Bedwood, Creative Partner
Gareth Beeson, Designer
Melonie Beeson, Director
Paul Belford, Creative Director
Andrew Bell, Creative Director
David Bell, Creative Director
Nick Bell, Designer
Stephen Bell, Creative Director
Zoë Bell, Head of TV
Madeleine Bennett, Designer
Marc Bennett, Creative Director
Simon Bere, Head Copywriter
Bruce Beresford, Creative Director
Adrian Berry, Creative Director
Giles Bestley, Designer
Victoria Beswick, Design Director
Gary Betts, Executive Creative Director
James Beveridge, Creative Director/Managing Partner
Ady Bibby, Creative Director
Coralie Bickford-Smith, Senior Designer
Kim Biggs, Creative Partner
Phil Bignell, New Media Consultant
Anthony Biles, Creative Director
William Bingham, Art Director/Copywriter
Graham Birch, Designer
Kevin Bird, Creative Director
Nick Bird, Copywriter
Fraser Black, Managing Director
Garry Blackburn, Creative Director
John Blackburn, Executive Creative Director
Joshua Blackburn, Managing Director
Paul Blackburn, Creative Director
John Blackwell, Designer
Stephen Bland
Stephen Blanks, Creative Director
Stephen Blenheim, Design Director
Sue Blitz, Head of Copy
Charlie Blower, Managing Director
Laurence Blume, Managing Director
Tony Blurton, Creative Director
Terence Bly, Copywriter
Helen Board, Art Director
Martin Boase, Former Chairman
Louis Bogue, Art Director
Mike Boles, Deputy Creative Director
Andy Bolter, Creative Director
Jim Bolton, Creative Director
Jane Bolton, Producer
Franco Bonadio, Creative Director
Mike Bond, Art Director
Mark Bonner, Director/Creative Director
Neil Boote, Digital Designer
Andy Booth
Allen Boothroyd, Managing Director
Emma Booty, Branding Director
Stephen Boswell, Creative Group Head
Cat Botibol, Creative Director
Mark Bottomley, Design Director
Shaun Bowen, Creative Partner
Darren Bowles, Design Director
Damian Bradfield, Client Service Director
Chris Bradley, Design Partner
Joel Bradley, Copywriter
Dave Brady, Head of Design
Barry Brand, Head of Art
Mike Brandt, Art Director
Catherine Brandy, Design Manager
Tim Braybrooks, Creative Director

Paul Brazier, Executive Creative Director
Paul Bretherton, Creative Director
Richard Brett, Design Director
Lise Brian, Associate Director
Amalia Brightley-Hodges
Paul Briginshaw, Creative Director
Tony Brignull, Copywriter
Adam Brinkworth, Designer/Managing Director
Curtis Brittles, Copywriter
Carl Broadhurst
Andy Brockie, Graphic Designer
Tony Brook, Creative Director
Danny Brooke-Taylor, Creative Director
Mike Brooking, Copywriter
Sheila Broom, Graphic Designer
Simon Brotherson, Creative Director
Newy Brothwell, Art Director
Warren Brown, Executive Creative Director
Tim Brown, Director
Craig Brown, Educational Technologist
Dave Brown, Chairman
Mark Brown
Stuart Brown, Art Director
Matthew Brown, Joint Managing Director
Rik Brown, Art Director
Sarah Brownrigg, Senior Copywriter
Bill Bruce, Chairman/Chief Creative Officer
Daniel Bruce
Uwe Brueckner, Creative Director
Richard Bryant, Architectural Photographer
Andy Buchan
Dave Buchanan, Copywriter
Peter Buck, Creative Director
Matt Buckhurst, Creative Director
Mark Buckingham, Creative Director
Frank Budgen, Director
Matt Buels, Managing Director
James Bull, Creative Director
Matthew Bull, Chief Creative Officer
Sheila Bull, Copywriter
Vicky Bullen, Chief Executive Officer
Martyn Bullock, Managing Director
Andy Bunday, Art Director
Samantha Burges, Account Manager
Johnnie Burn, Director/Sound Engineer
Colin Burns, Principal
Max Burt, Planning Director
Adrian Burton, Executive Creative Director
Liam Butler, Copywriter
Sarah Butler, Deputy Creative Director
Joel Butt, Interactive Designer
Dominic Buttimore, Executive Producer
Ian Buttle, Creative Director
Adrian Caddy, Managing Director
Brian Cairns, Illustrator
Mark Cakebread
Aziz Cami, Creative Director
Lucian Camp, Chairman/Executive Creative Director
Alister Campbell, TV Producer
Brian Campbell, Art Director
Michael Campbell, Creative Director
Milo Campbell, Writer
Wolf Peter Camphausen, Chief Creative Officer
Jon Canning, Creative Director
Simon Carbery, Creative Director
Paul Cardwell, Creative Director
Tom Carey, Designer
Stephen Carlin, Art Director
Richard Carman, Senior Copywriter

Alison Carmichael, Hand Lettering Artist
Fiona Carpenter, Art Director
Jeremy Carr, Creative Partner
David Carroll
Cameron Carruthers, Creative Director
Scott Carslake, Director
Mareka Carter, Art Director
Peers Carter, Creative Independent
Philip Carter, Creative Director
Sam Cartmell, Creative Partner
Luiz Fernando Carvalho
Ben Casey, Executive Creative Director
Dinah Casson
Martin Casson
Sasha Castling, Director
Ian Caulder, Creative Director
Michael Cavers, Executive Creative Director
Eduard Cehovin, Creative Director
Tony Chambers, Editor in Chief
Theseus Chan, Creative Director
Andrew Chappin, Art Director
Kellie Chapple, Client Services Director
Martin Charvat, Creative Director
Tej Chauhan, Designer
Andy Cheetham, Creative Director
Ed Cheong
Steve Chetham, Creative Director
Adam Chiappe, Art Director
Terry Childs, Creative Director
Peter Chodel, Creative Director
Sandy Choi, Design Director
Ben Christie, Designer
René Christoffer, Creative Director
Natalie Chung, Creative Director
Chris Church, Design Director
Paul Cilia La Corte, Senior Designer
Ben Clapp, Creative Director
John Claridge, Photographer
Bryan Clark, Level 2 Coordinator Graphic Design
Edmund Clark, Photographer
Nick Clark, Creative Director
Andrew Clarke, Executive Creative Director
Chris Clarke, Chief Creative Officer
Eoghain Clarke, Art Director
Neil Clarke, Copywriter
Phillip Clarke, Head of Interactive
Steve Clarke, Art Director
Steve Clay, Executive Creative Director
Kirsten Clayton, Business Director
Phil Cleaver, Creative Director
Nick Clements, Managing Partner
Anthony Cliff, Art Director
Sarah Clift, Creative
Tom Climpson, Art Director/Designer
Stephen Coates, Art Director
Barney Cockerell, Creative Director
Jonathan Coles, Head of Design
Peter Coles
Benjamin Collier, Art Director
Lucy Collier, Art Director
Damon Collins, Executive Creative Director
Barny Collis
Patrick Collister, Copywriter
Kevin Colquhoun, Art Director
John Commander
Denise Connell, TV Director
Jayne Connell, Design Director
Conor Connolly
Richard Connor, Art Director
Sebastian Conran, Design Director
Philip Contomichalos, Producer
Graeme Cook, Copywriter
Neil Cook, Lead Creative
Gary Cooke, Executive Creative Director
Gene Cooke, Designer
Brian Cooper, Creative Director
Roger Cooper
Steve Cope, Director

Michele Corcoran, Awards Manager
Dan Cornell, Creative Director
Lieve Cornil, Lettering Artist
Michael Coulter, Creative Director
Michael Courthold, Art Director
Jason Coward, Managing Director
Richard Coward, Director
Dulcie Cowling, Designer
Barry Cox, Director
Darren Cox, Designer
Neil Craddock, Head of Design
Jeremy Craigen, Executive Creative Director
Juan Cravero, Vice President/General Creative Director
Tom Crew, Creative Director
Chad Cribbins, Manager Information Architect
Mark Cridge, Chief Executive
Matthew Cridland, Creative Director
Martin Crockatt, Typographer
Lisa Cromer, Design Director
Stuart Cronin, Creative Director
John Cross, Copywriter
Mike Crowe, Writer
Charlotte Crumbleholme
Helen Cumberbatch, Editorial Manager
Karen Cunningham, Producer
Fiona Curran, Design Director
Alan Curson, Copywriter
Gavin Cutler, Editor
Robert D'Souza, Copywriter
Chris Dacyshyn, Senior Copywriter
Graham Daldry, Creative Director
Philippa Dale, Animation Director
Pip Dale, Deputy Creative Director
André Dammers, Copywriter
Senje Darbar, Art Director
Michael Darby, Designer
Matthew Darcy Hunt, Creative Director
Nicholas Darken, Executive Creative Director
Peter Darrell, Film Director
Ashted Dastor, Creative Director
John Davenport, Creative Director
Ian David, Writer
Andrew Davidson, Illustrator
Tony Davidson, Executive Creative Director
Gill Davies, Design Director
Justin Davies, Design Director
Pete Davies, Art Director
Steve Davies, Design Director
Steve Davies, Head of Design
Tivy Davies, Typographer
Jonathan Davis, Creative Director
Paul Davis, Creative Director
Peter Davis, Creative Director
Brendan Dawes, Creative Director
Claire Dawson, Art Director
Gary Dawson, Creative Group Head
Neil Dawson, Global Creative Director
Nigel Dawson, Creative Director
Nigel Dawson, Designer/Typographer
Andrew Day, Associate Creative Director
Derek Day, Executive Creative Director
James Day, Photographer
Gabriel De Abreu, Group Creative Director
Emma de la Fosse, Creative Partner
Thiago de Moraes, Digital Creative Director
John De Vries, Art Director
Ian Dean, Graphic Designer
Eduardo Del Fraile
Gregory Delaney, Chairman
Paul Delaney, Creative Director
Theo Delaney, Film Director
Tim Delaney, Group Chairman
Alan Delgado, Group Creative Head

Alessandro Demicheli
Mike Dempsey, Managing Director
James Denley, Copywriter
Richard Denney, Creative Director
Michael Denny, Director
Jonathan Dent, Designer
Mark Denton, Creative Director
Lisa Desforges, Copywriter
Tracy DeShiro, Awards Show Coordinator
Marion Deuchars, Illustrator
Simon Devine, Head of TV
Darryn Devlin, Creative Director
Martin Devlin, Creative Director
Stewart Devlin, Design Creative Director
Harriet Devoy, Creative Director
Shaun Dew, Creative Director
Sarah Dezille, Designer
Israel Diaz, Senior Vice President/Managing Partner/Creative Director
Mark Dibsdall, Account Manager
Lin Dickens, Managing Director
Mark Dickens, Art Director
Simon Dicketts, Executive Creative Director
Steward Dickinson, Creative Director
Kirsten Dietz, Managing Director/Creative Director
Rachael Dinnis, Director
Jon Dobinson, Copywriter
Keith Dodds, Designer
Patricia Doherty, Creative Director
Matt Doman, Creative Director
Marc Donaldson, Typographer
Liam Donnelly, Copywriter
Christine Donnier-Valentin, Photographer
Richard Donovan, Art Director
Elke Dossler, Design Director
Julian Douglas
John Dowling, Designer
Nick Downes, Art Director
Chris Doyle, Creative Director
Till Dreier, Head of TV
Bruce Duckworth, Creative Director
Malcolm Duffy, Creative Director
Belinda Duggan, Creative Director/Head of Account Management
Luke Duggan, Creative Director
Gert Dumbar, Creative Director
Rob Duncan, Art Director
Seb Duncan, Senior Art Director
Dick Dunford, Art Director
Iain Dunn, Writer
Marie-Catherine Dupuy, Chief Creative Officer/Vice Chairman
Michael Durban, Art Director
Helen Durham, Publications Manager
Nick Dutton, Account Director
Sonya Dyakova, Associate Art Director
Alan Dye, Creative Director
Dave Dye, Creative Director
Brian Eagle, Creative Director
Nick Eagleton, Creative Director
Hugo Eccles, Managing Director/Creative Director
Paul Edison, Executive Creative Director
Bryan Edmondson, Design Director
Gerard Edmondson, Creative Partner
Dominic Edmunds, Art Director
Andrew Edwards, Group Chief Executive
Ed Edwards, Creative Director
Garnet Edwards, Creative Director
Janet Edwards, Design Director
Steve Edwards, Creative Partner
Steve Eichenbaum, President/Creative Director
Jonathan Ellery
Simon Elliott, Creative Director
Adam Ellis, Design Director
Jamie Ellul, Designer
Simon Elms, Composer
Jon Elsom, Creative Director

Mark Elwood, Head of Art & Design
Ken Erke, Chief Creative Officer
Joseph Ernst, Art Director
Simon Esterson
Michael Evamy, Writer
Phil Evans, Copywriter
Richard Evans, Art Director
Michael Everett, Copywriter
Christoph Everke, Creative Director
Tom Ewart, Executive Creative Director
Markus Ewertz, Associate Creative Director
Anton Ezer, Creative Director
Mark Fairbanks, Creative
Corinna Falusi, Creative Director
Guy Farrow, Photographer
Mark Farrow, Creative Director
Nick Farrow, Managing Director
Gary Fawcett, Joint Head Creative Director
Sara Fearnley, Managing Director
Guy Featherstone, Senior Designer
Lisa Fedyszyn, Creative
Tim Fellowes, Designer
Chris Felstead, Art Director
Tim Fendley, Consultant Creative Director
Georgia Fendley, Managing Director
Verity Fenner, Art Director/ Copywriter
Dave Ferrer, Executive Creative Director
Joe Ferry, Head of Design
Mark Fiddes, Executive Creative Director
Sandy Field, Graphic Designer
Paul Fielding, Managing Director
Paul Filby, Interactive Copywriter
Graham Fink, Executive Creative Director
Kevin Finn, Director
Nick Finney, Creative Director
Christian Finucane, Creative Partner
Rodney Fitch, Chairman/Chief Executive
Fred Flade
Rob Fletcher, Creative Partner
Alex Flint, Creative
Richard Flintham, Executive Creative Director
Alan Flude, Creative Director
Suzanne Foerch, Group Head of Art
Brett Foraker, Network Creative Director
Dean Ford, Creative Director
Jonathan Ford, Creative Partner
Wayne Ford, Design Director
Chris Forman, Consultant
Jon Forss, Creative Director
John Foster, Art Director
Louise Fowler, Design Skills Senior Manager
Fiona Fox, Designer
Joseph Fraine, Copywriter
Lennart Frank, Copywriter
Simon Frank
Stephen Franks, Director
Brian Fraser, Joint Executive Creative Director
Paul Fraser, Copywriter
Susanna Freedman, Managing Director
Piero Frescobaldi, Managing Director/Creative Director
Fabian Frese, Creative Director
Mark Fretton, Senior Copywriter
Heiko Freyland, Creative Director
Vince Frost, Creative Director/Chief Executive Officer
James Fryer, Copywriter
David Fudger, Development Manager
Vikram Gaikwad, Executive Creative Director
Bill Gallacher, Deputy Creative Director

Martin Galton, Creative Partner
Alexandre Gama, President/ Creative Director
David Gamble, Art Director
Steve Gandolfi, Editor
Leigh Garland, Senior Interactive Developer
Surrey Garland, Head of Copy
Robin Garms, Interactive Creative Director
Jeremy Garner, Creative Director
Malcolm Garrett, Creative Director
Paul Garrett, Creative Director
Peter Gatley, Art Director
Nicholas Gawith, Associate Creative Director
Matt Gee, Executive Producer
Kim Gehrig, Creative Director
Michael Geoghegan, Creative Director
Phil Gerard, Director
Dan Germain, Head of Creative
Jan Geschke, Chief Creative Officer
Aftab Gharda, Deputy Head of Visual Communications
Holger Giffhorn, Designer
Colin Gifford, Director
Luke Gifford, Graphic Designer
Matthew Gilbert
Adam Giles, Designer
Kevin Gill
Nick Gill, Executive Creative Director
Gavin Gillespie, Executive Producer
Barry Gillibrand, Creative Director
Dexter Ginn, Creative Director
Marco Giusti, Vice President Programming & Marketing
Amanda Glasgow, Art Director
Joe Glasman, Composer
Felix Glauner, Chief Creative Officer
Gillian Glendinning, Creative Director
Simon Glover
David Godfree, Creative Director
Jonathan Goldstein, Composer
Adrian Goldthorpe, Vice President Strategy & Innovation
Rennie Gomes, Managing Director/ Composer/Sound Designer
Colin Goodhew, Graphic Designer
Jason Goodman, Managing Director
Franki Goodwin, Creative Director
Mark Goodwin, Deputy Creative Director
Gavin Gordon-Rogers, Creative Director
Michael Gore, Creative Director
Andrew Gorman, Creative Director
David Goss
Laura Gould, Head of TV Production
Marko Govorusa, Art Director/ Designer
Peter Graabaek, Creative Director
Alasdair Graham, Creative Partner
John Graham, Managing Director
Bruce Gray, Treasurer
Jonathan Gray, Designer
Nigel Gray, Creative Director
Malcolm Green, Creative Director
Stephen Greenberg, Creative Director
Paul Greeno, Art Director
Mark Greenwood, Art Creative Group Head
Peter Greenwood, Design Director
Shane Greeves, Executive Creative Director
Laura Gregory, Executive Producer
Richard Gregory, Graphic Designer
Andrew Griffin
Michael Griffin, Producer
Dylan Griffith, Creative Director
Sam Griffiths, Senior Designer
Martin Grimer, Executive Creative Director
Chris Groom, Art Director

Stephen Grounds, Executive Creative Director
Paul Grubb, Regional Executive Creative Director
Peter Grundy
David Guerrero, Chief Creative Officer/Chairman
Markus Gut, Chief Creative Officer
Zlatko Haban, Architect/Designer
Dennis Hackett, Editor
John Hadfield, Managing Director
Roland Hafenrichter, Executive Creative Director
Karen Hagemann, Art Director
Richard Hague, Copywriter
Jeremy Haines, Creative Partner
Tim Hales, Creative Director
Alistair Hall, Graphic Designer
Graeme Hall, Copywriter
Robin Hall, Creative Director
Simon Hall, Art Director
Clem Halpin, Designer
Geoff Halpin, Creative Director
Vivienne Hamilton, Creative Director
Warren Hamilton, Director/Sound Engineer
Damian Hamilton, Director/ Designer
Garrick Hamm, Creative Director
Jiaying Han, Design Director
Paul Hancock, Creative Director
Albert Handler, Innovation Director
Martin Handyside, Project Management Consultant
Harry Handyside, Designer
Sascha Hanke, Creative Director
Mike Hannett, Art Director
Maria Hanson, Designer
Mark Hanson, Art Director
Nicholas Hanson, Creative Director
Deborah Hanusa, Creative Director
Morihiro Harano, Creative Director
Matthias Harbeck, Executive Creative Director
Tony Hardcastle, Art Director
George Hardie, Designer/Illustrator
Ian Harding, Creative Director
Stuart Harkness
Carolyn Harlow, Creative Director
Liz Harold, Career Consultant
Peter Harold
Mark Harper, Creative Director
Julian Harriman-Dickinson, Creative Director
David Harris, Executive Creative Director
Elliot Harris, Creative Director
John Harris, Creative Partner
Tony Harris, Creative Director
David Harrison, Copywriter/Art Director
Adrian Harrison, Managing Director
Barbara Harrison
Dylan Harrison, Executive Creative Director
Glenn Harrison, Creative Director
Iain Harrison, Head of Copy
Jerry Harrison, Creative Director
Richard Hart, Design Director
Kim Hartley, Creative Director
Kiki Hartmann, Creative Director
Neil Harvey, Creative Director
Mark Harwood, Photographer
Laurence Haskell, Photographer
Ludwig Haskins, Owner
Lionel Hatch, Creative Director
Joachim Hauser, Creative Director
Ian Haworth, Global Chief Creative Officer
Antonia Hayward, Design Director
Richard Haywood, Packaging Designer
Jane Healy, Director
Ian Heartfield, Copywriter
Sam Heath, Copywriter/Art Director
Ted Heath, Copywriter
Paul Heaton, Creative Director
Tony Hector, Creative Director

Neil Hedger, Graphic Designer
Guido Heffels, Executive Creative Director
John Hegarty, Chairman/Worldwide Creative Director
Mat Heinl
Flo Heiss, Creative Partner
Bo Hellberg, Executive Creative Director
David Helps, Board Creative Director
Dave Henderson, Creative Director
Cathy Heng, Art Director
Norbert Herold, Executive Creative Director
Alexandre Hervé, Executive Creative Director
Margie Hetherington, Designer
Ralf Heuel, Executive Creative Director
Till Heumann, Designer
Chris Heyes, Designer
Peter Heyes, Writer/Art Director
Clare Hieatt, Senior Copywriter
Peter Higgins, Director
Sue Higgs, Senior Copywriter
Kevin Hill, Creative Director
Paul Hillery, Studio Manager
Robert Hillier, Designer
James Hilton, Creative Director/Managing Director
Nik Hindson, Film Editor
Adam Hinton, Photographer
Matt Hines, Campaigns Team Leader, Fire & Resilience
Melissa Hinves, Design Director
Neil Hirst, Creative Director
Paul Hiscock, Designer
David Hobbs, Senior Art Director
Jamie Hobson, Head of Marketing & Administrations
Nicholas Hockley, Designer
Anthony Hodgson, Art Director
Gary Hoff, Creative Director
David Hofmann, Creative Director
Paul Hogarth, Creative Director
Ken Hoggins, Creative Director
Michael Hoinkes, Creative Director
Jesse Holborn, Creative Director
Phil Holbrook, Art Director
Ruth Holden, Creative Director
Roger Holdsworth, Copywriter
Ton Hollander, Creative Director
Jerry Hollens, Creative Partner
Jon Hollis, Flame Artist/Director
Richard Holman
Adrian Holmes, Executive Creative Director
David Holmes, Designer/Art Director
Lucy Holmes, Creative Director
Gary Holt
Richard Holt, Senior Designer
Christos Hooper, Art Director
Iain Hope, Graphic Designer
Roger Horberry, Copywriter
Johnny Hornby
Andrew Horner, Director of Photography
Michael Horseman, Managing Director
Bonnie Horton, Creative
Charlotte Horton, Creative
Greg Horton, Creative Director
Mark Hosker, Design Director
Tom Hostler
Keren House, Creative Director
Steve House, Senior Designer
Jonathan Howard, Lighting Designer
Mark Howard, Creative Director
Gareth Howat, Creative Director
Gareth Howells, Creative Partner
Phil Howells, Creative Director
Rob Howsam, Creative Director
Adam Hoyle, Interactive Designer
Kai-Lu Hsiung, Producer
Tom Hudson, Assistant Creative Director
Will Hudson, Designer
Ringo Hui, Design Director

Gerry Human, Worldwide Executive Creative Director
Colin Hume, Managing Director
Barrie Hunt, Creative Director
Danny Hunt, Art Director
Patrick Hunt, Creative Director
Simon Hunt, Creative Director
Barry Hunter, Writer
Mark Hunter, Executive Creative Director
Natalie Hunter, Creative Director
Jon Hunter, Head of Design
Gavin Hurrell, Designer
Mark Hurst, Art Director
Mike Hurst, Director of Sky Creative
Dingus Hussey, Graphic Designer
Iain Hutchinson, Deputy Creative Director
Craig Hutton, Design Director
Kelly Hyatt, Creative Director
Charles Inge, Creative Partner
Daniel Ingham
Angela Inglis, Creative Director
Richard Irvine, Managing Director/Executive Creative Director
Richard Irvine, Managing Director
Richard Irvine, Executive Creative Director
David Isaac, Creative Director
Takashi Ishizu, Director
Jonathan Ive, Senior Vice President Industrial Design
Noriko Iwamoto, Curator/Librarian
Frances Jackson
Tania Jackson
Alexander Jaggy, Creative Director/ Managing Director
Marcus James, Head of Design & Editorial
Rob Janowski
John C Jay, Executive Creative Director
Victoria Jebens, Director
Adrian Jeffery, Creative Director
David Jeffery, Creative Director
David Jenkins, Designer
Nina Jenkins, Independent Branding Designer
Paul Jenkins, Creative Director
Dave Jenner, Art Director
Dave Jennings, Copywriter
Asbjorn Jensen, Designer
Andy Jex, Creative Director
Armin Jochum, Chief Creative Officer
Simon John, Managing Partner
Michael Johnson, Creative Director
Neil Johnson, Chief Creative Officer
Steven Johnson, Creative Director
Derek Johnston, Creative Director
Colin Jones, Art Director
David Jones, Creative Director
David Jones, Creative Partner
Gareth Jones
Michael Jones
Nick Jones, Creative Director
Penny Jones, Designer
Sarah Jones, Design Manager
Steve Jones, Art Director
Yann Jones, Art Director/Copywriter
Rupert David Jordan, Copywriter
James Joyce, Graphic Designer/Illustrator
Annabel Judd, Head of Design
Hellena Jun, Creative Director
Satoshi Kambayashi, Illustrator
Jon Kamen, Chairman/Chief Executive Officer
Jiri Karasek, Designer
Amir Kassaei, Chief Creative Officer
Diti Katona
Willy Kaussen, Creative Director
Seijo Kawaguchi, Art Director
Gareth Kay, Director of Account Planning
Matthew Kay

Adam Kean, Executive Creative Director
Nik Keane, Global Brand Director
Giles Keeble, Creative Director
Tris Keech, Product Designer
Jamie Keenan, Designer
Amelie Keller, Director/Creative Director
John Kelley, Creative Director
Steve Kelsey, Director
Steve Kelynack, Creative Director
Carol Kemp, Lettering Designer
Paul Kemp-Robertson, Editor
Adrian Kemsley, Creative Director
Malcolm Kennard, Design Director
Roger P Kennedy, TV Graphic Designer
Iain Kennedy, Global Category Director
Roger Kennedy, Creative Director
Simon Kershaw, Creative Consultant
David Kester, Chief Executive
Janet Kestin, Chief Creative Officer
Shailesh Khandeparkar, Illustrator
Pit Kho, Creative Director
Rick Kiesewetter, Writer
Yuki Kikutake, Art Director
Paul Kilvington, Designer
Sung Han Kim, Head of Office
Jeff Kindleysides, Designer
Jason King, Creative Director
Andrew Kingham, Graphic Designer
Rodney Kinsman, Art Director
Vanessa Kirby, Associate Creative Director
Janice Kirkpatrick, Director
Takayoshi Kishimoto, Creative Director
Matthew Kitchin, Producer
Alan Kitching RDI, Typographic Artist
Daniel Kleinman, Director
Jonathan Kneebone, Creative Director
Mary Knight, Creative Director
Paul Knott, Creative Group Head
Jonathan Knowles, Photographer
Claus Koch, Chief Executive Officer
Wolfgang Koeppel, General Manager
Tiffany Kosel, Creative Director
Joanna Kotas, Creative Partner
Tomiaki Kotsuii, President
Dennis Koutoulogenis, Copywriter
Denis Kovac, Creative Partner
Sajan Kurup, Chairman
Thomas Kurzawski, Creative Director
Ray Kyte, Design Director
Simon Labbett, Digital Creative Director
Benjamin Lambert, Industrial Designer
Martin Lambie-Nairn, Executive Creative Director
Alex Lampe, Creative Partner
Kevin Lan, Designer
Neil Lancaster, Creative Director
Justin Landon
Lisa Lanfranchi, Graphic Designer
Tanja Langgner, Designer
Kristina Brigitte Langhein, Creative Director
Nathan Usmar Lauder, Creative Director
Lucilla Lavender, Designer
Paul Lavoie, Chairman/Chief Creative Officer
Jason Lawes, Creative Partner
Martin Lawless, Creative Director
Amanda Lawrence, Graphic Designer
Andy Lawson, Creative Director
Cat-Tuong Le-Huy
Simon Learman, Joint Executive Creative Director
Diane Leaver, Copywriter
Christopher Lee, Creative Director
Dai Soo Lee, Designer

Lester Po Fun Lee, Photographer
Matt Lee, Copywriter
Peter Lee, Designer
Szu-Hung Lee, Executive Creative Director
Mark Leeds, Designer
Stephen Legate, Typographer
Richard Lemon, Art Director
Edwin Leong, Deputy Chairman/Executive Creative Director
Tan Yew Leong, Creative Director
Jeremy Leslie, Design Director
Timothy Leslie-Smith, Graphic Designer
Hendra Lesmono, Creative Director
Mark Lester, Creative Director
Matt Lever, Copywriter
Cam Levin, Head of Creative
Mary Lewis, Creative Director
Heidi Lightfoot, Director
Jon Lilley, Senior Creative Copywriter
Adrian Lim, Senior Copywriter
Chai Lim, Operator
Ted Lim, Executive Creative Director/Deputy Chairman
Leo Lin, Art Director
Graham Lincoln, Creative Partner
Joan Lind, Director of Account Management
Andrew Lindsay, Creative Director
Birger Linke, Integrated Art Director
Domenic Lippa, Design Director
Brenan Liston, Head Creative
Jason Little, Creative Director
Steve Little, Copywriter
Lydia Liu, Creative Manager
Tanya Livesey
John Lloyd, Consultant
Tom Lloyd, Designer
Jim Lobley, Creative Director
David Lock, Managing Director
Ian Logan, Creative Director
David Loosmore, Senior Art Director
Martin Loraine, Creative Writer
Martin Lore, Designer
Matthew Lowe, Senior Designer
Will Lowe, Art Director
Chris Lower, Creative Director
James Lowther
David Lubars, Chairman/Chief Creative Officer
Stuart John Lugg, Photographer
Sophie Lutman, Creative Director
David Lyle, Chief Executive
Anthony Lynch, Art Director
Andrea MacArthur, Managing Director/Editor
Alan MacCuish, Creative
Rob MacDonald, Creative Director
Paula MacFarlane, Design Director
Alex Machin
Holly Mackenzie, Broadcast Designer
David Mackersey, Art Director
Alan Mackie, Senior Art Director
Chris Maclean, Creative Director
Kevin MacMillan, Director
Vicki Maguire, Copywriter
Simon Maidment, Design Consultant
Dilys Maltby
Oliver Maltby, Creative Director
Clinton Manson, Regional Executive/Creative Director
Thomas Manss, Director
Gareth Mapp, Creative Director
Alfredo Marcantonio
Pearce Marchbank, Design Director
Andy Margetson, Director
Pedro Marin-Guzman, Creative Consultant
Fiona Marks, TV Producer
Nicolas Markwald, Art Director
Alan Marsh, Photographer
Jill Marshall, Managing Director
Guy Marshall, Design Director
Aaron Martin, Executive Creative Director

Amanda Martin, Managing Director
Greg Martin, Creative Director
Mark Martin, Creative Director
Paul Martin, Creative Director
Phil Martin, Creative
Richard Martin, Sound Designer/Composer
Natalia Martin Esteve, Creative Director
Charly Massey, Head of Innovation & Activation
Dave Masterman, Creative Director
Sónia Matos, Art Director
Jo Maude, Education & Professional Development Manager
Eva Mautino, Head of Digital & Executive Producer
Billy Mawhinney, Creative Director
Steve Mawhinney, Art Director
Andrew Maxwell, Art Director
Sigi Mayer,
Matthew Mayes, Creative Director
John Mayes, Editor/Managing Director
Thomas Mayfried, Director
David Mayo, President
Andy McAnaney, Creative
Ian McAteer, Managing Director
Jamie McCathie, Designer
Mark McConnachie, Design Director
John McConnell
Alexander McCuaig, Chairman/Creative Director
Duncan McEwan, Creative Director
Sam McGarry, Executive Producer
Richard McGillan, Design Director
Stephen McGilvray, Designer
James McGrath, Executive Creative Director
Shaughn McGurk, Senior Designer
Peter McHugh, Executive Vice President
Shaun McIlrath, Joint Global Creative Director
Ian McIlroy, Design Director
Adrian McKay, Creative Director
Bruce McKelvie, Head of Television
Ian McLean, Designer
Kylie McLean, Designer
Andy McLeod, Director
Jonathan McMahon, Creative
John McManus, Editor/Company Director
Brigid McMullen
John McWilliams, Chairman/Creative Partner
Ant Melder, Copywriter
Tim Mellors, Vice President/Chief Creative Officer
Jack Melville, Creative Director
Rob Messeter, Creative
John Messum, Creative Partner
Mike Middleton, Art Director
Marcia Mihotich, Graphic Designer
Ruan Milborrow, Art Director
Jeremy Miles, Chairman
Adam Mileusnic, Designer
Brian Millar, Creative Director
Simon Milldown, Creative Director
Chris Miller, Copywriter
Kathy Miller, Designer
Rodney Miller
Graham Mills, Creative Director
Howard Milton, Creative Director
Marcello M Minale, Managing Director
Dharmesh Mistry, Designer
Zubin Mistry, Director of Photography
Chris Mitchell, Illustrator
Gregory Mitchell
Peter Mitchell, Managing Director
Matthias Mittermuller, Creative Director
Richard Mitzman, Architect/Creative Director
Jumpei Miyao, Creative
Cosimo Moeller, Copywriter

Sarah Moffat, Design Director
Gerry Moira, Creative Chairman
Tim Molloy, Head of Creative Direction
Victor Monclus, Art Director
Sakol Mongkolkasetarin, Art Director
Dave Monk, Art Director
Anthony Moore, Creative Director
Jo Moore, Creative Director
Nick Moore, Chief Creative Officer
Tim Moore, Designer/Tutor
Daniel Moorey, Head of Art Buying
Paul Moran, Art Director
Karen Morgan, Designer
Richard Morgan, Associate Creative Director
Simon Moriarty, Studio Director/Creative Services
Matt Morley-Brown, Creative Director
Chris Morris, Programme Leader BA (Hons) Advertising Design
Dave Morris, Art Director
Debbie Morris, Creative Director
Tim Morris, Photographer
Nick Morrisey, Art Director
Simon Morrow, Design Director
Andy Mosley, Creative Director
Aaron Moss, Designer
Stephen Moss, Copywriter
Lana Mossel, Creative
Zak Mroueh, Creative Director
Fraser Muggeridge, Director
Chris Muir, Copywriter
Damian Mullan, Design Director
Dave Mullen, Creative Director
Steffen Müller, Photographer
Tony Muranka, Creative Director
Andrew Murdoch, Copywriter
Kevin Murphy, Managing Director
Rob Murphy-Martin, Executive Creative Director
Steve Mykolyn, Chief Creative Officer
Bob Mytton, Creative Director
Kentaro Nagai, Graphic Designer
Alexander Nagel, Art Director
Julian Nagel, Art Director
Paul Nagy, Creative Director
Andy Nairn, Planning Director
Ramsey Naja, Chief Creative Officer
Dave Newbold, Copywriter
Ronald Ng, Executive Creative Director
Victor Ng, Chief Creative Officer
Kenny Nicholas, Creative Director
Kate Nielsen
Rob Nielsen, Creative Director
Barbara Nokes, Creative Advertising Consultant
Alex Normanton, Head of Design
Simon North, Chief Executive Officer
Jim Northover, Chairman
Graeme Norways, Art Director
Richard Nott, Copywriter
Michael Nyrop-Larsen, Art Director
Gerard O'Dwyer, Creative Director
Mike O'Sullivan, Executive Creative Director
Timothy O'Brien, Creative Director
Nick O'Bryan-Tear, Copywriter
Marty O'Connor
Ciaran CC O'Hagan, Researcher
John O'Keeffe, Worldwide Creative Director
Tim O'Kennedy, Chief Executive Officer
John Anthony O'Reilly, Writer
Chris O'Reilly, Executive Producer
Dan O'Rourke, Executive Producer
Nick Oakley, Industrial Designer
Benjamin Oates, Creative Director
Chris Oddy, Art Director
Sebastian Oehme, Copywriter
Colin Offland, Managing Director
Peter Ogden, Deputy Creative Director
Michael Ohanian, Creative Director

D&AD Members

Yasumichi Oka, Creative Director
Craig Oldham, Designer
Sam Oliver, Creative
Rob Omodiagbe
Carol Ong, Senior Copywriter
Fabio Ongarato, Creative Director
Jeff Orr, Executive Creative Director
Richard Orrick, Film Editor
Mark Osborn, Creative Services Director
Deborah Osborne, Graphic Designer
Mark Osborne
Garry Owens, Photographer
Jaqueline Owers, Senior Designer
Ronald Packman, Director
Mark Padfield, Art Director
Mark Pailing, Design Director
Graham Painter, Senior Designer
Michael Paisley, Design Director
John Pallant, Regional Creative Director
Paolo Palma, Art Director
Dave Palmer, Creative Director
Rick Palmer, Chief Executive Officer/Chief Creative Officer
Yu-Yan Pal Pang, Creative Director
Laura Pannack, Photographer
Simon Panton, Art Director
Ronnie Paris, Music Composer
Alan Parker CBE, Director
Grant Parker, Head of Art
John Parker, Photographer
Mukesh Parmar, Senior Designer
Alex Parrott
Guy Pask, Creative Director
Claudio Pasqualetti, Art Director
Shaun Patchett, Head of Art
Shishir Patel, Art Director
Neil Patterson, Writer
Christopher Pattison, Director
Nicholas Pauley, Managing/Creative Director
Alix Paver, Creative Partner
Stephen Payne, Brand Consultant
David Pearce, Managing Director
Harry Pearce, Design Director
Jack Pearce, Executive Creative Director
Alex Pearl, Copywriter
David Pearman, Creative Director
David Pearson, Designer
Tim Peckett, Creative Director
Simon Pemberton, Creative Director
Fidel Pena, Creative Director
Robert Pendar-Hughes, Director of Photography
Serge Pennings, Art Director
Kelvin Pereira, Chief Creative
Joanna Perry
Scott Perry, Copywriter
Lorens Persson, Sound Designer/Engineer
Karin Peterson, Creative Director
Alastair Pether, Design Manager
Tor Pettersen, Designer
James Phelan, Director
Aled Phillips, Managing Director/Creative Director
Gemma Phillips, Art Director/Copywriter
Jay Phillips, Art Director
Simon Phillips, Manager/Copywriter
Tracey Phillips, Managing Director
Aaron Phua, Senior Art Director
Chomoi Picho-Owiny, Senior Art Director
Clive Pickering, Copywriter
Sarah Pidgeon, Designer
Marina Pietracci, Creative Manager
Palani Pillai, Chief Executive Officer
Joyce Pinto
Tony Pipes, Copywriter
Monica Pirovano, Designer
Luca Pitoni
David Pocknell, Creative Director
Spiros Politis, Photographer
Jane Pollard, Design Manager

Nicholas Pollitt, Creative/Managing Director
Ivan Pols
Hernán Ponce, Executive Creative Director
Jay Pond-Jones, Creative Director
Rob Potts, Creative Director
Dick Powell, Director
Eliot Powell, Creative Director
Kerrie Powell, Director
Julian Powell-Tuck, Director
Michelle Power, Senior Copywriter
Nadine Prada, Senior Art Director
Guy Pratt, Designer
Richard Prentice, Art Director
George Prest, Executive Creative Director
David Preutz, Photographer
Dave Price, Creative Director
Dean Price, Design Manager
Rebecca Price, Head of Brand
Richard Price, Producer/Managing Director
Tony Price, Creative Director
Ed Prichard, Creative Director
David Prideaux, Executive Creative Director
Ben Priest, Creative Director
Christopher Pring, Proprietor
Michael Pring, Joint Managing Director
Hamish Pringle, Director General
Jim Prior, Managing Partner
Horacio Puebla, Executive Creative Director
Graham Pugh, Creative Director
Tim Purvis, Creative Director
Laurence Quinn, Creative Director
Michael Quinn, Creative Director
Greg Quinton, Creative Director
Dom Raban, Managing Director/Creative Director
Stuart Radford, Creative Director
Andrew Rae
Rebecca Rae, Creative Head
Jochen Raedeker, Managing Director/Creative Director
David Rainbird, Creative Director
Kjell Ramsdal, Creative Director
Russell Ramsey, Executive Creative Director
Michael Rand, Art Director
Alexander Rank, Photographer
Harry Rankin, Director/Photographer
Rupert Rawlinson, Designer
Nathan Reddy, Head of Design
Carolyn Reed, Creative Director
Crispin Reed, Managing Director
Mike Reed, Copywriter
Nigel Reed, Creative Director
Sharon Reed, Joint Chief Executive
Noah Regan, Creative Director
Michael Reissinger, Visual Director/Creative Consultant
Lynda Relph-Knight, Editor
Erika Rennel Björkman, Graphic Designer
Jack Renwick, Creative Director
Roger Rex, Copywriter
Jan Rexhausen, Creative Director/Managing Director
Aaron Reynolds, Sound Engineer
Simon Rice, Art Director
David Richards, Senior Designer
Jill Richards, Recruitment Consultant
Jonathan Richards, Creative Director
Tom Richards, Art Director
Darren Richardson, Creative Director
David Richmond, Creative Director
Mark Riley, Creative Director
Tim Riley, Head of Copy
Adam Rimmer, Copywriter
Ian Ritchie, Executive Creative Director
Peta Rivero Y Hornos, Executive Marketing Services Director
Adam John Rix, Designer

Paul Rizzello, Creative Director
Mark Roalfe, Chairman
Dominic Roberts, Creative Director
Michael Roberts
Owain Roberts, Senior Associate & Design Director
Sarah Roberts, Senior Designer
Alastair Robertson, Writer/Creative Director
Dana Robertson, Creative Director
Melissa Robertson, Head of Account Management
Colin Robinson, Designer
Richard Robinson, Art Director
Simon Robinson, Art Director
Susan Robinson, Creative Director
Iain Robson, Head of Design
Paul Rodger, Director
Victoria Rodgers, Creative Designer
Hayden Rogers, Art Director
Justin Rogers, Copywriter
Jeneal Rohrback, Creative Director
Miguel Roig, Executive Creative Director
Joe Roman, Director
Marie Ronn, Creative
Peter Rose, Creative Director
Jeremy Rosenberg, Head of Brand Marketing
Jane Rosier, Head of Marketing
Andrew Ross, Designer
John Ross, Photographer
Paul Rothwell, Managing Director/Producer
Alexander Rotterink, Creative Director
Teresa Roviras, Graphic Designer
Simon Rowlands, Creative Director
Sebastian Royce, Creative Director
Stephen Royle, Creative Director
Jo Royston, Office Manager
Markus Ruf, Creative Director
John Rushton, Managing Director
Richard Russell, Creative Director
Andreas Ruthemann
Stephen Rutterford, Art Director
Chris Sainsbury, Art Director
Gerard Saint, Creative Director
John Salmon, Creative Director
Derek Samuel, Creative Director
Mike Sands, Art Director
Simon (Sanky) Sankarayya, Art Director
Yasuharu Sasaki, Interactive Creative Director
Lim Sau Hoong, Executive Creative Director
Matthew Saunby, Art Director
Joachim Sauter
Daniel Paul Savage, Senior Civil & Structural Engineer
Tiger Savage, Head of Art/Deputy Creative Director
Paolo Savignano, Copywriter
Robert Saville, Creative Director
Martin Schmid, Director
Hans Günter Schmitz, Creative Director
Wolf Schneider, Managing Director
Eric Schoeffler, Managing Director/Creative Director
Richard Scholey, Creative Director
Frank Schroeder, Design Director
Mark Schulz, Brand Experience Manager
Jonathan Schupp, Art Director
Boris Schwiedrzik, Art Director
Graham Scott, Design Director
Jordan Scott, Director
Julian Scott, Art Director
William Scott, Creative Director
Jim Seath
Linda Seaward, Head of Marketing & Publishing
Jack Sedgwick, Sound Engineer
Richard Selbourne, Group Creative Director
Bill Sermon, Vice President Multimedia Design

Christian Sewell, Acting Head of Art
James Sexton, Copywriter
Andy Seymour, Photographer
Richard Seymour, Director
Jonathan Shanks, Designer
Algy Sharman, Copywriter
Richard Sharp, Creative Partner
Gary Sharpen, Executive Creative Director
Adrian Shaughnessy, Art Director/Writer/Consultant
Tom Shaughnessy, Design Director
Harry Shaw, International Creative Director
Kevin Shaw, Managing Director
Peter Shaw, Managing Director
Graham Shearsby, Group Creative Director
Clare Sheffield, Senior Designer
Jaspar Shelbourne, Global Creative Director
Robin Shenfield, Chief Executive Officer
Duncan Shepherd, Editor
Simon Sherwood, Group Chief Executive
Paul Silburn, Creative Director
Peter Silk, Creative Director
Frances Silor, Managing Director/Producer
Luis Silva Dias, Creative Director
John Silver, Copywriter/Consultant
Scott Silvey, Typographer
Alistair Sim, Director
John Simmons, Director
Todd Simmons, Creative Director/Creative Services Contact
Dani Simonds
Anthony Simonds-Gooding
David Simpson, Creative Director
Paul Simpson, Elite Technical Director
Charlotte Sinclair, TV Producer
Jeremy Sinclair, Chairman
John Sinclair, Director
Simon Sinclair, Creative Director
Ajab Singh, Creative Director
Daljit Singh, Executive Creative Director
Kin-Wai Michael Siu, Associate Professor
Phil Skegg, Creative Director
Paul Skerm, Graphic Designer
Mark Slack
Emma Slater, Senior Designer
Anthony Smith, Creative Director
Charlie Smith, Graphic Designer
Colin Smith, Composer
Dave Smith, Creative Director
David Smith, Director
Debrah Smith, Designer
Don Smith, Creative Director
Gordon Smith, Creative Director
Jay Smith, Designer
Jeremy Smith, Producer
Katy Smith, Designer
Lee Smith, Art Director
Mark Smith, Creative Director
Martin Smith
Michael Smith, Design Director
Paul Smith, Regional Creative Director
Rick Smith, Creative Director/Chairman
Timothy John Smith, Executive Creative Director
Will Smith, Director/Designer
Ben Smithard, Lighting Cameraman
Sam Sneade, Editor
Lord Snowdon, Photographer
Emma Somerville, Head of Interactive Programming
Christian Sommer
Hunter Sommerville
Sine Brogger Sorensen, Graphic Designer
Frances Sorrell, Designer
John Sorrell, Chairman
Peter Souter, Vice Chairman
Claudia Southgate

Matthias Spaetgens, Creative Director
David Spears, Senior Art Director
James Spence, Group Creative Director
Charlie Spencer, Composer
Dörte Spengler-Ahrens, Creative Director/Managing Director
Martin Spillmann, Creative Director
Jonathan Spooner, Creative Initiative Director
David Sproxton, Executive Chairman
Alison Squire, Director
Alain St-Hilaire, Creative/Art Director
Dominic Stallard, Regional Executive/Creative Director
Horst Stasny, Photographer
Astrid Stavro, Art Director
Nick Steel, Creative Director
Guy Steele-Perkins, Marketing Manager
Hillary Steinberg, Manager
Christoph Steinegger, Creative Director
Mike Stephenson, Director
Peter Stephenson-Wright
Lucie Stericker, Creative Director
Jules Stevenson
David Stewart, Photographer
Brian Stewart, Art Director/Photographer
Derek Stewart, Design Director
Anthony Stileman, Designer/Art Director
Andrea Stillacci, President
Peter Stimpson, Designer Consultant
Ben Stockley, Photographer
David Stocks, Creative Director
Jim Stoddart, Art Director
Andrew Stokes, Design Manager
Garech Stone, Creative Director
Karl Stones, Creative Director
Richard Stoney, Senior Copywriter
Matthias Storath
Mark Stothert, Producer
Ben Stott, Creative Director
Stephen Stretton, Creative Director
Tony Strong, Copywriter
David Stuart, Designer
Phil Stuart, Creative Director
James Studholme, Managing Director
Suthisak Sucharittanonta, Chief Creative Officer
Frank Sully, Art Director
Jim Sutherland, Director
Jeff Suthons, Art Director
Linda Sutton
Nille Svensson, Designer
Per Magne Sviggum, Art Director
Alex Swatridge, Designer
Suzanne Sykes, Creative Director
Nick Talbot, Director
Toby Talbot, Executive Creative Director
Elisa Tan, Art Director
Jo Tanner, Creative Director
Amanda Tatham, Graphic Designer
Brian Tattersfield, Designer
Alexandra Taylor
Charles Taylor
Graham Taylor, Director
James Taylor, Copywriter
Richard Taylor, Typographer/Designer
Steven Taylor, Designer/Art Director
Alex Telfer, Photographer
Keith Terry, Art Director
Tham Khai Meng, Worldwide Creative Director
Jens Theil
Sallyanne Theodosiou, Senior Lecturer BA (Hons) Graphic Design
Katja Thielen, Creative Director
Parv Thind, Sound Designer
Allen Thomas, Copywriter
Andrew Thomas, Director
Graham Thomas, Chief Executive Officer
Trefor Thomas, Creative Director

Steve Thomas-Emberson, Design Writer/Editor
Ian Thompson
Neil Thompson
Sean Thompson, Creative Director
Ross Thomson, Chief Ideation Officer
Magnus Thorne, Creative Director
Lydia Thornley, Design Consultant
Jim Thornton, Executive Creative Director
Michel Tikhomiroff, Artistic Director/Film Director
Oscar Tillman, Creative Director
Stephen Timms, Copywriter
Justin Tindall, Creative Director
Richard Tindall, Director
Robbie Tingey, Interactive Designer
Neil Tinson, Graphic Designer
Sean Toal, Copywriter
Ken Luis Tobe, President
Gary Todd, Head of Design
Hugh Todd, Copywriter
Dave Tokley
Matthew Tolliss, Design Director
Gavin Torrance, Copywriter
Dave Towers, Head of Design
John Townshend, Creative Partner
Lynn Trickett, Design Director
Alfredo Trivino, Art Director
Damon Troth
Chuck Tso, Creative Director
Katherina Tudball, Designer
Barrie Tullett, Graphic Designer
Paul Tunnicliffe, Graphic Designer
Christian Tunstall, Typographer
David Turner, Head of Design
Paul Turner, Creative Group Director
Steve Turner, Creative Director
Christopher Turrall, Designer
Claire Tuthill, Designer
Glenn Tutssel, Executive Creative Director
Mark Tutssel, Worldwide Chief Creative Officer
Claire Tuvey, Designer
Mark Tweddell, Copywriter
Paul Twivy, Chief Executive Officer
Elizabeth Tyley, Creative
Favio Ucedo, Creative Director
Joel Uden, Creative Director
Joel van Audenhaege, Creative Director
Alexander van Gestel, Managing Partner
Jan van Mesdag, Managing Director
Tim Vance, Art Director
Christopher Vane, Creative Director
Simon Veksner, Copywriter
Pierre Vermeir, Creative Director
Guy Vickerstaff, Head of Art
Julian Vizard, Head of Art
Rankin Waddell, Photographer/Publisher
Peter Waibel, Chief Executive Officer
Christopher Waite, Course Leader, MA Creative Advertising
Mark Waites, Creative Director/Founder
David Wakefield, Designer/Typographer
Gary Walker, Copywriter
Melissa Walker, Managing Director
Neil Walker, Director/Creative Director
Pius Walker, Creative Director
Hayley Jane Wall, Senior Designer
Matt Waller, Copywriter
Michael Wallis, Graphic Designer
Martyn Wallwork, Creative Director
Martyn Walsh, Creative Director
Dick Walter, Composer
Frank Walters, Creative Director
Marc Ward, Serials Librarian
Richard Ward, Creative Partner
Emma Warner, Creative Team Head
Richard J Warren, Copywriter
Morten Warren, Chief Executive Officer
Graham Warsop, Group Chairman/Chief Creative Officer
Simon Waterfall, Creative Director
Dave Waters, Creative Director
Keith Watson, Creative Director

D&AD Members

Paul Watts, Film Editor
Mary Wear, Copywriter
Paul Wearing, Illustrator
Cameron Webb, Head of Design
Dean Webb, Copywriter
Graham Webb, Graphic Designer
Peter Webb, Photographer
Tim Webb-Jenkins, Creative Director
Michael Webster
Rob Webster, Copywriter
Stefan Weil, Art Director/Chief
Executive Officer
Paul Weiland, Director
Paul Weinberger, Chairman
Les Welch, Creative Director
Michael Werkmeister, Designer/
Managing Director
Wesley West, Model Maker/Art
Director
Shaun Westgate, Creative Director
Roland Wetzel, Copywriter
Mark Wheatcroft, Senior Designer
Adam White, Creative Director
Ben White, Planning Director
David White, Art Director
John White, Senior Lecturer
Marketing
Kerry White, Designer
Luke White, Creative Director
Paul White, Programme Leader BA
Comms Studies/Graphic Design
Bev Whitehead, Designer
Piet Whitehorne, Creative Director
Mark Wickens, Chairman/Creative
Partner
Valerie Wickes, Chief Executive/
Creative Director
Benji Wiedemann, Creative Partner
Lennart Wienecke, Creative Director
Chris Wigan, Designer
Regine Wilber, Creative Director
Brendan Wilkins, Creative Director
Darrell Wilkins
Greg Willcox, Film Editor
Don Williams, Chief Executive Officer
Huw Williams, Art Director
Jon Williams, Chief Creative Officer
Richard Williams, Director
Steve Williams, Senior Art Director
Jeff Willis, Deputy Head of
Department, Communication
Art & Design
Ryan Wills, Creative Director
Karina Wilsher, Managing Partner
Richard Wilshire, Associate Creative
Director
Charlie Wilson, Art Director/Creative
Partner
David Wilson, Designer
Dougal Wilson, Director
Gillian Wilson, Account Director
Peter Windett, Creative Director
Guy Wingate, Creative Director
Matt Wingfield, Creative Director
Dominic Winsor, Senior Information
Architect
Steve Wioland, Art Director
Michael Wolff, Designer
Stephen Wolstenholme, Art Director
Philip Wong, Managing Director
Spencer Wong, Executive Creative
Director
Timothy Wong, Senior Designer
Anne Wood, Creative Director
Benjamin Wood, Art Director
Peter Wood, Photographer
Rob Wood, Creative Director
Dave Woodcock, Creative Director
Malcolm Woodfield
Laura Woodroffe, Education
& Professional Development Director
Dave Woods, Executive Creative
Director
Julia Woollams, Designer
Matthew Woolner, Copywriter
Richard Worrow, Senior Art Director
Nick Worthington, Executive
Creative Director
Darren Wright, Copywriter
Heather Wright, Head of
Commercials/Executive Producer

Jimmy Yang, Creative Director
Clive Yaxley, Art Director
Matt Yeoman, Director
Wei Chen Yeung, Designer
Hei Yiyang, Creative Director
Andrew Young, Creative Director
Alan Young, Creative Partner
Robert Young, Designer
Stuart Youngs, Design Director
Darek Zatorski
Lawrence Zeegen, Head of Graphic
Design
Wolfgang Zimmerer, Managing
Director
Gerrit Zinke, Creative Director
Stefan Zschaler, Creative Director
Debra Zuckerman, Creative Director
Andrew Zulver, Design Director
Ulrich Zunkeler, Creative Director
Rik Zygmunt, Creative Director

Becoming a member of D&AD

Since 1962, D&AD has represented the world's creative community, supporting and nurturing its members at every stage of their careers.

Simply put, D&AD works tirelessly to ensure that you have creative opportunity, that creativity itself is valued, and that the brilliance you achieve in your own work is recognised. It's a movement that supports you, and which – if we can be pushy here for a moment – is one you should support too. That goes for everyone, from creative student to creative superhero.

So, become a member, and stay a member.

D&AD's membership community is an unashamedly elite group, comprising some of the most talented, engaged and passionate creative people on earth – all of them hell-bent on making the world a better place for creativity.

Of course, the tangible benefits of D&AD Membership are myriad, ranging from exclusive content and features on the D&AD website to valuable third-party offers and free invitations to members' events – as well as the opportunity to showcase your own work online.

But the real benefit is this: you'd be doing the right thing. For yourself, and for the world of commercial creativity.

How to join
For more information about the full range of benefits and to make D&AD part of your professional life visit:

www.dandad.org/join

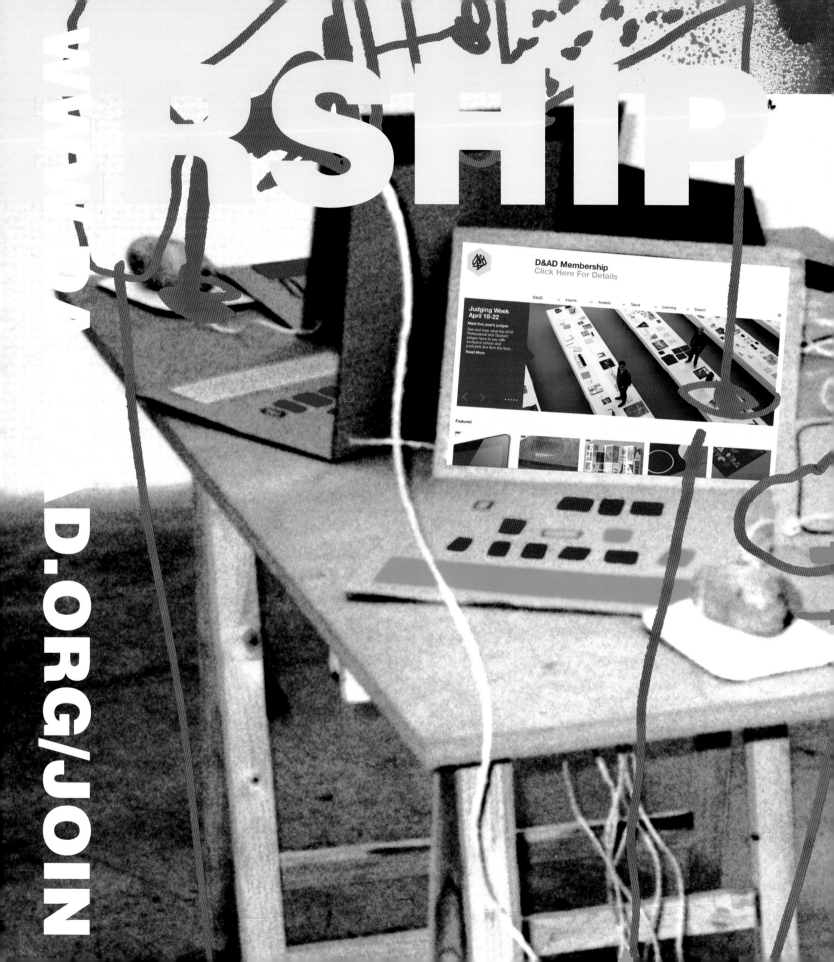

Acknowledgements

© 2010 D&AD
9 Graphite Square, Vauxhall Walk
London SE11 5EE
+44 (20) 7840 1111
www.dandad.org

D&AD is a registered Charity
(Charity No 3050992) and a
Company limited by Guarantee
registered in England and Wales
(registered number 883234) with
its registered office at 9 Graphite
Square, Vauxhall Walk, London,
SE11 5EE, UK
Phone: +44 (20) 7840 1111

The D&AD logo and the
pencil are the registered
trademarks of D&AD.

© 2010 TASCHEN GmbH
Hohenzollernring 53
D-50672 Köln
www.taschen.com

To stay informed about
upcoming TASCHEN titles,
please request our magazine
at www.taschen.com/magazine
or write to TASCHEN,
Hohenzollernring 53,
D-50672 Cologne, Germany,
contact@taschen.com,
Fax: +49-221-254919.

We will be happy to send you
a free copy of our magazine
which is filled with information
about all of our books.

Art Direction & Original Artworks
Bob and Roberta Smith
http://bobandrobertasmith.zxq.net
**Designed by and Messed
about with by**
Keith Sargent at IMMPRINT LTD
www.immprint.com
Templates & Grids Designed by
Jeremy Leslie, magCulture
www.magculture.com

Awards Director
Holly Hall
Coordination & Editing
Jana Labaki
Artworkers
Kim Browne
Guy Ralph Jackson
Senior Editorial Assistant
Claire Scott
Editorial Assistance
Peter Coles
Ana Garcia
Kat Leung
Image Production
Beatriz Hernández
Guy Porter
Faye Renshaw
Emma Volken
Sanne Winderickx
Production Consultant
Martin Lee
Origination
DawkinsColour, London

Editor in Charge
Julius Wiedemann
Editorial Coordination
Daniel Siciliano Bretas
German Translation
Jürgen Dubau
French Translation
Aurélie Daniel
for Equipo de Edición

Printed in China

ISBN: 978-3-8365-2499-5

GRAVE. EDIT. I. M. SHY. EVIDENT. MISERY. HAG. EVIDE
ME. GRAVITY. DEN. HIM. SEE. GRENADE. THEISM. IVY. G
MSTER. HANDSET. GEE. IVY. MR. I. HARVEST. GEMINI.
MY. VINE. HEADSET. NIGER. IV. MY. HEARING. EYES. DIM
RIVE. MAD. HYGIENE. DRIVE. MAST. HYGIENE. AT. ED.
AGERY. EVENT. DISH. IMAGERY. EDEN. HI. TVS. IMAGE
RED. TV. INSIGHT. EVERY. MADE. INSIGHT. ME. EVERY
SHY. INTEGER. DIVA. INVERSE. EIGHTY. MAD. MY. I
ED. MEANDER. GIVE. SHY. IT. METHANE. DIRGE. IVYS.
IVETE. GRID. NAIVETE. SIGH. EM. DRY. NAIVETY. DIRGE.
G. MY. VASE. NIGERIA. DEEM. SHY. TV. RAGTIME. DE
GIMEN. DIVEST. HAY. RESTIVE. MANGY. HIDE. REVENGE. D
D. THIS. MY. REVENGE. HAM. IS. TIDY. REVENGE. RHYMIN
RDINE. THIEVE. GYM. SEGMENT. DIARY. HIVE. SEGMENT
GE. HE. SERVING. DIET. YAM. HI. SERVING. MEAT. DYE
VENTY. RIGID. DIG. ME. SEVENTY. HAIR. SHAVING. REME
SHRIVEN. AIDE. SIDEARM. EIGHT. ENVY. YE. SIDEARM
INGER. HEAVY. DIME. I. V. STRANGE. EYED. HIM. A.
RINGE. HEAD. I. VE. MY. TARNISH. EDGE. TEHERAN. I
EREIN. DIG. MY. VASE. THEY. RE. SAVING. DIME. T
MARGIN. SIDE. DRY. THIEVES. ENIGMA. THIEVES. ANGRY
NGY. RIDE. THRIVEN. EASY. MIDGE. VARIETY. DESIGN. H
RY. MEND. ARID. VESTIGE. HYMEN. VESTIGE. HYMEN.
RESY. DIM. GEYSER. HE. D. VITAMIN. I. ADVISE. M
IDST. EVERY. HINGE. ARIGHT. DEMISE. ENVY. AVENG
. ME. DAINTY. GRIEVE. MESH. DANGER. IS. MY. THI
VEN. MYTHS. DEARIES. MIGHT. ENVY. MY. DEARTH. GIN
NITY. SHIM. SHY. DEGREE. MINI. VAT. DEMISE. IN. T
RIVE. ME. HASTY. GIN. DERIVE. SEAMY. THING. DERIVE.
SIGN. RHYME. VITAE. DESIRE. GAVE. IT. HYMN. DEVEIN